Romania and the European Union

MANCHESTER
1824

Manchester University Press

Romania and the European Union

How the weak vanquished the strong

TOM GALLAGHER

Manchester
University Press
Manchester and New York

distributed in the United States exclusively
by PALGRAVE MACMILLAN

Published by Manchester University Press
Oxford Road, Manchester M13 9NR, UK
and Room 400, 175 Fifth Avenue, New York, NY 10010, USA
www.manchesteruniversitypress.co.uk

Distributed in the United States exclusively by
Palgrave Macmillan, 175 Fifth Avenue, New York,
NY 10010, USA

Distributed in Canada exclusively by
UBC Press, University of British Columbia, 2029 West Mall,
Vancouver, BC, Canada V6T 1Z2

British Library Cataloguing-in-Publication Data
A catalogue record for this book is available from the British Library

Library of Congress Cataloging-in-Publication Data applied for

ISBN   978 0 7190 7743 2   *hardback*

First published 2009

18 17 16 15 14 13 12 11 10 09   10 9 8 7 6 5 4 3 2 1

Typeset in Minion
by Servis Filmsetting Ltd, Stockport, Cheshire
Printed in Great Britain
by MPG Books Group, UK

Contents

Acknowledgements

I gladly acknowledge the help and backing of Shaun Gregory and Davina Miller, the two colleagues who were heads of the Department of Peace Studies at Bradford University during the period when this book was researched and written, for giving me the space to pursue work on it. Owen Greene deserves thanks for ensuring that I obtained several small grants which enabled me to make research trips to Brussels in 2006 and 2007. A wide range of people were willing to talk to me on and off the record about the EU's engagement with Romania and the response of different political and social forces there. They included members of the European Commission, from junior to very senior levels, who had worked both in Brussels and Romania itself as members of different Directorates or else of the Delegation over a ten-year period. I am grateful to Monica Macovei and Madeleine Crohn for putting their knowledge about the struggle to reform the justice system before me and for allowing me to see first hand the commitment they showed towards trying to achieve that indispensable end. Liesolotte Millitz-Stoica was a constant source of encouragement, ensuring that my interest in Romania never flagged during the last three years. With Armand Goşu, Gelu Trandafir and Valentina Pop, I had engrossing discussions which helped clarify a number of my ideas about the subject of the book. Lavinia Stan and Mark Gilbert were two academics with whom I had very fruitful debates. During the final stages of the book I enjoyed several meetings with Vladimir Tismăneanu, who realises how crucial proper engagement with the rest of Europe is if Romania is to try and erase the destructive legacy of its communist decade, and I am glad that whatever misunderstandings occurred between us in years past have been laid to rest.

Jim Brooker ensured that I was free from many preoccupations and distractions that would have delayed the completion of the project and for such backing he deserves enormous thanks. Willie Huppertz provided me with a tranquil base in Portugal from which to work on this project over extended periods. Chris Ciupe was enormously helpful with editing tasks and helped to ensure the publication was delivered on time. Finally, responsibility for the contents of this book, and for any mistakes to be found in it, lies with me.

Tom Gallagher

List of abbreviations

AID	Asociația pentru Implementarea Democrației (The Association for Implementing Democracy)
ANI	Agenția Națională de Integritate (The National Integrity Agency)
ANSIT	Agenția Națională pentru Sprijinirea Inițiativelor Tinerilor (The National Agency for Youth Initiative Support)
APADOR	Asociația Pentru Apărarea Drepturilor Omului din România (The Association for Defending Human Rights in Romania)
APIA	Agenția pentru Plăți și Intervenții în Agricultură (The Agency for Payment and Intervention in Agriculture)
ASE	Academia de Studii Economice (The Academy of Economic Studies)
CFR	Căile Ferate Române (The Romanian Railroad Company)
CNI	Centrul Național de Integritate (The National Integrity Centre)
CNSAS	Consiliul Național pentru Studierea Arhivelor Societății (The National Council for the Study of the Archives of the *Securitate*)
CSM	Consiliul Suprem al Magistraturii (The Supreme Council of Magistrates)
CUPAR	The Central Unit for Public Administration Reform
CURS	Centrul de Sociologie Urbană și Regională (The Centre for Urban and Regional Sociology)
DA	Alianța Dreptate și Adevăr (The Justice and Truth Alliance)
DGA	Direcția Generală Anticorupție (The General Anti-corruption Directorate)
DLAF	Departamentul pentru Lupta Anti-Fraudă (The Department for the Struggle Against Fraud)
DNA	Departamentul Națională Anticorupție (The National Anti-Corruption Department)
EADS	European Aeronautic Defence and Space Company
ECE	East–Central Europe
EEC	European Economic Community

EP	European Parliament
EU	European Union
FSN	Frontul Salvării Naționale (The National Salvation Front)
GDP	gross domestic product
GRECO	Council of Europe's Group of States Against Corruption
IER	Institutul European din România (The European Institute of Romania)
IICR	Institutul de Investigare a Crimelor Comunismului în România (The Institution for the Investigation of Crimes against Communism in Romania)
IMAS	Institutul de Marketing și Sondaje (The Institute of Marketing and Polls)
IMF	International Monetary Fund
ISPA	Instrument pentru Politici Structurale Pre-Aderare (The Instrument for Structural Policies for Pre-Accession)
JHA	Justice and Home Affairs
MAI	Ministerul Administrației și Internelor (The Ministry of Administration and the Interior)
NACS	Agenția Națională a Funcționarilor Publici (The National Agency for Civil Servants)
OECD	Organisation for Economic Cooperation and Development
OLAF	Office Europeen De Lutte Anti-Fraude (European Anti-Fraud Office)
OSCE	Organisation for Security and Cooperation in Europe
PC	Partidul Conservator (The Conservative Party)
PCR	Partidul Comunist Român (The Romanian Communist Party)
PD	Partidul Democrat (The Democratic Party)
PDSR	Partidul Democrației Sociale din România (The Party of Romanian Social Democracy)
PLD	Partidul Liberal-Democrat (The Liberal-Democratic Party)
PMUs	Project Management Units
PNA	Parchetul Național Anticorupție (The National Anti-corruption Prosecutor's Department)
PNL	Partidul Național Liberal (The National Liberal Party)
PNȚCD	Partidul Național Țărănesc Creștin-Democrat (The National Peasant and Christian Democratic Party)
PRM	Partidul România Mare (The Greater Romania Party)
PSD	Partidul Social Democrat (The Social Democratic Party)
PUR	Partidul Umanist Român (The Romanian Humanist Party)
RICOP	Programul de Restructurare Industrială și Reconversie Profesională (The Enterprise Restructuring and Professional Conversion Programme)

SAR	Societatea Academică din România (The Romanian Academic Society)
SIE	Serviciul de Informații Externe (The External Information Service)
SIGMA	Support for the Improvement in Governance and Management
SOF	state ownership fund
SRI	Serviciul Român de Informații (The Romanian Information Service)
UCM	Uniunea Civică Maghiară (The Hungarian Civic Union)
UDMR	Uniunea Democrată Maghiară din România (The Democratic Union of Hungarians in Romania)
YPS	Proiectul Tinerilor Profesioniști (Young Professionals, Scheme)

Introduction

On the surface the European Union has been able to exercise strong and effective leverage over Romania. Probably no other candidate for membership has faced such a daunting range of obstacles since the fully totalitarian communist regime of Nicolae Ceauşescu ended in 1989. Many were taken by surprise when, exactly a decade later, in 1999 the EU agreed to open talks for full membership with a country whose unreadiness for the challenge had been plainly set out in 1997 by the EU when it assessed the state of reform in each of the Eastern European countries which had applied for membership. Second-ranking communists had directed the transition on a minimalist agenda for change. A sprawling bureaucracy remained unreformed and often appeared incapable of carrying out even routine administrative tasks. Years of economic decline and flagrant corruption had finally led to the former communists suffering electoral defeat in 1996. But a weak coalition of their opponents soon appeared to be in office but not in power, daunted by the challenges that they faced and divided about how to respond to them.

Nevertheless, in the eyes of the EU enough progress in meeting the political criteria for entry appeared to be taking place. Certainly, most of the authoritarian practices of President Ion Iliescu and the power networks which had kept him in power since the end of 1989 were renounced. In 1999, the assistance which Romania rendered both the EU and the North Atlantic Treaty Organisation (NATO) in their confrontation with Serbia over the mistreatment of the Albanian minority in Kosovo boosted the credibility of Romania. As long as the Balkans were going to be a critical arena for NATO, scarred by its previous failure to halt destructive warfare in Yugoslavia, and also for the EU as it acquired new foreign and security responsibilities concerned with stabilising its troubled eastern neighbourhood, it seemed unrealistic to overlook Romania. In addition, there was a political desire to complete the EU's 'big bang' expansion into Central and Eastern Europe. So by 2002 Romania (as well as Bulgaria) had been given a guarantee they could join in 2007 or 2008 at the very latest, even if they were not fully ready.

This involved a significant relaxation of the conditions required before EU membership talks could begin and then be completed. Political criteria were emphasised and Romania was given time in order to try and acquire a functioning market economy. Later, economic growth was given a higher priority over completing an onerous set of institutional reforms set out in the EU's road map for entry: the *acquis communautaire*.

In the late 1990s, Romania's GDP was only around one-fifth of the EU average. In 2003, Romania had the highest percentage of people employed in the agricultural sector (44.4%) and the lowest percentage employed in the service sector (29.7%) among all EU candidates, according to the EU. The EU's median percentage of those employed in the agricultural sector was 4.2%, while 67.2% of EU citizens were employed in the service sector.[11] So this weak peripheral country scarcely fitted the profile of a country which might be expected to enter the EU within a decade of membership talks getting started. Indeed, it is not unfair to say that the integration process had been designed for states that had a different social and economic profile from Romania's. This placed an obligation on the EU to reflect if it was really using the best instruments to enable this highly particular candidate to transform its circumstances so that it could be an effective full member of the European club.

Nobody questioned the assumption that the EU would be the dominant player in an asymmetrical relationship. Romania would be exposed to a process of Europeanisation involving a gradual transfer of values and capabilities that would enable it in time to enjoy the opportunities, and also assume the responsibilities, of full EU membership. The EU already appeared to have an impressive track-record of success in this regard. A Europeanisation process shaped around the promotion of economic and political pluralism had stabilised the former Southern European dictatorships of Spain, Greece and Portugal once they joined the EU in the 1980s. This reinforced the impression that consolidating fragile democracies and joining the EU were actually mutually reinforcing processes.

Officials in Brussels, the centre of EU decision-making, were aware that in no other former communist satellite state had power networks been preserved more completely than in Romania. But they seemed incapable of withstanding the transformative power of the EU. Accordingly, there was not undue alarm when the post-communists, by now renamed the Social Democratic Party (PSD) and still under their wily leader, Ion Iliescu, were swept back into office in December 2000.

On the surface, there appeared to be no lack of evidence that the EU was exercising considerable vigilance over Romania during the decade (1997–2007) in which it became increasingly actively engaged with the country. Along with Bulgaria, it was given a later target date for entry (2007–8) than the other candidates from Eastern Europe (which joined in 2004). In 1999 a medium-term economic strategy was unfurled in which it appeared that the

EU, along with international financial institutions, would actively steer what was still a state-dominated economy along the free market path. Several times, in 2001 and again in 2004, the EU delivered stern warnings to the government about its failure to abide by its undertakings to safeguard the welfare of children in institutionalised care. Suspension of talks was in the air during both occasions. Only in 2004 was the EU willing to concede that Romania had acquired a functioning market economy, a condition deemed as indispensable before entry negotiations could be closed. Along with Bulgaria, it was also subject to 'a safeguard clause' from the end of 2004: unless the pace of reform was maintained in crucial areas such as the justice system, the EU would impose this clause, postponing entry from 2007 to 2008 and imposing post-entry monitoring.

However, in this book I will try to show that the EU's multi-layered system of decision-making was unequal to the stark challenges presented by a candidate with as many problems as Romania. The three main pillars of the Union – its administrative corps, the European Commission, the member states grouped in the European Council, and the European Parliament (EP) – were unable to act effectively together to ensure that Romania joined with key reforms effectively in place rather than their delivery promised at some unspecified time in the future. Instead, the main entities of the EU allowed themselves to be misled and disarmed by a calculating local elite well versed in simulating change. Romania became the 27th member of the EU on 1 January 2007 on the agenda of minimal change which its post-communist leaders stubbornly clung to. Old political structures which had blocked reform were left substantially unchanged. An economy from which the state had extracted itself far more swiftly than in Thatcher's Britain nevertheless remained under the influence of a narrow set of forces closely allied to most of the major political parties. They were determined to prevent values cherished by the EU, such as political accountability, clean government and active citizenship, acquiring any real meaning in the Romanian context. Instead of a process of Europeanisation occurring, it is more accurate to think in terms of a process of Euro-Balkanism at work. Romania absorbed the laws, values and decision-making procedures of the EU only at a superficial or declaratory level. Under the surface, political power continued to be wielded by a narrow set of privileged players determined not to be accountable before the law or to face other constraints. The justice system continued to be a tool in the hands of the powerful ready to be used against rivals or indeed ordinary citizens who got in their way. Despite the EU paying belated attention to justice reform, a bogus separation of powers failed to prevent an army of judicial officials continuing the practice of absolving members of the political elite who had got into difficulties because of their corrupt behaviour. The administration also continued to be poorly performing and dominated by patronage structures. Most citizens found that they had little effective access to decision making and opportunities for political participation were blocked. A trans-party alliance whose leading members had acquired vast fortunes from politics had no intention of adopting better standards of conduct or retiring to the sidelines. They mocked the idea that power should be exercised with the consent of the governed or that citizens' taxes should be spent with their interests in mind.

So some of the classic features of Balkan politics, where narrow groups flagrantly imposed their will over society at large, were not only carried forward but reinforced as a result of Romania joining the EU. The previously isolated and peripheral country now belonged to the world's most successful regional political entity. Its influence and legitimacy were reinforced by joining this prestigious club. But after entry the EU would be unable to enforce standards of acceptable behaviour on Romania. As a sovereign state it enjoyed substantial autonomy and was only likely to face serious censure if it flagrantly violated EU rules. A sinuous elite adept at concealing its agenda was unlikely to offer such open defiance. Nevertheless, the first year of full membership, 2007, offered plenty of disturbing evidence that Romania would be a problematic member disinclined to implement previously agreed undertakings and constantly looking for opportunities and loopholes to enable it to pursue policies benefiting only restricted but powerful political groupings.

The EU prided itself on projecting its values, economic models and forms of governance eastwards in previously inhospitable terrain. But the story of a bilateral relationship in which the EU displayed far more naivety than cunning, and ruling parties took advantage of its carelessness and ultimately trusting disposition, has been one of democratic retreat even during the period, after 2004, when the EU was subjecting Romania to its closest scrutiny. It remains to be seen how great a setback for building a common Europe based on pluralistic principles will the admission of an unreformed Romania prove to be. But it cannot be ruled out that the EU's legitimation of forces in Romania that only adopted the trappings of Western democracy could prove to be an important staging-post in the resurgence of soft forms of political authoritarianism in Eastern Europe.

It is not the overt nor underlying assumption of this book that Romania, or the wider region it is a part of, is unable to overcome negative historical legacies and move towards installing Western models of democracy and institution-building. Nor do I assume that Romania was unfit for EU membership and therefore should not have been considered as a candidate. Nor that the task of preparing Romania to put its house in order was beyond the EU's capabilities. It did indeed have considerable leverage and in Romania there was a not insignificant pro-reform constituency with which the EU could have forged an effective alliance in order to provide powerful momentum for the Europeanisation process. But this would have involved the EU doing a number of things unpalatable for a centralised and indeed often complacent organisation which clung to specific bureaucratic processes with almost religious fervour. Nothing less than a profound culture shift would have been necessary if the EU was to engage effectively with a candidate which had the potential to be a constructive member but only if there were no illusions about the depth of the change which needed to be carried out.

The EU would have had to modify its customary approach to preparing applicants for membership to match the highly specific conditions to be found in Romania. Inevitably, this would have involved giving Romania much greater priority, not so much in terms of resources, but certainly in terms of time. But the EU refrained from asking the Romanian government for more powers of oversight and intervention in order to try to overcome the key blockages preventing Romania becoming a law-based state, one where citizenship mattered and the guardians of the state acted with restraint and showed a concern for wider national concerns rather than petty private ones. It could have created task forces to improve the capacity of key parts of ministries and regulatory agencies which need to function in a competent way if the country is to have a chance of holding its own against competitors. A different form of regional system could have been created in order to allow for the successful distribution of funds under the EU's three instruments of pre-accession support: Phare for institution-building, Ispa for environment and transport, and Sapard for agriculture. Conditionality might have been emphasised as much in political areas as economic ones. A longer period could have been allowed before particular areas of the national economy were opened to foreign competition. Rules for accessing pre-accession funds might have been customised to suit Romanian conditions (made far simpler, and the funding more resistant to interception by corrupt power-brokers).

But even though Romania was the second largest of the 12 new states which joined in the last wave enlargement, EU decision-makers in practice failed to devote major attention to it. They were preoccupied with the countries belonging to the 2004 entry wave, which included states like Poland and Hungary which the EU, and Western Europe overall, had much closer ties to. Romania was seen as an exotic and peripheral country with a clutch of deep-seated problems, one which had somehow been included in the enlargement process for reasons which nobody could quite recall as memories of the Kosovo conflict faded from view. The vigilance sporadically exercised after 1999 occurred when observant officials realised that in specific policy areas there were serious problems that would cause grave discredit to the EU unless they were addressed. But there was never any desire to subject Romanian membership to a more searching appraisal and many of the initiatives taken in Brussels with Romania specifically in mind had a declaratory aspect in which there was no sustained follow-up.

The political elite in Bucharest soon realised that the attention span of Brussels was rather spasmodic and it became adept at adopting a range of rituals and initiatives which were essentially nothing but public relations gimmicks in order to satisfy Eurocrats that Romania was indeed engaged in a process of socialisation enabling it to internalise European norms and values. It played off different tiers of the EU's multi-layered decision-making structure and lobbied avidly to secure entry on a minimal agenda of change. Gradually, instead of the EU imposing its agenda on Romania, it surrendered increasing amounts of terrain to the local elite, which was the most single-minded of the actors involved in the entry process. Instead of an asymmetrical process being at work, the EU gradually accepted large parts of the local elite's world view, namely that meaningful reform was bound to be a long-term process and only those who had been decision-makers for most of the time since 1989 could be regarded as effective partners. However suspect their antecedents and exasperating their behaviour could be, at least they understood the rules of power in Romania which had frequently baffled the EU. Perplexed, and weary of dealing with such an exacting candidate, there were no shortage of players in the EU system prepared to believe that Brussels must lower it sights and work with the available power structures, however unattractive their members were.

An alternative approach would have been to treat the government, once more from early 2001 controlled by the appointees of Ion Iliescu, the architect of the post-1989 transition, not as a partner but as a potential adversary. The EU's problems might have been eased considerably if it had recognised that Romania possessed a political elite that was cynical and amoral to an extent unusual even in the former Soviet satellites. Such awareness might have been acquired if the EU had realised that the old structures had regrouped after 1989 and that the communist system had been broken up far less completely than anywhere else outside the old Soviet Union itself. A network of political and economic forces determined to monopolise political and economic power was in place. Its influence often extended beyond the successor of the communists to include most of the major parties, especially during the final years of the negotiating process with the EU. Brussels might have saved itself considerable trouble if it had adopted a much firmer approach to regime backsliding. It could have looked for alternative interlocutors which, after all, is what it and also the USA had done in parts of the western Balkans and the Ukraine when trying to maximise the reform constituencies in those places. Above all, it could have made it clear that it was ready to suspend the entry process if irrefutable evidence had been required that the government in reality was averse to carrying out the undertakings it had entered into with the EU.

Greater vigilance and knowledge of local political realities would have served the EU well. It is surprising that Eurocrats for a long time recoiled from recognising that often what drove politics forward in Romania was the desire by highly motivated and resourceful people to channel public money into private hands. If such awareness had become more generalised in Brussels, then it is unlikely that the EU would have been so keen to impose large funding programmes in Romania which, in many ways, fed corruption rather than deterred it. Iliescu's PSD had already proven adept at camouflaging its intentions to rule primarily in the interests of an oligarchy which had emerged from the old structures behind a modernising rhetoric. The EU too often took this rhetoric at face value and failed to take the measure of the party or properly understand its origins. Its annual reports described PSD substitutes for reform, such as passing legislation and setting up new bodies meant to drive forward the EU agenda, that were not progressive steps but crafty delaying actions meant to lower the vigilance of Brussels. Only occasionally was the air of complacency about Romania punctured. No original thinking occurred about how to absorb the second largest former satellite state with a grim totalitarian legacy, a battered economy, and an administrative system defective in the area of problem-solving and bereft even of normal management capabilities.

In EU *communiqués*, Romania merely appeared to be behind the Central European candidates and was engaged in a process of catch-up. Frank European officials with experience in both Romania and countries less disfigured by communist rule knew this to be a highly euphemistic viewpoint. The quality of many of the politicians and civil servants in Poland, several of the Baltic states and Hungary, and their knowledge of what Europeanisation entailed, far exceeded what was to be found in Romania. Implausible assumptions about elite behaviour and a lack of sensitivity to the historical context served the EU very badly.

There was no desire to take stock when, quite early in the negotiating process, evidence emerged that the standard EU approach to candidates was not producing many beneficial results in the case of Romania. The roadmap for entry known as the *acquis communautaire* was not able to make a dent on problems of under-development, mal-administration and post-communist misrule. The forms of assistance the EU devised for candidates proved unsuitable for Romania. These often consisted of large funding projects which channelled funds to an unreformed central and local administration in the expectation that belated modernisation of the country would result. These pre-accession aid programmes were beset by delays, waste and corruption. The EU's reliance on regional structures dominated by reactionary politicians for the distribution of funds proved to be an astonishing admission of how little it understood the nature of political power in Romania.

The outcome was a set of incomplete and superficial reforms that were capable of being reversed. Even before Romania joined the EU, the government of Călin Popescu-Tăriceanu was trying to unpick some of the reforms meant to guarantee genuine economic competition in order to reward its supporters. By the time of entry, the bogus reform agenda pioneered by the PSD had been embraced by nearly all political forces except those aligned with President Traian Băsescu. Even as the EU's engagement with Romania intensified, this trans-party elite grew in strength and confidence and in the year before entry it was openly defying the EU by refusing to approve key anti-corruption undertakings. By contrast, civic actors with a democracy-building agenda and much of the independent media were entering into decline.

Unprepossessing local actors with a striking record of failure in policy terms nevertheless knew what they wanted. With Romania inside the EU, they would be able not only to access an El Dorado of foreign funds but also extend their rent-seeking activities to the heart of the EU thanks to the access to EU institutions that they would enjoy as one of the larger member states. Membership of one of the most prestigious global economic blocs could attract foreign investment to the country and enable a promiscuous domestic elite to try and induce major international firms to do business the Romanian way.

The EU was unable to match in coherence the vision of local political actors who were determined to bend the EU to their own purposes. In its published reports, the EU often adopted inflated rhetoric about the degree to which Romania was corresponding to its norms (this rhetoric was often at variance with the findings of classified peer reviews on important policy areas such as the justice sector). There was the ongoing assumption that recalcitrant postcommunists could be induced to accept the standards and values of the Union. But this was hardly possible if the domestic momentum behind genuine reform was so feeble.

The absence of decisive leadership and of coordination between the multi-layered bodies of the Union proved to be telling disadvantages. But they were avoidable ones. Middle-ranking EU officials existed who glimpsed all too clearly the emerging debacle. If senior colleagues had shared their realism or, more crucially, one or two key member states had displayed vigilance given the information being received about the fictional quality of many aspects of the Romanian reform process, then the EU could have avoided seeing the initiative being seized by a disreputable set of local actors.

Ironically, despite refusing to adopt a Romania-specific entry process, in practice the EU abandoned its rigid entry formula at key moments to try and drive the accession process along. This happened in 1999 when Balkan security considerations led to the economic criteria for membership talks getting underway being set aside. Later, when a government under Prime Minister Adrian Năstase began to return to past authoritarian ways, the EU failed to react. It was impressed by the PSD's purposeful approach to economic deregulation, overlooking the fact that this was a very convenient strategy for both the PSD and its economic constituencies. EU vigilance was eroded when Bucharest offered major investment opportunities on generous terms to top European firms which enjoyed close links to the political establishment in major continental EU states.

The EU's emphasis on rapid privatisation had two clearly unforeseen effects which were bound to adversely affect Romania's future role as a full member. Firstly, the resulting unemployment, on top of over a decade of falling real wages, provoked heavy emigration that led to a rapid shrinking of the labour market. The resulting steep fall in economically active sections of the population meant that there was soon the need to export workers in order to maintain vigorous growth rates in the low-skilled economy Romania had become. Secondly, EU-driven deregulation enabled different wings of the predatory elite to carve out domains of private power. These private fiefdoms are emerging as more influential than public agencies supposed to regulate and audit economic decision-making involving both the state and private enterprise. But the EU had insisted on rapid privatisation without ensuring that the political conditions would allow proper regulation. The result was the rapid emergence of an unregulated crony capitalism which poses a threat to the EU's own security given Russia's avid desire to draw a clutch of capitalist barons in its former satellites into its political orbit.

The EU may therefore shortly rue its short-sightedness. Post-communists had already been withdrawing resources from the state from the early 1990s. The EU then came along and demanded that the shrinking of the state occur at an even faster level, but it lacked the historical awareness and knowledge about the reality of power in post-communist Romania to realise how a policy of state extraction from the economy, in the absence of political reform, risked creating a system of private enterprise under the thumb of entrenched political networks.

Economic liberalism in the absence of genuine political liberalisation risked becoming a dead letter. By the time of entry in 2007, Romania had a smaller proportion of economic activity directly controlled by the state than Great Britain. But genuine economic competition was bound to be jeopardised by the survival of a political system dominated by immensely rich political cartels whose members often acted as if they were above the law. The EU never seemed to appreciate that economic pluralism depended on a strong system of regulations and institutions to enforce them so that powerful capitalists would be accountable to the rule of law. Russia under Vladimir Putin showed only too clearly what could happen if a ruthless cabal combining political and economic power managed to subvert state institutions and fatally erode checks and balances preventing concentrations of political power.

A mishandled privatisation process in Romania has enabled Russian influence to resurface unexpectedly, particularly in the energy sector. Leading Eurocrats used to argue that security was the chief rationale behind admitting Romania to the EU. But instead of closing a porous border with an unstable and authoritarian East, it looks as if, inside the EU, Romania could be a gateway for Russian economic influence. Elements in the Bucharest elite have woken up to the fact that a resurgent Russia defying democratic norms gives them an important bargaining lever with Brussels. If pressure for reform becomes too insistent then Bucharest can threaten to develop its links with Russia in a way that undermines EU solidarity against a large and currently troublesome neighbour. In 2007, when the Kazakhstan state oil company bought a controlling share in the largest private energy company in Romania, previously owned by a long-term ally of Prime Minister Tăriceanu, the EU started to realise that events in Romania might not be going according to plan.

Back in 2001, Romano Prodi, then President of the European Commission, had proclaimed: 'Our aim is, that in a few years, Romania will become a part of Europe, economically and politically speaking, and to invest here will be similar to investing in Germany, France, Italy, or any other European country'.[22] But instead of the economy becoming integrated with the rest of the EU, it is likely to remain a hybrid one, closely intertwined with Russia and its satellites and also the Third World. There is also the strong likelihood, for which evidence already exists, that Western companies investing in Romania, instead of being transformative agents improving business practices, will instead have to conform to local business practices if their operations are to enjoy any success.

Polling surveys regularly showed Romanians to be the most pro-European in sentiment of electorates in any recent candidate countries. But the EU was not an effective guardian of Romanian interests despite the rhetoric about partnership and about the benefits to be obtained through accepting painful economic sacrifices. There is no lack of evidence that (with the exception of child welfare) the EU usually only treated as a priority those reform objectives which member states saw as vital for their own wellbeing: a system of border security to stem the tide of illegal immigrants or contraband from Central Asia and the Middle East; improvement in environmental controls and hygiene standards in the agricultural sector to prevent contamination of air, river systems or food. But the pressure from the heart of the EU system to ensure state compliance with reforms that Romania's own citizens would primarily benefit from, particularly regarding the quality of the justice system and public services was far less systematic and intense.

It was mentioned earlier that I believe it is possible to see Romania as a constructive member of the EU enjoying the benefits and contributing to the overall cohesion of the entity. I should also place on record my support for the EU enlargement process extending to Romania and, indeed, adjacent countries. But its effectiveness depends on the quality of the engagement and the commitment of both bilateral partners to ensuring that the conditions for membership are not diluted, that Romanian citizens, rather than a narrow sector of the population, are the chief local beneficiaries of entry, and that citizens in established member states are not exposed to unnecessary inconveniences and threats as a result of the way in which Romania has been inducted into the Union. Unfortunately, these elementary precautions have not been adhered to. Instead, Romania joined with the accession criteria relaxed or even set aside in key areas. Victory was declared on a flimsy basis with reforms in vital policy sectors waiting to be accomplished and an elite with no appetite for this work reaping the main benefits of membership. Thus, it should not be surprising if I decline to see the accession process through the theoretical prism preferred by the great majority of scholars who have examined the EU's eastward enlargement. While there is substantial evidence that the EU has played a key progressive role in consolidating political and economic pluralism in most of the countries which joined in 2004, the evidence for it being a progressive harbinger of change at this systemic level in the case of Romania is far more elusive. So I think it is inappropriate to refer to a process of Europeanisation being sponsored by the EU in Romania. There is insufficient evidence that the EU has played a transformative role there, enabling a socialisation process to occur in which Romanian legislators, civil servants and other important actors absorb the normative values and procedures that are to be found at the heart of the EU system. Instead, I will reluctantly contend that a process of *pseudo-Europeanisation* has characterised the essence of the relationship between Romania and the EU for most of the period since 2000. I have called it Euro-Balkanism, in which negative local political characteristics which flout the EU's agenda based on transparency, accountability and ethical government are reinforced behind the screen of a direction-less Europeanisation process lacking real content.

The story of Romania and the EU helps to illustrate the unhelpful way that Western political concepts can be transferred to the South-East European context and how they have been diluted and even deformed in the process. The relevance of this unsuccessful transfer of values and procedures particularly for the western Balkans goes without saying. Here the European Union has become the lead-player in trying to move forward fragile peace processes in Bosnia and Kosovo as well as continuing to emphasise the possibility of full membership of the Union in future to states which adopt an agenda of reform not dissimilar to that proposed for Romania a decade ago. This book provides a detailed account of how the EU lost its way in Romania during that period. It shows how the apparently weak local forces opposed to substantially changing the political rules established after 1989 outwitted an unprepared and irresolute EU. The result was that Romania entered the EU on a minimalist agenda for change. The possibility of further democratic renewal may well have been blocked off and there are real risks that Romania could be a problematic member endangering the success of the eastern strategy unfurled by the EU over a decade ago in order to strengthen democratic values in its immediate neighbourhood. So there is strong justification for offering an in-depth assessment of the manner in which a local elite, hopeless at performing routine administrative tasks but extremely adapt at defending its group interests in uncertain times, hoodwinked the EU after 2004. There is little doubt that Russia will have observed the low-grade response of Brussels to the quiet defiance and subterfuge practised by the Bucharest elite and absorbed the appropriate lessons. But it is in the countries of the EU that a debate is overdue about the best means by which the EU can extend its influence and project its values in countries with an authoritarian past as entrenched at that of Romania.

Chapter 1 examines the first major steps in the relationship between the EU and Romania, culminating in the start of entry negotiations in 2000 and the return to power in 2001 of the Social Democratic Party, which would be the chief Romanian interlocutor with the EU over the next four years.

Chapter 2 shows how the government of Adrian Năstase succeeded in convincing the EU that it was committed to fulfilling many of the economic criteria for entry. I argue that this led key EU actors to overlook serious violations of the political criteria, especially in regard to freedom of speech and ensuring impartial trials and judicial investigations.

Chapter 3 explores the EU aid assistance programmes meant to drive forward the modernisation of the country so that it could compete effectively with existing members upon joining the Union. It argues that this externally sponsored assistance failed to decisively improve the country's institutional capacity or its infrastructure. Much of it was intercepted by venal local forces or else wasted, and the EU seemed disinclined to try to learn lessons from this debacle and adopt an approach that enabled ordinary citizens to see the benefit of such large infusions of aid.

Chapter 4 examines the failure of the EU's plans to promote a professional civil service able to assume the responsibilities of implementing legislation emanating from the EU in a transparent manner and preparing projects that would enable Romania to benefit from the fruits of membership. It chronicles the strategies that were used by local players to discredit and nullify reform initiatives and the irresolute response of the EU.

Chapter 5 examines the degree of political control that was exercised over the justice system in Romania and the degree to which this undermined meaningful prospects for reform. It shows how the courts and prosecution service remained adjuncts of the Năstase government and its allies even as negotiations with the EU were reaching their height. It argues that the willingness of the EU to accept, at face value, cosmetic changes which supposedly guaranteed judicial independence was perhaps its most serious blunder before entry talks were concluded with Romania in 2004.

Chapter 6 examines the strategy of duplicity exercised by the post-2000 government, both in its bid to join NATO and become a member of the EU. It shows how EU vigilance over child care briefly led to a crisis in relations between the EU and Romania at the start of 2004 and how failings in the EU's untidy system of decision-making enabled the PSD to regain the initiative after a short time.

Chapter 7 dwells on the manner in which the EU engaged with Romania during the final six months of negotiations in 2004, which I believe was the defining period of the bilateral relationship in which the initiative swung decisively towards the old structures in Bucharest. It examines in detail how the EU decided to close negotiations on the PSD's restricted agenda for change. The terms and conditions were relaxed and top Eurocrats hardly concealed their wish for the PSD to return to office. The EU's decision to overlook serious electoral irregularities not only showed the deeply unsatisfactory nature of a superficial process of Europeanisation but the disinclination of Brussels to establish a meaningful partnership with pro-reform constituencies in possession of skills and commitment that could have improved the quality of the accession process.

Chapter 8 examines the culminating two years of accession talks with a new government and a new Commission in place. It probes the last-minute safeguards introduced by the EU to try and inject fresh momentum into the reform process, especially in the area of justice reform. It shows how these were too weak to prevent a powerful anti-reform coalition involving the ruling Liberals, the PSD and smaller parties from sabotaging key reforms which the EU had insisted upon. The failure of the EU to react purposefully in the face of this defiance and instead set an entry date for 1 January 2007 showed the extent to which Romania was entering the EU on the restricted agenda of its unaccountable political elite.

Corruption has been a long-term and deep-seated problem in Romania. Its depth and prevalence have acted as a check on the country's economic development, impaired the state even in the performance of its normal duties, and created huge barriers of mistrust between society and the political elite. Chapter 9 surveys the degree to which EU-sponsored anti-corruption efforts made any difference to the scale of this chronic problem that dominated public life in Romania from 1989 until after it joined the EU. It shows that by insisting on the privatisation of large parts of the Romanian state without an effective regulatory system being in place, and by pouring huge amounts of pre-accession aid into the country which it could often not keep track of, the EU may have helped to exacerbate this vice. Overall, the measures it advocated in the anti-corruption struggle were not commensurate with the scale of the problem. In trying to eradicate it, the EU would be far less single-minded and resourceful than those powerful groups determined to ensure that corruption would be a way of life even with Romania inside the EU.

Chapter 10 examines the first year of Romania's membership inside the EU. This was a period when the Tăriceanu government drove out most reformers from office and linked up with its nominal opponents in the PSD to try and secure the impeachment of President Băsescu from office. As a result, urgent reforms to upgrade the administrative machine so that Romania could access post-entry EU funds ground to a halt. Despite the government's record of failure on the policy front, it grew increasingly defiant of the EU, which showed no real understanding of how grave a setback to its enlargement strategy the Romanian debacle was proving to be. Instead of European security being enhanced by Romania being inside the EU, this period furnished increasing evidence that it would be a problematic member capable of disrupting routine EU business and of being a disloyal member if tensions with an authoritarian Russia worsened.

In mid-2008, as this book approaches completion, Eurocrats are beginning to realise that they have been involved in a grand masquerade in which the former communists running Romania have outwitted them nearly every step of the way. They have grabbed at the opportunities to transform themselves into aggressive capitalists while scorning the restraints and wider obligations which have often made capitalism the economic underpinning for liberal democracy. The *acquis communautaire* as it applied to Romania can be compared to a complicated electronic system. When buttons were pressed, lights came on. But the wires at the back led nowhere. The switchboard was not attached to any operating system that could enable the EU to direct its energy towards the transformation of a country where resistance to its modernisation plans was deep-seated. The army of seconded officials, aid masters and diplomats who were supposed to promote the leap forward only had bare theoretical knowledge which rested on clichés like exercising 'soft power' and transferring the norms and values which enabled the EU to be an effective entity in a multi-polar world. The literature on enlargement has usually echoed this complacent Brussels perspective and refrained from subjecting the enlargement process to the kind of close scrutiny which it deserves. The main message of this book is that the low-grade and uninspired engagement with Romania has exposed a serious design flaw in the EU's effort to project its institutions and norms in unfamiliar terrain. Instead of promoting a fusion of sovereignty between established democracies and post-communist states, each wedded to building a progressive and effective European order that relegates the nation-state to the sidelines, European officials have caved in to a resourceful and predatory group who have nothing but contempt for the guiding principles that have animated the EU. The oligarchy which has established its control over the EU's seventh largest member exploited the unwieldy multi-layered system of decision-making in Brussels to join the European club on its own limited agenda. This is one of the biggest setbacks for democracy seen in Europe since 1945. Given the nearby location of a combative Russia wedded to nineteenth-century concepts of national supremacy whose potency the EU has forgotten in its infatuation with soft power, the debacle in Romania is likely to have repercussions capable of undermining the entire European project.

Notes

1 Radio Free Europe, *RFE-RL Newsline*, 21 December 2003.
2 *Nine O'Clock*, 17 January 2000.

1

The EU discovers Romania

Romania first made official contact with the European Economic Community (as it then was) at the height of the Cold War. In 1973 it managed to obtain preferential trading status from the EEC. This was long before Brussels established any formal ties of this nature with other 'People's Democracies' of Eastern Europe.[1] Geopolitical concerns motivated the EEC in its relations with Romania. It was a communist state, indeed a dogmatic one, modelled in its later stages on North Korea. But it was also a maverick one which appeared to have become semi-detached from the Soviet-led institutions of the Warsaw Pact and Comecon. Security issues would shape the relationship to an even greater extent in the late 1990s and beyond. Both under Nicolae Ceaușescu and most of his post-communist successors, the Romanian state had not dissimilar goals in relation to the EEC and later the EU. It wished to strengthen its international legitimacy by drawing closer to Brussels, acquire considerable economic benefits and strengthen its grip on the population at home. Before 1989, there was no interest whatsoever in wishing to transform state and society on the EU model (which was encapsulated in the 1993 Copenhagen criteria) and surprisingly little after 2000 when Romania found itself negotiating for full membership. Most of the time, Romania's rulers had a clearer understanding of what they wished to obtain from the EU than *vice versa*. Throughout the long bilateral relationship, the EU really only engaged with Romania through a narrow political elite which had an exploitative relationship with much of the rest of society. This proved to be a severe handicap which prevented the EU from acquiring an understanding of Romanian realities outside the corridors of power.

In the 1980s, Romania–EU relations declined as the Ceaușescu regime, in its last dark phase, became deeply repressive and idiosyncratic.[2] In April 1989, the EU suspended its trade agreement with Romania because of human rights abuses.[3] Within a year Ion Iliescu was well on the way to becoming the undisputed architect of post-communist Romania. He had been a contemporary of Mikhail Gorbachev's at Moscow University in the early 1950s and, after a decade as President of Romania (1990–96, 2000–04), showed no sign of wishing to relinquish influence in his own party. It had tired of his paternalism and readiness to intrigue against younger successors but in his absence was finding it hard to maintain its national influence.

Iliescu and his team were hopeless administrators unable to accomplish the modernisation of their country but they were skilful masters of manoeuvre, able to preserve the interests of the party and state bureaucracy in times of unexpected change. Iliescu, by grabbing the reins of power from the dictator who had marginalised him in the 1970s and then establishing a successor regime, had shown political abilities of a high order. He and other second-ranking officials of the state and Romanian Communist Party (PCR) came to prominence just over a week after the eruption of unrest in the western city of Timişoara on 16 December 1989. Once it spread rapidly to Bucharest and other large cities, involving large numbers of people and producing a confused but violent response from the dictator's arsenal of repression, Ceauşescu's fate was sealed. Three days after fleeing the capital with Elena, his wife and co-ruler, both of them were shot in an improvised trial ordered by Romania's provisional rulers on 25 December 1989. This sacrifice was meant to atone for their grotesque catalogue of misdeeds during the previous quarter of a century when Romania had become synonymous with their totalitarian exercise of power. They became the official scapegoats for a repressive system whose survival had depended on the active participation of millions of other large and small cogs in the dictatorial wheel.

Ion Iliescu's first task was to restore order and establish the authority of the new group exercising power over the state bureaucracy and the sprawling intelligence services. In theory, there was no need to bother about the 3 million-strong Romanian Communist Party. It had been dissolved in one of the first acts of the National Salvation Front (FSN), the political vehicle which would take Romania into a new and uncertain political era. Indeed Romania was the only former satellite state where no successor to the Communist Party emerged. Instead, the FSN used the infrastructure, resources and personnel of the PCR to launch its own bid for power. It acquired vital popular endorsement in elections held on 20 May 1990, less than 20 weeks after the violent transfer of power. The harsh conditions of life which had been the norm during the dictatorship's last years were relaxed by flooding the shops with consumer goods which had previously been exported in order to pay off the country's foreign debt. But even if the first of many such populist gestures by Iliescu had not been made, it is likely that he would have won a mandate. The bulk of the population was defined by residual communist attitudes. This was inevitable in what had been a fully regimented society, one in which the regime intruded deep into the private lives of citizens and had insisted on public conformity. The 20 May result, which led to Iliescu being elected President with 85% support in a massive turnout, was challenged by civic activists and the

remnants of pre-1945 parties. These protests were suppressed with considerable violence in June 1990. It was a sign of how ruthless Iliescu was prepared
to be in order to shape the transition Romania was embarking on around a
limited agenda of change. A procedural democracy would be permitted to take
shape provided the interests of the old structures which had regrouped at the
end of 1989 were not fundamentally affected. Iliescu was prepared to break his
own rules when he in turn used violence to get rid of a rival who appeared to
threaten his hold on power. In September 1991 the miners who had acted as
a praetorian guard to crush civic protests in Bucharest in the summer of 1990
were summoned back to the capital to drive Prime Minister Petre Roman from
office. By now, groups steeped in the ideological and institutional heritage of
communism saw Iliescu and the FSN as providing them with a comfortable
life insurance policy. Not only would they not need to account for their past
sins but they could fully expect to prosper if the regime managed to consolidate itself. In 1991, the Parliament adopted a law on national security, sealing
most of the Communist Party archives indefinitely. So there appeared scant
likelihood that figures compromised by their ignoble conduct before 1989
would ever have to account for their crimes.

Iliescu and the FSN devised a new Constitution under which the President
enjoyed more power than in any other former People's Democracy. His
authority extended to controlling senior appointments in the justice system so
that the separation of powers which enabled the judiciary to operate independently from the executive was set aside. State institutions were given a makeover
without, in most instances, any effort being made to increase their efficiency,
or their accountability to anyone other than the ruling group. Some actions
by Iliescu suggested that he was slow to assume that the West had emerged on
top in the long-running contest with the Soviet Union. In April 1991, Romania
became the only former Moscow satellite to sign a treaty of friendship with the
Soviet Union. It gave Moscow an effective right of veto over any Romanian
alliance with a Western country. If it had not been annulled by the collapse of
the Soviet Union six months later, it might have placed Romania more firmly
in the Soviet sphere of influence than it had been in Ceauşescu's time.[4]

Iliescu and his party devised the institutional architecture of post-
communist Romania without forming pacts with the opposition in order to
bestow legitimacy on the changes made. The National Peasant and Christian
Democratic Party (PNŢCD), which would be the largest party after 1996,
when Iliescu lost office, actually boycotted the 1991 referendum on the new
Constitution in protest at it being a vehicle to consolidate FSN rule. Iliescu
and the Party of Romanian Social Democracy (PDSR) went down to defeat
in 1996 elections against a coalition of all their opponents barring the ultra-
nationalists. The post-communists were penalised by voters for failing to
honour their promise of offering social protection to vulnerable sectors of

the population, the undertaking largely responsible for their earlier electoral successes. Runaway corruption and the incompetence of the 1992–96 government, led by Nicolae Văcăroiu, were impossible to conceal. An outspoken independent press, the main expression of the cautious liberalisation which gathered pace in the 1990s, exposed the shortcomings of those in power and helped to raise voters' expectations.

There were widespread expectations that in 1996 a turning-point had at last been reached which would enable a genuine transition to political and economic pluralism to get underway. Without the replacement of Iliescu, it is almost impossible to contemplate the European Union agreeing to include Romania in the enlargement process which got underway at the Luxembourg summit in 1997 or recognising that it fulfilled the political criteria for entry. But by now the new ruling group had consolidated its authority. The coalition was too fragile and preoccupied with surviving in office to be able to substitute a fresh set of rules capable of weakening the hegemony of the PDSR. It and its supporters continued to exercise control of the economy. Privatisation had hitherto been allowed only if the newly private assets mainly went to the PDSR's clientele. Prominent among the new capitalists had been former members of the intelligence services with access to hard currency and contacts in the unreformed state structure enabling them to benefit disproportionately from Romania's uncertain lurch towards a market economy. By the end of the 1990s, private sector share of GDP in Romania, at around 60%, was well below the Central European average of 70%.[5] The state sector of the economy provided another large support base for the PDSR. After a year of uncertainty, when the coalition attempted some bold economic reforms only to face social unrest and deepening internal strife, the PDSR may have had some cause to fear for the future. But by 1998 it was becoming clear that the government lacked the strength to uproot the old structures in any significant area of national life. Iliescu's strategy of cautious democratisation without meaningful de-communisation remained largely intact. His opponents were in office but not in power. Indeed, this bitter taste of office would reconcile not a few of them to the PDSR playing a dominant role in national politics, thus reducing the dimensions of the hitherto strong communist versus anti-communist cleavage in national politics.

During the years when Iliescu and his allies were building a new set of structures with which to take Romania into the post-Cold War era, the EU's attention towards Romania had only been spasmodic. The heroic images of demonstrators resisting Ceauşescu's tanks had suggested that Romania was on the verge of a hopeful new era at the end of 1989. In January 1990, Frans Andriessen, the EU's Foreign Affairs Commissioner, made the first official visit to the country following Ceauşescu's overthrow, during which he was told by Iliescu that the FSN would hand over power and disappear for ever after elections.[6] But the strong-arm methods used by the new rulers to assert their right to rule produced increasing foreboding in Brussels. Following the state-induced miners' rampage in Bucharest in June 1990, Bruce Millan, the EU's Trade Commissioner, stated that a deepening of ties would have to be put aside until 'the achievement of an economic and political system founded on the same principles prevailing within the Community'.[7] Romania was excluded from the Phare aid programme launched in 1989 to enable former Eastern bloc states to progress with the reconstruction agenda. Poland obtained 20.9% of the total Phare aid distributed up to 1996, compared with the allocation to Romania (which only had a slightly smaller population) of 10.9%.[8] Poland and Hungary signed European association agreements with the EU in 1991. But this breakthrough only occurred for Romania in February 1993.[9] The EU was of course preoccupied with completing the Maastricht treaty devoted to deepening cooperation in the areas of justice and home affairs as well as preparing the way for a common EU foreign policy. After 1991, a disproportionate amount of time put aside for Eastern Europe was devoted to trying to halt the escalating violence in the former Yugoslavia. Intransigent nationalism had been unleashed as a power-conserving strategy by conservative forces around Slobodan Milosevic, who wished to re-centralise the federal state around Serbia. Iliescu's own efforts to stir up nationalist tensions in order to weaken the political opposition and deflect popular attention from the looting of state resources by his supporters, would not have escaped the attention of Brussels. There were real fears that if relations between the state and the Hungarian minority deteriorated further, a new flashpoint in inter-ethnic tension could be opened in the Balkans. Romania only obtained full membership of the Council of Europe (COE) in October 1993 because of concerns over minority rights. Widely seen as a gateway paving the way for participating in the EU integration process, the COE's chief aims are to protect human rights and democratic freedoms. Unease about Romania's commitment to the COE's core values persisted, and from 1993 to 1997 its *rapporteurs* visited Romania every six months to assess progress in observing human rights.

A period of several years elapsed before the EU's intentions towards the former communist states of East–Central Europe (ECE) became clearly apparent. The Europe association agreements were gestures of goodwill in which Brussels offered to remove commercial and economic barriers as well as promote free trade in return for the ECE states passing legislation to guarantee property rights and ensure economic competition. Poland, Hungary and the Czech Republic were the states with which Brussels had the closest ties. They had formed the Visegrad group in 1990, committed to rapid economic reform and integration with Euro-Atlantic economic and security structures. Romania hoped to join this club for accelerated Westernisation. But its credentials were deemed insufficient by the other members and when Petre

Roman turned up uninvited to one of the summits, he suffered a humiliating rebuff. One top EU official closely involved with Romania early in the accession process, and who had spent a period negotiating the Europe agreements with the Visegrad states, could understand their reticence: 'these people were on another planet compared with their counterparts in Romania. The quality of the political forces and the civil servants in these countries could not be compared with what the EU found in Romania. Sometimes it seemed as if they knew the EU better than we did'.[10]

The Visegrad group challenged the EU to set out clear guidelines for accession or else justify their continued exclusion. In June 1993, the EU responded at the meeting of the European Council held in Copenhagen when it was agreed that the associated countries (which by now included Romania) were to 'enter into a structural relationship with the institutions of the Union . . .'. In a decisive turning-point in relations with the former Warsaw Pact satellites, it was decided that 'the association countries of central and Eastern Europe . . . that so desire shall become members . . . as soon as able to assume the obligations of membership by satisfying the political and economic conditions required'.[11] The Danish summit also witnessed the unfurling of the set of conditions for beginning accession negotiations. The Copenhagen criteria required candidates to demonstrate that

- they have stable institutions that guarantee democracy, human rights, the rule of law and protection of minorities;
- they have a functioning market economy capable of withstanding competitive pressures within the EU;
- they are able to take on the obligations of membership and adhere to the aims of political, economic and monetary union;
- their administrative and judicial structures will allow for the adoption and application of EU legislation.[12]

This process indicated the ability of the most reform-active states of ECE to influence the accession agenda and not be mere suppliants.[13] Formal applications for membership began to be submitted from March 1994. In December of that year, as a sign of the new relationship, the leaders of the association countries, including Ion Iliescu, attended the EU's Essen summit. It is reckoned that this occasion marked the start of the pre-accession strategy, with the Commission being asked to draw up a white paper on preparing them for integration and the internal market.[14]

On 21 June 1995, the Snagov statement was issued by the main political parties in which they appeared to agree on an integration strategy for Romania. Soon after, the Romanian Foreign Minister, Teodor Meleşcanu, submitted Romania's formal request for membership. A National Strategy for the Preparation of Romania's Accession to the European Union was drawn up in which it was stated that Romania expected to fulfil the criteria for accession by the year 2000. This was a rare example of still polarised political forces mobilising behind a common national objective. Romania's application was lodged with Brussels soon afterwards.[15]

Since 1993, the EU had already had a permanent delegation established in Bucharest. For the next five years it was headed by Karen Fogg, a British member of the European Commission who had been trained as a development economist. The need to strengthen the autonomy of the individual from the state was paramount in her view (given the legacy of rigid communism in Romania). Promoting levels of autonomous activity involving a range of social actors (or 'stakeholders') was seen as a useful way of breaking up the old system of central control.[16] Her procedures were innovative certainly for Romania and increasingly for the EU as it adopted unwieldy approaches to cope with the biggest expansion in its history. Fogg would devote considerable energy to setting up local partnerships involving elected officials, the community sector, the rest of civil society and local business in order to promote sustainable development at local level. She had known Romania before arriving as ambassador in 1993 and had more experience of Romania than most of the 25 or so members of her staff which steadily expanded in the years ahead. After 1989 she had been given sectoral responsibility for the Phare programmes being implemented in the former Warsaw Pact states. Large budgets were available for improvements in the areas of public administration, social policy and civil society. She was able to make use of good-quality local staff on her team, who were committed to change. Such people were not entirely absent on the government side, and included Mişu Negriţoiu, who as President of the Council of Reform in Romania coordinated aid emanating from the EU.[17] He knew the West through his trade background and was felt to be non-hierarchical in his approach to administration. The sociologist, Cătălin Zamfir, was an early champion of this kind of thinking as Minister of Labour after June 1990, but he left politics after being unable to influence the direction of policy. Aurel Dochia was an economic analyst with whom Fogg worked closely on Phare objectives. He was recalled by her as a tenacious person who stood up to political pressure regarding the fate of projects.[18] She herself fought a battle with the Văcăroiu government regarding the evolution of the civic agenda. Before her arrival in Bucharest, she had helped to launch a Civil Society Foundation which was designed to be 'a broad church' encompassing the most effective civic bodies. She had to manoeuvre and ensure that its existence be recognised in the Phare agreement with the government so that it could be funded while retaining important autonomy. Through various creative stratagems, the Delegation managed to get resources for non-governmental organisations (NGOs) without the government being intensively involved.[19]

At that time, there was a cross-national perspective shaping the evolving Phare projects which Fogg considered to be invaluable: 'We were all in such a rush to do things. We picked up ideas in the one country and applied them [with suitable modifications in some cases] in the other. The European Institute for Human Rights and Development (EIDHR) was a rich source of ideas due to the work it had done in post-authoritarian southern European states that later joined the EU'.[20]

Fogg looked back with satisfaction to her period in Romania: 'I was in Romania at a time when it was a creative clearing-house of ideas . . . If we could look back on our experience and start again, we could only do it worse'. She wanted to reach out beyond Western-looking NGOs: 'I wasn't just concerned with engaging with NGOs who were service deliverers or were trying to shape policy in the areas needed to accomplish a successful transition'.[21] Neighbourhood associations involving the residents of the high-rise block in which most city-dwellers lived were important in her view. Consortia of local 'stakeholders' were encouraged to set up local development foundations, income-generating activities and community associations. It was important for local authorities to become accustomed to doing this kind of work for their communities. Camelia Gheorghe, a community development specialist who shared her vision, recalled Fogg as 'a large brain on two legs'. Much energy was invested in trying to 'wake up sleepy and silent communities in order that they could realise their potential'.[22] Partnerships extended across the local public administration, decentralised services of the ministries, NGOs, the business world, churches and the education sector. In some districts, the synergy released enabled local communities to make effective use of later EU programmes.[23] This was a time when the EU had yet to firm up its mandate in countries seen as potential members and where Delegation heads initially had a fairly free hand to carry out their mission. It was also a period when the ruling post-communists were experiencing internal difficulties, so officials newly arrived from the West had greater opportunities to make headway with their plans than before or indeed later. But time would show the true extent of the EU's commitment to empowering communities to be able to do things for themselves without entering into a dependency relationship with either Bucharest, Brussels or local political forces.

Apparent indications that Romania was at last throwing aside its totalitarian legacy and striving to catch up with its Central European neighbours coincided with growing international interest in the Balkans. The West had learned the impracticability of allowing the Yugoslav conflicts of the early 1990s to be left to burn themselves out. A US-orchestrated move to end the conflict in Bosnia had culminated in the 1995 Dayton peace agreement. It would be the first of two costly international peace-keeping operations in the region. Perhaps unavoidably, it led to growing interest in the stability of the former communist states bordering ex-Yugoslavia among senior diplomats on both sides of the Atlantic. Their own ability to transcend corrosive nationalism appeared likely to contribute to the success of Western efforts to stabilise the Balkans. Encouragement was derived in both NATO and the EU from the readiness of Iliescu's successors to include Hungarian minority members in the government and respond to some of the principal grievances of that 1.7 million-strong community.

Important decisions were due to be taken in 1997 which would determine the pace and extent of Euro-Atlantic integration in Eastern Europe. NATO had announced that it would invite a number of candidates to open talks on membership at its July summit in Madrid. In December, the EU was going to extend invitations to open talks for full membership to former communist states which appeared capable of handling this responsibility. In Bucharest, the government headed by Victor Ciorbea decided to concentrate on convincing NATO of the fitness of Romania to join. The criteria for entry were not as strong as for the EU and, in 1994, when NATO announced a cooperation programme with prospective new members called the Partnership for Peace, Romania was actually the first former Soviet bloc state to join. This established a process of reforming the Romanian military and bringing it closer to the model of armies in long-established democracies. Greater civilian control was asserted and professional competence was given a higher priority than in other branches of the state.[24] But NATO also made it clear that a candidate nation's chance of joining the Western military alliance depended on its performance in democratising its society, reforming its economy and settling any serious differences with adjacent states. When Alexandru Herlea, Ciorbea's Minister of European Integration, visited Washington in the spring of 1996, he was told by Richard Holbrooke, the US State Department's chief envoy in the Balkans, that it was through continuing with a programme of bold economic reform that Romania stood the best chance of integrating with Euro-Atlantic institutions.[25]

Between January and April 1997, Ciorbea pursued a policy of shock therapy. Subsidies were removed from energy and food products and plans were drawn up to close loss-making state enterprises. The International Monetary Fund (IMF) offered a new loan in the hope that the Fund's seal of approval would attract international investors who had been avoiding Romania in favour of better-governed states in ECE. In May 1997, the London *Economist* appeared in no doubt that Romania's new ruling team 'have set about remaking Romania's economy, its polity, even its values, with almost Bolshevik zeal'.[26] But already cracks in the government's resolve were opening up. The Democratic Party (PD), which had once been part of Iliescu's FSN, was increasingly viewed as a Trojan Horse inside the coalition opposed to bold reform in case it harmed the interests of economic clients in the state sector.[27] However, it was President

Emil Constantinescu, whose power base derived from the Peasants' Party (PNŢCD) and civic forces, who discreetly slammed the brakes on reform. He feared that factory closures would result in social unrest that would extinguish Romania's chances of joining NATO in the near future. France was Romania's only major backer at the Madrid summit. The USA, Britain and Germany did not feel that Romania would strengthen the Alliance at this stage and the enlargement was confined to three Central European states.

Thereafter, progress with the EU application appeared to be the most realistic option for strengthening ties with the West. A Department of European Integration had existed since 1994, attached to the Prime Minister's office. But it generated little activity in the 18 months after the Snagov declaration. At the start of the coalition, it became a full ministry under Alexandru Herlea. He was a technocrat based in France after going into exile as a young man in 1972 who had taught the history of science and technology at universities in France and North America. Across Eastern Europe, *émigrés* who entered national politics made little impact after 1989 except in the Baltic states. Herlea was seen as an outsider by many in his own party, the PNŢCD. This image made even the pro-reform press suspicious of him. His commitment to radical reform made him anathema to the PD. During the year in which the PD's Adrian Severin was Foreign Minister, Herlea found himself trying to prevent his new ministry being absorbed by one well known for being a stronghold of officials dating from communist times. Ciorbea was an ally but he was unable to persuade him to strengthen the ministry by appointing fresh blood. He told Ciorbea that 'we are inexperienced. We need to recruit 5–10 specialists who can lead discussions with the EU and international financial institutions'.[28] But the Prime Minister was not strong enough to accomplish this. He also had to resist demands from the PNŢCD to sack the existing staff and hire replacements whose only criteria was their claim to be party loyalists. One of his key roles was to make the Council of Economic Integration which he headed into a major driving force behind reforms meant to keep alive Romania's EU hopes. But he failed to get the cooperation of other ministers and the Council became a dead-letter as Ciorbea's authority waned.

The multilingual Herlea was a good networker who was able to use his Franco-German links to obtain two counsellors, Francois Froment-Meurice and Christain Zschaber, whose salaries were covered by France and Germany. But EU hopes appeared to be receding for Romania by July 1997. In that month, the Commission published the so-called 'Agenda 2000', assessing the degrees of readiness for accession of the various candidates. The report acknowledged the progress Romania had made in the various fields, yet baldly expressed its 'uncertainty whether Romania will be in a position to assume the obligations of membership in the medium term'.[29] The overall assessment deemed Romania unprepared for membership and it seemed inevitable that

Romania would be excluded from the next wave of enlargement, even though it had been the third among the ECE states to apply for EU membership.

So the European Commission recommended that Romania, along with five other states, be left out of the accession process, due to commence shortly, because it was difficult to envisage when it could meet the terms of entry.[30] But in December 1997, at the Luxembourg summit of EU heads of government, it was decided to simultaneously extend invitations to all 11 aspirant members (nearly all from the East) but to proceed at a far slower pace with those falling well short of entry requirements, Romania standing out in this category. This was one of the first indications of the readiness of the European Council, or more especially leading member states, to disregard the Commission's advice regarding enlargement issues. It showed how effective lobbying could be, especially in the various groupings represented at the European Parliament. At the November 1997 meeting of the European Popular Party, Herlea managed to win over doubters and a motion was passed advocating that all candidate states be kept in the enlargement process even if some were less prepared than others for completing the EU roadmap. Adrian Severin has emphasised the efforts made at the time to persuade left-wing heads of government in Italy, Greece and Portugal to take a similar line.[31]

The volatile Severin left office after he was unable, or unwilling, to substantiate bizarre claims that leading press editors and also two current party leaders were spies who had been financed by intelligence services from abroad.[32] Ciorbea failed to survive beyond February 1998. He had impressed Francois Lamoureux, the Deputy Director-General for European enlargement, when what was supposed to be a ten-minute protocol meeting turned into a four-hour marathon in which Ciorbea thoroughly explained Romania's European strategy. Lamoureux said later to Herlea that 'I never thought I would meet a prime minister with such knowledge of the European brief'.[33] This was high praise coming from one of the most accomplished officials in the Commission who had been *Chef de Cabinet* of Jacques Delors at the height of the Maastricht process.[34] But despite his rectitude, capacity for hard work and elephantine memory, Ciorbea was a neophyte in the shark-infested waters of Bucharest politics. This Transylvanian lawyer lacked the versatility and craftiness to prevail in a land whose Levantine characteristics appeared increasingly noteworthy. Herlea lost his most substantial ally and very soon his ministry became little more than an agency for translating the *acquis communautaire*, the EU legislation which Romania would need to absorb, into the Romanian language.

Poland, Hungary, the Czech Republic and Estonia started full negotiations in 1998. Romania, Slovakia, Bulgaria and Slovenia were due to join them at a later date. However, even for these second-tier states, there was an emphasis on moving quickly forward with large-scale funding projects meant to prepare candidates for membership. There seems to have been no pause for reflection about whether such massive funding schemes could work as unwieldy national bureaucracies struggled to absorb the cash flow. Under the 'Agenda 2000' strategy unfurled in Brussels in 1997, countries near the end of the queue were due to receive disproportionately large amounts of pre-accession funds. The decision was also made to create regional development agencies, eight in all for Romania, which would be the main channels for pre-accession funds, especially for the Phare programme. This was the oldest of the EU's pre-accession instruments and it was meant to channel technical, economic and infrastructural expertise and assistance to recipient states. The aim was to try and ensure that these countries acquired economies based on free enterprise and private initiative. A regional strategy made sense given the country's size and the remoteness of the capital from districts most in need of external help. It was an admission that most central ministries were poorly equipped to be motors of development. But the EU appears not to have reflected very deeply about what kind of regionalisation process could advance its agenda. Initially, it backed a small number of regions based on the country's historic regions. Protests emanating mainly from the PDSR, but also some of the parties in government, that this could lead to the federalisation of Romania, resulted in the original plan being modified.

The first of no less than nine regular reports that the EU produced annually on each candidate's progress towards accession appeared in the autumn of 1998. It was gloomy about the potential for Romania to consolidate weakly based reforms and alarm was expressed about a deteriorating economic situation which saw sharp falls in GDP during the lifetime of the coalition. In July 1998, a Commission official had declared that 'Romania had the worst economic performance of any EU applicant over the past year'.[35] In August relations with Brussels were soured by the government's failure to submit economic data in time to enable the Commission to publish its annual report; when the data were finally submitted, they included contradictory estimates of the same indicators produced by different ministries.[36]

By now, the economy was starting to experience significant penetration by Western European firms. They benefited from the lifting of trade barriers under the association agreement signed in 1996 with the EU. Germany and Italy soon replaced Eastern European states as the main source of imports. This had adverse results, particularly for the large but inefficient agricultural sector. Romanian food markets and shops flooded by imports from heavily subsidised EU producers. In 1997 the country enjoyed the best harvest for a decade but much of it rotted in warehouses because EU produce was cheaper.[37] Mircea Ciumara, the Trade Minister, was soon calling for the renegotiation of the agreement and a five-year postponement in its full implementation, perhaps a sign that neither he nor his colleagues had understood what the full implications of it were likely to be for the vulnerable local economy.[38]

A partnership failed to arise between the Minister of European Integration and Fokion Fotiadis, who succeeded Karen Fogg as head of the European Delegation in August 1998. Herlea had decided to emphasise progress made by Romania in adhering to the Copenhagen criteria regarding democracy and human rights. The coalition's record was far from pristine, with the fate of children in state institutions being chief among the Commission's concerns. But it did not take long for Fotiadis to be convinced that no progress could take place unless the economy was fixed. Brussels was told by him within weeks of his arrival that the accession process would be a theoretical one with many reforms existing only on paper in the absence of solid economic growth.[39]

No EU figure as well connected and senior as Fotiadis would serve in Bucharest after formal ties had been established at ambassadorial level in 1993. Fotiadis enjoyed good access to Lamoureux who is widely seen by top Commission officials as being the moving spirit responsible for the success of Eastern enlargement. Indeed, one went so far as to say that 'It probably wouldn't have happened without him'.[40] Lamoureux had sent Fotiadis to Bucharest after a plea from Herlea to him for Brussels to appoint a heavy-weight figure. Lamoureux had said: 'I will do something for you and especially for Romania. I will send my best diplomat to help you, but don't forget that he has a special quality. He knows how to establish the best relations at the highest level'.[41] Perhaps understandably, given his lack of influence at home, Herlea was sidelined by Brussels and the new ambassador concentrated on establishing a smooth working relationship with Ciorbea's successor, Radu Vasile. A former academic specialising in economic history, Vasile was a political insider who proved to be a better crisis manager than his predecessor. His stiffest challenge undoubtedly was the politically inspired miners' march on Bucharest at the start of 1999. This influential group of workers had been used by Iliescu to vanquish anti-communist foes and his known internal rivals in 1990–91, and by now their leader, Miron Cozma, was aligned with the ultra-nationalists.[42] Commission officials at the Delegation recall the panic among the Romanian staff as militarised police units were vanquished by the miners. It took the active backing of the ambassador to enable Vasile to persuade his security advisers that it was worth negotiating with the miners, so strong was the defeatist mood high up in the government. These negotiations led the miners to retreat and eventually the army was able to bring their rebellion under control. The Commission had been prepared to fully support Vasile however much force was required to bring the miners to heel.[43] It was probably crucial that Lamoureux, the Director for Enlargement, was French and therefore was likely to reflect the strong support for Romanian membership emanating from Paris. He backed Fotiadis when the ambassador urged Vasile that it was essential to take decisive action in order to restore order.[44] Romania was fortunate that authoritative figures who enjoyed a close rapport were working in tandem in order to avoid disaster in Romania. Brussels failed to display the same degree of coordination at future key moments, especially in 2004, with baleful effects on Romania's role once it was inside the EU.

Within months of this crisis, NATO found itself involved in the first military action in its 50-year history, in the Balkans. In the spring of 1999, the ten-week confrontation between NATO and Serbia over Milosevic's maltreatment of the Albanian population of Kosovo increased Romania's importance in the eyes of key Western states. The EU threw its weight behind NATO's risky efforts to halt the 'ethnic cleansing' of the Albanians. Romania and Bulgaria closed ranks to assist NATO, denying Russia access to their airspace when it tried to rush support to Milosevic. The shift in the British position was particularly dramatic. Prime Minister Tony Blair, when addressing the Romanian Parliament on 4 May 1999, referred to Romania as 'an exemplary partner and future ally'.[45] Hitherto, Britain had displayed limited interest in Romanian political and economic matters. Robin Cook, the British Foreign Secretary, wondered aloud in 1997 if Romania had a common border with Greece.[46] But on 4 May, Blair informed his Romanian hosts that: 'At the meeting of the European Council in Helsinki in December, Great Britain is going to support an invitation being extended to Romania to begin negotiations to join the EU'.[47] He overrode the objections of his officials, most of whom believed that such an offer was inadvisable since the Copenhagen criteria were fundamental requirements that Romania failed to measure up to in economic terms. On returning home, he told MPs: 'It is essential that we begin work as soon as possible on a regeneration programme for the Balkans because many of the front-line states – such as Bulgaria, Romania, Macedonia and Albania – have given us support in circumstances of intense internal difficulty'.[48] These internal difficulties were a reference to the unpopularity of NATO's military action, with Iliescu's PDSR being the chief critic in Romania. A Stability Pact for the Balkans was launched in the summer. The EU was the main source of funds for a project designed to prevent future conflict and integrate the region with mainstream Europe. This poorly managed initiative was soon lost sight of and instead the EU integration process assumed centre stage.

Blair won the backing of previously sceptical EU member states like Germany for including the Balkans in the enlargement process. Romano Prodi signalled a clear softening of the official EU approach towards Romania in a speech he made on 13 October 1999, not long after becoming President of the European Commission. He stated that if the Copenhagen conditions were applied 'to the letter, it rules out opening negotiations with most of the remaining applicant countries since they do not fully meet the economic criteria'. This approach to Romania as well as Bulgaria, Latvia, Lithuania, Slovakia and Malta was described by Prodi as a 'hardline' one. He recommended instead that 'accession negotiations be opened in 2000 with all candidate countries' that 'are ready to take the necessary measures to comply with the economic criteria'. He described this as 'a bold step' needed 'to inject vital new momentum into the enlargement process'.[49]

As Prodi envisaged it, the road ahead was to be based on 'a fully-flexible, multi-speed accession process . . . We should look at the individual situation of each country and, on that basis, open only those chapters which can realistically be concluded in the short to medium term'.[50] This meant leaving to the end the difficult chapters, which in Romania's case would be justice and home affairs, competition policy and agriculture, to name only the most pressing ones. It increased the chance that if informal pressures, such as those springing from the Kosovo crisis, came into play in the future, then the demand for a flexible interpretation of the chapters would grow. This is indeed what had started to happen by the third year of entry negotiations. The EU's institutions of multi-level governance proved remarkably prone to lobbying from the Romanian state and the allies it had meanwhile cultivated in Western Europe in order to advance its cause. With challenging applicants like Macedonia in mind, the EU would later concede that it must start with the difficult accession chapters first and not allow negotiations on relatively unproblematic ones to be closed, thereby building up a momentum behind entry that lacked a solid basis.

The Economist presciently warned in 1999 that 'the EU does nobody any favours by admitting countries before they are ready to join'.[51] With Prodi backing an early start to talks, Gunther Verheugen, the Enlargement Commissioner, faced the risk of being overruled by the European Council if he maintained the Commission's sceptical line about the feasibility of absorbing both Romania and Bulgaria. Instead, he came up with a novel-sounding initiative which seemed to suggest that the EU was going to give sustained attention to Romania's economic difficulties and how to overcome them. In a letter to Prime Minister Radu Vasile sent on 26 October 1999, Verheugen proposed that working groups be set up composed of representatives from the EU, the IMF and the World Bank who, working in tandem with Romanian experts and officials, would draw up a medium-term economic strategy that would hopefully enable the economic impediments to joining the EU to be overcome.[52] It was clear that Verheugen envisaged international financial institutions playing a crucial role along with the European Commission itself, with Romanian ministers and experts being involved but not necessarily in a prominent role. This is certainly how the media in Bucharest viewed the approach. 'The West offers to "manage" Romania' was the view of the influential commentator, Bogdan Chirieac.[53] He saw the West's offer to become involved in directing the country economically over a period of five years as 'a kind of directorate' that was 'perhaps not the worst solution for Romania'. His close colleague, the outspoken commentator Cristian Tudor Popescu, soon afterwards declared that 'we have to choose between strict European monitoring and misery, death, violence, disaster, and perhaps the disintegration of the state. For any Romanian, I am sure that more precious than national pride has to be a single objective: "the survival of Romania'".[54]

Less than ten months earlier, during the miners' rebellion, Romania appeared to have the characteristics of a failed state in the heart of Europe, similar to Albania where state authority had dissolved in 1997, leading to an Italian-led NATO force being sent to try and restore order. Verheugen's plan was less dramatic but it stirred opposition. Ion Iliescu stated that Romania had enough competent people to single-handedly elaborate a reform project and only then was it advisable for the EU to get involved: 'partnership, negotiations, consultation and cooperation are one thing, but to have a committee of supervision is quite another'.[55] Paul Păcuraru, a government deputy representing the Liberals, branded the EU initiative as 'unnecessary and inopportune'.[56] Eight years later he would be Minister of Labour in a government resisting EU requests that Romania honour the obligations it had made in the area of justice reform in order to obtain membership in 2007. In February 2000 Iliescu sent a letter to Fokion Fotiadis, the head of the EU Delegation, in which he expressed his dissatisfaction with the lack of consultation with his party. Soon after, an alternative strategy appeared, entitled 'The PDSR, a Promoter of Social and Participatory Democracy'.[57]

Having briefly seemed to be destined for marginalisation in 1996, the PDSR was once again the most popular force in the country. It had stirred up opposition not only to Romania's engagement with NATO in the Kosovo conflict but also to privatisation measures which the government was implementing under EU and IMF pressure. Ordinary voters had paid a harsh price for poorly implemented or delayed reforms. In 1999, according to data released by the World Bank in 2000, 41.2% of Romanians lived on or below its poverty threshold compared with 25.3% in 1995, and those living in extreme poverty comprised 16.6% of the population – double the total for 1995 (8%).[58] Alarmingly, polling evidence in 2000 showed a wave of nostalgia for the period of communist rule in which the country had faced the greatest privations. The following answers were given to the question: 'When in the last 100 years did things go better for Romania?'[59]

	%
Before World War I	4.2
The inter-war period	13.5
The Dej years of communism	4.6
1965–79	34.3
1980s	18.4
After 1989	8.5

Double the number of respondents believed life had been better for them in the 1980s than it had been after 1989 and a majority, 52.7%, believed that life was better for Romanians under Ceauşescu than at any other time in recent history. The poll, carried out by the Centre for Urban and Regional Sociology (CURS) and the Romanian Academic Society, confirmed that the communist era remained the chief reference point for most Romanians: details of that time, such as the endless queuing for scarce basic commodities and a television output largely devoted to the public duties of the Ceauşescus, had faded from memory. In 2000, the all-important fact was that 44% of Romanians lived on an EU average poverty wage of $4.30 a day.[60]

The announcement that Romania was opening membership talks with the EU failed to evoke a strong response among Romanian public opinion. It was widely viewed as the weakest of the five applicants given candidate status at Helsinki. It had broken through from a position of marginality thanks to the unexpected opportunity provided by the Kosovo crisis for Romania to appear a useful ally of the West. As the Bucharest editor Cornel Nistorescu pointed out: 'It becomes obvious now that Romania's pro-NATO stand during the war in Yugoslavia substantially tipped the balance in our favour. It was a courageous move that showed a country that was the West's ally, though at home neither the people nor the opposition nor most of the press seemed to understand how much our support would contribute to . . . success in Helsinki'.[61]

Shortly beforehand, *The Economist* had written that 'Romania . . . needs to be told that it still has a decade of work ahead'.[62] If this message was passed on, it did not appear to have been heeded in Bucharest. Within hours of the completion of the Helsinki summit, President Constantinescu ousted his Prime Minister in a doubtful constitutional manoeuvre.[63] It led to weeks of infighting before a new government was formed. Much lengthier political paralysis would follow within months of full membership occurring in 2007. This revealed how introspective and fractious the political elite was and perhaps also how insincere was the commitment of the parties set out in the 1995 Snagov pact to work to make Romania's engagement with the EU a success.

Romano Prodi made a high-profile visit to Romania in January 2000 during which he recognised Romania's strategic importance: 'Romania is a key country for stability in this delicate region of Europe'.[64] Perhaps the greatest favour the President of the Commission could have made to Romania was to point out that success in realising its hopes for full membership was far from certain and that it could only be guaranteed by the elite showing a genuine commitment to the Europeanisation of political standards and to rebuilding the country economically, which had been largely conspicuous by its absence in the previous decade. Instead, after a round of meetings with political leaders, he adopted almost a festive air, declaring that he had 'discovered a powerful unity of opinions among all representatives of Romanian society and members of political parties for Romania's accession to the EU. 'Together', he proclaimed, 'we have initiated a great thing', which was a very fanciful claim, given the polarisation between and within the parties and the fact that there were very few figures who understood what the process of Europeanisation actually meant for Romania.[65] It was inevitable that politicians who had mainly fled from carrying out national responsibilities in favour of bolstering their own privileges would draw comfort from the undemanding words of an indulgent EU chief. Iliescu's PDSR, which looked increasingly likely to be returned to power at the end of 2000, was bound to have noted them carefully. Even during Prodi's visit, Iliescu indicated how anachronistic his thinking was when he told the press: 'the EU needs Romania because it is in competition with the US and must consolidate its position'.[66] It was far from clear how reaching out to a country whose GDP (in 1997) was just 27% of the EU average could assist the EU in any competition with the USA, or indeed anyone else. Iliescu was displaying the Romanian penchant for manoeuvring between different big powers and trying to extract the most favourable conditions from them. It hardly suggested, as one academic later wrote, that 'Iliescu changed significantly during the . . . four years of opposition when he read widely and reflected. This resulted in a changed mentality about the EU'.[67]

It probably never occurred to Prodi that such opportunistic behaviour might even continue once the country was fully inside the EU. At Bucharest's Academy of Economic Studies (ASE: from which most of the country's economic elite had graduated in communist and now post-communist times), instead of adopting a stern pose, Prodi was elegiac and even utopian about the future: 'what we need to do in the coming years is to develop a completely new culture which will allow the spontaneous integration of as many as 25 or 30 national states in the one single political entity'.[68] He seemed to have little grasp of how deficient the elite was in carrying out many of the rudimentary tasks without which a nation-state was unable to function effectively. Perhaps being given Romania's top honours as well as being made an honorary doctor of the ASE had prompted him to postpone a tough lecture about the fundamental transformation which the country would have to undergo until a later time. Instead, when declaring that 'the process of European expansion is irreversible' he indulged in rhetoric which did no favours at all for Romania or its people. It suggested that room would be found for the country in the exciting new European edifice and that success depended on pan-European efforts not on the rate of progress that occurred on the ground in Romania.[69]

The EU opened negotiations for Romania on 15 February 2000 at a time when reformist forces were in disarray. A deeply divided four-party coalition, unpopular because of its austerity policies, was struggling to stay in office.[70]

Post-communist rivals who had dictated the exit from the hardline national Stalinist rule on a limited agenda for change were on the verge of a resounding electoral comeback. The annual progress reports on a candidate's perform-ance issued in 1999 and 2000 by the Commission painted a sombre picture of Romania's ability to shoulder the responsibilities of membership. Both drew attention to the 'widespread problem of corruption' and the absence of effective steps to counter it.[71] They saw the chronic weakness of the public administra-tion as a huge barrier in enabling the country to prepare for eventual acces-sion.[72] In 2000 the establishment of a functioning market economy appeared far off because 'many institutions required . . . do not exist or are too weak to be effective'.[73]

The medium-term economic strategy that Verheugen had placed such emphasis on during the previous autumn was adopted in March. In May the EU accepted the 'Action Plan', which included a strategy for the broad orientation of economic policy in the 2000–04 period.[74] But Aurel Ciobanu-Dordea, appointed at the start of 2000 as Romania's chief negotiator with the EU, recalled that the document had become little more than a chain of banalities.[75] The new Prime Minister, Mugur Isărescu, felt he had no alterna-tive but to actively involve the opposition in the long-term planning process. He was a man with roots in the old system who appeared to have adapted well to the new opening towards private enterprise. Since 1990 he had been head of the Romanian National Bank and he wished to return to that post if his foray into politics proved unsuccessful. Accordingly, he was sensitive to PDSR concerns and he agreed that an advisory council of economists nomi-nated by all the parties be formed to shape the strategy. The leading figure was probably Tudorel Postolache, who had helped to design the Snagov strategy promoted by Iliescu. He was an economist who had obtained a PhD from Moscow University in the 1950s. The cross-party advisory group was wedded to obsolete economic strategies but without its consent nothing could be incorporated into the Action Plan. A 'useless strategy' was the end result to which Verheugen, the Enlargement Commissioner, gave his blessing.[76] But the EU lost interest in the medium-term economic strategy. It would be just one of a number of initiatives, such as the 'Roadmaps for Romania and Bulgaria' announced with a lot of fanfare in 2002 or the 're-orientation' in the negotiations announced in March 2004, which appeared in retrospect to be mainly public relations exercises. Such gestures were required usually when the EU intensified its engagement with Romania and needed to demonstrate that it was taking appropriate measures to move the process forward.

But the EU's weakness for such essentially superficial publicity exercises would not be lost on Romanian officials, especially after 2000. It was a major error to display such an improvised approach towards a country much of whose elite were past masters at merely simulating reform. The EU's position was also weaker than it should have been owing to the failure to establish an effective partnership with the World Bank and the IMF (something that was not necessarily chiefly the EU's fault). They were supposed to be the main midwives of the strategy which Verheugen launched in 1999. But by 2001 it has been claimed that they were not even sharing information with each other about Romanian matters, never mind trying to pursue a common reform approach.[77] In its annual reports, the EU urged the ministries and key policy-making agencies to coordinate their approach to completing the EU roadmap. But external entities lacked credibility if they were disinclined to practise the very advice which they insisted was essential if a state with such poor administrative capacity was to make progress.

Ciobanu-Dordea is remembered with respect by many of those with whom he came into contact during his year as Romania's chief negotiator. He decided to be a tough negotiator, trying to obtain as much advantage as possible for Romania in the talks opened for the early chapters. Thus, he advocated that compensation for Romanian consumers with defective products should start at a lower base rate than elsewhere because of the lower standard of living. A common negotiating approach was coordinated with Poland because of similar problems, such as a large and relatively unproductive agricultural sector. Indeed, it looked as if an informal Polish–Romanian alliance might emerge in the negotiating process. It certainly suited the Poles to have Romania on the same side since it increased the likelihood that greater transition periods could be obtained for industries that needed time to adapt to the challenge of EU competition. But the Polish–Romanian *entente* was discontinued after 2001 with Iliescu's party focusing on building partnerships with political forces in existing EU states.

The European Institute of Romania (IER) had been set up by Alexandru Herlea in the late 1990s in the hope that it would act as a think-tank stimulating effective approaches to enable Romania to make good progress in the entry talks. From 2000, the EU expected all of the national ministries in Romania to do 'impact studies' that would contribute to the satisfactory completion of the negotiating chapters. A lot of money was set aside for this process and Ciobanu-Dordea envisaged that the IER and its team of specialists could play a coordinating role in this process.[78] But the reformist character of the IER started to be diluted upon the replacement of Herlea at the end of 1999. He was sent to Brussels as Romania's ambassador to the EU, replacing Constantin Ene, who had enjoyed the grade of ambassador in the Foreign Ministry since 1972 and had been ambassador to the EU continuously since 1993.[79] This communist-era war-horse became head of the administrative council of the IER and also rector of the Diplomatic Academy. From such positions, this old-school bureaucrat exerted an influence over young diplomats moving to the expanding Brussels mission. Overall, he was unwilling to adopt new operating procedures even as Romania faced the unprecedented challenge of transforming the machinery of government to suit EU requirements. Soon the IER was just doing technical studies with Brussels money.[80]

Throughout the years of engagement with the EU, it became normal for power-holders in Bucharest to abolish, amalgamate or found new ministries and agencies as if such actions were proof of their commitment to moving the European process forward. Petre Roman, the leader of the PD, was in charge of European issues in the Isărescu government which existed to the end of 2000. His first major preoccupation was to restore the European portfolio to the Ministry of Foreign Affairs. This involved not only moving the ministry files to a new building but the staff in the old Ministry of European Integration had to pass an exam merely to work in the Foreign Ministry and have access to its files.[81] The whole process took three months to complete and something similar would occur exactly one year later, following the change of government, when the Ministry of European Integration was re-established and a new incumbent spent a lot of time ensuring that it operated in the way that best suited her.

In May 2000 Verheugen declared that negotiations with Romania were well on track and he gave a positive assessment of the Action Plan.[82] But with President Constantinescu refusing to run for a second term because of disastrous poll ratings, it was soon apparent that the most outwardly reformist of the parties were unlikely to remain in power beyond the winter. Isărescu, despite having been a state official before 1989, was drafted to run as a presidential candidate by the PNŢCD. But he could only manage fourth place when the elections were held on 26 November 2000. The PNŢCD was wiped out as a political force and many supporters of the ruling coalition switched to the extremist Greater Romania Party (PRM) as a gesture of protest over the way their living standards had tumbled in the late 1990s. The PRM registered a strong second place, producing murmurings of unease in Brussels, but the PDSR emerged as the largest party with 36% of the votes and around 45% of the seats.

Conclusion

By the time the EU had begun to strengthen its bilateral ties with Romania, ruling groups with their roots in the pre-1989 communist system were busy establishing a power-base that extended from the political sphere to the economy, and indeed it encompassed the justice system and even large parts of higher education. It is not clear the degree to which the EU realised that a process of restoration might be occurring behind a façade of democratisation and concessions to Western norms of behaviour. The EU, along with other external agencies trying to stimulate change in transition states, often overlooked local political fault-lines, underestimating how entrenched groups opposed to meaningful change were capable of indefinitely sabotaging their plans. Karen Fogg, the first EU ambassador, had innovative ideas about how the EU could contribute to the breaking up of totalitarian structures. She saw the need to promote autonomous activity involving a range of social actors whose voices had hitherto counted for little. Promoting social and economic partnerships at grassroots level fitted in well with the EU's championing of the principle of subsidiarity, that power be distributed to the lowest level practicable. But it was bound to be a lengthy and involved process before major results could be noticed. When Romania moved from being a peripheral country in the European neighbourhood to one that was being considered for membership, a new approach was already being adopted by Brussels. The work of the Phare programme was geared towards the accession objectives as set out in the *acquis communautaire* and projects designed to strengthen democracy or promote community partnership were drastically scaled back. There was an emphasis on allocating and then rapidly dispersing substantial funds for projects with highly specific time-lines. This was a strategy applied to all candidate countries but there seems to have been little thought about what its consequences would be in Romania, where the capacity of the public administration remained desperately weak long after 2000 according to each progress report published by the European Commission.

Officials who adhered to the managerial strategy emanating from Brussels and proved capable of helping accession states to fulfil the spending targets set by the EU had more chance of rising in the Commission hierarchy than original thinkers like Fogg, who had shown a strong desire to concentrate on grassroots change. Concentrating on economic criteria became more important than ensuring that political criteria continued to be adhered to (unless aspects like child care had well-placed advocates). This placed the 1996–2000 government at a disadvantage. It could demonstrate progress in tackling political problems which had made Romania an object of concern. However, its ability to promote economic reform was limited. This was due to its own internal weaknesses and the baleful economic legacy inherited in 1996. But a crucial factor was the influence that Iliescu's PDSR exercised over the hybrid economy even when in opposition. The EU does not appear to have evaluated the balance of forces within the country and what would be the outcome of insisting on a radical set of market-led changes. Its detachment was understandable because Romania was one of a dozen countries in the queue for membership and it looked as if many years would elapse before it reached the front. But the unexpected conflict in Kosovo abruptly upgraded the importance of Romania. The EU's own criteria for starting talks were put aside. Romano Prodi, the incoming President of the European Commission, described it as a 'hardline' one.

Full negotiations commenced in 2000. The EU was usually at its most powerful when it was deciding whether or not to begin accession negotiations with a particular state.[83] But it failed to press home its advantage over Romania by recommending a comprehensive set of reforms that were undoubtedly unpalatable to the old structures, and then linking compliance with them to progress in negotiations. It might even have contemplated a plan B, which would have given Romania a long transition period for entry and made the ability to play an increasing role in all EU activities conditional on demonstrable progress in carrying out fundamental reforms. But the EU never had a plan B for Romania and it proved to be a telling weakness as time went on.

The 1999–2000 medium-term economic strategy proved to be an ephemeral document and the EU failed to prioritise vital areas such as administrative reform. The breakthrough announced at Helsinki which transformed Romania from being a peripheral partner to the second largest country negotiating for entry had stemmed from unexpected events and was driven forward by a few top-level European politicians. But thereafter Romania only spasmodically crossed their radar screens and they failed to see what was required to ensure that the enlargement process was a high-grade one which enabled Romania to assume the responsibilities of membership rather than a superficial one, consisting merely of ticking a set of bureaucratic boxes. Just after his successor Romano Prodi had talked in elegiac terms in Bucharest about the partnership between Brussels and Romania, Jacques Delors, who had revived the integration process in the late 1980s, warned that a process of economic and political convergence would be impossible if the EU grew to have '27 or 30 members, with the new members having been absorbed in the same way as the original six or nine'.[84] But his attention was focused on the consequences for the EU project as a whole of an enlargement process which did not take account of the formidable challenges that some of the new candidates posed.

The EU's multi-layered decision-making system failed to produce a hard-headed cost–benefit analysis, showing the consequences of enlargement for both Romania and the EU as a whole. No particular notice appears to have been taken of the fact that the EU's strong implantation in Romania would coincide with the comprehensive rout of the very forces Brussels had singled out as its main local partners for reform. In February 2000, Verheugen, at a joint press conference with Foreign Minister Roman, had declared that Romania had the worst heritage when it came to democratic institutions.[85] But thereafter the EU would rarely behave as if this fact was at the forefront of its thinking on Romania. Indeed, emphasis on political conditionality would diminish. This was despite the previous record of the party with which the EU would strive to establish a working partnership. From January 2001, the EU would find itself negotiating with Iliescu's post-communists, who had created a political system with outwardly democratic features designed to minimise changes that threatened the hold on power of the old structures for which it acted as the legate. By now, the PDSR had acquired quite close understanding of the EU approach to decision-making on the basis of how it had already engaged with Romania from 1996 onwards. It found the content of the Europeanisation agenda based on a union of laws, values and economic processes baffling or distasteful. But there is evidence (as shown by the acceptance of the medium-term strategy) that outward compliance with EU requirements was not viewed as threatening its grip on Romania's transition process. Time would quickly show what would be the response of the EU to the arrival in office of a party which had until recently been a regional byword for authoritarian and state-orientated policies, especially after it started to revert to aspects of its previous behaviour.

Notes

1 Ronald Linden, 'After the Revolution: A Foreign Policy of Unbounded Change', in Daniel Nelson (ed.), *Romania After Tyranny*, London and San Francisco: Westview Press, 1992, pp. 203–4.

2 See David Phinnemore, 'Enlargement to the East: Romania', in Hilary and Mike Ingham (eds), *EU Expansion to the East: Prospects and Problems*, Cheltenham, UK: Edward Elgar, 2002, p. 223.

3 Peter Siani-Davies, *The Romanian Revolution of December 1989*, Ithaca and London: Cornell University Press, 2005, p. 51.

4 See Tom Gallagher, *Romania After Ceauşescu: The Politics of Intolerance*, Edinburgh: Edinburgh University Press, 1995, chapter 4; also Phinnemore, 'Enlargement to the East', p. 224.

5 John Gray, *Evaluation of DFID Country Programmes, Country Study: Romania 1997–2003*, London: Department for International Development, 2004, p. 99.

6 *El Pais* (Madrid), 15 January 1990.

7 Dimitris Papadimitriou, *Negotiating the New Europe: The European Union and Eastern Europe*, Aldershot: Ashgate Publishing, 2002, p. 125.

8 Tom Gallagher, *The Balkans Since the Cold War: From Tyranny to Tragedy*, London: Routledge, 2003, p. 34.

9 Phinnemore, 'Enlargement to the East', p. 226.

10 Interview with European Commission official, Brussels, 2008.

11 Phinnemore, 'Enlargement to the East', pp. 226, 227.

12 Fitch Ratings, 'EU Enlargement – Its Impact on the Accession Countries', 26 September 2002, www.fitchratings.com.

13 Tim Haughton, 'When Does the EU Make a Difference? Conditionality and the Accession Process in Central and Eastern Europe', *Political Studies Review*, Vol. 5, No. 2, 2007 (seen in manuscript form).

14 Phinnemore, 'Enlargement to the East', p. 227.

15 See G. Prisăcaru, 'The National Strategy Preparing Romania's Accession to the EU', *Romanian Journal of International Affairs*, Vol. 2, No. 4, 1996, pp. 31–55.

16　Interview with Camelia Gheorghe, Romanian development adviser, Bucharest, 14 June 2007.
17　His career began at the Ministry of Foreign Commerce in 1978. He was a Secretary of State from 1990–92; in the government 1992–93; from 1994–96 Presidential counsellor; in 1997 he became Director and later Executive Director, ING Bank in Romania and he was also Professor at the Academy of Economic Studies (ASE). See Gheorghe Crişan, *Piramida puterii, Vol. II*, Editura Pro Historia, Bucureşti, 2004, pp. 269–70.
18　Interview with Karen Fogg, Brussels, 25 April 2007.
19　Interview with Karen Fogg, Brussels, 25 April 2007.
20　Interview with Karen Fogg, Brussels, 25 April 2007.
21　Interview with Karen Fogg, Brussels, 25 April 2007.
22　Interview with Camelia Gheorghe, Bucharest, 14 June 2007.
23　See Rupert Wolfe-Murray, *Partners for Europe: Getting Together to Get it Together*, Glasgow: DFID/Romania, 2005.
24　Tom Gallagher, *Theft of a Nation: Romania Since Communism*, London: Hurst & Co., 2005, p. 128.
25　Interview with Alexandru Herlea, Paris, 30 December 2007.
26　'Romania Starts to Rebuild', *The Economist*, 3 May 1997.
27　Gallagher, *Theft of a Nation*, pp. 194–6.
28　Interview with Alexandru Herlea, Paris, 30 December 2007.
29　See European Commission, 'Commission Opinion on Romania's Application for Membership of the EU', DOC 97/18, Brussels, 15 July 2007; www.ec.europa.eu/ enlargement/archives/Romania/key_documents_en.htm.
30　*Evenimentul Zilei* (Bucharest), 17 July 1997.
31　*Ziua* (Bucharest), 3 November 1999.
32　Gallagher, *Theft of a Nation*, p. 195.
33　Interview with Alexandru Herlea, Paris, 30 December 2007.
34　Anne Corbett, *The Guardian* (London), 21 December 2006.
35　*Romania: Country Report*, 3rd Quarter 1998, London: Economist Intelligence Unit, 1998, p. 19.
36　*Adevărul* (Bucharest), 13 March 1998.
37　Alina Mungiu-Pippidi, 'Identity Crisis', *Transitions*, April 1998, p. 76.
38　Alina Mungiu-Pippidi, 'Identity Crisis', *Transitions*, April 1998, p. 77.
39　Interview with Fokion Fotiadis, Brussels, 20 February 2008.
40　Interview with European Commission official, Brussels, 2008.
41　Interview with Alexandru Herlea, Paris, 30 December 2007.
42　See Gallagher, *Theft of a Nation*, pp. 202–8.
43　Interview with European Commission official, Brussels, 2008.
44　Interview with Fokion Fotiadis, Brussels, 20 February 2008.
45　*Ziua*, 5 May 1999.
46　*Adevărul*, 25 November 1997.
47　*Ziua*, 5 May 1999.
48　Hansard (Record of the proceedings in the House of Commons), 8 June 1999, p. 468.

49 *Ziua*, 15 October 1999.
50 *Ziua*, 15 October 1999.
51 'Enlarging the European Union. A New Pace?', *The Economist*, 1 October 1999.
52 *Ziua*, 3 November 1999.
53 *Adevărul*, 30 October 1999.
54 Cristian Tudor Popescu, 'Sovromizarea inversă', *Adevărul*, 4 November 1999.
55 *Ziua*, 2 November 1999.
56 *Ziua*, 2 November 1999.
57 *Nine O'Clock*, 23 February 2000.
58 *Adevărul*, 29 January 2001.
59 *Revista 22*, 28 March–3 April 2000.
60 'A Bitter Romania Seeks Election-Time Revenge', *Inside Romania News*, 22 September 2000.
61 *Evenimentul Zilei*, 13 December 1999.
62 *The Economist*, 2 October 1999.
63 Gallagher, *Theft of a Nation*, pp. 226–7.
64 *Nine O'Clock*, 17 January 2000.
65 *Nine O' Clock*, 17 January 2000.
66 *Nine O'Clock*, 14–16 January 2000.
67 Geoffrey Pridham, *Designing Democracy: European Enlargement and Regime Change in Post-Communist Europe*, London: Palgrave, 2005, p. 81.
68 *Nine O'Clock*, 14–16 January 2000.
69 *Nine O'Clock* (Bucharest), 18 January 2000.
70 By 2001, overall production had dropped to 75% of its 1989 level and Romania had attracted only 7 billion dollars worth of foreign investment. Radio Free Europe, RFE-RL *Newsline*, 6 July 2001.
71 Commission of the European Communities, *1999 Regular Report on Romania's Progress Towards Accession*, Com (1999), 13 October 1999, p. 13; *2000 Regular Report on Romania's Progress Towards Accession*, Com (2000), 8 November 2000, p. 87.
72 *1999 Regular Report*, p. 80; *2000 Regular Report*, p. 89.
73 *2000 Regular Report*, p. 88.
74 *2000 Regular Report*, p. 28.
75 Interview with Aurel Ciobanu-Dordea, Brussels, 1 December 2006.
76 Interview with Aurel Ciobanu-Dordea, Brussels, 1 December 2006.
77 Interview with Vasile Puşcaş, Bucharest, 20 December 2006.
78 Interview with Lucian Branea, journalist and manager of the Romania-EU–list (a blog on Yahoo, a clearing-house for information on civil society issues in Romania), 21 December 2006.
79 Crişan, *Piramida puterii*, p. 144.
80 Interview with Alexandru Herlea, Paris, 30 December 2007.
81 Interview with Aurel Ciobanu-Dordea, Brussels, 1 December 2006.
82 *Nine O'Clock*, 16 May 2000.
83 Haughton, 'When Does the EU Make a Difference?'.
84 *Reuters* (Paris), 18 January 2000.
85 *Nine O'Clock*, 16 Febuary 2000.

2

Crafty natives lead the Eurocrats astray

For Romania, the accession process was to be identical to that for the candidate countries joining in 2004 and indeed for those which joined in earlier rounds. It centred around the need to absorb the entire body of regulations of the EU which have been accumulated and revised over the last 45 years: the *acquis communautaire*. Thirty-one chapters would have to be opened and completed before it could be concluded that a candidate country had fulfilled the entry terms.

This chapter will examine the strategy which the PDSR employed in order to boost its credibility in Brussels. It will argue that it pursued a twin-track approach, conceding the need for economic restructuring but seeking to ignore or dilute important aspects of the 1993 Copenhagen criteria concerning the need for candidate countries to have stable institutions guaranteeing democracy, the rule of law and human rights. The EU, it is argued, either failed to note the slippage that was occurring or else was prepared to accept a reversal to semi-authoritarian behaviour in return for what appeared to be overdue and impressive progress in terms of economic reform.

The EU had only conceded that Romania fulfilled the Copenhagen criteria in 1997 once Iliescu and the PDSR had left office. It was a gesture of encouragement for the new government rather than a statement of reality. The fractious coalition only had a tenuous grasp on important areas of the state. Romania had experienced democratisation without de-communisation. The political system was meant to safeguard the interests of powerful networks which traced their origins back to the pre-1989 period and had regrouped in the aftermath of the collapse of Ceauşescu's totalitarian regime. In terms of political liberties Romania had enjoyed undeniable progress, but the emerging political system failed to safeguard the public good, however loosely this term is used, and instead enabled a determined and resourceful set of players to set about transferring state assets into private hands on a massive scale. To succeed, while at the same time drawing closer to the EU which required behaviour from new members at variance with what was the norm in Romania, a strategy of dissimulation was adhered to.

In the end, the EU's expectations about what could be achieved in Romania were lowered thanks to nimble manoeuvring by the PSD. It managed to convince its EU interlocutors that its own unimpressive standards of behaviour mainly reflected those of the Romanian people as a whole. The political criteria were lost sight of at important moments and allowed to be diluted.

This type of grand camouflage was something the PSD had a lot of experience in. It ought to be remembered that an over-stretched central agency with radical ideas but without the reach to implement them was something that Romania's leaders were familiar with. Most of those exercising power in the 2000–04 period had gained their experience of politics and decision-making in the last decade of Nicolae Ceauşescu's arbitrary rule (1965–89). His state had gargantuan ambitions for the country but ambitious targets were met on paper and often ignored in practice. Officials became adept at misinforming a dictator increasingly out of touch with reality. So when the EU arrived on the scene there was already a recent tradition of non-compliance with unrealistic targets for change imposed by central decision-makers. The EU's decision-making machine is sleek and efficient compared with Ceauşescu's. But comparisons are valid. Like Ceauşescu, the EU had ambitious targets but did not have the means to easily implement them. Nor were its powers of oversight so good as to be able to deal with non-compliance. It lacked the flexibility to modify its approach to a problem when the approach was obviously an inappropriate one. It has been too absorbed with its own ideological model and therefore reluctant to make modifications in order to respond effectively to the stark challenges presented by Romania. Bureaucracies which encounter such difficulties only have a limited number of options. They can admit failure and try a new strategy. Such candour has been on display more often in some communist states, such as Poland and Hungary, than in the EU. Or else, they can reduce their expectations and declare success when many of the key targets have been met only in a superficial sense.

So, in some ways the pre-accession era, instead of being a revolutionary new phase in Romania's modern history, was more like 'back to the future'. Once the rulers of the post-communist state became familiar with EU ways, they did not find it such an alien entity. They found that the EU was not unduly intrusive or exacting if gestures were made to its modernisation programme that did not undermine the ruling party's grip on power. Over four years, a blizzard of activity was launched in which much legislation was passed, action plans were drawn up, and ministries and state agencies were formed, amalgamated or broken up, all in the name of fulfilling the EU's transformative agenda for Romania. These initiatives were favourably commented on in regular EU reports but there were also nagging complaints (usually expressed in a lower key) that Romania did not appear to be moving decisively forward in switching from being a post-communist state to one able to assume the responsibilities of EU membership, benefiting from the opportunities provided and contributing to the success of the integration process.

Against the EU, the PDSR showed the same traits of improvisation and adaptation it had displayed when it had grabbed hold of the reins of power in 1990. It was like a matador who used his skills in the bullring first to tire out and then subdue his opponent, who in this case were millions of pro-Western Romanians impatient for change. The EU was a hugely important external power with temporary sovereignty over the development of Romanian policy in major respects, but the PDSR hoped that adept footwork in the bullring of EU negotiations would similarly disorientate a potentially disruptive opponent.

The PDSR's first gesture, camouflaging the nature and intentions of the party, was to drop its old name and re-christen itself the Social Democratic Party in July 2001. Social democracy had been historically weak in Romania and it was hoped that under Western European influence, the PSD might embrace a genuine social democratic vision rather than merely mimic it. But there had been determined resistance in the past to abandoning neo-communist conceptions of power. In 1997, a group which would have been seen as cautious reformers elsewhere in the old communist bloc had broken away from the party in 1997 due to the unwillingness of Iliescu either to retire or embrace an unambiguous non-communist stance. After his presidential victory in December 2000, Iliescu was once again the dominant political figure. He was beginning the last presidential term permitted under the Constitution and as Prime Minister he appointed Adrian Năstase, probably the most competent of the officials to whom he had given major state responsibilities earlier in the 1990s. Năstase belonged to an elite family: his father-in-law had been ambassador to China under Ceauşescu, as well as a long-serving Agriculture Minister. He had trained in international law, specialising in human rights. During the most repressive phase of the communist regime, he was trusted to attend international conferences, where he insisted that basic norms of human rights were respected in Romania. In the closing months of the dictatorship, he even took part in a delegation to the Soviet Union where he was zealous in his defence of the communist system. An account was published in a Soviet newspaper, *Komsomolskaya Pravda* on 25 November 1989 of an interview with Năstase. Asked for his views on *perestroika*, he indicated that Gorbachev's ideas might not be suitable for Romania, claiming that Romania had actually started to move in such a direction as early as 1960. He characterised Romania, still under Ceauşescu, as a democracy, saying: 'The essence of our democracy lies in the fact by means of various social organizations which practically include the whole nation, every citizen can participate in solving the most important national objective – the building in Romania by 1995 of the multi-laterally-developed socialist society'.[1]

These inconvenient facts would emerge in 2004 when he would be a candidate for the presidency. But in 2001, he sought to re-invent himself as a genuine practitioner of pluralist politics. A protocol was quickly signed with the Democratic Union of Hungarians in Romania (UDMR) which gave his government a working majority in Parliament. Given the emphasis that Prodi and other officials had placed on respecting minority rights during their visits to Romania, this gesture was bound to impress Brussels. In the past, Iliescu's party had marginalised the Hungarian party and branded it the enemy within.[2] As late as 1999, Năstase had insisted that 'Hungarian revisionism' was a threat to the region's security and he had even predicted a 'hot autumn' in Transylvania, arguing that socio-economic frustrations could bring ethnic antagonisms to the surface.[3] So deciding to keep the UDMR in the mainstream of politics and shelving years of anti-minority rhetoric appeared to be big concessions on the part of the PDSR. But the deployment of the chauvinist weapon had always been a tactical one. Iliescu's party in fact possessed few fixed principles, except for retaining control of the political process as much as possible. Whipping up hysteria about the claimed threat to the unity of Romania posed by the UDMR had been a useful tactic, enabling attention to be diverted from the systematic theft of state assets by the PDSR and its allies in the early 1990s. By 2000, it had ceased to fulfil any usefulness. Most voters no longer took Hungarian irredentism seriously as a threat and many saw through the manipulation of their emotions by the PDSR. Moreover, the UDMR had become heavily involved in the economic spoils systems. It had economic barons like Attila Verestoy who were as resourceful and authoritarian as any to be found in the PDSR. Indeed, the cohesive group in charge of the UDMR from the early 1990s onwards would enjoy a marathon span at the centre of decision-making after 1996 when the party entered the centre-right coalition. The alliance with Năstase proved remarkably smooth, with the UDMR being viewed almost as the Transylvanian Hungarian wing of the ruling party by 2004. An equally unruffled partnership with Călin Popescu-Tăriceanu, Prime Minister for four years from December 2004, then got underway and the UDMR became a chief mainstay of his government when it began to obstruct key EU reforms, especially in the justice sector. It is unlikely that the EU imagined the most prominent minority force in Romania would become such an obstacle to its plans to bring Romanian institutions up to European standards. EU rhetoric viewed minority movements as progressive bodies that were vital partners in the integration process. The UDMR played up to that image until its absorption in oligarchical politics proved impossible to conceal, proving an invaluable ally of Năstase during his Premiership.

A good working relationship also appeared to be developing with Emma Nicholson, the British Liberal Democrat member of the European Parliament (MEP) who was its *rapporteur* for Romania. In this capacity she monitored

Romania's performance in complying with the EU entry conditions and would issue biannual reports during the five years she carried out this responsibility (1999–2004). Initially, she had a positive view of the government's performance, declaring in February 2001 that its reforms were 'excellent'.[4] But her attitude towards the government diverged sharply over the plight of as many as 100,000 children placed in dilapidated state institutions often run by venal officials. The Commission had been taking this situation extremely seriously for several years. Its 2000 report had warned: 'Romania fulfils the Copenhagen political criteria although this position will need to be re-examined if the authorities do not continue to give priority to dealing with the crisis in their child care institutions'.[5]

Nicholson was bound to treat the plight of many of these children as a major priority. She had been a tenacious defender of the rights of vulnerable children across the world, and her willpower and lobbying skills had ensured that an international operation to rescue huge numbers of Kurdish children whose lives were in jeopardy at the end of the 1991 war between Western powers and Iraq's Saddam Hussein swung into action. To Năstase and his colleagues, it is unlikely that Baroness Nicholson de Winterbourne appeared destined to give them particular difficulties during four years of negotiations with Brussels. Aristocratic in her bearing, suffering from chronic deafness in one ear, her initial statements did not suggest that she would be a major obstacle in the way of Romania joining the EU on the PSD's terms. But if Năstase thought he could easily outmanoeuvre the Baroness, he proved mistaken. She proved a determined adversary who made particular difficulties for his government in 2001 and 2004, in both cases over child care. In her draft report, submitted to Parliament in May 2001, the possibility of breaking off negotiations with Romania was openly raised. State officials were accused of exploiting institutionalised children for vast cash sums. She told the *Financial Times*: 'It is a well-oiled system which rests upon the abandonment of children. Far from stopping abandonment or offering contraception or stemming it by introducing child welfare payments, there is clear evidence that the state is encouraging child abandonment'.[6]

She was particularly concerned that officials profiting from an unregulated system were placing children in the hands of foreigners prepared to cause them harm. But the initial reaction of the government was complacent, even dismissive. Năstase talked obliquely about politicians using the issue to pursue their own agenda. Vasile Puşcaş, the normally surefooted chief negotiator with the EU, was more explicit. He stated that she wished to appear resolute in the eyes of the voters in the British general election: 'favourable news regarding institutionalised children would not have the same impact'.[7] But Nicholson was not a candidate and she amplified her concerns on 4 June, declaring: 'Most certainly I have met with officials myself, and I have been given evidence by highly credible sources, of other officials in the system who in the last five years have done things that have been contrary to the best interests of the child and have certainly made a lot of money for those officials. I have put to the new government the strong recommendation, privately, that these officials should be charged and the full weight of the law should be taken'.[8]

But in light of claims that a Romanian child advertised on the internet could fetch anything between $3,000 and $49,000 on the black market, Hildegard Puwak, the Minister for European Integration, said the government expected Nicholson to produce evidence to back up her 'serious accusations'.[9]

On 12 June Nicholson stated that her harsh report might be modified, suggesting that a more cooperative response from the government was occurring. In fact Năstase acknowledged that the government lacked information on child care and an independent enquiry was speedily launched. The small enquiry team included Alin Teodorescu, the head of the IMAS polling agency, long associated with democratic opposition forces. Around 8,000 children had been sold abroad prior to 2001 and Teodorescu relates that when he saw the files for some of them, he was horrified by the absence of safeguards to ensure their welfare once taken from Romania: 'there was nothing about the intermediaries or the destination of the children. It was just a business'.[10] Nicholson herself acknowledged the thoroughness of this lightning enquiry: 'they found out things that made my own report pale into insignificance'.[11]

The government agreed to the EU's request for immediate steps to be taken to end the trade in children and Teodorescu paid many trips to Brussels in the second half of 2001 to convince officials that comprehensive safeguards were being put in place.[12] Child care was made a priority for the secretary-general of the government and the portion of the national budget devoted to it was sharply increased. A high-level group, partly international in composition, and including Nicholson as well as representatives from UNICEF and the WHO, was set up to monitor progress.

The Commission in its October 2001 report declared that 'reform of the child care system is well underway'.[13] Its main reason for this level of confidence was the decision, earlier in the year, to impose a moratorium on international adoptions. The EU and the government began to promote a child care policy based around placing children in 'substitute families' – either relatives or foster families. A ban would later be imposed on placing a child under two in child care institutions, many of which would be designated for closure. Nicholson 'lit a fire under their bums' was the view of a Brussels official who admired her implacable attitude to Bucharest politicians, many of whom knew people involved in the lucrative trade in children.[14] But it was notable that in Bulgaria, where adoption agencies and also criminal gangs were also busily engaged in taking children abroad, far less action was taken.

Nicholson's criticisms of the Năstase government were much milder for nearly the entire duration of its life. The Prime Minister had learned that child welfare was an *idée fixe* for her and however outlandish this might appear for unsentimental post-communist officials, she needed to be humoured and, at least on the surface, serious commitment needed to be demonstrated in saving vulnerable children from harm.

In July 2002, with the child welfare crisis out of the way, Năstase asked the EU to establish a clearer timetable for Romania's entry. He even declared that he hoped to close all negotiating chapters by the end of 2003, even though several had not even been opened.[15] But in December 2000, at the EU's Laeken summit, Romania, along with Bulgaria, had been offered a suggested entry date of 2007. No chance therefore existed that they could join along with countries whose negotiations were further advanced than Romania's and who would soon be given 2004 as a provisional entry date. Năstase ought not to have been surprised as the Commission had hitherto been guarded in its public comments on Romania. It was still sizing up the PSD and was obviously influenced by its prior record in office. On 19 March 2001 Verheugen had said that Romania has a 'long and difficult road ahead' before it could join the EU.[16] Very different were his views on Bulgaria, which he visited several days later. He publicly stated that Bulgaria had made better progress than expected, remarking that Bulgaria does 'exactly what we want it to do', acting as a 'factor of stability'.[17] But Fotiadis, the head of the EU Delegation, held out a lifeline for Romania when he said in the same month that 'joining the EU will be less influenced by closing all chapters in the *acquis communautaire* and more by the evaluation of economic performance'. Here was an indication that a flexible approach might be taken to key sections of the EU roadmap if Romania acquired a 'functioning market economy'. Fotiadis said that its absence, owing to continued state domination of much of economic activity, was in fact 'the chief impediment' to Romanian membership. He mentioned that the way to overcome scepticism in Brussels was to simplify legislation on foreign investments, continue efforts for achieving macro-economic reform, introduce strict fiscal and budgetary discipline, and act to reduce the rate of inflation.[18] Here was a sign that if the PSD used the leverage it enjoyed in the system and over social forces who had challenged the previous government when it proceeded with painful reforms, then it might not have to wait such a long time in the entry queue.

Workers protesting in Braşov over impending lay-offs were spoken to in unprecedently blunt terms on 18 March 2003 by Năstase, when he said that the privatisation of loss-making firms could no longer be delayed and that the state could no longer keep on subsidising them.[19] EU officials were bound to take notice because such language had usually been absent from the PSD and its centre-right predecessor.

In 2002 the government took steps which suggested that it meant to proceed with economic restructuring along the lines desired by the EU. It announced plans for the privatisation of the largest bank (Banca Comecială Română) by early 2003, though this would not take place until much later.[20] A law passed in March 2002 could accelerate the privatisation and liquidation process; it established no minimum price and provided new financial arrangements concerning past arrears to the state budget. But its effects would depend on the way it was implemented. In 2004 the Năstase government passed an *ordonance* withdrawing from insolvency the Dacia-Felix Bank, the first private bank to fail in Romania. This paved the way for its sale to the Israeli businessman, Freddy Robinson for a nominal sum (the state having gained little from the transaction).[21]

Inter-enterprise indebtedness was treated as an issue that could no longer be avoided (such arrears being still around 40% of GDP). The energy sector had amassed the largest debts to the central exchequer and the government announced that it intended to break up the energy utilities, ensuring that prices would no longer be subsidised. The OECD welcomed this step but urged price increases to be followed by effective payment discipline of energy bills with all bad payers suffering disconnection.[22] Such a tough, even-handed approach clashed with the Romanian practice of allowing exemptions for clients enjoying political favour and the PSD would be slow to match rhetoric with action. Nevertheless, these were bold steps in the direction of reform.

In 2001 Năstase had already achieved a significant breakthrough that improved his government's international image by accomplishing the privatisation of 80% of Romanian steel production. Much of it was located in Galați in eastern Romania. Here in the early 1960s the nationalist-minded communist regime had built what would become the largest steel complex in South-Eastern Europe as a gesture of independence from the Soviet Union (which under Khruschev had wanted Romania to concentrate on agricultural products). Lacking reliable markets for expensively produced steel, the Sidex plant at Galați had debts totalling $900 million by 2001.[23] Amidst chronic mismanagement, the state was required to subsidise it annually to the tune of $250 million.[24] Closure would have devastated the city of Galați – 60% of the population depended on the wages earned by the 27,000 Sidex employees.[25] Negotiations with a foreign buyer were in train under the Isărescu government. But it would have probably been difficult for the centre-right government to conclude a deal which had the support of the powerful trade unions. Năstase and the PSD had no such credibility problems and Sidex was sold to the British-registered company, LNM Holding, owned by the Indian steel magnate, Lakshmi Mittal. Steel production was preserved and a significant portion of the workforce would be kept on. But controversy surrounded how the project was negotiated and the role of the British government. With the contract due to be signed on 20 July 2007, the government in Bucharest announced its postponement the day before. A visit by Prime Minister Lionel Jospin of France was imminent and it was to show diplomatic sensitivity that the Romanians claim the contract was postponed.[26] But a French company was interested in the project and Jospin was expected to lobby on its behalf. Against this background, Tony Blair signed a letter, on the advice of the Foreign Office, urging acceptance of the LNM bid. When eventually the transaction was completed in November 2001, Richard Ralph, the British ambassador to Romania, actually read out the Prime Minister's letter at the signing ceremony.[27]

A brief but intense political row resulted, with Blair's Conservative opponents accusing the Labour government of doing a blatant favour for a businessman who was a party donor. The 'Steelgate' affair appeared to be the forerunner of other deals involving major firms keen to invest in Romania which enjoyed close ties with an EU government and would benefit handsomely from the transaction (in the case of LNM, it would obtain lavish subsidies from the EU). But the claims of sleaze do not appear to stand up to close examination, at least in this case. Mittal's donation to Labour Party funds was no secret because it had to be disclosed by law. The letter was no secret either because the ambassador had read it out. Moreover, the Foreign Office had for some time seen itself as a champion of British businesses abroad (although only 81 of Mittal's 125,000 employees were actually in the UK). Nevertheless, the perception that a major EU player like Britain had ulterior motives for backing Romania's EU entry were hard to dispel, though the Sidex affair would in time be forgotten as really dubious transactions occurred which suggested that major economic players were determining the pace and timing of Romania's EU membership.

Even before the Sidex deal had been signed the EU's regular report on Romania for 2001 declared that 'Romania's policy towards industry is moving towards the principle of EU industrial policy, i.e. market-based, stable and responsible'.[28]

Another significant boost for the image of the PSD was its ability to strengthen the control system on its borders in order to check illegal immigration from Moldova. Until mid-2001, Moldovan citizens had been able to enter Romania without producing a passport and merely showing their ID cards. Most of the country had been part of Romania until Stalin occupied it in 1940 and in Romania most Moldavians were considered fellow Romanians. But the perception that Romania's borders were insecure meant that Romanian citizens required a visa to visit EU states. Obtaining one entailed considerable expense and inconvenience. Indeed, by 2001 Romania was the only candidate for accession whose citizens needed a visa, which according to the well-known commentator Cristian Tudor Popescu, 'speaks volumes about how Europeans regard us'.[29] But in June 2001, the European Commission recommended lifting this requirement because of progress in border and immigration control.[30] All the EU states which were party to the Schengen agreement would have to agree to the Commission's recommendation before it could be ratified. They were conscious that once the current accession round was completed around 25% of the EU's border with eastern states would be controlled by Romania. There were fears that if checks continued to be lax, it would be a channel for people-smuggling and the illegal importation of drugs and weapons, contributing to burgeoning crime in existing EU states. But on 7 December 2001, the EU formally agreed to lift visa requirements, starting on 1 January 2002. Romanian efforts to harmonise its legislation with the EU, strengthen border and passport security, and sign re-admission treaties with all EU states except Britain and Portugal, led to a unanimous decision by 15 justice and interior ministers to abolish visa requirements.[31] The EU had said that Romania had made 'precise and concrete commitments to guarantee security and prevent illegal immigration'.[32] Indeed border security was probably the area where Romania would go on to show most consistency in complying with EU requirements. It would lead to the signing of a contract with the defence giant EADS in 2004 for 'an integrated border security system' which the EU Commission in an internal document drawn up in October 2005 admitted was 'extremely expensive' and went 'way beyond the Schengen requirements'. After several years of steady economic growth, it was doubtful 'about the financial capacity of a country like Romania to secure the required financial means' needed to provide 'extremely expensive . . . running and maintenance costs'.[33] The EADS contract would also be politically explosive because it was concluded without a tender, thus infringing EU competition rules, which had recently passed into law. Nevertheless, progress in border management which could be traced back to 2001, along with the Sidex privatisation, boosted the image of the Năstase government in Romania. These successes began to popularise the view across the system of multi-level governance in the EU that it was better to negotiate with a government in Bucharest that was able to control the machinery of state and meet important targets even if it had some authoritarian tendencies. An official involved in the negotiating process with Romania recalled that these breakthroughs in 2001 lowered the guard of top officials in Brussels and made them more tolerant of PSD misbehaviour in other areas than perhaps they ought to have been.[34]

Child care, reconciliation with the Hungarians, convincing visa controls and a bold privatisation venture in heavy industry were essentially secondary concessions which improved the image of the PSD without forcing it to alter its methods of rule. It remained determined to defend its primary sources of influence and control. These were to be found in the justice system and the vast public administration at both central and local level. Contrary to the hopes of some in Brussels, a genuinely home-centred reform process that would propel the country towards a well-prepared entry failed to emerge. There were a series of impressive-looking economic initiatives, the sheen of which would start to wear off some of them when the time for delivery came. There was little commitment to progress on the political, legal and administrative aspects of reform.

This caused frustrations for the Delegation head Jonathan Scheele, in place for most of the pre-accession period from 2002 until the end of 2006. A gap of several months followed the departure of Fotiadis in mid-2001 and Scheele's arrival. He had the unenviable task of putting pressure on government officials if funding programmes were not working well. As one of his senior colleagues stated: 'Success depended on whether ministers treated EU accession tasks as a priority or instead viewed them as a burden that had been imposed on them. If projects were not obtaining co-financing promised, or else were stuck or moving in the wrong direction, we had to intervene'.[35]

Fotiadis had had more leverage because he was dealing with a relatively weak administration during almost the whole of his three years in Romania. He also enjoyed senior contacts at the Commission which Scheele appeared to lack. Năstase sensed this and allowed his hauteur to show, most notably when he told the Delegation head to mind his own business after he had expressed concern in late 2002 that the government was refusing to carry out EU-funded infrastructure work in Bucharest because the funding would be administered by the opposition mayor.[36]

By its first anniversary in office, there was no sign of the PSD improving its habits and purging the state of the inefficiency, corruption and hyper-bureaucracy which meant that fundamental change occurred exceedingly slowly. By contrast, the start of a Năstase personality cult could be detected, with one of the Prime Minister's first actions being to order the archive department of state television to erase all film footage of the former president Constantinescu. This led the well-known television director Lucia Hossu-Longin to remark that 'for them history had to begin after 2000'.[37] In early 2002 prosecutors were ordered to crack down heavily on opponents who published information about Năstase's private wealth and by now the justice system was being purged of figures committed to bringing corruption under control.[38] Since the PSD was not abandoning its authoritarian ways or its pro-prietorial attitude towards the state, the integration process was destined to become instead largely a Brussels-centred diplomatic effort.

The Commission's annual monitoring report for 2002 had found that Romania still could not be considered as a functioning market economy, unlike Bulgaria, which had just been recognised as having one. Nevertheless, the report made no mention about disquieting aspects of PSD rule which indicated a resurgence of authoritarian tendencies, notably the Armageddon II affair. This was the title of a report which had been distributed electronically to foreign embassies and news agencies in January 2002 and which focused on the personal wealth of the Prime Minister and his family, and his connections with controversial businessmen.[39] Most of the claims had already been published by the press or aired in parliamentary debates. Nevertheless, the Prosecutor-General's office ordered the detention of the man alleged to have distributed the document and searched the office of Mugur Ciuvică, the former chief of staff of ex-president Constantinescu whom the authorities claimed to be its author. Romania's main human rights watchdog, Apador, accused the Prime Minister of confusing defence of his own reputation with national security and warned that it was only the most serious example of a renewed authoritarian trend in state behaviour.[40] Soon prosecutors investigating top-level anti-corruption cases would be taken off them on orders of the Minister, but this was an issue also left unmentioned in the EU's report.

It soon became clear that the power base of the PSD was shifting under Năstase. Whereas in the 1990s, the managers of state enterprise had been the dominant economic pressure group inside the party, this role was being increasingly assumed by private businessmen who were emerging as the pace of economic activity quickened after the recession years of the late 1990s. These new capitalists in the construction and other fields were very much dependent on the state for their success, such as obtaining preferential treatment in auctions for state contracts.[41] Dan Matei Agaton, a long-term ally of Năstase's, had made it clear that he expected private firms to make an unconditional expression of support to the PSD in campaign contributions and not favour any other parties with them.[42] Nicolae Mischie, the best-known regional boss of the PSD at this time, did not hide the fact that his pen favoured those districts which had given electoral support to the PSD.[43] Indeed, the realisation that the PSD was ready to distribute local resources on a partisan basis led to a stampede from the opposition to the ruling party in the world of local government. Between 2001 and 2003 alone, the number of mayors affiliated to the PSD went up from 35.5% to 64.4%.[44] The EU did draw attention to the grip that the PSD was establishing at the local level of politics where more revenue was flowing due to decentralisation measures adopted in the late 1990s. Aware that more attention was starting to be paid to the sleazy aspects of PSD rule, Năstase assumed a stern pose in mid-2002. Noticing that in very many localities, 'things are not in order', he pointed to prefects and county council heads who rigged auctions, allowed public money to be channelled in a suspect manner, or who adopted an opulent lifestyle not in keeping with their office.[45] He delivered a warning that 'Romania is nobody's private estate and we are not in power forever'. In the same month, he promised that 'firm measures' would be taken against party members who were guilty of corruption and, to root them out, 'operative groups' would be set up in each county.[46] But no purge of tainted activists or officials occurred. Instead, the PSD expelled four of its own deputies who had made accusations of corruption against colleagues.[47] Năstase remained loyal to Şerban Mihăilescu, the Secretary-General of the government until he was forced to resign in October 2003. This PSD official was by then openly described as 'Micky Baksish' in the press. A subordinate, Fane Pavelache, one of the few senior figures to be given a prison sentence for corruption, filed a complaint to the National Anti-Corruption Prosecutor's office that he had obtained a government post in 2001 after giving €28,000 to Adrian Năstase, the deal allegedly being mediated by Mihăilescu. Pavelache's down-fall had occurred in 2002, when he was arrested for trying to manipulate the bankruptcy proceedings in favour of a bank in return for receiving a size-able bribe. He was sentenced to six years in prison but a court set Pavelache free in 2006 after he had agreed to cooperate with prosecutors over more serious corruption allegations which he had knowledge of.[48] Mihăilescu con-tinued to face legal proceedings, one of his main claims to fame being that he inaugurated an EU project, using money from the ISPA fund, to supply the village of Cornu, one hour north of Bucharest, with running water. It contained the holiday home of Năstase and other leading PSD notables and the project cost over €1 million.[49] Năstase stood by his colleague, taking him to Rio de Janeiro for the meeting of the Socialist International at which the PSD was going to be formally inducted into the global family of left-wing parties. Mihăilescu had already been awarded the *Legion d'Honneur* by the Jospin government in France, an early sign that some core EU states were prepared to extend the hand of partnership to local figures persistently dogged by controversy.

The government practised the arts of dissimulation not only in the phantom struggle against corruption but in the more delicate area of internal surveil-lance. In Romania acquiring compromising information on potential and actual opponents became a widespread practice after 1989. One of the PSD's most resourceful political chiefs employed a team of journalists after 2004 to gather intelligence and spread disinformation and he was probably by no means alone in that regard. It would have been naive for the European Commission to assume that it would be spared such attentions, either in Bucharest or indeed at its Brussels headquarters. Romania had growing dip-lomatic missions in Brussels, based at NATO and the EU, and it would have been a total break with practice before and after 1989 if at least some envoys were not engaged in gathering information which could enhance Romania's chances of joining the EU with minimum effort at reform. Confirmation of exactly such surveillance came in July 2002 from an unlikely source. Trying to fend off accusations that he was prejudiced towards the Roma, Corneliu Rusu-

Banu, the Prefect of Iaşi County, blurted out to journalists that the phone of Jonathan Scheele, head of the EU Delegation, was being tapped by operatives from the main domestic security agency, the SRI.[50] Rusu-Banu said that an SRI officer had informed him this was the case, which prompted Scheele to ask the authorities if this were true or not. The reply came from Ion Stan, head of the parliamentary commission overseeing the SRI, who declared that Rusu-Banu (who was a fellow PSD official) had been mistaken and that a phone tap could only be authorised by the Prosecutor-General's office.[51] But in early 2004, Emma Nicholson complained to the press that she was being openly trailed by secret servicemen, which the authorities once again denied.[52]

It would have been normal for the EU, at the start of negotiations, to have pointed out to the Romanian authorities that any form of spying on the activities and movements of EU officials would have been viewed as a highly unfriendly act. The intelligence sector would probably not have been surprised to receive such a warning since the spying role of Ceauşescu's secret service in NATO, and indeed inside certain Western governments, was well known. Charles Hernu, the French Defence Minister who had given the order for the sinking of the Greenpeace ship, 'Rainbow Warrior' in New Zealand in 1982, had, it has been claimed, been on the communist Romanian payroll.[53] But the EU does not appear to have adopted such an elementary measure of self-defence. One senior official pointed out that he and his colleagues were indeed under the impression that communications between the Delegation and Brussels, and even within the Delegation, were not 100% safe. He said that it had been decided to live with this awkward situation rather than make a fuss. Sometimes it was hoped that leaks from the Delegation would assist the EU by showing the political bosses of the eavesdroppers what senior EU officials in fact thought of them. At the other extreme, the precaution was taken of always holding meetings of EU ambassadors in a special sealed room of the German Embassy, even when Germany was not holding the EU Presidency.[54]

The same source mentioned that there were at least two members of the locally recruited Delegation staff who could not be relied upon. But it is possible to argue that such a nonchalant attitude might only have spurred on the Romanian controllers of what remained a sprawling intelligence sector with at least seven separate agencies to be even more brazen. One well-known EU official acquired a mistress from among the local Delegation staff while another peripatetic individual reviewing Romania's performance is widely believed to have succumbed to the charms of a suave and much younger Romanian to whom an introduction was expertly arranged while on a provincial visit of inspection. It is through such stratagems that a wily and resourceful government hoped to cross the finishing line in 2007 without undue expenditure of effort. But there were also parts of the system ready to display ruthlessness usually associated with a bygone era. In 2002, the Defence Minister warned journalists not to pry too deeply into sensitive areas, stating publicly that 'life is too short and your health has too high a price to pay to be endangered by debating highly emotional subjects'.[55]

The Năstase government saw the advantages to be gained by building up an effective lobby spearheaded by diplomatic missions and by a range of front organisations in key EU states designed to promote Romanian membership even if many key reforms existed only on paper. This was done by throwing open the economy to multinationals which became advocates of early membership on informal terms. Lucrative contracts were offered to top firms which in the era of declining party memberships were a vital source of funding for major Western European parties (see chapter 7).

A historic debt to Sweden offered a novel way of building influence in a European capital where, according to the chief EU negotiator, Vasile Puşcaş, Romania suffered from an image problem.[56] Parliament agreed to pay back the debt, worth $120 million, and offer economic benefits for a Swedish company in the energy sector worth another $20 million. Năstase, accompanied by close colleagues, flew to Stockholm on 29 May 2002. This was at a point when Romania's membership bid had recently seemed under threat because of its failure to honour commitments to safeguard children in state care. Yet Goran Persson, the Social Democratic Prime Minister, hailed Năstase as 'a special politician', 'Adrian, my dear friend' and declared that 'Romania's reform process is regarded as a successful and courageous one'. No other European leader at such an early stage in PSD rule had been as forthright as Persson in support of Romania's EU bid.[57]

The PSD was also able to manipulate the workings of the Commission by drawing closer to major political forces at the heart of the elaborate EU system. It succeeded in inserting advisers high up within the Commission whose brief was to argue that Romania ought to join on the basis of the promise of future reforms (see chapter 5). It joined the largest of the European political families, the Socialist group, in 2003 when it was formally admitted to the Socialist International. It successfully reached out even to ruling centre-right parties in EU states. Luxembourg is a useful case in point. Despite its small size, this founder member is an influential member. Romania found it relatively easy to deploy its lobbying skills because the elite is small and consensual. The PSD had enjoyed a breakthrough in the 1990s by cultivating the country's elder statesman, Pierre Werner (1913–2002), a former banker who had led the Christian Social Party in government for many years. Werner was one of the most ardent champions of a European super-state and in 1970 launched the Werner plan which was designed to achieve European Monetary Union within a decade. Tudorel Postolache, an economic adviser to Ion Iliescu, was the key intermediary. He was ambassador to Luxembourg for two lengthy periods after 1990, during which he became on close terms with Werner, even becoming Honorary Co-president with him of the 'Romania–Luxembourg Centre for Study and Documentation' in 1995.[58] Jean-Claude Juncker, Werner's successor as Prime Minister and the dominant figure in centre-right politics over the last 15 years, proved a steadfast defender of the Romanian case for early EU membership. In 2002, he was one of the few EU figures who consented to receive the country's highest decoration, granted by Iliescu, for his services in this regard.

Such connections were invaluable for Năstase whenever he encountered difficulties with the Commission over implementing the *acquis*. Bilateral links with EU statesmen were used to bypass the Commission.[59] This caused a well-connected journalist to observe that 'cynical Bucharest politicians quickly understood that political sympathies with capitals could trump the worries of Brussels technocrats'.[60]

But it was the Socialist connection which proved most advantageous to Năstase and the PSD. Gunther Verheugen, the Commissioner for Enlargement, increasingly viewed Năstase and the PSD as partners and seemed oblivious of the fact that their most vocal champion among the EU members was Silvio Berlusconi, Italy's emphatically right wing Prime Minister from 2001 to 2006.[61]

Academic studies, while not overlooking 'the opportunism and career-ism' entrenched in Romanian politics, argued that leading politicians who possessed these traits in abundance could still opt for 'Euro-Atlantic integration'.[62] The British academic Geoffrey Pridham cites Ion Iliescu, whom he sees as having 'become converted to the cause of European integration though not unreservedly to all its conditions'; in the case of Adrian Năstase, Pridham draws on close aides who told him that 'his . . . commitment to Euro-Atlantic integration grew . . . from autumn 2000; and . . . this came from holding direct responsibilities for Romania's fortunes and from close and regular contact with EU representatives'. He even goes on to claim that 'unqualified elite commitment' to European enlargement 'was present in Romania'.[63] But what lay behind the commitment if it really existed in any tangible form? Was it enthusiasm for being part of a European community of laws, a community of values, a common internal market and a political union? Or did this commitment spring from a cynical calculation by an elite numb to these sentiments that the Union provided unparalleled opportunities for acquiring legitimacy, fresh sources of material wealth and perhaps even geopolitical leverage of the kind exercised by Ceaușescu during the Cold War? The weight of evidence regrettably points in the direction of the second viewpoint.

By contrast, the EU, after the start of negotiations, failed to engage in strenuous lobbying in Romania to build up a pro-reform constituency which could have exercised pressure on Năstase's government in areas where it was proceeding slowly with reform, or indeed actively sabotaging it. Jonathan Scheele, Fotiadis's successor as head of the EU Delegation, was mindful of the need to boost his own image as an EU official who cared deeply about the future of Romania. But he restricted his contacts with opposition journalists, at least during the period in which the PSD was in office. It tended to be mainly, but not exclusively, journalists who were close to the PSD who received invitations for informal talks over drinks at his home. It was only after the PSD lost office that he widened the invitation list to include figures from the media who had been thorns in the side of Năstase such as Armand Gosu and Gelu Trandafir.[64] The restricted nature of his contacts was often revealed by the bland answers which he gave in interviews in which the journalist often focused on the government's disdain for upholding human rights and preserving political pluralism. Sorin Moisa, his chief adviser on domestic politics, appears to have been a crucial influence on Scheele's outlook. They became close friends and indeed Scheele acted as best man at his wedding. Moisa had started out as a critic of PSD domination, having written blistering commentaries on PSD ethics and strategy while working as a journalist for the respected *Monitorul* chain of newspapers. He had been a supporter of the EU evolving in the direction of a federal state, perhaps influenced by the need to contain a rogue political force like the PSD which was a stranger to Europeanisation. However, he grew closer to the PSD, especially after the Foreign Minister Mircea Geoană started a public relations offensive to win over EU officials to the idea that, with all its blemishes, the PSD was the one force capable of placing Romania on the road of long-term modernisation. He wrote detailed reports for Scheele about political matters and if these are ever published it will be fascinating to see what kind of political advice was being conveyed to him and indeed to the upper levels of DG Enlargement. Certainly, officials to whom I have spoken were impressed by the quality of the analyses of political developments coming from the Delegation in Bucharest. There is some evidence, however, that by 2007, with Romania now a full member, Moisa had moved away from his previously held federalist position and believed in the need for Romania to resist directives from Brussels which could be seen as infringing its national sovereignty. [65]

The PSD barely concealed its desire to neutralise all the opposition parties which had been in office from 1996–2000 in much the same way as it had succeeded in co-opting the UDMR. Under Traian Băsescu, a tough and resilient leader, the Democratic Party, which had once been part of Iliescu's National Salvation Front, managed to retain its freedom of action despite defections of senior figures to the PSD. But the National Liberal Party (PNL) proved more amenable, or at least the powerful wing which answered to Dinu Patriciu, fast emerging as Romania's wealthiest businessman. He admitted in 2006 to having given a generous donation to the PSD's campaign funds before the 2004 election.[66]

Patriçiu was the classic example of a talented businessman who had prospered thanks to having connections right across the political spectrum. Under communism, he had practised as an architect, designing houses in the Middle East, an unusual privilege to have been given since the Ceauşescu regime usually restricted such foreign contacts to trusted insiders. He had gone into business with his long-term political and business partner Calin Popescu Tăriceanu in 1990 and faced no serious obstacles despite not belonging to the ruling FSN. It has been claimed that Tăriceanu and Patriçiu lobbied the left-wing Prime Minister Petre Roman in March 1990 in order to obtain state backing to launch Romania's first private firm.[67] In 1998, Patriçiu had led an investors buy-out of the Rompetrol group and in 2002 he had become its CEO. Without powerful connections in the centre-right coalition and the subsequent PSD government, he would have found it difficult to transform Rompetrol from an oil-servicing company into one of the top 25 oil operators in the EU. His crucial breakthrough occurred in 2001, when he purchased a major stake in Petromidia, the owner of the most modern refinery and petro-chemical complex in Romania, for $50.1 million. He was then a Liberal member of Parliament and he admitted that political connections had played a part in his economic success.[68] The acquisition of Petromidia transformed the company's prospects. By 2004, it was worth $1.44 billion, second in the domestic energy sector only to the oil and gas company Petrom SA, which had been privatised and sold to OMV AG of Austria.[69] Patriçiu had managed to beat competition from Western firms which were buying up important strategic sectors of the economy. His partner Tăriceanu would later, as Prime Minister, express concern about an excessive concentration of foreign ownership. Such a view was bound to be shared by the PSD, which in the 1990s had retained a modified version of Ceauşescu's strongly nationalist outlook on major political and economic issues. It made sense for the trans-party alliance of political figures active in business to keep some strategic economic sectors under local ownership. Patriçiu was seen as a reliable figure unlikely to allow his party to change the rules of the game which allowed politics to be one of the most lucrative professions in the country. Năstase showed his trust in Patriçiu in 2003, when his government allowed Petromidia to turn its $600 million debt to the government, dating from the time it had been a state-owned company, into bonds with a 20-year maturity.[70] But under a maverick President, Traian Băsescu, who appeared intent on cutting down to size the politico-economic moguls like Patriçiu, he suddenly faced difficulties from the authorities. In May 2005, he would be detained for questioning concerning alleged irregularities in the post-privatisation activities of Petromidia.[71] He was already under investigation for tax evasion and money laundering, to which was added a charge of manipulating the stock exchange.[72] The contest between Patriciu and prosecutors encouraged, by both the head of state and the EU to investigate alleged top-level corruption, turned into a trial of strength which had enormous ramifications in politics.

EU insistence on a quick series of privatisations to reduce the state's economic role appeared to have had consequences which Brussels mandarins had never intended. It reduced the extent of political competition as erstwhile political rivals closed ranks to safeguard broad elite interests. The democratic process did not benefit as Năstase realised that important elements in the political centre-right could be tempted by overtures to enjoy concessions and opportunities usually monopolised by the governing party. Indeed, it is not an undue exaggeration to say that already by the year of Petromidia's purchase by Rompetrol, much of the opposition was a pale version of the PSD. The opposition forces usually represented only narrow social interests. They were usually also driven by the will to acquire, or remain in power and benefit from access to state wealth and the patronage possibilities that it provides. Parties absorbed with the spoils system usually had little in the way of a programmatic agenda.

But when a political upset allowed Traian Băsescu, the PSD's chief opponent, to narrowly win the Presidency, it led to major infighting at the very heart of the political system over the degree to which major entrepreneurs could be made accountable to the law. Light was shed on some dark corners but the resulting power struggles greatly slowed governmental efforts to prepare Romania to withstand the challenges of membership. It also led to feverish efforts to take over independent media outlets by powerful figures who perhaps stood to be inconvenienced by investigative reporting into the degree to which party politics and the emerging capitalist system – dominated by a few foreign and local giants – were tightly enmeshed. So the deepening engagement of the EU in Romanian policy matters, instead of stimulating a renaissance of political activity, with new parties being launched and existing ones cleaning up their act, seemed to reduce the choices available. This retarded the level of pluralism in politics.

The EU itself impeded the chances of Romanian politics growing more representative by some of the decisions which it took. Perhaps this was most clearly demonstrated by its enthusiasm for promoting a regional level of administration midway between central institutions and the local authorities. The chief motive was to identify new tiers of government through which a large part of pre-accession funding would be channelled, thereby bypassing unwieldly and often partisan central ministries. Regionalisation was in line with the EU's own commitment to distributing power to the lowest level practicable, known as subsidiarity. It would also be another way of reducing the influence of central government, especially in large states where there was resistance to ceding further powers to Brussels. After 1997, each candidate country was being pressed to adopt regional elected structures in order to comply with the EU approach. A green paper on regional development in Romania was published in 1997. It was dawn up by Rambol, a Danish firm expert in decentralisation issues. In the annex of the report, it was pointed out that Romania's 41 counties were too numerous and small to act as a channel of pre-accession funding.[73] Instead, it proposed eight regional development zones which would in time become the country's main territorial units if the regionalisation process made headway in Romania. But first, they would function as funding outlets for the Phare budget. It would be the largest of the three pre-accession instruments designed to modernise the country before entry. As pre-accession assistance was stepped up, especially after the start of entry talks, the Phare programme would comprise half the assistance, well over €3 billion euros.[74] Central and local government, as well as NGOs and private bodies, would be able to contract for Phare funding. Strengthening regional infrastructure was seen as vital in order to quicken the pace of economic and social development and make up for the chronic neglect that had characterised the last decades of communism and indeed Iliescu's period of influence. But the Commission failed to carry out an impact study of its own on the effects of regionalisation in a country where the only organised force across much of the country remained the successor of the Communist Party.

Nor did Brussels ensure that the regional aid bodies had transparent funding structures. Their status was in fact unclear. Neither were they an extension of central government nor could they be described as a non-governmental organisation. Not surprisingly, they were to provide the biggest opportunities for corruptly misusing pre-accession money and it must have seemed a stroke of amazing good fortune for unethical politicians that EU controls proved so feeble.

Even before the electoral defeat of the centre-right, the PDSR was beginning to acquire control of most of the eight Regional Development Councils (RDCs). They comprised presidents of the county councils and mayors of the county capitals as well as representatives of other towns and smaller districts. They made the funding decisions that were implemented by the Regional Development Associations (RDAs). Each RDC comprised between four and seven *judeţe* (counties) and it soon emerged that the advantage lay with the *judeţ* (county) whose capital had been designated the headquarters of the RDA. It benefited disproportionately in terms of funding opportunities and the politicians controlling the county council found themselves enjoying considerable influence as the funding cycle got underway from about 1999 onwards. Instead of regional solidarity slowly taking root, sharp resentments grew up, as in Muntenia and the Central region. Regional barons acquired national renown as Nicolae Mischie in south-west Oltenia and Dumitru Sechelariu in the North-East appeared to set up lucrative regional fiefdoms. They made headlines because of the way they flaunted their influence and acquired power and wealth. The press provided detail of the wealth the Mischie family had acquired from Phare projects.[75] A dossier on his activities drawn up by anti-corruption prosecutors revealed the pressure he was able to exert on local officials in order to ensure that contracts went in the direction of particular private companies.[76] Mischie was forced to step down in 2004 upon being charged and he would eventually be found guilty of corruption and sentenced to a prison term (which at the time of writing he has yet to serve).[77] Sechelariu would be rejected by the citizens of Bacău in the 2004 local elections and afterwards his own difficulties with the law would begin. But the centre of gravity shifted towards local and regional chieftains in part because of the EU's decision to impose regional structures on the country without any forward planning. This was shown in April 2005, when chieftains' votes prevented the party's founder Ion Iliescu from re-occupying the leadership after he could no longer serve a further term as President. Phare funds are complex and difficult to track which meant that the regional barons grew to be an enormous headache for the EU Delegation. But it was the Commission's own strategy which meant that it would struggle to keep track of a large portion of funds stemming from the Phare programme. It would face embarrassment when it emerged that relatives of PSD barons were applying successfully for funding. The regionalisation strategy arguably strengthened the oligarchical character of the PSD and the direction of funds to agencies which had all too easily been captured by local politicians deepened the already massive problem which Romania had with corruption.

Vasile Puşcaş, the chief negotiator for Romania in talks with the EU during the PSD government, was in no doubt that the regional experiment had failed in Romania and that it had been the politicisation of the regionalisation process which prevented it making a positive contribution to Romania's entry preparations.[78] Some RDAs performed better than others though. Surprisingly, the most highly praised was located in the North-East, the poorest area of the country where PSD methods of control had often been extremely crude. It benefited from a good administrative team and reasonably committed staff, which meant it built up an institutional memory that was not dissipated as in so many other branches of administration where staff turnover was extremely high. The funds appeared to be well managed, it initiated other projects apart from Phare ones, and even held regular annual investment fairs to put the region on the map. The British Department of International Development (DFID) had done a lot of preparatory work in the North-East to try and promote local and regional partnerships. This was also done in South Muntenia but the synergy was far less apparent there because of a sharp cleavage between the more prosperous north of the region, which enjoyed a strong industrial and also tourist base, and the more underdeveloped southern plains.[79]

By 2002, it was clear that Brussels was not happy with the government's regional planning approach. There was no correlation between local, regional and national planning. Progress with completing chapter 21 on regional policy was slow. In response, the Năstase government announced a working-party to prepare a National Development Plan which would be implemented between 2004 and 2006. Octavian Cozmâncă, the Minister of Public Administration, had announced in October 2002 that it was hoped to create directly elected regions which would have considerable administrative responsibility. Meanwhile Năstase called for 'an ample debate on what regionalization, regional development, and decentralization really mean'.[80] Partnership structures at both national and regional levels were then set up by the government, including the universities as well as economic and social actors.[81] The Ministry of Regional Development was dissolved and located in the Ministry of European Integration, still under a firmly centralising Minister, Hildegard Puwak.

These rituals appeared to be the classic response of a government playing for time in the hope that the EU's bizarre enthusiasm for regionalisation would burn itself out. By the time it unexpectedly lost office in 2004, plans for the regionalisation of Romania were hardly much further advanced. This left the EU with a growing headache because negotiations by now had been completed and regional structures were still thought to be the best means of delivering structural and cohesion funds which were due to dwarf in size pre-accession funds.

The Ministry of European Integration was in charge of all EU-related affairs and responsible for contracting and overseeing a large proportion of the pre-accession projects ensuing. Hildegard Puwak held the job for the best part of three years. She had a background in financial management stretching back to communist times and, appropriately for someone whose administrative career originated then, her approach to the ministry was rather authoritarian. Staff were recruited on the basis of their loyalty and reliability rather than their skills and readiness to accomplish very demanding targets. The European Institute of Romania, instead of being encouraged to function as a powerhouse of ideas enabling Romania to make progress to complete the *acquis*, languished under her. It became little more than an agency which was used to translate the *acquis* into Romanian and it even lacked control over which companies this task was sub-contracted to.[82] In September 2001, she appointed Leonard Orban as deputy negotiator with the EU, primarily so he would watch over his chief, Vasile Puşcaş.[83] Puşcaş, who had joined the PSD only a short time before becoming chief negotiator, had made sure that he would enjoy freedom of action, being answerable to the Prime Minister and enjoying a seat in the cabinet. As well as negotiating in Brussels, he worked closely with producer groups in Romania, reported back to parliamentary committees, and drew up numerous position papers on *acquis* chapters for consideration by the government. He found the Commission was usually unwilling to modify its negotiating position and adopted 'a take it or leave it approach' on many technical and economic aspects of the *acquis*. At least one Commission official replied by arguing that if he had been more tenacious in some aspects of negotiation more could have been achieved. He was most proud of the progress accomplished in the chapter on the environment, where Romania had found itself in a very weak position when negotiations first started.[84] This was a policy area where some cooperation occurred with NGOs. But usually, Puwak kept the NGO community firmly at arm's length, which was ironic because her downfall occurred when it emerged that an NGO run by close family members had broken the law in order to obtain a large sum of money from a Phare programme.

On 26 August 2003 the BBC Romanian Service revealed that companies ran by Iosif, the husband, and Mihai, the son of Mrs Puwak had obtained from the Leonardo da Vinci training programme €150,000, part of which had been granted after she had been appointed Minister.[85] An audit team from OLAF, the EU Anti-Fraud Office, began an investigation.[86] On 20 October Mrs Puwak resigned from the government, a decision publicly welcomed by Jonathan Scheele. In the same month, the Commission ordered her family to pay back €150,000 obtained from the Leonardo da Vinci training programme. But in December 2003, Iosif Puwak was exonerated by the anti-corruption prosecutors of the PNA: the funds had apparently been spent in conformity with the programme for which they were allocated.[87] So the law had not been broken. But further investigations revealed that large sums had been embezzled and in December 2007 Puwak was sentenced to two years in prison. His wife's political career had ended when she had been forced to leave office in October 2003, an obscure job being found for her in the state bank after she retired from Parliament. The departure of two other Ministers posed doubts about the ethical standards of those holding high office under Năstase. Mircea Beuran, the Health Minister, resigned after a medical ethics commission found him guilty of plagiarising American and French medical textbooks. Meanwhile, Şerban Mihăilescu, a close ally of Năstase, resigned after prosecutors alleged that two aides on trial for seeking bribes to facilitate business deals had done so in his name.[88] Năstase insisted his ministers were blameless, but accepted their resignations 'to avoid creating any problems for the government'.[89]

These embarrassing resignations occurred shortly after the holding of a referendum to seek approval for constitutional changes. The main one ensured the supra-national authority of the EU in areas where previously only Romanian laws applied. The campaign illustrated the failure of European issues to have an impact on the electorate and the inability of the PSD to mobilise voters even though the referendum was held over two days, on 18 and 19 October 2003 to try and ensure a large turnout. For the vote to be valid 50% of voters had to cast ballots. But on the first day only 14.29% bothered to vote. On the morning of the second day, Octavian Cozmâncă, the PSD Secretary-General, held a video conference with the county leaders of the party, warning of dire consequences unless they took exceptional steps to obtain a satisfactory turnout.[90] Mobile polling booths intended to allow the elderly and handicapped to vote from home appeared and they were used in supermarkets, railway stations and airports. Reports indicated widespread efforts to woo voters with food, drink, supplies of winter wood, and even tombolas.[91] A turnout of 55% was declared and the referendum was easily approved. But several NGOs drew up a detailed report claiming fraud, only for it to be greeted with silence in Brussels.[92] Official EU documentation later welcomed the fact that no constitutional impediments prevented the *acquis* and other EU documents becoming law, but the manner in which this result had been obtained was passed over in silence.

Conclusion

What motives did the PSD have for wanting to take Romania into the EU? I once startled a leading member of the EU Delegation midway through the negotiation process by asking him this question. He finally replied that it was a desire for respectability on the part of the PSD combined with not wanting to be left out of a process that was gathering momentum everywhere in the region, except in former Yugoslavia.

It did not appear to have occurred to the official that EU membership was highly desirable because it did not really threaten the form of control that the PSD exercised over the country, and indeed offered it scope to replicate its negative behaviour traits on the European stage. Adrian Năstase was able to discover that the EU was not going to pay overmuch attention to the political criteria for entry. As one academic expert has written: 'All three main Copenhagen conditions are very broad and open to considerable interpretation . . . the conditions are very general; they do not, for example, define what constitutes a market economy or a stable democracy'.[93] It would probably be enough for the PSD to avoid the repetition of events as gory as those in June 1990 when a rogue army of coal miners, on state orders, savagely dispersed opposition protestors.

The EU was prepared to lower its guard after the PSD dropped its anti-Hungarian rhetoric and seemed prepared to accept Baroness Nicholson's strategy on child protection. There was mounting relief in Brussels that a government had reached office which appeared to control the state and understood large parts of the EU's accession agenda. By 2002, the EU was prepared to overlook reversals to authoritarian behaviour and it actually welcomed the result of the 2003 referendum on the Constitution, even though there was compelling evidence that the required 50%-plus turnout was obtained by highly unorthodox means. A top official in the EU Delegation whom I interviewed in 2003 expressed his impatience with the opposition forces and stated baldly that 'I cannot act as the opposition for them'.[94]

A blossoming partnership with the PSD was maintained thanks to its willingness to swallow unpalatable economic medicine. Năstase slashed state subsidies to private firms and engaged in a rapid privatisation drive in an economy which was still two-thirds state controlled in 2001.[95] But the EU failed to see, or else overlooked, the enhanced benefits likely to accrue to the PSD from opening up the economy to outside forces. Năstase and much of his party were confident that many of the PSD's local economic clients could establish lucrative ties with major European businesses needing expert guidance to steer them through the Romanian economic maze. Commissions would be earned, local board places would be filled, structural funds would irrigate the businesses of politicians from the oligarchy, and there were many other ways in which adaptable post-communists would become players in economic transactions extending beyond Romania. This was an exciting big league compared with preserving state companies, their incompetent managements and obsolete workforces. Too late did the EU realise that the regional structures which it had set up for the delivery of Phare funds were a perfect opportunity to PSD barons to help themselves to the very same funding.

The PSD hoped that the EU and leading Council members would accept economic reform in the context of a state still subject to strong one-party influence. The party was determined not to relax political influence over the justice system, nor was the EU prepared to act resolutely to ensure that serious judicial reform and a real, as opposed to synthetic, separation of powers occurred. The PSD realised, probably quite early on, that the EU had no plan B for Romania. For Brussels, it was a question of muddling through somehow and declaring victory. The suspension of talks was not to be contemplated and no thought was given to a process of phased entry.

It was the PSD and its economic allies who probably did the most strategic thinking about what Romania's place in the EU should be. They could see themselves establishing fruitful links with major businesses in order to exploit Romanian resources and take advantage of the European and domestic funds available for major infrastructure projects. Thanks to establishing alliances with leading members of the European social democratic family, they

managed to obtain political protection for pursuing a form of rogue capitalism with recourse to authoritarian measures whenever these were absolutely
unavoidable.

The EU was preoccupied with bigger accession challenges than Romania.
Extra managerial resources from Brussels were not even available when it
was clear how hard it was to keep track of pre-accession funding. The partnerships which the PSD built up at European level were not replicated by
the EU in the domestic arena, where it remained isolated from pro-European
opinion.

It was the PSD's mission to convince the international bodies that its own
irregular standards of behaviour were an accurate reflection of the debased
standards which it was suggested applied across state and society in a Balkan
country burdened by an unfortunate history. By 2002, it had made progress.
The EU was faced with a resourceful candidate government which was busy
building alliances inside the EU system in order to join without complying
with many entry requirements. But Brussels shrank from tough measures and
instead gave increasing emphasis after 2002 (in the words of Alina Mungiu-
Pippidi) to 'socialisation as a tool meant to secure the candidate's compliance
with EU goals'. This has been described as engaging accession states, besides
also ones in the EU neighbourhood, 'in multiple personal and institutional
contacts and joint activities, offering a model for successful transformation'.[96]
The twinning process was the most obvious example of this deployment of
'soft power' and in Romania its result would prove distinctly mixed (see chapters 3 and 4).

The EU failed to see that economic liberalisation was likely to be distorted
if there was no genuine reform of political institutions, with separation of
powers a key priority. In 2006, Geoffrey Pridham wrote: 'Depending on the
determination of new democracies to accede, the EU is provided with a compelling leverage over their political elites'.[97] Elsewhere, he argued that 'once
negotiations have actually started, a country's state system becomes locked
into a dynamic and this in turn acts on a constraint on new parties in office'.[98]
But the PSD's engagement with the EU, in my view, offers scant evidence of
the EU's ability to project its values and governance standards in this transition state. The EU failed to make use of the leverage at its disposal when it
became obvious that this particular candidate wished to accede with major
reforms left undone in as many areas as possible. Romania's state system
remained one that was opaque, inefficient and a prisoner of special interests.
The PSD did not feel constrained by any dynamic pull from Brussels pushing
the country in the direction of fundamental reforms. Instead, Năstase and his
allies saw the EU as a transient force to be confused, offered inducements and
sidetracked until its ability to lecture the Romanian elite ceased once the goal
of full membership had been reached.

Notes

1 *Evenimentul Zilei*, 3 December 2004.
2 See Gallagher, *Romania After Ceauşescu*, chapters 2 and 3.
3 *Adevărul*, 5 July 1999.
4 *Cotidianul*, 19 February 2001.
5 *2000 Regular Report*, p. 14.
6 Phelim McAleer, 'Romania Urged to Deal with Unwanted Babies', *Financial Times*, 30 May 2001.
7 *Evenimentul Zilei*, 4 June 2001.
8 Eugen Tomiuc, 'Romania: EU Report Assails Nation over Treatment of Orphans', *Radio Free Europe*, 4 June 2001.
9 Tomiuc, 'Romania'.
10 Interview with Alin Teodorescu, Bucharest, 18 December 2004.
11 Rupert Wolfe-Murray, 'A True Revolution', *Transitions Online*, 2 January 2006, www.tol.cz.
12 Interview with Alin Teodorescu, Bucharest, 18 December 2004.
13 Commission of the European Communities, *2001 Regular Report on Romania's Progress Towards Accession*, Com (2001), 13 November 2001, p. 101.
14 Interview with European Commission official, Brussels, 2008.
15 Radio Free Europe, *RFE-RL Newsline*, 29 June 2001.
16 Radio Free Europe, *RFE-RL Newsline*, 20 March 2001.
17 Radio Free Europe, *RFE-RL Newsline*, 22 March 2001.
18 Radio Free Europe, *RFE-RL Newsline*, 28 March 2001.
19 Radio Free Europe, *RFE-RL Newsline*, 19 March 2003.
20 OECD Economic Assessment 2002, *Romania*, Paris: Organisation for Economic Cooperation and Development, 2002, p. 7.
21 *Gardianul* (Bucharest), 16 June 2007.
22 OECD Economic Assessment 2002, p. 10.
23 Phelim McAleer, 'Romanians Find Little Fault with the Sidex Steel Deal', *Financial Times*, 16 February 2002.
24 *Adevărul*, 25 July 2001.
25 *Adevărul*, 25 July 2001.
26 McAleer, 'Romanians Find Little Fault'.
27 Editorial, 'Slamming the Gate on Donors', *Financial Times*, 16 February 2002.
28 *2001 Regular Report*, p. 72.
29 *Adevărul*, 1 June 2001.
30 Radio Free Europe, *RFE-RL Newsline*, 29 June 2001.
31 Eugen Tomiuc, 'Romania: Travellers Ponder Gains, Losses from EU's Visa-Free Regime', *Radio Free Europe*, 12 December 2001.
32 *Nine O'Clock*, 10 December 2001.
33 EU internal memorandum, 2005.
34 Private information.
35 Interview with European Commission official, Brussels, 2008.
36 Gallagher, *Theft of a Nation*, p. 348.

37 *Adevărul*, 7 April 2006.
38 Gallagher, *Theft of a Nation*, p. 323.
39 *Evenimentul Zilei*, 21 January 2002.
40 Gallagher, *Theft of a Nation*, p. 323.
41 Alexandru Lăzescu, *Revista 22*, 26 June–2 July 2001.
42 *Evenimentul Zilei*, 18 November 2003.
43 Cristian Ghinea, *Dilema Veche*, 31 October 2003.
44 Cristian Ghinea, 'Povestea primarului rătăcitor', *Dilema Veche*, 31 October 2003.
45 *Ziarul de Iaşi*, 20 July 2002.
46 Radio Free Europe, *RFE-RL Newsline*, 16 July 2002.
47 Radio Free Europe, *RFE-RL Newsline*, 15 October 2002.
48 Andreea Pocotila, 'Ex-government Aide Released from Prison', *Bucharest Daily News*, 24 June 2006.
49 *Ziua*, 6 September 2003.
50 *Ziarul de Iaşi*, 20 July 2002.
51 *Ziua*, 3 August 2002.
52 *Evenimentul Zilei*, 5 February 2005.
53 *L'Express* (Paris), 31 October 1996.
54 Private information.
55 David Cronin, 'Homing in on Reform', *European Voice*, 11 December 2003.
56 Geoffrey Pridham, 'Between Rhetoric and Action: Reflections on Romania's European Accession and Political Conditionality – the View from Brussels and Bucharest', *Romanian Journal of European Affairs*, Vol. 6, No. 3, 2006, p. 12.
57 *Evenimentul Zilei*, 23 May 2005.
58 'Welcome to Tudorel Postolache', http://romania on-line.net/postolacheTudorel/.
59 Pridham, 'Between Rhetoric and Action', p. 18.
60 Andrei Postelnicu, 'Why Romania Needs Help to Stay on Track', *European Voice*, 27 October–2 November 2005.
61 Interviews with EU officials based in both Brussels and Bucharest, 2005 and 2007.
62 Pridham, 'Between Rhetoric and Action', p. 15.
63 Pridham, 'Between Rhetoric and Action', p. 17.
64 Private information.
65 Information from Bucharest-based civic activist.
66 *Adevărul*, 7 August 2006.
67 See Mihai Nicuţ, 'Adam şi Eva ai capitalismului', *Cotidianul* (Bucharest), 8 August 2006.
68 Cristi Cretzan, 'Romania's Probe of Big Oil Firm Prompts Concerns', *Dow Jones Newswires*, June 2005.
69 Cretzan, 'Romania's Probe of Big Oil Firm Prompts Concerns'.
70 Cretzan, 'Romania's Probe of Big Oil Firm Prompts Concerns'.
71 *Bucharest Daily News*, 21 July 2005.
72 *Evenimentul Zilei*, 19 February 2004.
73 Gabi Moroianu, 'Regionalizarea ca în Regat', *Ziua*, 15 October 2002.

74 See Sorin Ioniţă, *Too Much to Handle? Review of EU Funds Absorption Capacity*, Bucharest: Romanian Academic Society, 2006.

75 See *Gazeta de Sud* (Craiova), 21 December 2002.

76 *BBC Romanian Service*, 18 May 2004.

77 *Gândul*, 13 July 2007.

78 Intervention at a conference held at Birmingham University on 19 March 2007.

79 Information derived from Wolfe-Murray, *Partners for Europe*, and an interview with Camelia Gheorghe, Bucharest, 14 June 2007.

80 Ovidiu Bancheş, 'Regionalizarea Romaniei', *Ziua*, 8 October 2002.

81 Commission of the European Communities, *2003 Regular Report on Romania's Progress Towards Accession*, Com (2003), p. 94.

82 The view of several European Commission members interviewed.

83 Information from a Romanian with a senior role on the EU Delegation staff at this time.

84 Interview with Vasile Puşcaş, Bucharest, 20 December 2006.

85 *BBC Romanian Service*, 26 August 2003.

86 Radio Free Europe/Radio Liberty, *Newsline*, 3 September 2003.

87 *Gazeta de Sud* (Râmnicu Vâlcea), 22 December 2003.

88 *Le Monde*, 22 October 2003.

89 Dana Spinant, 'Romanian Ministers Quit', *European Voice*, 23 October 2003.

90 *Evenimentul Zilei*, 20 October 2003.

91 Christopher Condon, '3 Ministers Resign after Graft Allegations', *Financial Times*, 21 October 2003.

92 Gallagher, *Theft of a Nation*, p. 350.

93 Heather Grabbe, 'Challenge of EU Enlargement', in Dominic Lieven and Dmitri Trenin (eds), *Ambivalent Neighbors: The EU, NATO, and the Price of Membership*, Washington DC: Carnegie Endowment for International Peace, 2003, pp. 72, 77.

94 Meeting with a senior member of the EU Delegation, June 2003.

95 Radio Free Europe, *RFE-RL Newsline*, 6 July 2001.

96 Alina Mungiu-Pippidi, 'EU Enlargement and Democracy Progress', in Michael Emerson (ed.), *Democratisation in the European Neighbourhood*, Brussels: Centre for European Policy Studies, 2005, p. 17.

97 Pridham, 'Between Rhetoric and Action ', p. 8.

98 Pridham, *Designing Democracy*, p. 111.

3

The futility of EU funding

Romania was allocated €6.5 billion of pre-accession funding by the EU between 1990 and 2005.[1] Most of this assistance was meant to ensure that a process of economic and social modernisation was accelerated. This involved modernising the infrastructure of the country, neglected under Ceauşescu and left in disrepair afterwards. Assistance was also meant to ensure that Romania acquired a market economy based on free enterprise and private initiative. Overall, it was correctly assumed in Brussels that a large-scale absorption of aid was required if the country was to relate to EU norms and standards and narrow the developmental gulf with existing members. If the aid was wasted, stolen, or was unable to be applied because of the incapacity of the state to channel it in the right direction, then there was the real risk that Romania would end up as a net contributor to the EU budget during its early years of membership. Such an outcome was bound to confirm it as a peripheral member of the EU. Due to be the seventh largest member in terms of population, it was likely to remain a laggard unless there were creative and well-planned efforts to use EU assistance to focus on the development priorities which had been blocked for many years due to ideological rigidity and later political instability, and the lack of any coherent reform momentum.

But this chapter will try to show that the assistance model adopted for the Eastern European candidates had serious flaws. Preliminary academic assessments suggest that it failed to strengthen the capacity of the new candidates in important respects. Large funding schemes in which money was hurriedly dispersed without the Commission being able to track its impact only scratched the surface of many of the developmental problems faced by former communist states. In the case of Romania, where institutional failings were more systematic owing to the totalitarian nature of the communist system, the rigid and superficial approach to pre-accession assistance had particularly harmful effects. As the Commission's annual reports showed, there was no real growth in administrative efficiency across much of the public sector. Indeed, there is no shortage of evidence that political forces and their bureaucratic allies were content to mimic change and turn key tools of the EU strategy, such as the emphasis on regionalisation, to their own advantage. From quite early in the accession process, the EU had plenty of evidence that its plans for modernisation were encountering severe obstacles in Romania. But rather than carry out a fundamental review and consider adopting a customised approach that targeted attention on the reform blockages, it preferred to improvise and produce euphemistic accounts of the impact of pre-accession instruments on an applicant whose structural problems often appeared impervious to its centralised approach to institutional reform and improving a low-grade infrastructure.

It was unfortunate that the aid strategy for the applicants, mainly from Eastern Europe, was drawn up and finalised when there were few in the European Commission who were ready to assume that Romania could be joining as a full member in the foreseeable future. By 1995 the Commission had produced a blueprint detailing the various forms of financial and technical assistance to be provided for candidate states during the process of negotiations.[2] The EU insisted that these pre-accession instruments were non-negotiable. If it had been envisaged that a country with such an inefficient and politicised public service was going to be catapulted from a peripheral applicant to a serious contender for entry, then the EU might have re-thought its plans. It might have been reasonable to expect that it would come up with a customised strategy to strengthen the capacity of the state before embarking on wholesale privatisation and the distribution of pre-accession funds. Less emphasis might have been given to establishing regional structures as a conduit for large amounts of EU funds given the dominance the kleptocratic post-communists enjoyed over much of local government. There might have been strong emphasis placed on modernising the education system so that it became geared towards producing far greater numbers of skilled and motivated graduates capable of strengthening the capacity of the public service; directing funding and expertise to sectors of the educational system capable of working in partnership with the most vibrant sectors of the economy, particularly in the information technology sector, might have contributed to the emergence of a genuine home-centred reform process.

But there were acute problems in getting projects started on time and a limited capacity to manage EU funds which would not significantly improve as the years rolled on. Throughout the pre-accession period, there was a massive turnover of staff from different ministries and agencies involved with EU assistance programmes. Officials who obtained training and expertise often moved into the private sector where salaries were usually higher and working conditions less uncertain and onerous. This meant institutional memory was lost and, in the absence of proper feedback and evaluation, few lessons were learnt that could be applied to improve the next stages of modernisation programmes. At cabinet level, effective coordination of EU funding initiatives was usually lacking. The Ministry of European Integration was not the most efficient of ministries and, under Hildegard Puwak, a minister drawn from the pre-1989 bureaucracy, it did not became a magnet for talent.

The Phare programme was the oldest of the EU's pre-accession instruments and it was meant to channel technical, economic and infrastructural expertise and assistance to recipient states. During the first half of the 1990s, it had focused on technical assistance usually at ministerial level. Phare was 'demand driven' and responded to requests for help from governments. There was a proliferation of projects across many areas. Each one had a Project Management Unit (PMU) involving local civil servants and external advisers. Tight financial monitoring by the Commission meant that delays built up between when funds were committed and actually paid out. This and the proliferation of unwieldy small projects reduced the enthusiasm of national bureaucracies in candidate states for Phare-driven reform.[3]

After 1997, PMUs were scrapped and replaced by National Funds, usually located within national finance ministries. Phare was increasingly orientated towards making the enlargement process work. Accession partnerships drawn up after the 1997 Luxembourg summit made this clear. A National Programme for the Adoption of the *acquis* was at the heart of the partnership. Phare was to focus on enabling the pre-accession priorities identified by the Commission to be met. Administrative reform and institution-building were identified as key objectives, and after 1997 the Commission pledged 30% of its entire Phare budget for work in these areas.[4] The end goal was to ensure that the institutions of new member states had the capacity to absorb the large quantities of structural funds which would become available upon entry.

But Phare assistance did not settle into a stable pattern. After the resignation of the Santer Commission in 1998, Commission monitoring of funding programmes grew even tighter, so delays in funding projects were not significantly reduced. Around half of the funds allocated to Romania between 1990 and 2005 were channelled through greatly varying Phare programmes. This was a very unwieldy and complex development tool. The final beneficiaries could be central government institutions, local government, or private profit-making or non-profit-making groups. Phare covered an extensive range of activities: capacity-building at the central or local level, grant-giving schemes for civil society or small firms, social programmes to tackle unemployment or assist marginalised groups, projects to boost local and regional infrastructure, and many others besides. Projects were supposed to follow a three-year cycle: this involved two years for programming and contracting and one year for implementing and payments. But, especially with larger infrastructure projects, funds were re-allocated to respond to other contingencies and the timetable was frequently extended in response to delays in meeting targets. In Romania, programmes for which the last disbursements should have been made at the end of 2003, 2004 or 2005 still had activities going on and payments outstanding in December 2005.[5]

From 1998, the Phare programme had an important twinning element. Civil servants in candidate states were linked up to counterparts in established members to work together on specific projects. Twinning was meant to transfer knowledge and competence in areas that were seen as crucial for ensuring success in the adoption of the *acquis*. Astonishingly, civil servants who might be seconded to Romania for up to 24 months received no specific training in the local administrative culture, which they soon found out was a highly specific one. According to scholars who studied aspects of the twinning scheme, as a result of this oversight most of them 'faced a long and difficult period of adjustment to their new working environment'.[6] Besides it was often hard to keep up with the administrative demands placed upon them by EU accounting methods. Many complained that their hands were full with form-filling when they should have been trying to realise the project's objectives.[7] Not surprisingly, the EU's haphazard approach to institution-building, as shown by the twinning exercise, ensured that progress was slow in enabling candidate states to absorb the meritocratic and efficiency-based norms that it was assumed animated bureaucracies in existing members. Whether the experiences of policy-making of established EU members were successfully assimilated is hard to say but the evidence for this happening in Romania would often be hard to detect.

The Delegation was entrusted by the Commission with the task of monitoring the twinning exercises. The Commission and the Delegation both found it difficult to keep track of Phare projects since they were run by different bodies: central government institutions, private contractors and through the eight RDAs. The misallocation of funds by venal politicians who dominated several of these RDAs proved a real source of embarrassment for the Delegation (see chapter 2). The rank favouritism shown to clients, who included close relatives, meant that it was often an uphill task for small entrepreneurs to apply for funds, however worthwhile their projects. Non-governmental organisations tended to have a much better track record in devising projects that were completed according to schedule and left some worthwhile results in their wake.

But once a candidate started to consolidate its bid for entry, the EU increasingly delegated the task of coordinating the distribution of funds to the NGO sector to the government in charge. Brussels must have realised that applying this rule to Romania was fraught with peril given the desire of the PSD to colonise all available public spaces. Although attempts were made to ensure that independent-minded NGOs still benefited from EU support, constant vigilance had to be exercised. This was confirmed by the scandal that emerged around the funding of the National Agency for Youth Initiative Support (ANSIT). Between 2000 and 2005, it had received €7.84 million from Phare's

Leonardo da Vinci programme to provide training for young people. But an investigation carried out in 2006 by the Department for the Struggle Against Fraud (DLAF: a recently formed corruption agency meant to work in partnership with the EU's OLAF) discovered grave irregularities in its accounts since ANSIT could only account for €5.8 million.[8] But the EU had been alarmed at the situation for some years, having suspended funding for the youth programmes that ANSIT was overseeing as early as 2003–04. The Commission's 2004 progress report on Romania laconically stated that improvements in ANSIT's financial management 'remains the condition to resume the normal implementation of the programme in Romania'.[9]

The DLAF report claimed that over €1 million had been spent in other areas. But as long as the PSD was in power, there had been no progress in discovering the fate of the missing funds. Cristian Rizea, the Director of ANSIT, was well connected politically. Indeed, he was the god-child of Alexandru Athanasiu, the PSD's first Minister of Education after 2000. With investigations still dragging on in 2008 into one of the murkiest episodes in pre-accession funding in Romania, it is unclear whether anyone will pay a penalty if the fate of these funds is ever established.

In 2004, the development economist John Gray commented aptly about the superficial and wasteful strategy of the EU in trying to strengthen youth expertise through various training programmes involving exchange schemes with Western European bodies: 'little can be shown in the way of results for all the educational programmes financed by [the] EU in Romania in the last decade – Socrates, Erasmus, etc. Hundreds of students and teaching staff were toured around Europe, all in non-degree programmes too short to make a difference to someone's professional development. The main beneficiaries of this form of academic tourism were these second-rate Western European universities who were paid for hosting East Europeans. With less money, the World Bank programme of financing alternative textbooks or the Soros Foundation's strategy of financing advanced degrees in western-type universities are likely to have a much more substantial and long-lasting impact on these societies'.[10]

But World Bank projects were not always suitable for Romania's needs, even though often conceived differently from those of the EU. In the late 1990s, there was a big flow of sectoral experts to work with the government. Though the World Bank director in Romania was a Frenchman, Francois Ettori, they were mostly from the USA. The Bank's funding was mainly in the form of loans and was only a fraction of the EU's non-reimbursable assistance. Nevertheless, its Washington chiefs expected to play the dominant role in shaping structural reforms. Sharp differences arose over Washington's prescriptions for energy, which the Commission believed were in contravention of the *acquis*, and also agriculture. One Commission official with extensive experience in Eastern Europe said: 'If they did business in Romania as if it was

Zimbabwe, we could not live with this. We thought we were on the right side of the equation in terms of policy and the future of the country'.[11]

With the IMF, relations were more mixed. But a successful collaboration occurred over the protracted issue of child protection. Fotiadis recalls that, while driving through Bulgaria on his way back to Greece, he received a phone call from Radu Vasile. His hard-pressed government had been unable to provide sufficient funds for the child care programme agreed with the EU. On a Bulgarian roadside, Fotiadis rang up IMF chiefs and managed to persuade them to contribute finance by stressing the importance of proper child care for the future of Romania.[12] But such examples of smooth coordination between the different international players were relatively rare. Not surprisingly, the mixed messages proved confusing for the Bucharest authorities but, under a Machiavellian figure like Năstase, they also provided scope for playing off one international institution against the other.

Easily the largest Phare project was the Enterprise Restructuring and Professional Conversion Programme (RICOP) scheme designed to alleviate the impact of industrial plant closures in vulnerable communities facing a collapse in earnings and large-scale unemployment. Its genesis can be found in the 1999 miners' revolt which Prime Minister Vasile helped to contain by promising an EU-funded social recovery programme for the Jiu Valley. Francois Lamoureux, the senior Commission official responsible for enlargement issues, could see the sense in the initiative when it was explained to him by Fokion Fotiadis, the Delegation chief in Bucharest.[13] Thus RICOP was born. The scheme covered 17 of Romania's 41 counties and in total €170 million was spent. It did not operate through the much-criticised RDAs but involved local actors ranging from councils to unemployment offices and NGOs. The Danish consultancy overseeing RICOP was committed to pushing funds towards low-income groups in communities reeling from closures. But a lack of coordination among the different partners reduced its effectiveness, especially in the area of small business creation.[14] By the time RICOP was supposed to be fully functioning, the problems which had led to its creation were in decline. Large-scale unemployment was being absorbed by a sharp upturn in economic growth after 2000. The effects were not strongly felt in economic blackspots but with the relaxation in visa restrictions from 2001 onwards, their unemployed inhabitants had the opportunity to emigrate and a huge exodus gathered momentum in the years to come so that at least 10% of the national labour force had relocated to the rest of the EU by the time of Romania's accession.[15]

Senior Commissioners looked askance at RICOP, which was viewed as a wasteful 'leviathan'. But at least one middle-level Commission official involved with its implementation had no hesitation in offering a vigorous defence, mainly due to ancillary benefits derived from it. It led, in 2001, to the flagship privatisation of Sidex, which had been losing €1 million a day. Trade-union resistance had crumbled because of the severance payments RICOP could fund. The efforts made to provide alternative means of employment were also not without success and it was a way for local authorities to obtain experience in community renewal programmes. In addition, the Commission acquired substantial information about the opaque accounting practices in state companies. This enabled effective strategies to be developed that were to enhance economic competition and prevent covert and direct state funding of both private and state firms which were supposed to be self-sufficient.[16]

The RICOP project appeared not to be part of a wider development strategy and seemed concerned to overcome specific short-term problems that threatened to delay progress with meeting the accession terms. This was true also of ISPA. It was supposed to improve infrastructure in transportation, water and waste management, and pave the way for effective absorption of structural funding in these areas upon accession being achieved. It functioned on a project basis and, unlike Phare, each individual project and each stage of implementation had to be pre-approved by the Commission. External audits discovered problems with organisation, human resources and internal auditing which resulted in massive delays.[17] This delayed the goal of Romania acquiring a decentralised implementation system for ISPA to pave the way for management of the much larger structural funds it was due to acquire after 2007. Transportation projects were rated very poorly. Auditors found problems with all contracting authorities, especially the state railways (CFR).[18] Chronic mismanagement was apparent and there was no proper quality screening. Staff from the EU Delegation were often required to intervene to try and salvage projects that had run into difficulties. The poor quality of tenders was often the main reason for acute delays in launching projects which meant that the absorption of ISPA funds was usually poor. Environmental projects were usually more successful than transportation ones but there were serious doubts about whether local authorities would be able to maintain new infrastructure properly. No less than 35% of ISPA funding was from the national budget, so the failure of many of these projects to have a direct impact on pressing developmental issues was a loss which, to a large degree, was carried by the Romanian taxpayer.

By the time the Commission proposed 'roadmaps' for both Romania and Bulgaria in 2002, it was aware that the state lacked the capacity to absorb pre-accession funds and use them effectively in the way intended. There were gifted officials within the administration such as Daniela Gheorghe who, from her base in the Ministry of Finance, had key roles from 2001 to 2007 in trying to ensure that pre-accession funds were effectively used and contributed to a strategy of national development. Her administrative methods based on team-work and delegation chimed in well with those of Brussels officials with Romanian responsibilities.[19] She tried to ensure that at least some lessons learned from the managing of EU funds were applied to the administration of domestic finances. But there were insufficient people with her outlook, encouragement was lacking from political office-holders, and she and a handful of others like her were isolated modernisers within a stagnant administrative culture (see chapter 4). In 2007, she became the first Romanian official to become a Director-General in the Commission and, in an interview shortly afterwards, she made it clear that the unwillingness of politicians to curb efforts to politicise the civil service was doing immense harm to its ability to play an effective role in modernising the country.[20]

To try to stimulate both Romania and Bulgaria to undertake greater efforts in order to achieve the goal of membership, the Commission had published roadmaps for both of them in November 2002. The aim was 'to support the two countries' efforts to meet the remaining criteria for membership by iden-tifying the tasks ahead and providing increased financial assistance'.[21] The governments of both countries had pressed for such maps, perhaps on the assumption that tough criteria would not be laid down and they would be assured of the irreversibility of the enlargement process.[22] At the time, this initiative was taken as an indication of a deepening commitment in Brussels to ensuring that the challenges both these 'laggard' applicants posed for the integration process would be tackled directly and not swept under the carpet. Romania had still to begin negotiations on some of the toughest chapters in the *acquis* and 'the roadmap provided benchmarks against which . . . progress can be measured' for those still to be opened and then closed.[23]

The roadmap failed to face up to the institutional problems in Romania preventing the accession objective being met. Accordingly, it deserves to be viewed as one of a number of initiatives, such as the 'Medium-Term Economic Strategy' announced with a lot of fanfare in 1999, or the 'Re-orientation' in the negotiations announced in March 2004, which appeared in retrospect to be mainly public relations exercises.

The Commission proposed to increase financial assistance to both coun-tries, to an additional 20% in 2004, 30% in 2005 and 40% in 2006 compared with the average assistance they received from 2001 to 2003.[24] If it had con-cluded in the light of its sobering experience in Romania that the level of funding could not be stepped up because of a poor absorptive capacity, then it threatened to throw out the timetable for entry. To safeguard 'the cred-ibility of the accession process', according to an internal document from the Directorate for Enlargement seen by the author in 2002, new ways to improve absorption would have to be considered. The accession priorities could be changed to include national development ones, such as infrastruc-ture projects. This would involve the allocation of more resources to ISPA. In addition, the national budget could be financed on a temporary basis, but this would almost certainly merely relieve pressure on the state to improve its tax-raising capacity and eliminate arrears.

Ultimately, the Commission decided to maintain its existing strategy based on hope that Romania would somehow begin to catch up with other applicants and would be ready to assume the responsibilities of membership by the time entry occurred.

Radical ideas such as those occasionally floated by the first head of the EU Delegation, Karen Fogg, continued to be spurned. In 1998, she made it clear that active external engagement was necessary in order to provide decisive backing for the reform process. She had told a journalist that if Romanian officials were incapable of managing a programme of reform designed to take the country into the EU, then they would have to be 'temporarily replaced' by European technocrats.[25] But there was no appetite among Commission officials for this level of engagement with such a problematic candidate, nor did high-level political backing for it exist inside the EU. Nor were opportunities to move beyond the *acquis* and examine proposals to modernise the education and health sectors taken up. Failings in these areas were already greatly accelerating a brain drain and a flight of labour which would impose major developmental constraints after entry. Incredibly, the decision to accelerate the flow of funding was not accompanied by a willingness to increase the number of officials able to ensure the money was correctly used and not stolen or wasted. By 2002, the EU Delegation in Bucharest was already responsible for overseeing funds valued at around €600 million per year. But there were only a handful of staff allocated to overseeing this task (there was only one dealing with agriculture when a senior official estimated there should have been three).[26] By contrast, in African and Caribbean countries, where less funding was being provided, there was a higher density of EU officials. DG-Relex, which made these personnel decisions, was criticised as a 'black hole' ready to pamper the EU's growing foreign service but neglect a 'frontline' theatre like Romania where the success of a highly risky enlargement exercise depended on an effective EU presence on the ground. But resources followed projects very slowly, as illustrated when one Delegation head in Bucharest hosted a very successful visit by Commission President Romano Prodi, culminating in a private dinner at his home. At the end of the evening Prodi turned to his host and said, 'just ask if you need anything'. The Delegation head said: 'what about a few more staff?' to which Prodi replied, 'not even a Commission President can achieve that'.[27]

Surprisingly, the Commission did not encourage, or insist upon, close collaboration between the Delegations in Bulgaria and Romania, even though both of them were grouped in the same accession round. No regular consultation appears to have occurred at Commission or Delegation level between the teams dealing with both countries. A twinning process in which members of the Bucharest and Sofia Delegations pooled knowledge about the intractable issues to be found in these post-Stalinist states, and ways of overcoming them so as to move the accession process forward, might not have been such a bad idea. But Delegation heads only appear to have met on an annual basis when there was a reunion of all of those from candidate countries.

The roadmap appeared when there was already clear evidence that Bulgaria was moving ahead of Romania in entry preparations. By mid-2002, it had closed 21 out of 31 chapters and opened all the rest, including those on agriculture, industry, and Economic and Monetary Union. Romania, by contrast, had concluded negotiations for only 13, had still to open three, and was widely recognised as not having made much progress on crucial issues.[28]

In the published roadmap, the administrative capacity of both countries was compared and it was impossible to hide concern about the state of the Romanian public service.[29] Paradoxically, eight areas considered as reform priorities were set out for Bulgaria while no such list of critical issues was provided for Romania. Perhaps this was an indication that in Romania external bodies trying to strengthen capacity still found it difficult to know where to start. EU Delegation officials were often in the dark about the stage that pre-accession programmes had reached.[30] This is not necessarily a reflection on their quality or motivation but on the arduousness of their task. One well-respected Bulgarian NGO commented sharply in 2006 about the efficiency and ethical standards deployed by the EU Delegation in Sofia, criticism rarely made in Romania about the EU Delegation there.[31] But the tempo of administrative reform was clearly faster in Bulgaria than in Romania, probably irrespective of the role of the EU. Certainly, in Bulgaria there had been a turnover of officials from the pre-1989 period, people unable to adapt to new conditions in a number of important ministries, something which either failed to occur in Romania or happened much more slowly.[32]

Significantly, the roadmap failed to re-iterate what had been emphasised at the EU General Affairs Council in December 1998 that 'the existence of credible and functioning structures and institutions' was a pre-condition of membership.[33] Implementing the *acquis* consisted of passing through four stages of reform: transposition, application, compliance and enforcement. Transposition was by far the easiest, requiring that a great many laws pass through Parliament. Due to its bicameral Parliament, the law-making process in Romania was often protracted, which meant that the government often preferred to issue Ordinances and Emergency Ordinances rather than tabling draft laws for debate. EU regular reports frequently drew attention to such practices but at least laws were passed whereas the application and enforcement of reforms often appeared to be an aspiration rather than an established fact. Already by the time of the roadmap's appearance, the Romanian tendency to focus on minor aspects of the accession criteria and proclaim major successes, while avoiding resolute action on the more substantial chapters, was well established. But the roadmap tended to play into the hands of Năstase's government by offering praise for changes which ultimately were ephemeral while withholding criticism for the failure in fulfilling pre-conditions which supposedly determined whether a country was enrolled as a full member or not. Already by the spring of 2002, it was possible to hear different Commission officials with important responsibilities for Romania saying, 'We are committed to Romania playing a full part in the European integration process. There is no alternative'; someone who contributed to the writing of a regular report during the mid-point in entry negotiations said that, 'political criteria are a nuclear option, which means we cannot be too critical since it might blow enlargement off course'.[34]

By 2004, it was clear that no improvement in absorption was noticeable to top EU players. The European Parliament's annual report on Romania noted that 'there has been a slight increase in the absorption rate of the pre-accession funds during the reporting period, but ... the overall capacity for programmes, operational management and financial control remains insufficient'. Its author, Emma Nicholson, was 'concerned about this in view of the need for Romania to administer steadily increasing funds in the next years of the pre-accession strategy and substantial funds after accession'.[35]

In September 2006, the EU Court of Auditors published a report which indicated that less than half of Phare funds allocated to Romania had been used for the purposes for which they had been intended. They checked 48 contracts through which Romania obtained €51 million and Bulgaria €14 million. The audited projects were generally in line with the investment objectives of Phare. The EU experts also found that results lagged behind the schedule, sometimes by up to two years. These shortcomings were due to a continuing lack of administrative capacity and national resources.[36]

The Court of Auditors criticised the EC's management of projects in three ways. Firstly, the management capacity of public authorities was over-estimated which led to over-ambitious targets and deadlines. Second, the principles of sustainability and co-financing were neglected, often a weakness of such assistance with the recipient not having the funding or motivation to provide long-term support. Finally, the EU managers did not give sufficient consideration to added value and the broad impact of these projects.[37]

Herbert Bosch, the influential Vice-President of the budgetary control committee of the European Parliament, endorsed the criticisms.[38] Most clearly in the firing line was the Delegation in Bucharest which had a major role in overseeing the Phare instrument and contained the bulk of officials in the Commission with Romanian responsibilities. The Commission overall had been criticised by the Court of Auditors for its general management of investment projects in Romania. It was seen as over-estimating the capacity of public authorities to implement Phare projects. It often failed to take account of the fact that projects which were approved often were not reinforced with Romanian money (despite co-financing being a condition).[39] A Romanian newspaper claimed that someone involved with the audit had stated that 'an internal restructuring of the Delegation is going to take place' and anyone who has not performed effectively 'is going to be transferred to other duties'.[40]

Scheele reacted angrily to such press reports strongly criticising his conduct, saying that the Court of Auditors report had been distorted by them.[41] To the surprise of many who assumed he would remain in his post at least until after Romania joined the EU in 2007, he quit as Delegation head several months later. His replacement was Donato Chiarini, a Commission official on the verge of retirement whose knowledge of Romania was far from extensive.

The third pre-accession aid instrument which was the channel of EU aid to Romania was Sapard (Special Pre-Accession Programme for Agricultural and Rural Development). It was meant to help the ten beneficiary countries of Central and Eastern Europe to deal with adjustment problems in their agricultural and rural sectors as well as the implementation of the *acquis* concerning the agriculture chapter. This meant trying to promote greater productivity in the countryside and strengthen the rural infrastructure. It was crucial that Sapard made a dent in Romania's rural problems because they dwarfed those of any other candidate country.

The EU's Jonathan Scheele was in no doubt that 'Romania has probably the biggest problem in structural terms in agriculture compared with other European candidate countries'.[42] The economist, Ilie Şerbănescu, writing in 2004, reckoned that the rural population comprised 47.8% of the total. Thirty-six per cent of the population were directly employed in agriculture and the share of the population dependent on this sector was no less than 70%, while its contribution to GDP was a mere 12%.[43] Another source claimed, two years earlier, that 35% of the population eked out a living from farming, largely on a subsistence basis. By now, 85% of agriculture was privately owned but the average size of holdings was only 2.8 hectares, a fraction of the size of plots in Poland, where dwarf holding had been identified as a real obstacle in the way of rural development.[44]

EU Agriculture Commissioner Franz Fischler on a visit to Romania in October 2004 declared: 'if you look at the structure of agriculture, you see only small farms and very big farms. What's missing is the medium class farm'. He also added: 'Your position and prospects in the EU marketplace will be jeopardised as long as your agri-food establishments and veterinary physio-sanitary standards fall below par'.[45]

The PSD had blocked rural recovery after 1989 by limiting the amount of land that could be restored to former owners and their descendants to amounts that made commercial farming unviable.[46] One reason why small and medium-sized farmers could generate little income was because they did not have access to a national market for their produce. The close relationship between state farms and food-processing companies kept this beyond their reach.[47] Iliescu and his party relied on rural backing, especially in the south and east of the country. They were determined to keep the peasantry dependent on the state and ensure that the party's rural power-brokers and their clients were the chief beneficiaries of any change that occurred in the countryside.

The EU was sympathetic to the PSD's argument that modernisation could come only from promoting large-scale farming. But it was unhappy at the methods involved. This involved communist-era collective farm managers and other fixers from the old system acquiring the right to rent high-yield land and gradually obtaining title deeds to it from compliant courts. The EU failed to insist on a transparent and thorough process of restitution to previous owners, which would have been difficult outside the province of Transylvania because of the absence of a land registry. Brussels was not prepared to insist, as in the industrial sector, that the state beat a permanent retreat from land ownership. It observed a mock privatisation of state farms, probably being fully aware that the new landed gentry would be entitled to generous grants from the EU once Romania was a member. Given agricultural trends in Western Europe, Brussels was bound to be sympathetic to the idea that land-holdings would have to be amalgamated. Indeed, Ilie Sârbu, the PSD's Agriculture Minister, openly recommended this in 2004.[48] He wished to tie rural subsidies to output. The aim would be to induce peasants to sell their holdings to private associations which would enjoy tax breaks as well as access to EU funds. In the same year he predicted that by 2005–06, 'agro-businesses controlling big properties will be making their mark in agriculture'.[49] Carol Sebastian, a noted critic of his government, complained about 'naïve European bureaucrats' and that they must 'understand that their funds are fattening rural authorities'.[50]

Sapard proved to be very slow to get going in Romania because the Minister of Foreign Affairs, Petre Roman (once Iliescu's closest ally), had challenged the Agriculture Ministry's entitlement to manage the Sapard programme. In 2000 Roman denounced the ministry for its well-known inefficiency and tried to place Sapard under the control of the Prime Minister's office, accusing Mugur Isărescu of 'fleeing from responsibility' when he demurred.[51]

The programme was 36 months late in starting owing to the need to properly organise the payment agencies for successful applications.[52] Scheele, often one to look on the bright side, tried to console Romanians by pointing out that it took Belgium no less than four years before it successfully put in place an effective payments agency for EU agricultural funds.[53] Normally funding allocations had to be spent within a year and those for 2000–02 were merged with the one for 2003 and contracted by 2005.[54] The programme was fully operational from 2002 to 2006 and the money for 2004, 2005 and 2006 had to be contracted between January and December 2006. The national share was one-quarter of the €600 million total that went into the Sapard programme. Most of it was designed to be spent on infrastructure and diversifying the rural economy. It was not difficult to absorb funds allocated for rural infrastructure. The state had historically neglected public services in Romanian villages, many of which lacked running water and sewage disposal services. Local authorities did not need to make any contribution to these infrastructure projects while private applicants for Sapard funds had to pay 50% of the total project. But it wasn't clear if the 350 infrastructure projects completed by late 2005 would be properly maintained by local authorities since they would have to find the funding from their own resources. Already by 2005, there were worrying signs: severe flooding in that year showed that money towards building or reinforcing dykes in vulnerable areas had been wasted. This was the view of Kaj Mortensen, the EU official monitoring Sapard from Brussels after a verification visit to Romania in May 2005 to study 16 large-scale Sapard projects.[55]

The rate of success in contracting funds was unimpressive across much of the rest of the rural sector. Peasants found the complicated paperwork and the fact that they had to provide money (usually around half the project's value) a disincentive to taking part because banks were unwilling to supply credit except on exorbitant terms. This was the message coming from Sibiu County in 2005, one with a modern socio-economic profile, at least compared with much of the rest of the country. An information campaign mounted by the Agriculture Ministry in 2004 had failed to raise much interest.[56] When it was later renewed, one management consultant described the atmosphere when over 120 peasants crammed into a hall in Sibiu to listen to officials from the ministry extol the merits of its 'Farmers' Programme'.[57] It was similar in conception to Sapard, involving applications for credits for agrarian projects but financed nationally. Initially, the audience was alert but the inaccessible language of the officials dampened enthusiasm. Spirits plunged as it was pointed out that the peasants would have to come up with a feasibility study or a business plan. The banks, whom most deeply distrusted (and not without cause), would have a big role in administering the assistance. No audio-visual material was used to simplify the message and nor were any explanatory materials distributed. The audience of farmers grew sceptical and ironic. Chaotic bureaucracy, the inability of officials to transmit their message and peasant obduracy all combined to turn the event into a fiasco. However well meaning the authorities might now be, with a Minister in place, Gheorghe Flutur familiar with some of the sector's needs, they were completely unable to market their scheme to its target audience. The event revealed the vast social gulf between the world of officialdom and that of peasant communities, with the state unable or unwilling to build alliances with a social sector that it had traditionally exploited in order to obtain capital for urban projects.

It was clear by 2004 that the blockages in the Sapard programme meant that the resources allocated for rural development were not effectively addressing critical local needs. There were huge challenges in terms of absorption capacity and spending the funds in a transparent and effective way was proving far from easy. Jonathan Scheele had declared at the start of the year that if the agriculture chapter wasn't closed by the end of 2004, it would cause a political shock.[58] Nevertheless, it was quietly closed in the middle of the year as an essentially political decision was taken by Commissioner Verheugen to admit Romania with crucial reform in some policy areas implemented only on paper (see chapter 7). The wisdom of Verheugen's lax attitude to Romania at this time would be questioned by his successor as Enlargement Commissioner, Olli Rehn. In May 2006, an interim report by EC officials on Romania's entry preparations imposed three red warning flags in the field of agriculture which would need to be eliminated by September. The first one concerned the need for the agricultural payments agencies that issued direct payments to farmers to be far better administered. Up to 1,400 competent staff needed to be found, IT systems put in place and improved office space found in order for the Agency for Payment and Intervention in Agriculture (APIA) to start doing its job effectively. Efficient systems of collecting, treating and disposing animal waste also needed to be implemented by the ministry. Finally, Brussels called for an Integrated System of Administration and Control in Agriculture to be speedily formed in order to be able to identify that claims of land owned by applicants for rural funding were correct, something that would hardly be an easy undertaking, given the lack of a land registry over much of the country.[59]

In September 2006, Brussels in its final pre-entry report declared that these problems had been dealt with. This was essentially a political decision in order to pave the way for admission several months later. The problems with the malfunctioning of the payments agencies would prove to be unresolved, in key respects, after membership. But at least, towards the end of its cycle, improvements had occurred in the way Sapard funds were managed. From 2005, simplifications were introduced in order to move the backlog of funds: the following steps had to be taken by an applicant, most typically a small farmer. First he had to submit a project at a regional bureau, where the first assessment was made in the presence of the potential beneficiary. After that, the agency checked the farmer's documentation and inspected his land to see that the details conformed with the application. If everything was in order, it was declared a Sapard project and finance could be made available.[60] Usually, the EU paid 50% of the value of the project. If a zone had been affected by a natural calamity, it rose to 75%. Flooding in 2004–05 delayed projects and completed ones slumped to half the previous rate.

For young farmers, those aged under 40, and for those in upland regions, the amount of EU support rose to 60%. If a candidate was both young and living in an upland zone, it was 65%. Gheorghe Flutur, Agriculture Minister from 2004 to 2006 and one of the few to have direct knowledge of agriculture, was keen to ensure that peasants living in hilly and mountainous regions benefited from EU funds. From 2006 80 euros was allocated for each hectare of land reforested. Young urban-dwellers were eligible to receive subsidies to move into the agricultural sector as farmers, perhaps as much as 18–20,000 euros a year according to Cornelia Harabagiu, the Director-General in the ministry.[61]

But banks were still proving unwilling to lend to many small firms and individuals hoping to apply for EU funding. This kept obtaining such funding beyond their reach, especially if they were located in small or medium-sized communities which banks were uninterested in. One month before Romania joined the EU, Nicolae Davila, the President of the Romanian Commercial Bank, declared that banks, the bulk of which were now foreign-owned, would have to alter their lending priorities if they were to contribute positively to the success of Romanian engagement with the EU.[62]

By 2006, it was taking around 90 days between depositing an application to Sapard and the arrival of funds in an applicant's bank account. Consultancy firms had sprung up to help farmers with their applications when the process had been more complex. They usually claimed fees that were around 10–12% of the value of the project. Inevitably, there was a growing list of firms blacklisted because of sharp practice. Projects were audited not by Sapard, but by state regulatory agencies such as the Financial Guard.[63] Many colourful ones were submitted. The head of the Târgoviște bureau received applications to rear guinea fowl, open a centre of oriental massage and even restore a church.[64] These were rejected but justified doubts hang over whether those accepted will contribute to the revitalisation of the agrarian sector or in many cases prove of ephemeral importance. In Ialomița, a poor county heavily dependent on agriculture, not one successful application had been made by the spring of 2005.[65]

The allocation of the last Sapard funding was swiftly followed by the sacking of Samoil Szabo, who had presided over an increased absorption of funds in 2005–06. This was on the grounds of 'inefficiency' according to the minister, Gheorghe Flutur.[66] But initially nobody was willing to come forward to replace him and administer the numerous funded projects which were to have a life of at least two more years. This was a sign that the agricultural sector continued to be regarded as a career graveyard by economic managers.

All three pre-accession instruments, Phare, ISPA and Sapard, were meant to try and narrow regional economic disparities which had quickly emerged after Romania began to experiment with market economics in the early 1990s. But it is not surprising that little progress occurred in realising this objective. A report on Romania published by the British Department For International Development in 2004 criticised the EU's pre-accession instruments for their negligible impact on structural reform. It stated: 'the EU is geared towards big programmes which, once started, must move a lot of money within a specific deadline. There is little flexibility or room for feedback and assessments tend to be made in terms of inputs rather than outcomes. Hence the obvious preference for infrastructure projects or big programmes that make substantial resources available for Romanian public institutions for them to play with rather than use . . . in order to reform the institutions and make them more efficient – a tendency that well suits the Romanian authorities and aggravates the problem of clientelism'.[67]

The EU often struggled to obtain reliable information on the implementation and impact of its programmes.[68] This was due to their complicated nature, the unwillingness of Brussels to provide resources to ensure that they were managed effectively, and of course to the under-performing public administration at central and local level. Unfortunately, the regional development structures hurriedly set up under EU auspices in the late 1990s proved to be among the worst performing of all. Indeed, it may not be too much of an exaggeration to say that using bodies often dominated by venal local politicians was just offering an incentive for making corruption worse.

In this light, it may not be surprising that the regional disparities which the EU was pledged to contain actually widened considerably during the main period of its pre-accession funding after 2000. The Nicholson report issued in January 2004 had expressed 'concern . . . that regional income disparities are fast increasing with Bucharest having nearly three times the GDP per capita levels of the poorest regions'. She asked the government to focus particular attention on economically backward regions.[69] By 2006, the Bucharest region was the only one where economic growth was forecast to surpass the national average. The only other regions enjoying comparable growth rates were several in the west and centre of the country assisted by being close to Western European markets or by a lower than average dependency on agriculture.[70] After 2007, the south and east of Romania were due to receive the most European money for regional development. Priority was to be given to such economically weak regions which are concentrated in these parts of Romania. The inhabitants of Oltenia would receive the most, on average €258 for each inhabitant compared with €160 for each of the inhabitants of Bucharest.[71] It was also believed worthwhile to place an emphasis on stimulating the economy in poor districts that belong to relatively prosperous regions. But there were dissenting voices. The Romanian Academic Society recommended that funding should be concentrated on areas already exhibiting strong growth in order to consolidate their position and enable them to compete at European level. The think-tank believed that there was strong likelihood that the existing strategy would fail to cure disadvantages which have hampered progress in economically peripheral areas. Romania's poorest regions were simply too far behind. Of the 15 least developed regions in the EU by 2005, no less than six were in Romania. The North-East region was actually the poorest in the entire EU. The only one which did not belong in the 'very poor' category was Bucharest–Ilfov, which had 74% of the average GDP for the EU.[72]

Conclusion

One senior Commission figure conceded that, from his experience, the PSD knew much better than the EU what it wanted from their relationship. Not a few of its local chieftains, and more senior figures who faced prosecution after 2005, had no qualms about corruptly intercepting EU funds. But the EU could never adequately demonstrate how its three pre-accession aid instruments would transform the economic face of the country. Large funding schemes in which money was hurriedly dispersed without the Commission being able to track its impact, failed to decisively improve the country's institutional capacity or its infrastructure. When drawn up in 1995, the EU had insisted that its pre-accession instruments were non-negotiable. But their effectiveness depended on the willingness of candidate states to take them seriously. Certainly, in the case of Romania the evidence is lacking that governments felt that they had ownership of these programmes and saw them as a vital adjunct for fulfilling development goals. Romania had a limited capacity to manage EU funds which would not increase significantly as the years rolled on.

The roadmaps of 2002 for Romania and Bulgaria set accession criteria but then placed the onus for accomplishing reforms on domestic elites.[73] If the EU had accepted co-responsibility, the limited amount of progress in key elements of the Phare, ISPA and Sapard aid programmes would have been embarrassing. The 2006 report of the Court of Auditors on the Phare programmes was able to deliver some hard-hitting criticisms. This suggested that progress was to some considerable extent bound up with the quality of EU engagement. The Delegation carried a heavy burden and did not seem always to be adequately supported by Brussels. Romania appeared to be a Cinderella in terms of human resources at important moments in the pre-accession cycle. A lot of improvisation occurred in order to meet planning targets, but there is scant evidence that decisive progress took place with accomplishing genuine reform. Funding continued to pour in even though the roadmap document of 2002 indicated that 'additional assistance will . . . be conditional on making progress in line with the roadmaps and improving significantly the capacity to manage and use funds effectively'.[74] There were few signs of such progress and when it was impossible to conceal the disappointing results of pre-accession work in Romania, there was no desire to carry out a fundamental review and consider adopting a customised approach that targeted attention on the reform blockages.

Instead of 'a process of significant Europeanisation' occurring, it is more apt to refer to 'pseudo-Europeanisation' involving minimal gestures towards reform, and the survival and upgrading of old structures, particularly in the public administration. Pre-accession funding could not settle into a stable pattern against such a troubling background. The EU's incoherence and unwillingness to engage in searching evaluations when its projects fell far short of target gave the initiative back to those who had given the old communist structures a democratic makeover. Two scholars more at ease with aspects of the EU's performance in Romania than I am nevertheless wrote that the 'fragmented and diverse manner in which the EU chose to "police" administrative reform' reinforced the significance of domestic factors and the ability of elites to sabotage or veto outright reforms 'designed to strengthen accountable and transparent policy-making'.[75]

Pre-accession funding did not settle into a stable pattern. In January 2006, Onno Simons, the deputy head of the EU Delegation in Romania, expressed his deep misgivings about the ability of the state to absorb EU funds. He argued that the central state should have a greater say in managing these funds because of the higher quality of public functionaries at this level. But he acknowledged that a centralised approach to distributing funds in an already hyper-centralised country had obvious disadvantages. At all levels of the bureaucracy, there was a need for better-motivated and well-paid bureaucrats. 'It is rather late, but there might still be some time available to improve entry preparations'.[76] Otherwise, Romania risked losing much of the pre-accession funding allocated to it due to its inability to devise feasible projects. Externally sponsored modernisation in Romania was never going to be easy but the instruments adopted by the EU with surprisingly little foresight or planning in many cases broke in its hands, as they were plunged into the rocky Romanian soil. It is a tragedy that the main beneficiary of Phare funds often turned out to be dishonest politicians but hardly surprising given that the EU failed to mobilise backing for its ambitious project beyond the narrow and unrepresentative political elite.

Notes

1 Ioniță, *Too Much to Handle?*, p. 3.
2 John O'Brennan, *The Eastern Enlargement of the European Union*, Abingdon: Routledge, 2006, p. 29.

3   David Bailey and Lisa de Propris, 'A Bridge Too Phare: EU Pre-Accession Aid
    and Capacity-Building in the Candidate Countries', *Journal of Common Market
    Studies*, Vol. 42, No. 1, 2004, pp. 79–80.
4   Dimitris Papadimitriou and David Phinnemore, 'Europeanization, Conditionality
    and Domestic Change: The Twinning Exercise and Administrative Reform in
    Romania', *Journal of Common Market Studies*, Vol. 42, No. 3, 2004, p. 624.
5   I rely strongly on Ioniţă, *Too much to Handle?* in this paragraph, especially p. 31.
6   Papadimitriou and Phinnemore, 'Europeanization, Conditionality and Domestic
    Change', p. 630.
7   Papadimitriou and Phinnemore, 'Europeanization, Conditionality and Domestic
    Change', p. 632.
8   *Evenimentul Zilei*, 28 February 2006.
9   Commission of the European Communities, *2004 Regular Report on Romania's
    Progress Towards Accession*, Com (2004), p. 109.
10 Gray, *Evaluation of DFID Country Programmes*, p. 112.
11 Interview with European Commission official, Brussels, 2008.
12 Interview with Fokion Fotiadis, Brussels, 20 February 2008.
13 Interview with Fokion Fotiadis, Brussels, 20 February 2008.
14 Ioniţă, *Too Much to Handle?*, p. 34.
15 Ioniţă, *Too Much to Handle?*, p. 35.
16 Interview with EU official familiar with Phare operations in Romania, Brussels, 4
    June 2007.
17 Ioniţă, *Too Much to Handle?*, p. 21.
18 Ioniţă, *Too Much to Handle?*, p. 21.
19 Interview with EU official familiar with Phare operations in Romania, Brussels, 4
    June 2007.
20 *Hotnews* (Bucharest), 8 February 2008.
21 *Roadmaps for Romania and Bulgaria*, Communication from the Commission to
    the Council and the European Parliament, Brussels, 13 November 2002, 624 final.
22 Aneta Spendzharova, 'Bringing Europe In? The Impact of EU Conditionality on
    Bulgarian and Romanian Politics', *Southeast European Politics*, November 2003,
    p. 148.
23 *Roadmaps for Romania and Bulgaria*, p. 2.
24 Radio Free Europe, *RFE-RL Newsline*, 14 November 2002.
25 Ciprian Ciucu, *Observatorul Cultural* (Bucharest), 17 May 2006.
26 Interview with European Commission official, Brussels, 2008.
27 Private information.
28 'Romania Country Report', *Economist Intelligence Unit*, October 2002, p. 18.
29 *Roadmaps for Romania and Bulgaria*, pp. 24–5.
30 Ioniţă, *Too Much to Handle?*, p. 12.
31 *Anti-Corruption in Bulgaria: Key Results and Risks*, Sofia: Centre for the Study of
    Democracy, 2007, p. 62; www.csd.bg.
32 Personal observation.
33 Vienna European Council, *Proceedings of 11–12 December 1998*, Brussels:
    European Council, 1998.

34 Conversations with Commission officials, Brussels, 16 April 2002.

35 See *2003 Regular Report*.

36 The full report can be found at www.europe.bg. See also the article on the same site 'European Court of Auditors, Phare Projects in Romania and Bulgaria Over-Ambitious', 23 June 2006.

37 Mihai Istrate, 'EU Critical of PHARE Fund Application in Romania and Bulgaria', *Bucharest Daily News*, 21 June 2006.

38 *Ziua*, 22 September 2006.

39 See *Special Report N 4/2006 concerning Phare Investment Projects in Bulgaria and Romania*, Brussels: European Court of Auditors, 2006, p. 7.

40 Daniela Filipescu and Gabriela Burlacu, 'Scheele a păcălit Comisia Europeană', *Adevărul*, 21 September 2006.

41 *Nine O'Clock*, 23 September 2006.

42 *Ziarul de Iaşi*, 27 February 2003.

43 Ilie Şerbănescu, 'The Two Romanias', *Nine O'Clock*, 8 June 2004.

44 Radu Marinaş, 'What's In It For Me? Romania's Farmers Wary of EU', *Reuters*, 4 January 2002.

45 Radu Marinaş, *Reuters*, 5 October 2004.

46 See *Early Warning Report Romania*, No. 5, Bucharest: UNDP/Romanian Society, 2002, p. 9.

47 Ron Synovitz, 'Agriculture Review Has Praise for Bulgaria, Misgivings about Romania', *Radio Free Europe/Radio Liberty*, 16 January 2001.

48 *Nine O'Clock*, 8 June 2004.

49 *Adevărul*, 8 May 2004.

50 *Evenimentul Zilei*, 15 August 2003.

51 *Nine O'Clock*, 8 November 2000.

52 Adrian Vasilache, Interview with Samoil Szabo, *Hotnews*, 20 June 2006.

53 *Ziua*, 21 January 2004.

54 Ioniţă, *Too Much to Handle?*, p. 13.

55 *Adevărul*, 21 May 2005; *Bucharest Daily News*, 7 June 2005.

56 *Ziarul Objectiv* (Sibiu), 18 February 2006.

57 Private letter, 3 February 2006.

58 *Ziua*, 21 January 2004.

59 *Bucharest Daily News*, 18 May 2006.

60 *Cotidianul*, 8 August 2006.

61 *Cotidianul*, 8 August 2006.

62 *Hotnews*, 2 December 2006.

63 Information from the above two paragraphs derived from an interview with the the Sapard chief, Samoil Szabo in *Hotnews*, 20 June 2006.

64 *Hotnews*, 3 July 2006.

65 *Cotidianul*, 6 April 2005.

66 *Hotnews*, 4 July 2006.

67 Gray, *Evaluation of DFID Country Programmes*, p. 112.

68 Ioniţă, *Too Much to Handle?*, p. 11.

69 See *2003 Regular Report*, p. 7.

70   *Bucharest Daily News*, 12 June 2006.
71   *Cotidianul*, 29 January 2007.
72   Laura Rădulescu, 'North-East Romania in 2005 was the Poorest Region in Europe', *Hotnews*, 12 February 2008; www.hotnews.ro.
73   Aneta Spendzharova, 'Bringing Europe In? The Impact of EU Conditionality on Bulgarian and Romanian Politics', *Southeast European Politics*, November 2003, p. 149.
74   *Roadmaps for Romania and Bulgaria*, p. 4.
75   Papadimitriou and Phinnemore, 'Europeanization, Conditionality and Domestic Change', p. 636.
76   Delia Budurca and Onno Simons, 'Centralizarea, o soluţie pentru absorbţia fondurilor europene', *Adevărul*, 30 January 2006.

4

Labour of Sisyphus:
administrative reform in Romania

It took the EU some time to realise just how inadequate the justice system in Romania was for upholding the rule of law and offering the most basic level of protection to Romanian citizens and also to those of existing EU states coming into contact with the country. But from the outset, there was an understanding that the administration of the country was in a particularly deplorable condition. This was the legacy of over 50 years of rigid political oversight under the communist system. A survey carried out for the British government in 1999 summarised the mentality and practices of the Romanian bureaucracy:

> The cultural pattern of the west is broadly-speaking one which promotes individualism whereas Communism promoted collectivism. Individualism involves risk assumption while collectivism promotes risk-avoidance . . . The latter is a feature of much of the present Romanian bureaucracy. Furthermore, the bureaucracy is characterised by the rigidity of its structure – officials do not move between posts and in many cases have occupied the same post for twenty years or more. Officials lack performance incentiveness, hence they are often inefficient. Moreover, they feel unconstrained by the letter or the spirit of the law. Low salaries and career stagnation engender corruption. Such conditions militate against policy initiatives.[1]

Fundamental change was necessary if Romania was to be capable of carrying out, even to a minimum degree, the tasks necessary to obtain full membership of the EU. Because the power and competences of the EU had vastly increased in the preceding decade, Romania found itself having to make sharp adjustments and transform the nature of its bureaucratic system far more completely than those Mediterranean countries (also former dictatorships) which had joined in the 1980s. The changes were required not just in central ministries and regulatory agencies but at the level of local administration. It was at local level that compliance with EU standards across a whole range of indicators would need to be demonstrated. A process of decentralisation was instituted from the late 1990s onwards, increasing powers of decision-making at local level and expanding the amount of revenues that could be raised. In addition, provision was made for the setting up of six regions that were meant to be channels for billions of euros of EU funding with which it was intended to transform the face of Romania. Such changes would require a new civil service ethos based on professionalism, political neutrality and dedication to maintaining the public interest rather than furthering the interests of a narrow set of political or bureaucratic players. Nothing less than a revolution in outlook and methodology was required if the bureaucracy was to move away from rigid political control and a low level of competence and motivation.

Externally led efforts to stimulate administrative reform had quite a long pedigree in post-communist Romania. Karen Fogg, the first EU Delegation head, had considerable experience at trying to strengthen administrative capacity in the region as a whole before taking up her post in 1993. She had realised that important reform objectives could not be met because of the lack of capacity in particular government departments. Project Management Units, which contained experts able to focus on specific objectives, were widely used in the ex-satellites willing to rely on EU expertise. The Romanian state was unhappy with such arrangements. There was a risk of parallel structures emerging and state interlocutors argued that another negative consequence was the de-motivation of mainstream officials. Iliescu and his allies had not hesitated to create parallel structures in a range of policy fields in order to block or slow down change, so such complaints were disingenuous. Where they were created PMUs tried to utilise the best knowledge of public administration procedures (drawn from Spain and Greece in the 1980s). A particular concern was how to promote top-level administrative coordination across government; another priority was to consolidate a permanent management structure in the ministries which was not dismantled with a change of government. Ideally, this would enable officials to provide neutral advice to their political superiors about the necessity of reforms.[2] But upon the departure of Fogg to head the EU Delegation in Turkey, the momentum behind this type of reform slackened visibly.

The context in which public service reform began to be prioritised was not a benign one. Legislation paving the way for increased professionalism and greater decentralisation was drawn up as the centre-right government spluttered towards the end of its life, divided and demoralised. Most of the impetus for change came from outside. But the quality of advice emanating from external donors was variable. Many were involved in offering advice about how to proceed with institutional reform. Sometimes, their programmes evolved independently of each other even though their advice might be broadly similar. This led to 'assistance fatigue' on the part of recipients.[3] Often the different philosophies behind assistance schemes, reflecting the contrasting administrative traditions of member states, proved disorientating for Romanian officials. Particularly when the PSD was in office from 2000 to 2004, the incoherence of these programmes enabled a government with a strong tendency to mimic reform to play off different donors. The quality of engagement of Brussels and the agencies it hired to provide information about the state of the public administration was often variable. The 1996–2000 non-PSD coalition lacked the authority to pass much of its own legislation midway through its time in office. This was due not least to defections and absenteeism among its supporters. Thus it was unable to make a promising start on this vital reform front. Evaluating the impact of the assistance the Department for International Development was giving to public sector reform at this time, John Gray noted in 2004 that 'the government's commitment to reform and its capacity for policy formulation was weak' (probably an understatement).[4] Senior functionaries often proved unresponsive. They knew that the government was reaching the end of its life and was likely to be replaced by Iliescu's party, which was unlikely to gladly implement its opponents' ideas. In some ministries, the influence of the PSD had never been displaced even after its 1996 electoral defeat. The largest one, the Ministry of the Interior, was a good case in point. The minister, Gavril Dejeu, an elderly member of the PNŢCD, proved to be a marionette in the hands of reactionary officials. They had no intention of disbanding networks of influence, which meant that the proceeds from customs scams at the frontier continued to flow to senior officials, nor of demilitarising the police force so that it could be more responsive to citizens' needs. When the hapless Dejeu was replaced because of his failure to keep order in the 1999 miner assault on Bucharest, a younger minister, Constantin Dudu Ionescu, tried with greater success to exercise authority over a ministry full of officials with an anti-democratic outlook capable of sabotaging any reforms they didn't like. But it was an uphill task to keep under control, the generals and colonels in charge of a ministry where they would be a law unto themselves for almost another decade.

In the Justice Ministry, an energetic minister, Valeriu Stoica, who served a full four-year term, was able to rally the forces of reform. But they found themselves outnumbered by judges, prosecutors and ministerial officials who were enmeshed with shadowy interests linked to the PSD that had prospered because the law was so open to manipulation. In the Ministry of Agriculture, staff continued to be selected on the basis of political criteria. The 2000 regular report observed that '[H]igh-turnover and insecurity of staff and limited career development perspectives have resulted in low motivation'.[5] For years to come, this neglected ministry would struggle to implement one of the main pre-accession instruments for preparing Romania for EU entry, Sapard. Before 2001, the only negotiating chapter where clear progress was evident was that of transport. Traian Băsescu, the minister since 1996, had recruited good-quality younger officials. Infrastructure projects in transport moved forward smoothly. Indeed, in the area of transport there were only two other candidate countries that aligned their legislation with the EU blueprint ahead of Romania. Cooperation with EU officials coordinating pre-accession assistance was good. One of them recalled: 'He was a man you could do business with. He listened, he responded constructively and tried to work with you. That was rare'.[6] EU officials noticed the sense of team spirit between Băsescu and his officials. Thanks to World Bank funding rules which enabled recipients to use part of the grant or loan to pay bonuses for additional work, high-performing staff were able to receive 500–1,000 euros a month. It was impossible to find such incentives in other parts of a demoralised public sector.

The EU hoped that the adoption of a Civil Service Law in November 1999 would mark a relaunch of the civil service so that it could deal with the urgent new tasks it would soon have to handle in a coherent and more disciplined manner. The law emphasised open and competitive recruitment practices in order to create a stable, professional and independent civil service with a performance ethos.[7] After the return of the PSD to office, the Commission could barely conceal its relief that some order might characterise the decision-making process after a debilitating period of confusion and infighting at the top. It welcomed the establishment of a new Ministry of European Integration which coordinated functions previously shared by separate and rival entities: the implementation of the pre-accession strategy, management of EC financial assistance and the conducting of the accession negotiations. The position of chief negotiator with Brussels had been raised to a cabinet rank and a secretary of state responsible for European integration had been appointed in each line ministry. They were all supposed to meet regularly in an inter-ministerial committee, and at the civil servant level inter-ministerial working groups were established to deal with the preparations for each of the 31 negotiating chapters. The 2001 regular report declared almost ecstatically: 'These changes, combined with a situation where all ministers now belong to the same political party, have significantly improved the policy-making capacity of the government'.[8]

But perhaps more significant were the sweeping changes in civil service personnel that occurred during the PSD's first months in office. Ministries were restructured and this would be a regular occurrence throughout Năstase's Premiership and indeed that of his successor. Numerous redundancies and resignations occurred, the government announcing that it intended to reduce staff numbers in the central ministries by 30%. According to the EC, there had been no evidence of undue over-staffing and with staff numbers cut by 22% by September 2001, 'this measure had reduced the already low levels of administrative capacity and left several important ministries under-staffed'.[9] It would not have been out of character if a party with such a large retinue of supporters who regarded a position in the bureaucracy as their entitlement in return for political support had not inserted many of them in vacant positions. The dismissals followed written tests (drawn up in each ministry) and there was disagreement about whether they complied with the provisions of the Civil Service Law. The government thought so and so did the courts after a number of sacked officials who considered that they had been victimised sought legal redress against Năstase's government. But John Gray, who advised DFID on its Romanian strategy, thought otherwise. He believed officials in whose training the EU had invested money had been purged after 2000. He also felt it striking that the response of the EU was so irresolute given that the 1999 Civil Service Law had been one of the key conditions for ensuring that Romania would be invited to open membership talks in 1999.[10]

A National Agency for Civil Servants (NACS) had been set up at the same time as the 1999 statute was formulated. It was designed to take the steps that would enable a corps of well-qualified public servants, with opportunities to increase their skills and enjoy security of tenure, to come into existence. But despite its role being that of guardian of the statute, it was not involved in the sweeping change of personnel. Indeed, it watched helplessly as many of the responsibilities held by director-generals were given to secretaries of state who were political appointees and whose numbers significantly increased.[11]

Commissioner Verheugen had declared in June 2001 that the administrative system needs to be 'totally reformed' to enable the country to 'battle corruption' and it would not have been surprising if the authorities had told him that the radical changes in personnel were a major step in that direction.[12] In the revised version of the accession partnership published in early 2002, 'the achievement of an adequate level of administrative and judicial capacity by the time of accession' was identified as the chief priority over the next two years.[13] But during and indeed beyond this period the EU often appeared like a bewildered spectator as it observed Bucharest announcing numerous initiatives in the field of administrative reform, none of which appeared to make a significant dent in the scale of the problem. It was a customary reflex of governments of all colours, upon assuming office, to announce a shake-up of ministries and ancillary agencies. This occurred in 2000, in 2004 and later when the ruling centre-right alliance fell apart. Put at its kindest, it reflected an assumption across the political class that 'the quickest way to bring change in top management was to restructure the institution'. But too often it was a device to block overdue change or to reward clients with a state salary in return for their political services to a party in power.[14]

The most consistent motive behind a series of such initiatives between 2001 and 2003 was to increase the control of the Prime Minister's office over the state machine. By 2002 Năstase had established an inter-ministerial committee on administrative reform under his personal authority.[15] But it rarely met, and according to one observer of the government system such a gathering would have been a futile exercise since the PSD had no understanding of what a discussion exploring policy alternatives entailed; as for Năstase, he found it hard to listen to the advice of others and saw his role as issuing instructions to his minions.[16] The Commission was encouraged by this move and believed that 'the government has demonstrated itself capable of effectively distributing responsibilities for major reforms between ministries'.[17] But the next year it was forced to report that this inter-ministerial committee had met only once in the intervening reporting period.[18] Half-hearted attempts at coordination across ministries mainly took the form of strategy papers or action plans which were strong on rhetoric and good intentions but vague about implementation and how the process would be monitored.[19] Coordinated planning to enable negotiating chapters to be successfully closed was an urgent necessity but it was hard to see how the PSD could provide leadership in that respect. It was a party dominated by powerful factions which only cooperated in order to tighten their stranglehold on power and material resources. Ministers displayed an adversarial attitude to one another if special interests were challenged.[20] The example came from the very top – where Iliescu sought to maintain a semi-presidential system whereas Năstase tried to ensure that the fulcrum of power lay in the Prime Minister's office.

Năstase recruited foreign technocrats, such as the former World Bank consultant Ken Sigrist, to advise him on administrative reform, and respected local figures who were unaligned in party political terms, such as Emil Hurezeanu, were recruited to work in his office on a general reform agenda. But these appear to have been gestures entered into for image purposes. The PSD showed no desire to break with a clientelistic approach to administration. The services of SIGMA (which stood for Support for the Improvement in Governance and Management), a mainly OECD-led initiative financed in large part by the EU's Phare programme, were not heavily utilised. The Commission's directorate of enlargement regarded SIGMA as a useful brains trust available to candidates that wished to strengthen their public institutions and attract well-qualified and committed officials to stable and professional working environments. Such an approach to public administration was regarded as vital if progress was to be made in closing particularly the most difficult chapters of the *acquis* within the period scheduled. But a review of SIGMA's efforts to strengthen capacity-building and coordination among senior officials concluded in 2004 that they were having little impact: 'the administrative system continued to be characterized by weak analytical and coordinating capacity and often ignored procedures'. The result was the proliferation of low-grade and contradictory policies, which made their implementation and enforcement fraught with difficulty.[21] Parliament was a key player because it needed to show a capacity to draft effectively worded bills that could ensure reforms were smoothly implemented. But this was beyond the cumbersome bi-cameral legislature even with the PSD firmly in control from 2000 to 2004 (and despite programmes initiated by SIGMA and others to strengthen parliamentary efficiency).

It was starting to be clear before the midway point of the PSD government's tenure had been reached that no alteration of bureaucratic methods or mentalities was taking place. Lip service was paid to improving the quality of human resources in the civil service but this was left to line ministries which often lacked any commitment to this goal or else were overwhelmed with numerous other tasks. Only central government was capable of improving the quality of officials but its own methods of operation suggested this was not a priority. Policy coordination was supposed to occur at the weekly cabinet meetings; however, many decisions occurred that did not follow normal internal procedures.[22] In early 2002, Năstase borrowed money from abroad without even informing the Ministry of Finance.[23] 'Special funds' allocated for local projects that often had a political objective were allocated by particular ministries.[24] Such loose accounting was not normally seen as the hallmark of a state intent on joining an economic union where trust depended on the fiscal probity of all its members. Finance remained one of the weakest central ministries. It contributed little to economic policy formulation even in areas where there were significant financial implications, such as major infrastructure projects or the financing of local government.[25] It was one of the ministries which, in the words of a foreign consultant struggling to improve administrative capacity in Romania, 'contained a lot of lonely and frightened people . . . averse to taking a decision in case it rebounded badly on them personally'.[26] The case of Alin Giurgiu was not easily forgotten. He was a former academic with a physics background from Cluj, whose linguistic skills and knowledge acquired of transition economies while working on international consultancies in Russia and elsewhere enabled him to be appointed deputy head of the state privatisation agency, the State Ownership Fund (SOF) in 1999. He worked hard to sell off or liquidate state companies incurring huge losses, but soon after the PSD retuned to office he was arrested on serious corruption charges in 2001 and spent three months in prison. Only the intervention of foreigners, who had known Giurgiu to be a dedicated public official, managed to secure his release in 2002 and nothing further was heard of the charges.[27]

By 2004 soft budgetary procedures were a major concern of the Commission, as was the government's practice of legislating through emergency ordinances. Unlike the previous government, which had a shrinking majority and towards the end found it hard to mobilise its supporters, Năstase enjoyed a strengthening majority due to defections from the opposition. *Ordonances* were used 'excessively and often in cases where there are no obvious grounds for urgency'.[28] They entered into force immediately and only needed retrospective approval from Parliament. The transparency of the legislative process suffered because bills often failed to obtain proper scrutiny, nor was there consultation on draft versions with stakeholders.[29] Consultation with interest groups was extremely variable anyway. The government had an aversion to involving NGOs in serious dialogues over policy. Some of the most effective critics of its authoritarian style came from policy-orientated NGOs such as the SAR. In 2001, only with the greatest reluctance had it agreed to the proposal of the UN Development Programme (UNDP) that SAR act as the UNDP's chief research partner in Romania, something which involved cooperation with the administration in order to produce a series of 'early warning' papers on reform priorities. Cooperation did exist between the authorities and NGOs over issues such as child protection and environmental protection that were not heavily politicised and where the EU was insisting on swift implementation of targets. With the trade-unions, a PSD support base, intensive contacts occurred. This led to the renewal of a Social Pact in 2002 at a time of mounting redundancies, especially in the heavy industry sector.[30] With business, contacts were far less frequent.[31] Employers' federations existed but lacked a strong presence in a sector dominated mainly by small firms whose viability often depended on informal arrangements with local authorities or particular ministries. In order to develop an industrial strategy which would strengthen the private sector, the Commission pressed for coordination between various ministries and economic stakeholders, but efforts at policy coordination proved shortlived.[32] In 2003 the Commission hoped that the passage of an act which would require the publication of a new draft law in advance and allow the public and NGOs to participate in the decision-making process (in some instances) might improve transparency. However, it went on to report that 'most departments of both central and local government have continued to issue legislation without respecting the new rules'.[33]

The government showed an undiminished desire to regularly redesign new laws rather than attempt to implement them as they currently stood. Thus a comprehensive reform of the 1991 Civil Service Law occurred in March 2003. The new version was not without positive features. It established the principle that recruitment procedures had to be competitive and based on transparency, merit and equal access. It also defined the conditions when conflicts of interest might occur and identified provisions for the declaration and control of the wealth of civil servants.[34] But the unwillingness to put into practice measures designed to regularise the recruitment and allocation of civil servants was shown at the end of 2002 when a decision was taken to recruit 500 specialised advisers in the field of European integration. They were to be taken from the Ministry of European Integration and seconded to line ministries. But as the 2003 regular report pointed out: 'the procedures for making these appointments lack transparency and these initiatives were taken without full consultation with the bodies responsible for civil service management and reform'.[35]

NACS, the body responsible for implementing civil service reform, had little authority over line ministries and its ability to influence events in its own area of competence was limited.[36] Civil servants lacked a transparent salary structure, the one still in use in 2003 being described as 'inconsistent, discretionary, and lacking in transparency'.[37] This helped to account for the high turnover in staff and the fact that many who stayed in post were often very demoralised and under-motivated. The Central Unit for Public Administration Reform (CUPAR), a body responsible for *designing* civil service reform, was described as having 'no real authority over the rest of the Romanian public administration, and with only eight staff members, is under-resourced to carry out a reform of the entire administrative system'.[38] Nor were prospects bright for the National Institute for Administration, responsible for the training of civil servants, since it had not been given the resources to carry out such a task effectively.[39] So a clutch of bodies were in place to design and implement civil service reform and carry out training to strengthen professionalism but each had a lifeless air according to the Commission, the body without whose pressure it is unlikely they would have come into existence.

In 2004, a further round of structural changes occurred in the government. One year before, a considerable number of state bodies had been placed under the direct control of the Prime Minister's office. But less than a year later, in March 2004, a new institution was appointed which took charge of many of them. This was the Chancellery, which was in the Prime Minister's office under his then close ally, Alin Teodorescu. There was uncertainty about its role. Was it supposed to coordinate and monitor the activities of government or make policy?[40] The General Secretariat of the government already existed in order to promote horizontal cooperation and realise objectives that needed inter-ministerial cooperation. But such a task was alien to the still-dominant administrative culture, and the personnel capable of promoting it did not exist in a heavily politicised civil service. The creation of the Chancellery had less to do with administrative streamlining and more to do with the fact that Năstase was preparing for a likely run at the Presidency in November and therefore needed to concentrate on political tasks. Often hastily drawn-up ordinances still dominated the legislative process to the detriment of Parliament. After a temporary drop in their number following the adoption of a revised Constitution in October 2003, they rose to their customary level in the first half of 2004.[41] Laws continued to be hastily prepared 'without a sufficient assessment of feasibility, impact and budgetary implications'.[42] SIGMA had observed as early as 1998 that 'weak implementation and poorly-drafted law places power in the hands of "street-level" bureaucrats who are often underpaid, poorly-trained and ill-equipped to understand their responsibilities, duties and rights'.[43]

Inter-ministerial coordination remained lacking in substance which often led to poor quality laws that were difficult to implement. This was the dismal prognosis in a report issued just a few months before Romania was due to close negotiations for entry. In March 2004, Jonathan Scheele had stated that adherence to the EU depended on the emergence of a depoliticised and professional public administration.[44] It is doubtful if his words carried much weight in government ranks, but they went through the motions of heeding his concerns a few months later by launching a public administration reform strategy in May. It included the buzz words of 'policy coordination', 'decentralisation' and greater 'professionalism'. With elections less than six months away, the Commission presumably hoped that priority would be given to its implementation.[45] But the authors of the 2004 regular report conceded that there was a mountain to climb when they wrote in the very same paragraph: 'the public administration is characterised by cumbersome procedures, a lack of professionalism, inadequate remuneration and poor management of human resources'.[46]

By 2005, there was confusion in Brussels about the role of the various agencies supposed to be directing policy at the centre: the Chancellery, the General Secretariat of the government and the Public Policy Unit.[47] The plethora of laws and ordinances gave officials discretion in the way they chose to interpret the law. Jonathan Scheele openly pleaded for a greater emphasis on delegating tasks in light of the growing burden of responsibilities the central administration had to shoulder: 'If you don't have the necessary people who know what to do and benefit from a certain degree of autonomy, then creating new structures is absolutely pointless'.[48]

It was difficult to retain competent people in light of the politicisation of the civil service and the lack of a fulfilling career structure. The drift of able officials to work in the more remunerative and more predictable private sector was not halted despite the emphasis the EU placed on strengthening the civil service after 2000. The whole administrative system continued to display an extremely limited capacity for policy formulation and execution. There was usually little concern with evaluating performance or trying to learn from mistakes in order to improve. Instead, the chief preoccupation was often with following procedures. A foreign consultant based in one of the largest ministries from 2004 to 2007 observed: 'Half the time of civil-servants is spent trying to cope with the law. Indeed much of their whole approach to administration is determined by the law – what is allowed, what can be done, what must be done . . . The system is totally orientated around rules, procedures and not results'.[49]

Since 1995, the Commission had promoted an organisation called Taiex whose role was to provide assistance with overcoming problems such as over-bureaucratisation in order to assist candidate countries to complete the *acquis*. Nearly a decade later, Taiex was closely involved with seconding officials and experts from member states to ministries and agencies in candidate countries in order to strengthen their administrative capacity. This process was known as 'twinning' and from 1999 it was seen in Brussels as a key tool for enabling candidates to adapt to membership requirements by assimilating the experiences of policy-making of established EU members. The policy transfer was supposed to occur through the secondment of civil servants from existing EU members to the accession states.[50] The projects they were involved with were designed by the Commission, but it was the candidate state which decided which bids from member states it would accept. Not surprisingly, in a country like Romania, where official scepticism about EU intentions was deeply ingrained, there was a preference for twinners from countries which could hardly be said to be paragons of reform in key areas like the justice system. But these civil servants often proved highly variable in ability and motivation and a large number were home officials nearing the end of their active careers whom their line managers were often happy to re-assign elsewhere.[51] They were no substitute for permanent EU staff in the field able to play a very direct role in the design and administration of the programmes it was financing. But the EU failed to budget for such a corps of 'front-line' staff, perhaps assuming that the entry challenges posed by accession countries would be of a temporary duration. Parachuting in officials who would act almost like 'district officers' in former British and French colonies would also challenge the sovereignty of the candidates. But this sovereignty was already heavily diluted by the sweeping economic changes candidates were required to implement; if the Commission (with the backing of senior member states) had been determined to impose such rigorous oversight on its spending programmes, it is doubtful if even the PSD would have held out against such a *demarche*.

The twinning process also enabled many officials in candidate countries to gain experience of working in ministries and justice systems of established member states. Working in parallel with twinning was a Young Professionals' Scheme (YPS), launched in 2003 in order to try and create a corps of professional public managers who would be 'change agents' in the policy process.[52] This was the brainchild of CUPAR, which had a secretary of state heading it.[53] Until the end of 2004, this was Marius Profiroiu, a PSD appointee who showed detachment from party politics and worked well with key foreign consultants seeking to get the YPS scheme off the ground. Practical training, study and experience in EU member states as well as Romania would hopefully enable promising young graduates to be a catalytic force who could wake up a sleepy system. They would modernise public administration by performing tasks and adopting patterns of behaviour which had been alien to the civil service up to now. They would be able to devise innovative ideas to respond to policy challenges and have the capacity to implement them effectively. This would involve working effectively in a team environment outside the normal hierarchical structures. A bottom-up chain of communication would gradually emerge. The emphasis would be on outputs and results, less on procedures.

The quality and cost-effectiveness of services would improve. Politicians would be willing to place more trust in administrators able to deliver effective results. Under-performing state sectors, such as health and education, would cease to be bywords for corruption and gross inefficiency. Above all, a revitalised civil service would be able to devise, implement, cost and evaluate projects that would ensure Romania would receive the share of structural funds allocated to it by the EU for the modernisation of the country.[54]

But the obstacles in the way of such a transformation soon proved to be immense. The PSD even set up a rival scheme under which young people, mainly the children of prominent public figures, were selected, given free postgraduate education or training abroad, and afterwards integrated into the bureaucracy; to provide respectability, the UNDP was persuaded to endorse it. Profiroiu resisted attempts by the PSD to absorb the YPS into the government-led rival. He indicated that he was committed to changing the civil service culture. But there were immense obstacles and they would spring from surprising sources, especially after the 2004 change of government. A civil service whose senior members were appointed on merit and promoted on account of their performance was a bold concept. It challenged the right of politicians to interfere and influence the appointments process for their own ends. Their ability to interfere would also be much reduced if policies were based on long-term planning rather than short-term electoral calculations. Moreover, bureaucrats who thought their primary role was to comply with procedures would also have to adapt to a new era where successful design and implementation of policy was what really counted. Inevitably, many would seek any pretext to postpone the advent of such an era.

Progress proved painfully slow. NACS, set up in 1999 to be a wind of change within the public administration, gradually instead became a force dedicated to blocking radical changes. It recoiled at the need for a career path for civil servants based on training along Western European standards rather than on absorbing legal knowledge. Under Jozsef Birtalan, a UDMR deputy who had previously been its Vice-President, it appeared obsessed with defending the pay, conditions and pensions of existing members. Strengthening human resources, by introducing special training and regular evaluations, was of little interest. There was barely hidden suspicion towards the new recruits who had joined through the YPS programme in case they would be the harbingers of unwelcome change. Given the tribal desire to preserve existing cultures in key line ministries, irrespective of whether they were appropriate for Romania inside the EU, it was hardly surprising that the public managers who had emerged from the YPS stable were viewed as an invading force by established officials. Inevitably, their integration into established ministries was going to be fraught with difficulty unless they decided to shed their reformist skin and go native. They were better trained and were going to be better paid.[55] Some were even blocked from joining the civil service on the pettiest of procedural grounds, but many were in time absorbed. The Justice Ministry got some of the best young professionals but they were mostly purged in 2007 under an anti-reform minister.

The political infighting which soon overtook the variegated non-PSD coalition enabled those who wished to sabotage reform to fight back. Profiroiu's successor, Liviu Radu, had his own agenda which did not extend to implementing difficult reform projects at central level. The PNL scarcely concealed its belief that a professional civil service was hardly required given that the job of officials was to implement policies devised by their political masters, irrespective of their competence.[56] A Commission for Public Managers, meant to audit the management of public policy, increasingly got involved in politicking. The presence on the commission of well-known figures from the world of civil society proved to be no barrier against this. Indeed, several of the most assiduous NGO personalities on the commission showed that their reputation for transparency was completely misplaced. One figure, prominent in publishing data on the extent of corruption, strove hard to absorb into the civil service the young people trained abroad under the PSD's rival scheme, even though many of the courses they had done were not suitable for an administrative career. Others tried to position their NGOs to pick up contracts for training in public policy and management.[57]

Bureaucratic procedures impeded reform at each step. Arranging coffee for conferences and day-schools proved to be a 'strategic' issue that involved lengthy discussions between the management of the YPS scheme and the National Institute of Administration, a body specifically set up by Profiroiu to offer a long-term academic foundation for the civil service reform process.[58] So the structures for the new institutions were proving just as archaic as those for the older ones. The failure of pillars of the reform process to agree on who was responsible for supplying refreshments showed how difficult it was even for them to behave as a team and coordinate their activities. NACS, the key agency, increasingly defended the legalistic *status quo ante*. The essence of effective management was obeying the plethora of rules which governed the activities of civil servants. Team-building, consultation, delegation, leadership, problem-solving and multi-disciplinary thinking were optional extras which had no place if they threatened the time-honoured rituals of Romanian bureaucracy. Thus, even in the midst of a period of unprecedented innovation in the administrative process, the old top-down arrangements were preserved in what was a process of simulated change.

An important incentive for proclaiming the triumph of the new, while stubbornly hanging on to the old methods, was the amount of money being devoted to 'administrative capacity-building'. As much as 1% of the structural funds allocated for each new member is allowed for this purpose, provided a matching figure comes from the government. In early 2006 the Tăriceanu government published an emergency ordinance whereby 8,500 new civil servants would be appointed by the summer to deal with accession issues. Professional managers and financial experts would have to be found and urgently allocated tasks which would ensure that structural funds would start flowing into Romania in the near future. The new appointees were to receive a 75% bonus on top of the basic salary. One consequence, which should not have been unexpected, was that there was a rush to be selected for these coveted jobs in Bucharest from other tiers of administration, especially at the *judeţ* and *prefectură* level. The recruitment process was transparent, but in Romania there were still lots of ways nepotism could be used to short-circuit any open recruitment process. The prevalence of favouritism was shown when a law was passed in November 2006 which allowed parliamentarians to be automatically entitled to a senior position in the public administration after completing one full parliamentary term. It was proposed by a PNL deputy, Mihăiţă Calimente, and was easily passed.[59] It meant that parliamentarians who had drawn up laws could console themselves with the knowledge that they would be able to apply them as well. By agreeing to such a proposal, the political elite made it abundantly clear that it viewed the bureaucracy not as an agency for solving the problems of the nation, but instead as a gigantic employment exchange where politicians could place their own supporters and even themselves once they tired of Parliament or were denied a fresh place by their own party.

For Romania, the consequences of this irresponsible approach towards the civil service could be devastating. Lots of capable officials will be needed for the many rounds of negotiations already taking place in Brussels for the allocation of structural funds. Without being able to devise projects, they will be crushed by sharp and determined civil servants from France and other member countries. These mandarins will be determined not to give up their contributions to poorer members without seeing evidence that the money will be well spent. Therefore it will be a huge struggle to extract the structural funds which in theory Romania should look forward to enjoying for years to come.

Secondly, public sector officials will be required to regulate private enterprise. This is a cornerstone of the EU approach to the capitalist system. Romanian officials will cause immense harm if they view the private sector through the narrow legalistic lens that they apply to other sectors of society. In France and Britain, the practice is long established of bringing business types into the civil service for some years and sending civil servants into the private sector. Mutual understanding is increased so that both sectors can try to work in partnership. But in Romania such innovations are seen as too disruptive of venerable bureaucratic procedures. Instead, there is a real likelihood that officials will impose crippling procedures on the business world that do not protect consumers but simply increase red tape. If so, the rhythm of economic activity will decline. Investors (at least the non-corrupt ones) will shun the Romanian market because of these difficulties. Of course, in order to enable Romania to acquire the label of a functioning market economy, starting a business became a less nightmarish process around 2002–03. But the old statist mentality could be reasserted if bureaucrats interpret EU legislation, designed to get capitalists to behave responsibly, in an unduly rigid way. Already, by 2007, there were signs this was happening. One survey carried out by Spanish and Bulgarian economists found that Romania was near the bottom of a list of 26 countries in Eastern Europe regarding its attractiveness to foreign economic investors.[60] Guy Barrow, President of the British–Romanian Chamber of Commerce, had declared pointedly in 2004 that administrative reform exceeded any pro-market measures by the state in boosting the private sector in Romania.[61] But in 2006 the dismal verdict of Sorin Ioniţă, an independent policy analyst knowledgable about the CUPAR project, was that 'we don't have a corps of public functionaries but a list of sectoral bureaucrats who operate according to the rules that they manage to negotiate around each particular issue'.[62]

Local government should not be overlooked when assessing the fate of administrative reform. Upon assuming office in 2000, the PSD found that it had inherited a sweeping decentralisation of power to local government. Laws had been passed by 1999 which devolved major responsibilities to local government in the fields of welfare assistance, health, pre-university education, transport, emergency services and public utilities. Funding in the form of transfers from the state budget and enhanced tax-raising powers at local level were authorised in order to make this devolution of competences work. The process clashed with a centralising tradition going back to the formation of the state but also with the power-conserving instinct of a party which was the direct heir of the defunct Communist Party. But the EU had pressed strongly for a transfer of power from a low-grade set of central ministries situated in the south-east of the country in order to hopefully bring into being a new administrative ethos based on effective service delivery. However, the obstacles in the way of a local government system taking much of the administrative load from the centre were immense. The 2000 regular report noted that 'the administrative capacity of local government is limited and in most cases there is a serious shortage of the qualified staff needed to manage newly assigned tasks'. From January 2000, local authorities had been responsible for the collection of local taxes but the ability to do so had been impeded by a lack of human capacity and the limited legal sanctions they could draw on to deal with non-payment. This created a danger that essential services would simply not be met and the Commission noted that 'improvement was a matter of priority'.[63]

In March 2001 the Năstase government published a new law on Local Public Administration. It upheld the principle of local autonomy, allowing local authorities to levy local taxes and elaborate and approve their own budgets. It sought to overcome shortcomings in the decentralisation process, and crucially central government was prohibited from devolving additional responsibilities to the local tier without also providing the necessary financial means.[64] The EC felt it necessary to avoid a situation where central government happily rid itself of unglamorous and demanding responsibilities, such as the care of children in large institutions, without providing adequate financial support to local service providers.

By 2003, Brussels was noticing that the decentralisation process wasn't working well. The legislative framework was unclear and open to contrasting interpretations. The central state showed little readiness to consult with the representatives of local authorities on draft legislation that would have a major impact at local level. The transfer of responsibilities was not combined with an adequate transfer of resources to local level. The ability to raise local revenues remained limited. This obliged many local authorities to concentrate resources on current expenditures inherited from Bucharest while neglecting capital expenditures on the maintenance of infrastructure.[65] Matters had not improved by 2004 despite the EC presumably making clear its worries to Năstase. Lacking information technology skills or equipment to manage new responsibilities led to some local authorities feeling overwhelmed. The turnover of local civil servants was inevitably high. The 2004 regular report stated baldly: 'Systems for managing human resources are underdeveloped, remuneration is low, and training is limited. Given this situation, local authorities find it difficult to implement newly decentralised responsibilities'.[66]

By 2003, the EC was prepared to express its misgiving that political criteria were often a major factor in deciding the allocation of resources to local government. The process lacked transparency, especially given the existence of 'special funds' managed by central government for local investment projects. The role of the prefect, the representative of central government at county level, was often crucial in determining the extent to which underhand practices existed. Since they were political appointees, it is hardly surprising that many viewed the position as a sinecure from which to profit. In 2005, the UK's Quinton Quayle, one of the best-informed EU diplomats in Romania, observed: 'You see the President of the County Council, the Mayor and the Prefect dining out together often with important business leaders and owners of the local media. They can form a charmed circle, each of whom protects the other's interests'.[67] The most controversial county council President until his suspension in 2004 had been Nicolae Mischie, of Gorj County in Oltenia. In 2003, when interim local elections were taking place, he had openly declared that his pen would favour communes and districts where the electorate selected a PSD mayor.[68] The PSD did nothing to discourage the widespread perception that allocation of local expenditure would be determined by the political complexion of localities. Since county council presidents like Mischie also had control over pre-accession EU funding (see chapter 3), making peace with the PSD or surrendering completely to it was seen as the price to be paid in order to have a chance of accessing EU funds. The 2004 regular report gave credence to this viewpoint. It also showed that huge migration to the PSD had occurred between June 2000, when 30% of mayors belonged to it, and June 2003, when the figure had risen to over 65%.[69]

EU-sponsored decentralisation failed to sponsor the birth of local democracy. The local elections held on 1 June 2008 showed that the presidents of county councils had emerged with enhanced powers. By now directly elected, they enjoyed tight control over public spending and in each of Romania's 40 counties they had, on average, control of budgets worth 2 billion euros. With such an incentive to consolidate their influence at local level, it is not surprising that local barons managed to be re-elected in 2008, usually standing for the PSD and enjoying the greatest success in the politically backward south and east of the country. It is difficult to see how such figures can easily be dislodged in the future. They have already shown a determination to allocate funding on the basis of the political loyalty of a district. They are sure to strengthen control over public contracts, which already go disproportionately to firms that enjoy family, political or business ties with those at the top of local government in counties where one party has been dominant. It is likely that these provincial barons will also increasingly determine the composition of members of the national Parliament, wresting this power from party bureaucracies in the capital. So the march of local power, launched by the EU, appears likely to drain competitive democracy of much of its content across large parts of the country.

Conclusion

'Romania needs to be active across the spectrum of EU business and to do that it needs a qualified, competent, and impartial public administration. Has it got one? Honestly, the answer today is "no". But I would like to put it more positively and say, "not yet"'.[70] These words of Ambassador Quayle were uttered late in the pre-accession process when the leverage of the EU in this and other key areas was beginning to diminish.

Before the PSD's return to office, the Commission had seriously considered deploying Phare funds to buy in a thousand professionals and place them in ministries where reform was vital if the accession process was to succeed. But this had already been tried in selected countries and once it was apparent the results were poor, it was abandoned. 'There was "omerta" around these people', one Commission official recalled, and a truly Herculean effort would have been needed to overcome resistance in the Bucharest ministries.[71]

Fokion Fotiadis recalled that one of the main lessons he had learned during his time in Romania was that: 'There is no way that you can impose reform if the goal is not shared by the government. It needs to feel a sense of ownership. We have to help these people if they genuinely wish our assistance. If they don't, it isn't for us to interfere with the decision-making process'.[72] His successors and top Commission officials did not deviate from that view and there was no appetite for completely rebuilding ministries and agencies, vital if accession was to work, from the ground up. Inevitably, the policy of tinkering with a bureaucracy deeply hostile to most forms of change meant that the Commission soon lost the initiative to the state agencies which were responsible for trying to implement the roadmap.

The sectoral nature of the *acquis*, with negotiating chapters encompassing different ministries, required horizontal cooperation across government. In Romania's case, only lip-service was paid to this objective. Inter-ministerial committees were set up that rarely met and were there to appease Commission officials. Presumably the Bucharest authorities noted how the authors of the regular reports were prepared to assume that new structures might indicate that the bureaucratic culture was at last becoming responsive to the EU's demands for greater professionalism. So new innovations kept occurring most years, but no corner was turned in terms of changing mentalities and bureaucratic habits. The Romanian civil service remained stubbornly orientated towards observing manuals of procedures that grew ever thicker with the passing of new laws. Ministries preserved their own behavioural styles and newcomers were socialised into adopting the language and cultural mores of these fortresses, the Ministry of the Interior and Internal Administration being a particular case in point.

The EU failed to react when it was clear that a professional civil service able to assume the responsibilities of implementing legislation emanating from the EU in a transparent manner was not going to emerge without a titanic struggle in which it would need to play a decisive role. It had shown its irresolution in 2001 by refusing to react when Năstase purged numerous senior officials who were supposedly protected under the 1999 Civil Service Law. The EU never succeeded in mobilising counter-elites committed to delivering effective reforms through state action. Indeed, it does not appear to have ever regarded this as an essential requirement if its reforms were to have an enduring footprint in Romania. It relied unduly on specific policy-orientated NGOs such as SAR. It failed to energise the rest of civil society to enable it to be an effective ally in pursuing deep-seated reform at macro level. Plenty of initiatives and funding opportunities were announced by the EU to push civil society actors to the forefront of the reform process but they had an abstract and disembodied feel to them. Similarly, the EU failed to reach out to the higher education sector and seek to build a community of policy analysts in the university world able to be a 'resource bank' for deepening administrative reforms. Its powers of persuasion were poor and its sanctions ineffective.

Writing in 2008, there is compelling evidence that the old structures and behaviour patterns in the Romanian bureaucracy have been consolidated beneath a modernising façade. A surprising amount of the old communist approach prevails: good management essentially consists of obeying the rules. To overcome problems, fresh laws and regulations are regularly devised. Newcomers rise in the civil service primarily by displaying ability to master the legal labyrinth not due to possessing any wider abilities. It is hardly surprising that promising junior officials who have been trained in the West are sometimes treated as subversives upon their return and find it hard to fit back into the Romanian bureaucratic world. Teamwork, delegation, consultation, a multi-disciplinary approach to problem-solving are dangerous qualities which should not be displayed too readily. They disrupt the civil service obsession of being guided by procedures and laws every step of the way. It will be a titanic struggle to ensure that the bureaucracy becomes comfortable with evaluating performance and promoting a team culture.

The Romanian authorities under Năstase and later during the Tăriceanu Premiership – when a tight-knit anti-reform alliance sprang up determined to roll back reforms that threatened rent-seeking behaviour – rarely displayed much fear of the EU. Skilful political operators manipulated the EU by displaying outward compliance to its recommendations but going their own way in practice. They viewed the EU, probably correctly, as a transient actor in the Romanian policy-making process. Năstase, Tăriceanu and those around them soon noticed that when the deadlines for implementing programmes drew nearer, not just the EU, but other donors as well, were prepared to relax the conditions for their successful conclusion. The Commission feared declaring failure because it only drew attention to its own lack of professionalism. As John Gray, the evaluator of DFID's projects, noted, 'the Romanian politicians and top politicians have developed good role-playing skills, knowing that their attrition skills will enable them to prevail in the long run'.[73] Indeed, the EU Delegation became a peripheral force for change on the eve of Romanian membership of the EU being confirmed in late 2006. It was left to individual EU states, like Great Britain and the Netherlands, which were concerned about the effects on EU stability and their own national security of granting an unreformed Romania full membership rights, to exercise vigilance. But their influence was only a shadow of what the EU's could have been had it been alive to the need for a single-minded approach to obtaining demonstrable progress in the area of administrative reform. Indeed, given the amount of attention paid to public administration reform in successive EU annual reports on Romania, one can only conclude that a chapter devoted entirely to securing this objective should have been part of the *acquis* for Romania.

Notes

1 *Good Government Assessment Romania*, London: Department for International Development, 1999, pp. 31–2.
2 Interview with Karen Fogg, Brussels, 25 April 2007.
3 Claudiu Crăciun, *The Learning Government Research Project: Assessing Policy-Making Reform in Romania*, Budapest: Central European University, 2005/06, p. 22.
4 Gray, *Evaluation of DFID Country Programmes*, p. xiv.
5 *2000 Regular Report*, p. 50.
6 Interview with a Commission official involved with pre-accession funding in Romania after 1999, Brussels, June 2007.
7 *2000 Regular Report*, p. 16.
8 *2001 Regular Report*, p. 17.
9 *2001 Regular Report*, p. 18.
10 Gray, *Evaluation of DFID Country Programmes*, p. 112.
11 *2001 Regular Report*, p. 18.
12 Radio Free Europe/Radio Liberty, *Newsline*, 13 June 2001.
13 Commission of the European Communities, *2002 Regular Report on Romania's Progress Towards Accession*, Com (2002), p. 132.
14 Crăciun, *The Learning Government Research Project*, p. 16.
15 *2002 Regular Report*, p. 21.
16 Private information.
17 *2002 Regular Report*, p. 22.
18 *2003 Regular Report*, p. 16.
19 *2002 Regular Report*, p. 22.
20 Crăciun, *The Learning Government Research Project*, p. 7.
21 See M. Ben-Gera, *Legislative Process and Policy Coordination in Romania: Synthesis of Reports 1998–2003*, Brussels: SIGMA, 2004.
22 *2002 Regular Report*, p. 22.
23 Private information from an official then attached to his office.
24 *2003 Regular Report*, p. 17.
25 *2004 Regular Report*, p. 15.
26 Private information.
27 See Gallagher, *Theft of a Nation*, p. 320.
28 *2003 Regular Report*, p. 16.
29 Crăciun, *The Learning Government Research Project*, p. 9; *2002 Regular Report*, p. 21.
30 *2003 Regular Report*, p. 22.
31 *2003 Regular Report*, p. 22.
32 *2002 Regular Report*, p. 92.
33 *2003 Regular Report*, p. 17.
34 *2003 Regular Report*, p. 15.
35 *2003 Regular Report*, p. 15.
36 *2003 Regular Report*, p. 15.
37 *2003 Regular Report*, p. 15.
38 *2003 Regular Report*, p. 15; see also Crăciun, *The Learning Government Research Project*, p. 8.

39 *2003 Regular Report*, p. 15.
40 Crăciun, *The Learning Government Research Project*, p. 7.
41 *2004 Regular Report*, p. 15.
42 *2004 Regular Report*, p. 15.
43 'Sustainable Institutions for European Union Membership', *SIGMA paper No. 26*, CCNM/SIGMA/PUMA (98)57, Brussels, 1998.
44 *Evenimentul Zilei*, 18 March 2004.
45 *2004 Regular Report*, p. 16.
46 *2004 Regular Report*, p. 16.
47 Commission of the European Communities, *2005 Regular Report on Romania's Progress Towards Accession*, Com (2005), p. 8.
48 *Bucharest Daily News*, 29 September 2005.
49 Private information.
50 Pridham, *Designing Democracy*, p. 125.
51 Interview with official involved in developing the Taiex initiative, Brussels, 6 June 2007.
52 For details see 'Young Professionals' Scheme, Programme of Excellence in the Field of Public Management', British Council, Romania, www.britishcouncil.org (accessed 14 October 2007).
53 For the role of CUPAR, see www//modernizare.mai.gov.ro.documente.scurt %20istoric.pdf, which is on the Ministry of the Interior website (accessed 14 October 2007).
54 *2004 Regular Report*, p. 16.
55 Crăciun, *The Learning Government Research Project*, p. 14.
56 Private information.
57 Private information.
58 Private information.
59 *Gândul* (Bucharest), 6 November 2006.
60 *Sofia Echo*, 10 October 2007, www.sofiaecho.com.
61 *Ziua*, 21 January 2004.
62 Sorin Ioniță, 'Ce ne facem cu funcționarii publici?', *Evenimentul Zilei*, 14 November 2006.
63 *2000 Regular Report*, p. 17.
64 *2001 Regular Report*, p. 19.
65 *2003 Regular Report*, p. 17.
66 *2004 Regular Report*, p. 17.
67 Alecs Iancu, 'UK Ambassdor: Romanian Public Administration Incompetent', *Bucharest Daily News*, 29 September 2005.
68 Cristian Ghinea, *Dilema Veche*, 31 October 2003.
69 *2004 Regular Report*, p. 17.
70 Iancu, 'UK Ambassador'.
71 Private information.
72 Interview with Fokion Fotiadis, Brussels, 20 February 2008.
73 Gray, *Evaluation of DFID Country Programmes*, p. 114.

5

Justice clings to its chains, 1989–2004

A compliant justice system was absolutely instrumental in enabling the post-communist regime to consolidate itself. It is hard to identify any other branch of the state which rendered such assistance to entrenched power structures determined to maintain their grip while adapting to new rules and conditions. No separation of powers applied in Romania, limiting executive control over the judiciary and prosecuting service until the regime installed by Iliescu had entered its second decade. In light of this fact, it is surprising that the EU accepted in the late 1990s that Romania fulfilled the political terms of the Copenhagen criteria. This chapter will seek to show that the EU was painfully slow in discovering the extent to which the justice system was manipulated by old political structures which had successfully regrouped to remain the principal players in a Romania embarking on the democratic path. It will argue that when the EU discovered a major problem existed with the justice system and the manner of its politicisation, it remained complacent. The PSD was allowed to dictate the pace of change largely on its own restricted agenda. The measures which the EU promoted to try and ensure balance and transparency were ineffectual counterweights. Only a few EU officials realised that, as one of them put it to me, 'a disjuncture existed between the normal and visible process of decision-making and other subterranean forms of decision-making which were in the hands of unseen and powerful groups'.[1] This disjuncture was not broken by the 2003 Constitution supposedly freeing the justice system from executive control. Arguably, it would be easier for the PSD and its allies to exert decisive leverage over the justice system after 2003 than it had been before then when the post-communist system was still evolving. It was not easy for the EU to impose legal structures on Romania since those of long-term member states were far from uniform. Nevertheless, it could have used the authority it undoubtedly enjoyed in the pre-entry period to ensure that principles guaranteeing a justice system which was not manipulated by political forces were more fully adhered to. The irresolution and naivety which the EU displayed in this vital field distorted the accession process in numerous ways and will reverberate long into the future.

There were isolated challenges from the courts to the PSD's readiness to manipulate the political system, such as a 1995 judicial ruling stating that Ion Iliescu was ineligible to stand for another term as he had already served the two allowed him by the Constitution. But such judicial defiance was unusual. In communist times judges and prosecutors had been recruited on the basis of their acquiescence with the one-party system and the intelligence services had carefully watched over the legal world. Much of the sprawling state apparatus rallied around Iliescu as a guarantor of their professional interests in the uncertain times that had opened up after 1989. It is not surprising that judges and prosecutors often proved loyal subalterns, approving controversial decisions concerning the regime's wish to establish a capitalist system initially based on the discreet transfer of state assets to supporters of the Iliescu regime. International financial institutions and the EU were slow to realise how important a compliant legal system was for autocratic rulers determined that the experiment with democracy would have definite limits. Much more emphasis was placed by the IMF on the rapid establishment of a market economy than on ensuring that a neutral and transparent legal system which provided impartial justice emerged in Russia and its former satellites. The first annual reports published by the EU on Romania's progress towards accession did not single out the justice system as a problematic area. Indeed, the one for 2000, which was otherwise bleak about reform efforts, stated that 'Romania has achieved stability of institution guaranteeing democracy and the rule of law'.[2] Chapter 24 of the *acquis* concerned justice and home affairs, but the Commission could not make specific recommendations about the nature of the legal system. In existing member states, where the rule of law was felt to be guaranteed, there were important variations in the way that the justice system was organised. After 2000, the degree of resistance in Romania emanating from deeply conservative forces in the justice system and their political allies clearly took EU officials by surprise. It soon became clear that Romania could not assume its responsibilities as a full member without radical change in the judicial system that went much further than many senior figures were prepared to go. Perhaps if the degree of resistance to creating a set of institutions that were professionally run and enjoyed freedom from political interference had been anticipated in advance, the EU might have substantially modified the *acquis* in the case of Romania. This might have involved including tough safeguards about judicial reform at the outset of the negotiating process rather than attaching them after seven years of frustrating efforts to promote worthwhile change in a field vital for the functioning of the state and ensuring that it was a reliable custodian of its citizens' interests and those of its European partners.

The lack of independence of the main branches of the justice system from the government of the day was the issue that most concerned Commission officials. The 1991 Constitution placed 'Courts of Law' and the 'Public Ministry' under the single heading of 'Judicial Authority', which blurred the distinction between the judiciary and the executive.[3] The revised Constitution of 2003 was supposed to ensure a complete separation of powers but the institutions designed to ensure the independence of the justice system remained under the influence of tight-knit political forces which often proved reluctant to make a complete break with the communist past. Judges and prosecutors who had begun their careers in communist times, when advancement was often based more on ideological criteria than professional merit, continued to exercise leadership in what were a hierarchical set of institutions in which a spirit of independent enquiry was frowned upon. Before it officially became independent of the executive, starting in 2005, the Supreme Council of Magistrates (CSM) nominated judges and handled their promotion and transfer. It consisted of ten judges and five prosecutors elected for a four-year term by Parliament.[4] But its composition was drawn heavily from the higher courts where judges with a communist past predominated. The CSM was not representative, in age and gender terms, of the judiciary which many young female jurists joined as the 1990s wore on. It was also chaired by the Minister of Justice, who appointed one-third of its members.[5] The minister could impose disciplinary sanctions on judges and prosecutors and authorise investigations and prosecutions against them. Judges were also appointed for renewable terms of only six years. This made them vulnerable to executive pressure and the Council of Europe's Group of States Against Corruption (GRECO) viewed it as a cause of concern.[6] Presidents of the court enjoyed powers of oversight over judges. Indeed, until 2005 they had a role in the distribution of cases between judges and even in their promotion process. They were appointed by the minister with the agreement of the CSM and were widely regarded as the 'eye' of the executive in the courtroom. A 2004 report for the EC stated that they were often seen as 'surveillance agents, for the executive, not particularly motivated by the quality of judicial work'.[7] The 1992 law on the organisation of the judiciary, which remained in force until 2005, gave the minister the right to determine jurisdiction and organisation within the courts and the right to be informed of the functioning of each court through the presence of inspectors.[8]

There was no groundswell of reform from within the system, certainly nothing comparable to that seen in Italy from the 1970s onwards when younger magistrates banded together to try and limit the influence of figures in the justice system who had been trained in the fascist era. Interestingly, Monica Macovei, the minister who endeavoured for over two years (2004–07) to change the culture and operating procedures of the justice system, was a human rights lawyer and not someone whose career had developed within the conventional legal framework. Senior figures in the judiciary went on record in 2002 to say that radical reforms were not necessary and such sentiments resurfaced many times in vitriolic exchanges between Macovei and a CSM with enhanced powers but still dominated by old-guard figures. In a focus group on the functioning of the judiciary organised by a public policy NGO in 2002, a Supreme Court judge declared that: 'negative evaluation of the Romanian courts comes only from people who lose trials'. A secretary of state in the Ministry of the Interior stated on the same occasion that from attending meetings of GRECO his conclusion was that 'Romania has no special problems compared to the other states present'. This official counselled that radical reform should be avoided in order not to turn the judiciary into 'a state within a state'.[9] Many judges had grown content with a 'big brother' residing in the Ministry of Justice. The days were not far removed when, before 1989, in sensitive cases, judges used to be informed by a secret serviceman or other official what the level of sentence should be, a situation by no means confined to communist Romania. The idea that the ministry should be the watchdog of the legal process, not the watchdog of judges, was hard for important figures in the justice system to accept.

The consequences of a judiciary which was a conveyor belt for decisions by the party in power was shown in March 2001, when the minister Rodica Stănoiu issued a letter to all appeal courts in the country, advising judges to favour the rights of tenants over landlords in property restitution cases.[10] This was an issue on which her mentor, President Iliescu, had strong views. This emerged into the open in 1995, when court decisions in favour of former owners trying to recover property nationalised in communist times started to be made. Iliescu characterised these court verdicts as 'unlawful' and urged local administrative bodies not to carry them out. The courts were pressurised by the executive to halt the process of property restitution: the Prosecutor-General filed numerous complaints. The Supreme Court, which had confirmed lower court decisions over property restitution, quickly reversed itself and ruled that these courts had over-stepped their authority.[11] The EU stated in its 2001 regular report that the government had admitted this action was in breach of the 1991 Constitution.

On 5 June 2001, the day that President Iliescu appointed the husband of Mrs Stănoiu to be a judge on the Constitutional Court, the man whom he was replacing, Judge Lucian Mihai, declared that his experience on the bench had shown him that Romania is 'still a partially totalitarian country'. He said that the executive and legislative branch of government display 'arrogance towards the judiciary and handle it as if it were merely a decorative artefact'.[12]

Article 131 of the 1991 Constitution stipulated that 'Public prosecutors shall carry out their activities in accordance with the pursuit of legality, impartiality and hierarchical control, *under the authority of the Minister of Justice*'.[13] Special emphasis was given to the last clause in a 2002 UNDP report on the justice system because the Minister, Mrs Stănoiu, had exercised her authority in this sphere in a ruthless manner within months of taking office in 2001. She quickly removed the Prosecutor-General, the Chairman of the Military Prosecutor's office and the Chief Prosecutor with anti-corruption responsibilities. All of them had been involved in investigating important cases involving senior politicians or civil and military officials. Dan Voinea, who combined the rank of General with Prosecutor, had pursued cases against military officers involved in acts of repression during the final days of the communist regime in 1989. Two successive Defence Ministers, Generals Mihai Chiţac and Victor Stănculescu, had been sentenced to 15 years in jail without the right to appeal. But the new Prosecutor-General, Tănase Joiţă, suspended these sentences.[14] Joiţă also moved quickly and recommended in 2001 that the sentence dismissing Răzvan Temeşan as head of the bank known as Bancorex be quashed. During his period in charge this bank had issued soft loans to many rising politicians and members of the new economic elite. In less than a decade, the state lost $1.2 billion as a result of the mal-administration of Bancorex.[15]

The dismissal that attracted most media attention was that of the prosecutor, Ovidiu Budeşan. He had re-opened several highly controversial cases upon being given a brief to pursue high-level corruption by the previous government. He was dismissed because he sent to the French authorities documents relating to a money-lending investigation without respecting the legal procedures. This operation had been carried out by a group which had produced election literature for Iliescu in 1996.[16] But Budeşan had challenged the secret power structures which controlled the passage of money and information from behind the scenes by re-opening the 'Dunărea File'. The Dunărea group of companies contained foreign currency for Ceauşescu's own personal use under the control of a wing of the *Securitate* (the communist secret services) involved in foreign trade. Budeşan was interested in the connection between Dunărea and the Crescent companies owned by Dan Voiculescu, one of the most successful post-1989 businessmen who in 2006 was officially unmasked as an informer for the *Securitate*.[17] Voiculescu continues to be pursued by the media about his wealth which enabled this official, earning a modest salary up to 1989 in the foreign trade sector, to launch a media empire in the 1990s that netted him the largest selling daily newspaper and arguably the most influential television channel. By 2000 Voiculescu had formed his own party, then known as the Humanists, which through a pre-electoral alliance with the PSD had obtained seats in Parliament and sustained Năstase's government with its votes. So Voiculescu became virtually untouchable and it was Budeşan who was not only removed from his post but stripped of his position as a prosecutor.[18] This led him to request diplomatic asylum in France in March 2001.[19]

A senior EU official who dealt with Rodica Stănoiu for most of her period as Minister of Justice had no hesitation in describing her as 'a formidable obstructive force . . . no judicial class with a sense of identity, backbone, integrity, competence' was visible during her period in charge of the Justice Ministry.[20] An even more damning verdict came from Alin Teodorescu, the technocrat who helped rescue Romania's EU bid after her sacking in 2004. He attacked her record in February of that year stating that, 'reform is completely lacking in the field of justice . . . clear action against corruption is lacking, especially corruption at the very top'.[21]

Stănoiu was a force to be reckoned with because she enjoyed the full confidence of the President and was unrepentant about packing the justice sector with her own supporters, even as the EU was calling for an end to such practices. Her most controversial appointment was to place General Marian Ureche in charge of the ministry's intelligence bureau. This former *Securitate* officer had been linked with acts of repression in 1989. Their association also went back to her period as a law student when Ureche had spied on her institute.[22]

Mini-fiefdoms invariably emerged in areas of national life where the PSD was determined to implant its influence, and Stănoiu was among the most assiduous of Iliescu's *protégés* in establishing her power base. She brought with her from Oltenia, often seen as the region with the greatest difficulty in breaking with the communist past, two close allies who would be thorns in the side of legal reformers for a long time to come. Maria Huza (the wife of an ex-PSD prefect) was appointed to the key position of head of the Bucharest Tribunal. Lidia Bărbulescu became Vice-President of the Court of Cassation and Justice, where she was expected to watch over its head Paul Florea who, despite having matured as a judicial official in communist times, showed an inconvenient desire to resist PSD dictates.[23] Stănoiu's exploitation of her position was flagrant even by PSD standards and prompted media critics to refer to the rise of 'judicial–political cartels based on the spirit of the clan . . . which merits the description of "the justice mafia"'.[24] Sharp criticism even came from party colleagues, perhaps an indication of how confident the party was that it would be in power for a long time, so it could allow such inner rivalries to spill out into the open. Antonie Iorgovan, the chief architect of the 1991 Constitution, stated in public that Stănoiu ought to stand down on the appointment of her husband to the Constitutional Court. He argued that Romania must convince the Western world that it had escaped from 'Balkanism and nepotism'.[25] But this was not the desperate cry of a reformer but the resentment of someone who believed that Stănoiu had snatched a position which was rightly his. He had devised a Constitution on Iliescu's orders full of ambiguities and contradictions which made the business of government enormously complicated but suited the wishes of someone who wished to preside over the resultant confusion. The 'father of the Constitution' was also someone who did not hesitate to defend in court controversial figures with very serious charges hanging over them, usually of an economic nature.

The tainted ethics of the justice system were no more sharply on display than during the Panait affair. Cristian Panait was a young prosecutor who tried to defend an older colleague, Alexandru Lele, after the wrath of the regime came down on him, when he challenged the immunity from prosecution of one of its political families. Lele ordered the arrest of the son of Adrian Tărău, a former prefect of Bihor County who was considered the head of an oil cartel in the north-west of the country. Soon Lele found himself dismissed from the case and investigated for abusive conduct. Panait, sent from Bucharest to close the investigations on Lele, lifted the charges against him.[26] On 28 March 2002 Stănoiu overrode the prosecutor and simply reimposed them.[27] The press later reported that she made numerous phone calls in the days ahead to Panait, who was also visited by one of her henchmen, Ilie Picioruş.[28] Panait flung himself from his high-rise apartment on 10 April 2002. It was clear that he was a model of honesty, someone who had left Picioruş's office with tears in his eyes, stating 'I swear I'll never step into this justice system again'.[29] Năstase took his family to the funeral, which became a national event.[30] But there was no investigation into the sharp disagreements with superiors which had led Panait to end his life. Instead Joiţă Tănase asked for psychiatrists to try to investigate what his state of mind had been and prosecutors came forward to claim, against the insistence of his family, that he was mentally unstable.[31]

There were districts and towns where families or tight-knit alliances had a stranglehold over local decision-making through having members or well-wishers in strategic positions in the town hall, the police and the court-house. Cornel Nistorescu, the most outspoken media critic of 'local mafias' singled out the south-western city of Craiova, which had been Stănoiu's launching pad, as the worst example of a city where the law was at the mercy of vested interests. In 2004 he described a 'politico-judicial mafia' at work, which enabled the teenage children of a former prefect to run amok and the son of a judge to crash a car he had no licence to drive, injuring several people, but without facing charges. Nistorescu said that if anyone doubted the veracity of the statements made by the EP member Arie Oostlander that in Romania there is no such thing as the rule of law, they should take a look at Craiova. There, he insisted, 'they will discover a new Romania, different from that in official reports, a Romania where the law is negotiated and where legal institutions intervene only to a certain extent. If the EU negotiated with the Romania of the provinces, and not with that of the politicians in Bucharest, 2050 would probably be a much too optimistic accession deadline'.[32]

A report submitted to the European Commission just several months later vindicated this editor's outspoken charges. It was clear by its wording that the extent of the crisis in judicial standards came as a surprise to the Italian jurist who drew it up. She wrote:

> After meetings held with representatives of the Magistrates Association and some NGOs in Bucharest significant information about the independence of judges and prosecutors was obtained . . . Magistrates or at least some were not free and do not feel free and independent and neither do they really trust one another. Some examples were given where judges were removed from their own office without their consent and from one day to another assigned another role and in some cases a different field; where influences were endured regarding sentences to be emitted. It was said that 'bonuses' could be the most diverse: career advancement, [including] the right to participate at courses abroad . . .[33]

Judges and magistrates also complained about economic pressures being imposed so that it was uncertain whether they were entitled to medical assistance or bonuses. A survey carried out into the outlook in the judicial system and published in May 2004 revealed a profoundly demoralised profession. The National Institute of Criminology and the civic group, Pro-Democraţia, sent a survey to judges and magistrates, of whom 3,400 responded. Seventy-seven per cent complained of overt political pressure. Eighty-one per cent insisted that there was no independence and 79% believed that prosecutors were also subordinate to the executive. Thirty per cent even admitted that they themselves were vulnerable to corruption and 16% said they had direct knowledge of colleagues whose court decisions were influenced by informal pressures.[34] It was well known that low salaries increased the temptation for corruption or the desire to move to better-paid professional employment. The salaries for judges and prosecutors were actually frozen during the first two years that Stănoiu was in her post. They were increased by 21% for most categories in January 2003 but this hardly compensated for the inflation rise which had occurred in the same period.[35]

But old-guard forces who had long been content with decisions in the justice system being made on informal criteria shaped by powerful political influences were entrenched in the system. This emboldened the PSD to bow to EU requests for the executive to stop meddling in judicial issues and ensure a proper separation of powers. The party knew that the legal world included plenty of officials who could be relied upon to preserve old practices under the guise of supposed judicial independence. With Stănoiu by now gone and the PSD recently having experienced electoral defeat, old-guard figures were still able to emerge on top in elections for the Superior Council of Magistrates held in December 2004. Only the presidents of courts could put up the posters of candidates and, in a hierarchical system where juniors could be pressurised and intimidated in numerous ways, subtle and not so subtle pressures to vote for the conservative slate resulted in victory going to it. One month into her job and with plans radically different from those of Stănoiu, Monica

Macovei found that she had to work alongside dinosaurs totally opposed to change. Ion Popa, in charge of human resources in the Justice Ministry from 2002–04 (when conditions of service were frequently criticised by the EU) was elected Secretary-General of the CSM and his deputy was none other than Ilie Picioruş, not only involved in the Panait affair but linked with the even more controversial Gheoghe Ursu case of 1985, when this critic of the communist regime was beaten up and killed while in detention.[36]

It is not surprising that among many citizens there was a 'generalised perception that Romania is governed by vested interests rather than by the rule of law'.[37] A World Bank report published in 2000 found that 65% of all businessmen polled agreed that all or most officials in the judiciary engaged in corruption, making the judiciary the second most corrupt state institution in the Bank's estimation (after the health service). Fifty-five per cent of ordinary citizens and 53% of public officials shared the same opinion of the judiciary as those in business.[38] A 2002 poll conducted by the Romanian polling agency CURS found that two-thirds of the public were of the view that the justice system did not serve the public interest, 29% stating 'not at all' and 40% 'hardly'.[39]

If the disastrous condition of the justice system had been apparent to the EC in 1998, it might not have been inclined to rule that Romania now fulfilled the political conditions for entry.[40] The recommendations in the 1998 report concerning justice and home affairs consisted of a single sentence dealing with the need for stronger action to tackle corruption and organised crime and improve border management. There was no mention of deep-seated problems in the justice system.[41] The 1999 report stated that 'the justice system remains weak with low levels of technical skills' but executive control went unmentioned.[42] From 2000, Romania was engaged in membership talks and successive reports, under chapter 24, dealt with a checklist of issues – visa policy, border control, migration, asylum, police cooperation and the fight against organised crime, drugs, and the customs service.[43] But each year increasing space was devoted to the shortcomings of the justice system, sometimes dwarfing the normal chapter 24 requirements, and the tone of the commentary was often very sombre in places. New problems were unearthed which suggested that the EC had underestimated the extent to which the communist system had imposed its influence on this key branch of state activity, often in profound ways. A justice system where many officials were the tools of political interests with an anti-democratic outlook and agenda continued to exist, even when other institutions such as the armed forces and the police started to be reformed. The 1999 miners' assault on Bucharest had been made possible by the decision of a judge to give a derisory sentence to their leader Miron Cozma, who had been arrested and charged in 1997 for leading previous such actions that had led to deaths and numerous injuries and the forced resignation of a government. Judge Dinu Marin had been a lathe operator in communist times whose membership of the militia, rather than any advanced qualifications, had enabled him to reach the bench. Despite being a judge he had spoken at public meetings in favour of Iliescu's FSN after 1990 and was an archetypal example of a judge with a strongly politicised outlook who had been promoted for ideological criteria.[44] Valeriu Stoica, Justice Minister from 1996 to 2000, had sent a large package of laws, enshrining major changes to the criminal code, to Parliament in 2000 but by now the failing coalition lacked the authority to get any substantial laws passed.[45] But the 2001 annual progress report from Brussels stated that 'Romania has made considerable advances in reforming its judiciary over many years'.[46] The report did not revisit the concerns expressed in the spring by Verheugen, who emphasised the importance of maintaining the independence of the judiciary. Radio Free Europe had traced these concerns of his back to the dismissal of top-level judges and prosecutors.[47] However, Verheugen devalued their impact by stating that after talks with Iliescu and Năstase he had accepted their assurances that the judiciary was independent and not subject to political pressure.[48] It is hard to see how the EU's goals in Romania were advanced by indicating in public that he accepted their good faith on such a crucial issue. He had no evidence other than their word that the judiciary was free and there was plenty to suggest that it was still under a tight executive leash. The 2001 progress report made no mention of the dismissal of the anti-corruption prosecutors, merely noting that many posts in this area of anti-corruption work had not been filled.[49]

However, concern in Brussels about the independence of the judiciary clearly existed as the 2001 report was being issued. In January 2002, improving administrative and judicial capacity was identified as the main goal of the accession partnership published that month. These partnerships identify the priority areas for further work set out in the previous regular report, setting out the financial assistance that will be available and the conditions that will apply to it. The target of the 2002 partnership was 'the achievement of an adequate level of administrative and judicial capacity by the time of accession'.[50] The wording was an eloquent indication of the inadequacy of the state machine in these vital areas. The 2002 regular report, giving details of this initiative, quoted a 1997 'Opinion' of the Commission which had pointed out how far Romania then was from 'meeting the necessary conditions of the justice and home affairs *acquis*'.[51] A close reading of the report suggests that nothing fundamental had changed. A sentence was inserted in the conclusion to the review of chapter 24 that 'Romania is now in the process of developing various multi-disciplinary strategies and [it has] started important reforms aimed at improving the functioning of its law enforcement bodies', but no concrete examples were given. Nor was an indication given of how the EC expected fundamental progress to be made in the chapter 24 areas where

Romania was deficient, in two years (2002–03), when the partnership and the accompanying action plan were supposed to be implemented.

The 2002 report identified a daunting series of problems which far from exhausted the list. Judges worked under a crippling workload which inevitably hampered their efficiency. The Ministry of Justice continued to appoint under-qualified judges and prosecutors who had not passed a competitive exam which the Commission described as 'political appointments'. The Prosecutor-General continued to enjoy the discretionary power of being able to appeal against judicial decisions even before other legal remedies had been exhausted. His powers to do so had actually recently increased and the situation had been found contrary to the European Convention of Human Rights.[52] On issues such as economic crime, money-laundering and the fight against corruption, where Romania needed to ensure that it did not import insecurity into the EU, the authorities showed no sense of urgency about introducing specialised training for relevant personnel in the justice sector.[53]

By the spring of 2002 (if not indeed earlier), the Commission had realised that in Rodica Stănoiu they were dealing with an exceptionally obdurate and wilful minister. She had achieved professional fulfilment in a heavily politicised and centralised justice system which was viewed as an aberration by European experts who saw it at close quarters. She had no wish to collude in the liquida-tion of that system and was quite prepared to withhold her cooperation from European officials.[54] Given the impasse, the Commission decided to try several round-about routes in order to reach their destination of a modernised justice system free from executive control. After initial opposition from Stănoiu, it was agreed that individuals with a justice sector background could come from EU states and try to inculcate good practice in the Romanian justice sector. Various twinning projects were worked out, the main one concerning how the Supreme Council of Magistrates could have a managerial role in the justice system free from executive interference. But improving the capacity of the justice system through this mechanism depended on many factors, not least the readiness of the authorities to have a constructive approach and the professionalism and dedica-tion of the seconded officials from the EU who were on these expert missions.

Later in 2002, another initiative was taken to drive forward change. France was the country that was most demanding about candidate countries com-plying with EU rules. It was also the one whose legal system Romania's most closely resembled if the deeply communist overlay was somehow discounted. In 2003, Pierre Trouche, a respected and recently retired senior judge, was sent to Romania to try to obtain progress with the justice and home affairs *acquis*. His formal position was counsellor to the Prime Minister on legal reforms. He had a very academic approach and was out of his depth in the Romanian context. He soon found himself side-tracked by Corinne Coman, a French citizen of Romanian origin who was already working as a French-backed adviser. Prime Minister Lionel Jospin had earlier promised to assist Năstase with law reforms, but nobody important was prepared to work in Romania and instead Coman was sent. She proved to be close to the Romanian authorities and the latter pulled off a coup by being seen to accept foreign help but then nullifying its impact by manipulating the personalities involved.[55] This doleful episode showed how member states could undermine vital policy objectives by engaging in initiatives that were well meaning but clumsily executed. The EU's unwieldy accession process, with many actors engaged and communication between them often tenuous, was a Godsend for a regime skilled in mimicking reform and at playing off different EU actors so as to dissipate whatever good intentions they had.

Tănase Joiţă, a Prosecutor-General who encapsulated the communist-era approach to the justice system, was eased out in the autumn of 2002 and, with a growing realisation that Stănoiu was impossible to work with, the Commission hoped that she might not be long in following. Indeed, she promised Năstase that she would retire by September 2003. But on her return from holiday, she dug in her heels and was able to count on Iliescu's support to keep her job.[56] The Commission's 2003 regular report barely concealed frustration about the limited independence enjoyed by the judicial system. The ability of the minister to directly appoint judges was raised as an issue of concern for the second year running. For the first time, the unclear way in which cases were distributed to judges was raised as a matter of concern. The ability of court presidents to enjoy 'influence over the handling of cases in the courts' was alluded to.[57] The report acknowledged that in September 2003 a judicial reform strategy had been adopted by the government but it pointedly mentioned that it 'needs to address these issues as a matter of priority'.[58] The best that the report would say about Stănoiu's reform strategy was that '[W]hile there are important issues that the strategy does not address in sufficient detail, it nevertheless represents a significant acknowledgement that further judicial reform is necessary'.[59] But it left no doubt that there was some disagreement between Brussels and the minister about what was the best way forward: 'A next step will be to agree upon a definitive action plan that provides sufficient human and financial resources to effectively implement the strategy'.[60] The impression conveyed was one of drift and stalemate. But it was clear that change had been halting and carried out in the face of feet-dragging from the very top of the ministry. In the report's Conclusion, the lack of progress was clearly set out: '[T]he judicial system needs to improve the management of cases and the consistency of judgments as well as to increase the independence of the judiciary. These key issues must be urgently addressed'.[61] But once again the Commission provided a confusing message by declaring in the same paragraph that 'the political will to address administrative and judicial reform exists'.[62] On past performance, the government could be expected to emphasise this positive viewpoint while minimising Brussels's strictures about the lack of real progress in practice. It is hard to see why the Commission diluted its concerns in this way unless there was pressure from top officials who had been won around to the Romanian position that substantial reforms could await the country acceding to the Union.

Stănoiu was finally sacked in March 2004 in the midst of the crisis that accompanied the release of the critical Nicholson report. But it was clear that she remained a force to be reckoned with since Iliescu immediately chose her as his chief adviser on security issues. She had simply been reassigned, as had Tănase Joiţă who in 2003, after being removed as Prosecutor-General, was appointed Romanian Consul in Strasbourg. By sending this reactionary official to the seat of the European Court of Human Rights, where so many desperate Romanian citizens had lodged appeals after the justice system at home had been unresponsive to them, Bucharest was delivering a calculated snub to the European vision of human rights, which it was using every stratagem to ensure would be kept well out of reach of most citizens for a long time to come.[63]

Stănoiu's replacement as minister was a middle-aged judge, Cristian Diaconescu, whom the government's publicity machine projected as a reformer keen to modernise the justice sector. But an EU official who had to work closely with him found him an insubstantial figure with whom it was hard to discuss technical aspects of reform.[64] He lacked standing in the party and would later bitterly denounce the EU for continuing to monitor judicial reform in the months after Romania's accession.[65] After four months in the post, old-guard forces won a major victory by obtaining the retirement of the only senior judge to consistently display an independent outlook towards the PSD. This was Paul Florea, the head of the Court of Cassation and Justice. He had made influential enemies after securing the release of a young judge, Andreea Ciucă, who had been imprisoned on corruption charges after colliding with members of the local oligarchy in her home city, Târgu Mureş.[66] He had reached the pensionable age of 70 in 2004, but the CSM could permit him to remain in his post for another two years. However, at a time of acute shortages in the judiciary and with the CSM supposedly in the process of acquiring independence from the executive, it turned down Florea's application to remain in post. Viorica Costiniu, the Honorary President of the Magistrates' Association, wrote to Verheugen about the matter, but the Enlargement Commissioner failed to make any public mention of it and instead praised what he viewed as impressive progress made by the government in meeting accession criteria.[67]

Conclusion

Geoffrey Pridham wrote in 2005: 'the Romanian government at last made a real effort to set in place the legal framework [for the 2002 anti-corruption strategy], although the country has a reputation in EU circles for producing fine-sounding documents that remain on paper'.[68]

This British academic built up close links with figures in the EU Delegation during the course of researching his 2005 book and it is likely that he was reflecting the views of several people whom he interviewed. However, the justice system was the one area where the PSD was unwilling to relax its control in the face of EU requests to loosen its tight grip on political and economic structures. Rodica Stănoiu, one of the most hardline PSD politicians, was appointed Justice Minister and she survived in that post until near the end of the government. Under her, independent-minded prosecutors were hounded and purged. There is plenty of evidence from her years in office which shows just how determined the PSD was to maintain direct control over the justice system. Well-informed Romanians keen to see the country play a responsible role in a European political process were aghast when negotiations were concluded with Brussels that left the justice system still heavily politicised. '"We don't deserve to join the club of civilised nations," Maria Antonescu, a 34-year-old Romanian engineer [said]. "It's too early. Just look at our lame justice system. Look at how corruption dominates everything"'.[69]

There was a striking overlap between senior members of the political class and the legal profession. A well-known press editor observed in 2004, 'All the important hierarchies in the justice system are filled with the wives, in-laws, cousins, nephews . . . of the political–financial clans represented by the ruling party'.[70] But, at the same time, perhaps the ideological commitment to the communist system was more pronounced in the justice system than among party activists where an opportunistic and amoral approach to politics prevailed before 1989. Judges and prosecutors had been constantly engaged in maintaining an arbitrary and hypocritical system of legal ethics and many would become true believers who informed EU analysts that they found it hard to see the necessity for any radical change. The prosecutor who had taken the decision to condemn Nicolae Ceauşescu to death not long afterwards took his own life, perhaps because he was unable to handle the enormity of what he had done. The politicians involved in what amounted to the judicial lynching of Ceauşescu and his wife had no such qualms.

The EU seemed to feel that the partisan steps taken by Stănoiu and her aides were the dying gasps of the old politicised legal system and that a more transparent one would prevail in line with changes occurring in the economy and elsewhere. Its 2002 roadmap beamed a searchlight on entry requirements in the justice sector and the area of administrative reform which had been eclipsed by the attention paid to economic criteria in the previous three years. But too much faith appeared to be placed in legal changes and action plans and not enough in implementing reforms so that these vital aspects of state activity began to escape from the control of special interests. It claimed with a confidence that was scarcely justified by its experience that 'once a comprehensive reform strategy, including an action plan, has been developed and finalised, Phare projects will be developed to implement specific reforms'.[71]

In times of frustration, it was consoling to assume that no group, however well entrenched, could hold out against the transformative power of the EU. This was a rather naive attitude to take. Romanian officials determined to preserve a justice system which served the privileged were often Machiavellian figures, which could not be said of very many of their EU interlocutors. Certainly, the twinning programmes, designed to import greater capacity and higher standards into the justice sector, along with other branches of the state, hardly troubled old-guard legal officials. But they were only approved with the greatest reluctance by Stănoiu, even though twinners were usually unable to transform the attitudes and approaches of influential judges and prosecutors favoured by the old structures. Instead of proving to be a dinosaur, she in fact was the first minister to openly challenge the EU reform agenda and she would have emulators after membership was achieved in 2007.

The revised Constitution of 2003 was supposed to set the justice system free from political control. But the different judicial tiers meant to guarantee its autonomy were dominated by PSD appointees or allies which would later prove crucial in seriously weakening the reform drive when it appeared to gather speed after 2005. This was particularly true of the CSM, supposed to ensure the autonomy of the judiciary but packed with old-guard figures. An EU peer review report on the justice system issued in 2006 would describe the CSM as 'conspicuously silent when Parliament repeatedly tried to block anti-corruption legislation, while at the same time being quite vocal when its own integrity was questioned'.[72] The Commission should have been aware long before this point that change was bound to be vestigial as long as the PSD had packed the judiciary with its own loyalists. It made demands for resolute action against high-level corruption risible if judges simply found excuses to quash prosecutions against figures with whom they were often in active solidarity. Sometimes daylight broke through, as when the Delegation head, Jonathan Scheele expressed the need, in 2004, for improvements in political governance and a deep-rooted reform of the legal system which he saw as crucial features of a fully functioning democracy currently absent in Romania. But for most of that year the Commission did not act as if a key aspect of the Copenhagen criteria for entry was being flouted. It is hard to recognise Pridham's account of 'the severity of EU approaches to Romania over conditionality problems'.[73] Afterwards, it was probably too late to try and undo the damage done, by insisting on belated justice reforms. The EU could only have recovered the initiative if it had admitted that it had been wrong to assume that a revamped Superior Council of Magistrates could ensure judicial independence and improving standards, demanding instead a completely fresh approach. But this would have damaged careers and reputations and the EU possessed little of the desire, to be found in the better-run democratic states, to subject its performance to such critical examination.

Notes

1 Private communication dating from 2006.
2 *2001 Regular Report*, p. 15.
3 *Monitoring the EU Accession Process: Corruption and Anti-Corruption Policy in Romania*, Brussels: Open Society Institute, 2002, p. 494.
4 *Monitoring the EU Accession Process*, p. 494.
5 *2001 Regular Report*, p. 20.
6 *Monitoring the EU Accession Process*, p. 494.
7 Human Resources, Training of Magistrates and Ethics', in *Draft Report of an Advisory Visit under Chapter 24 in the fields of Justice and Home Affairs in Romania, 29 March–2 April 2004*, Brussels: European Commission, April 2004, p. 111.
8 'The Establishment of an Independent, Reliable and Efficient Judicial System', in *Draft Report of an Advisory Visit under Chapter 24 in the Fields of Justice and Home Affairs in Romania, 29 March–2 April 2004*, Brussels: European Commission, April 2004, p. 80.
9 'Bad Politics Prompts Bad Justice', *Early Warning Report Romania*, No. 5, Bucharest: SAR/UNDP, 2002, p. 7.
10 *Evenimentul Zilei*, 3 April 2001.
11 Monica Macovei, 'The Procuracy and its Problems', *East European Constitutional Review*, Vol. 8, Nos 1–2, Winter–Spring 1999.
12 Radio Free Europe/Radio Liberty, *Newsline*, 6 June 2001.
13 'Bad Politics Prompts Bad Justice', p. 12.
14 *Evenimentul Zilei*, 16 March 2001; *BBC Romanian Service*, 16 June 2006.
15 'Bad Politics Prompts Bad Justice', p. 11; Gallagher, *Theft of a Nation*, pp. 235–6.
16 *Monitorul*, 26 May 2001.
17 *Evenimentul Zilei*, 5 June 2001.
18 *Monitorul*, 26 May 2001.
19 *Evenimentul Zilei*, 30 March 2001.
20 Private information.
21 *Evenimentul Zilei*, 18 February 2004.
22 Radio Free Europe/Radio Liberty, *Newsline*, 6 November 2003.
23 Christian Levant, 'Justiția, "mortul din fereastră"', *Dilema Veche*, 20 April 2004.
24 Levant, 'Justiția, "mortul din fereastră"'.
25 *Monitorul*, 7 June 2001.
26 *Evenimentul Zilei*, 19 January 2005.
27 *Evenimentul Zilei*, 9 May 2002.
28 *Evenimentul Zilei*, 20 April 2005.
29 *Evenimentul Zilei*, 9 May 2002.

30 *Evenimentul Zilei*, 16 April 2002.
31 *Evenimentul Zilei*, 28 May 2002.
32 *Evenimentul Zilei*, 11 February 2004.
33 'The Establishment of an Independent, Reliable and Efficient Judicial System', p. 81. Despite the poor punctuation and grammar, it was felt to be worth including these sentences since they provide, from an official source, a vivid account of some of the main problems resulting from executive infringement on the judiciary.
34 Răzvan Savaliuc, '"Alba-neagra" din Justiţie', *Ziua*, 21 May 2004.
35 *2003 Regular Report*, p. 19.
36 *Evenimentul Zilei*, 27 January 2005.
37 *Monitoring the EU Accession Process*, p. 456.
38 *Monitoring the EU Accession Process*, p. 496.
39 'Bad Politics Prompts Bad Justice', p. 6.
40 Commission of the European Communities, *1998 Regular Report on Romania's Progress Towards Accession*, Com (1998), p. 50.
41 *1998 Regular Report*, p. 52.
42 *1999 Regular Report*, , p. 13.
43 *2000 Regular Report*, pp. 73–5; *2001 Regular Report*, p. 85.
44 See Gallagher, *Theft of a Nation*, p. 201.
45 'Bad Politics Prompts Bad Justice', p. 14.
46 *2001 Regular Report*, p. 20.
47 Eugen Tomiuc, 'Romania: EU Enlargement Commissioner Says Bucharest Must Press Ahead with Reform', *Radio Free Europe/Radio Liberty*, 27 April 2001.
48 Tomiuc, 'Romania'.
49 *2001 Regular Report*, p. 21.
50 *2002 Regular Report*, p. 132.
51 *2002 Regular Report*, p. 113.
52 *2002 Regular Report*, p. 24.
53 *2002 Regular Report*, pp. 23–5.
54 This was made clear to me by Commission officials during the spring of 2002.
55 Information from a range of EU officials with experience of Romania.
56 Interview with Alin Teodorescu, Bucharest, 18 December 2006.
57 *2003 Regular Report*, p. 18.
58 *2003 Regular Report*, p. 18.
59 *2003 Regular Report*, p. 19.
60 *2003 Regular Report*, p. 19.
61 *2003 Regular Report*, p. 121.
62 *2003 Regular Report*, p. 121.
63 *Evenimentul Zilei*, 2 September 2003.
64 Interview with official from the European Commission's Justice and Home Affairs Department, Brussels, 5 June 2007.
65 *Hotnews*, 17 March 2007, www.hotnews.ro.
66 Rodica Culcer, ' Răzbunarea', *Revista 22*, 22–28 June 2004.
67 *Cotidianul*, 24 June 2004.
68 Pridham, *Designing Democracy*, p. 138.

69 Radu Marinaş and Tsveteli Ilieva, 'Romania and Bulgaria Gloomy about EU Invite', *Reuters*, 18 December 2004.

70 Cornel Nistorescu, *Evenimentul Zilei*, 20 February 2004.

71 *Roadmaps for Romania and Bulgaria*, p. 25.

72 *Third Peer Review Romania: Report on Corruption and Money-Laundering*, Brussels: European Commission, March 2006, p. 6.

73 Geoffrey Pridham, 'The Scope and Limits of Political Conditionality: Romania's Accession to the European Union', *Comparative European Politics*, Vol. 5, 2007, p. 363.

NATO, the EU and Romania's strategy of duplicity

Running parallel with the EU accession negotiations during the PSD's years in office was an accelerating process for Romanian membership of NATO. Talks commenced in 2002 after Romania was invited to open negotiations for membership and concluded in April 2004 when the country became a full member of the Atlantic alliance. Until a few years previously such a prospect had seemed a far distant one. Romania had actively sought to join NATO in the late 1990s, claiming that it fulfilled the military conditions for membership, only to be rebuffed. But after the attacks by Al-Q'aida on the East Coast of the USA on 11 September 2001, the strategic importance of countries like Romania, as important staging-posts close to the Middle East, increased, especially in American eyes. Thirty-six months later, with its entry to NATO, Romania accomplished a major step in the process of Euro-Atlantic integration.

At first sight, it appears that the comparisons between accession to NATO and negotiating for EU membership can only be lightly drawn in the case of Romania. After 2001 NATO enlargement was driven by the USA. The conditions for membership were less onerous than for completing the EU roadmap and indeed had been scaled down since the previous enlargement round of 1999, during which the Central European states of Poland, Hungary and the Czech Republic had joined. But as will be shown here, it is possible to argue that the Romanian response displayed broad similarities. There was strong official commitment to embracing the goals of NATO and Romania tried to exceed the other applicants in its zeal for identifying with the policy aims of the alliance's strongest member, the United States. But not much time would elapse before Romania started to qualify its backing for US international aims, especially when the policies of the Bush administration faced mounting opposition in the Middle East. In 2006, the government led by Călin Popescu-Tăriceanu attempted to engineer a sudden pull-out of Romanian forces from Iraq, without giving any warning to Washington. The existence of a head of state, Traian Băsescu, with important powers in the defence realm and who was committed to building a strategic partnership with the USA and Britain, foiled such a move. But it enjoyed considerable support across the political spectrum, including in the PSD under whom Romania had joined the Western security community. When this crisis erupted in 2006, a decision had yet to be made by the EU on the timing of membership for Romania. If all the existing members had agreed, entry could have been postponed beyond 2008. So alert Eurocrats could also have derived lessons from Romania's fickleness in complying with security undertakings entered into with countries that had been the keenest backers of Romania's inclusion into NATO. When it joined the EU on 1 January 2007 only a matter of a few weeks would elapse before unmistakable signs would appear of deep unwillingness to honour obligations to the EU which it had undertaken in order to join in that year. So it is worth paying attention to how the PSD handled the push for NATO membership and how its successors in office dealt with their membership responsibilities since it can shed important light on the much more complex and protracted engagement with the EU.

It is worth recalling that during the communist era, Romania had a track-record of engagement with a range of Western states and multilateral institutions. It lasted from the mid-1960s to the early 1980s, when the hardline nature of the dictatorship presided over by Nicolae Ceauşescu brought renewed isolation. During these years, Romania was projected as a maverick communist state where national interest took precedence over loyalty to Soviet bloc goals. Convinced that a weak link in the chain of Soviet power had been found, the West invited Romania into institutions that were closed to other communist states such as the International Monetary Fund and the World Bank.[1] Furious efforts were made by a resourceful intelligence service to acquire Western economic know-how through industrial espionage. At least one academic has argued that the Soviet Union obtained valuable intelligence and access to high-technology goods thanks to Bucharest's close Western ties.[2]

After 1989, it was not immediately obvious that the second- and third-echelon former communists who rallied around Ion Iliescu and the National Salvation Front were ready to disavow the politics of duplicity in their relations with the West. As head of the Foreign Intelligence Service, Iliescu appointed Mihail Caraman in 1990. He must have been aware of the record of espionage of this officer in the communist intelligence services. From his base in Paris in the 1960s, he had successfully infiltrated NATO headquarters, obtaining invaluable information about the strategic operations of the alliance. Manfred Woerner, Secretary-General of NATO, made it clear to Iliescu that he would never set foot in Bucharest as long as Caraman was in this sensitive post and he had gone by the spring of 1992.[3]

In the spring of 1991 Romania became the only former satellite to sign a comprehensive treaty of friendship with the Soviet Union. The terms gave Moscow an effective veto over any Romanian alliance with a Western country had it not been abrogated by the collapse of the Soviet Union six months later.

Once it became clear that the West was going to be a dominating presence in Eastern Europe (at least as long as Russia was in political and economic disarray), Iliescu adjusted his external strategy. Greater emphasis was given to the fact that for over a century Russia had been seen as a historic foe of Romanian independence. Under Stalin, the Romanian-speaking lands of Bessarabia and Northern Bukovina had been occupied in the wake of the 1939 Molotov–Ribbentrop Pact. NATO started to be welcomed by prominent figures close to the government as a check on any resurgence of Russian imperialism. Overtures to NATO started to be made by President Iliescu himself once its enlargement towards the East appeared an increasing possibility from 1994 onwards. Membership was seen as a largely cost-free undertaking, largely involving the need to downsize and modernise the armed forces. Such technical adjustments were unlikely to really affect the way political power was exercised in Romania.

Romania sought to court the USA not by speeding up reform but by responding with alacrity to foreign policy initiatives from Washington. Thus, it was the first former communist state to formally apply to join the Partnership for Peace programme launched in January 1994. The Partnership opened the possibility of future NATO membership without allowing any real participation in NATO's current decision-making. Romania showed similar zeal in August 2002, when it sought to impress Washington as a dependable ally by becoming one of the first countries in the world to sign a bilateral agreement with the USA under which it would not hand over any American personnel if indicted by the International Criminal Court.

A process of reforming the Romanian military and bringing it closer to the model of armies in long-established democracies slowly got underway.[4] Greater civilian control was asserted and professional competence was given a higher priority than in other branches of the state. By early 1996 invitations had been extended to former Warsaw Pact states to apply to join NATO and Romania applied in April of that year.

In 1997, the Foreign Ministry's *White Book on Romania and NATO* was emphasising that: 'Defence policy is made by civilian authorities. The military do not decide what are the national security risks, nor do they make the decisions on the ways and means to counteract them. Under the current legislation, the Armed Forces cannot impose their point of view with regard to any particular problem of interest to the society as a whole'.[5]

From 1994 to 1999, NATO had become increasingly interested in South-East Europe largely out of a need to promote a stable environment to support its peace-making efforts in ex-Yugoslavia. At the June 1997 Madrid summit, Romania, by now led by the first government since 1989 not under the influence of Ion Iliescu, actively sought admission. But against British, and particularly American misgivings in 1997, that Romania would be a consumer rather than a provider of NATO security that could weaken the cohesion of the alliance, Bucharest's entry bid failed.

For the rest of the 1990s Romania appeared to have all the hallmarks of a fissile state as reformists in government lost the initiative to Iliescu's forces and indeed to ultra-nationalists. Then in the spring of 1999 NATO's aerial campaign against Serbia transformed it from a troubled Balkan backwater to a 'front-line state'.[6] NATO requested and obtained military facilities from Romania (as well as Bulgaria) in its drive to compel Slobodan Milošević to give meaningful autonomy to the Albanian majority in Kosovo and to halt the expulsion of many of them from the disputed territory. The importance of the South-East European flank to NATO's security, something that many NATO planners had underestimated, seemed vindicated by the Kosovo war.

Along with Romania, Bulgaria denied Russia permission to over-fly its air-space to reinforce and supply troops it had rushed to Pristina at the end of the NATO campaign. Western leaders were appreciative but NATO membership was not on offer. Key NATO states still assumed that Romania was in no position to shoulder the responsibilities of full membership. Instead, the invitation to open talks for eventual EU membership issued at the summit in Helsinki in December 1999 to Romania and Bulgaria was the Western reward for both of them for their high-level support during the previous spring.

During the Kosovo crisis Iliescu had made clear his unhappiness about NATO's action. The PSD returned to office in the 2000 elections and several months later a new American President, George W. Bush, was inaugurated. He seemed to prefer a rapid scaling down of the US military presence in Europe's trouble-spots. It appeared difficult to imagine that a US president with his sights set at home and on Asia would be even likelier than his Democratic predecessor to allow into NATO countries still with armed forces of doubtful effectiveness. But all assumptions about the US foreign policy agenda were thrown into disarray by the terrorist attacks on New York and Washington carried out on 11 September 2001 by operatives of the radical Islamic Al-Q'aida movement. It was soon clear that the United States increasingly saw foreign policy dangers and threats through the lens of terrorism. It judged its allies and partners on their readiness to show purposeful engagement in countering that threat.

This new security landscape provided unexpected opportunities for NATO membership for Balkan aspirants like Romania. With the prospect of US-led military operations in the Middle East increasing steadily through 2002, countries bordering, or adjacent to, the Black Sea were in a position to act as important bridgeheads for the USA and its NATO allies. There were likely to be strict limits to the cooperation existing NATO members in the area could offer. Greece, because of deep-seated anti-US feeling among public opinion, and Turkey, owing to its *de facto* status as an Islamic country, couldn't offer unconditional support to US-led actions in the region.

Mircea Geoană, the Romanian Foreign Minister, underscored the new-found importance of the Black Sea when he declared on 4 April 2002: 'After September 11, the Black Sea has become relevant as a natural springboard towards regions of possible future terrorist threats'.[7] By now, both Romania and Bulgaria had made clear their readiness to assist the USA in countering that threat. Accordingly, their chances of being invited to join NATO went from slim in 2001 to increasingly bright by the time of the 26–27 March 2002 summit in Bucharest of the candidate countries: Romania, Bulgaria, Slovakia, Estonia, Latvia, Lithuania and Slovenia. Richard Armitage, a US Deputy Secretary of State for the first time gave a clear official indication that the USA desired the largest possible NATO enlargement. He also declared that no country would be left out of NATO on geographical or historical criteria or due to pressure from any outside power.[8]

After 2001, the Balkan NATO aspirants were faced with a set of conditions for NATO membership that appeared less daunting than those that had been on the table since the mid-1990s. Concrete engagement in the war against terrorism in fact as well as in words was the primary consideration. This meant a retreat from the message contained in the 1995, 'Study on NATO Enlargement', which made it clear that only states characterised by 'democracy, individual liberty, and the rule of law' could be serious contenders to join NATO.[9]

The entrenched nature of corruption in Romania had damaged its efforts to get close to NATO in the late 1990s. George Robertson, the Secretary-General of NATO, had indicated that the prevalence of corruption threatened Romania's chances of accession to NATO.[10] As late as 23 January 2002, the American ambassador, Michael Guest, was ready to deliver a strongly worded speech on this failing: he warned that 'corruption has become endemic in Romanian society', that confidence in the justice system had collapsed because of it, and that large amounts of money had gone to the political parties from unknown sources.[11] But from then on, as Romania's chances of joining NATO blossomed, criticisms of such directness about governing standards were made far less often by the heads of multilateral organisations or representatives of Western states.

In the autumn of 2002 Romania offered more concrete backing to the USA in its confrontation with Iraq than any other NATO aspirant. On 13 September the cabinet declared that it shared the American view about what needed to be done in the crisis.[12] Shortly afterwards, Donald Rumsfeld, the US Defence Secretary, was told by his Romanian counterpart that US troops could use Romanian territory in the event of a conflict with Iraq.[13] By the end of September, Romania had made it clear that it would provide all that was necessary for the USA other than Romanian combat troops. Bulgaria also delivered similar undertakings but the time-scale was often a little behind Romania.

Romania argued that it was in a strong position to assist the USA following the removal of the Saddam regime because, in the words of Geoană, 'Romania built more than one-third of the Iraqi economy in the old communist days. More than half of the technical infrastructure – electrical grid, power generation, refineries – was built by Romanian engineers'.[14]

Following the invasion of Iraq in March 2003, it was clear that top US officials believed that Romania could prove a useful role model offering lessons for enabling a democracy to sink durable roots in Iraqi soil. Paul Wolfowitz, Deputy-Secretary for Defence, was frequently singled out as the chief ideologue in the Bush administration behind confronting repressive regimes opposed to Western interests which had been branded as 'the axis of evil' by 2003. While on a visit to Romania in May 2003, it was evident that he considered Romania had successfully put its authoritarian past behind it: 'Romanians are an inspiring example to people in Iraq and elsewhere in the world in what you can achieve with freedom'.[15] In the same press conference, he declared: 'I think that Romania's effort to pass from a totalitarian regime to a democracy can offer an example to Iraq'.[16] Earlier in the same month he had claimed that the way the security services had been allegedly neutralised in Romania after 1989 was also a model for post-Saddam Iraq.[17] The relaxed attitude coming from the second-highest US defence official about the intelligence sector in Romania was significant because in some quarters there had been concern about allowing Romania to join NATO specifically because of the nature of its secret services.

Both Romania and Bulgaria had sprawling intelligence sectors with agencies linked to different ministries and the armed forces as well as large independent bodies dealing respectively with domestic and foreign intelligence. There had been concern among Western diplomats stationed in Bucharest about the effectiveness of Parliament in scrutinising the intelligence world and above all about the implications for NATO security if intelligence operatives had access to confidential NATO dossiers.[18] In Bulgaria, there was also concern about the presence of communist-era holdovers in sensitive posts, but the intelligence services there had been less crucial in formulating policy during the communist era and they had not played a particularly disruptive role during the post-communist transition. But neither claim was true of Romania, where a bloated intelligence apparatus that Ceauşescu used to crush dissent continued to be a disruptive force in national politics, seeking to discredit genuine reformers. In 2001 Prime Minister Adrian Năstase had caused uproar when he tried to appoint a close aide, Ristea Priboi, as head of the parliamentary commission monitoring the foreign intelligence service,

SIE. It soon emerged that Priboi had been a high official in the *Securitate's* foreign intelligence wing.[19] After one opposition figure described Priboi's appointment as showing 'a lack of responsibility' towards Romania's NATO aspirations, it was withdrawn. But the issue of the *Securitate* refused to die down. At least 15% of operatives in domestic intelligence and 20% of those in the foreign intelligence sector had practised their occupations in communist times and had been encouraged to view NATO as one of Romania's principal enemies.[20] It had been widely expected that they would be discreetly removed from the intelligence service prior to the Prague summit. But on 3 April 2002, President Iliescu denied any approach from NATO regarding the need to remove former *Securists* still in the secret service and he said he would be unhappy for such an approach to be made: '*Securişti* are an internal problem of Romania', were his words. NATO officials appeared satisfied by government assurances that sensitive intelligence matters were being handled carefully and that former agents would probably disappear from prominent positions as generations changed. NATO, it seemed, had dropped a thorough revamping of the intelligence services as a condition for Romanian membership.[21]

Indeed, in September 2003 Nicholas Burns, the US ambassador to NATO, described Romania as one of the most important partners of the alliance, quoting in his support NATO experts who said that Romania had undergone the most effective military restructuring process of all future NATO members.[22] Early next year, on the eve of the US entry into Iraq, Romania was one of ten NATO candidates which signed a declaration backing the impending US action. In February 2003 France's Jacques Chirac roundly criticised the candidates for missing 'a good occasion to keep silent'. He referred to their 'very superficial attitude', adding that, 'if they intended to diminish their chances of reaching Europe, they could not find a better method'. In particular, he singled out Romania and Bulgaria, saying the two neighbours 'were particularly flighty to launch out on this campaign while their position is still very delicate regarding the European Union'.[23] There were some fears that France would retaliate against Romania for spurning its line on an issue which would gravely impair transatlantic relations for nearly the remainder of Bush's time in the White House. But Năstase may have calculated that the advantages particularly in the economic sphere which Western European states would quickly obtain as Romania drew closer to the EU would deflect any backlash even by a member as powerful as France. Besides, with the EU acquiring foreign policy instruments whose success depended on defusing difficult problems in the Balkans, it would have been self-defeating to place the largest state in the region in quarantine. The words of Gunther Verheugen in 2004 indicated the importance of the strategic factor: 'Through receiving Romania, the European Union is going to promote economic and political stability in one of the most important and dangerous regions of the continent. This is in our strategic interest and it is the principal motive for Romania being part of the accession process'.[24]

Scaled-down versions of US bases were re-located from Germany to Romania and Bulgaria after 2005, and in December of that year Secretary of State Condaleeza Rice came to Bucharest to sign an accord allowing for the establishment of US bases in Romania.[25] But doubts were cast about the fidelity of Romania as an ally in June 2006 when, without any attempt to notify the USA, Teodor Atanasiu, the Defence Minister, instructed embassies to announce that Romania's 890 peace-keeping troops in Iraq were being withdrawn. The decision had been taken over dinner the previous evening by Prime Minister Tăriceanu and some of his closest supporters in the National Liberal Party, supposedly an unambiguously pro-Western force. A key foreign policy commitment had become a casualty of chronic political infighting between the Prime Minister and his chief rival Traian Băsescu, President since the end of 2004. He had promoted Romania as a strategic partner of the United States, that could be fully relied upon in the Middle East and in the Black Sea region even in difficult times. Tăriceanu was keen to try and sabotage such a policy but the move was doomed to failure since the power of initiative in foreign and security matters rested with the President under the Constitution. When US and British embassy officials publicly lauded the decision of the Supreme Council for National Defence, which the President chaired, to cancel any pull-out from Iraq, Tăriceanu took the unusual step of publicly criticising them on 3 July for their interference in Romania's internal affairs. Relations between his government and these powers would deteriorate, culminating in a furious outburst in November 2007 by the President of the Chamber of Deputies, Bogdan Olteanu (a godson of the Prime Minister) that the US ambassador Nicholas Taubman had obtained his position through corruption.[26] This followed an expression of concern by the ambassador that proposed changes to the criminal code backed by a parliamentary majority would make it more difficult to eradicate high-level corruption, a stance that had the public support of the British embassy.[27]

Unless the rival parties rose above their internecine quarrels over the distribution of political powers and also economic spoils, it looked unlikely that a coherent foreign policy vision for Romania could be sketched that enjoyed broad-based consensus. The population was solidly pro-Western in its preferences, but a fragmented elite increasingly influenced by business moguls looking to Russia and Central Asia for markets and partners showed signs of being tempted by very different political alliances.

This was almost certainly not what Western officials had expected. Henry Kissinger, who visited Bucharest in December 2007, perhaps might not have been surprised by such a *denouement*. In the 1970s, when he was the dominant influence over US foreign policy, he had harboured few hopes that Eastern Europe could orientate itself towards the West. Indeed, he had associated himself with the view that a peaceful world order partly depended on the West reconciling itself to the fact that the Soviet Union would be a pivotal presence in Eastern Europe for a long time to come. During the 1990s, he had also been cautious about any forceful Western moves to confront Slobodan Milosevic, as he tried to establish brutal control over much of Yugoslavia. In light of his long-term pessimism about Eastern Europe, it is perhaps not surprising that his hosts on his Romanian visit were not pro-Western figures like President Băsescu, but instead business moguls like Dinu Patriciu and Sorin Ovidiu Vântu.[28] They were ambiguous about Romania's strategic orientation and in the case of Patriciu had sold the leading share of much of the recently privatised energy sector to the state oil company of a Central Asian country closely influenced by Russia. Perhaps a cynical master of *realpolitik* like Kissinger was not actually surprised by such a development.

An American diplomat who was stationed in Romania when it was negotiating to join NATO reckons that the EU could have learned a great deal from Romania's relationship with NATO. A short time after obtaining full membership, it was clear to the US State Department that Romania was starting to forget previous undertakings it had made. Jonathan Scheele received US overtures in 2002 about the need for a common transatlantic push on strengthening the rule of law. But he was lukewarm to the idea and EU ambassadors from countries keen to view the EU as a counterweight to American power rather than as a continuing boon for Europe were even more so.[29] It is interesting that there was no desire to invite any US diplomatic official to the monthly strategy meetings on EU negotiations held by EU ambassadors. If any US envoy had attended, he or she would have seen how unfocused the agenda usually was. The US diplomatic mission in Bucharest had closer ties with individual EU missions such as Britain, the Netherlands and Spain than it did with the EU Delegation.

The European Union's relationship with Romania would show that much higher officials in the EU were willing to compromise some of the principles that they insisted Romania comply with when it appeared that nobody was looking. This was most glaringly shown in the contentious area of child protection. The 2001 strategy on child welfare worked out between the Năstase government and the European Parliament's *rapporteur* for Romania, Emma Nicholson, had been the first major indication that the PSD was going to be responsive to EU pressure for change in areas where its standards fell far below those existing inside the EU. This was the policy breakthrough in Romania which the EU seemed most proud about in its 2002 and 2003 regular reports and statements by visiting officials. From the first of its annual progress reports on Romania, issued in 1998, Brussels had devoted considerable attention to the plight of as many as 100,000 children placed in dreadful state institutions often run by venal officials. The Năstase government's apparent intention to eradicate international adoptions and close orphanages made it seem pioneering in relation to the rest of the region in the child protection field. This led to difficulties with the USA, the destination of many adoptees. Congressmen were lobbied by families and by law firms in order to try and get Romania to end the moratorium. It became a sensitive issue in bilateral relations because Congressional support was needed for Romania to join NATO after being invited to open negotiations in 2002. But in 2002 and 2003, favourable assessments of the child care strategy in the EU's progress reports of those years suggested that no backsliding was occurring. It therefore came as a shock, not least to Baroness Nicholson, when it was revealed that the international moratorium had been broken. Moreover, among the chief violators were top EU politicians and officials.

In December 2003, Adrian Năstase agreed to the adoption of 105 children who were in state care to Italian couples. He had received a personal appeal from Italy's Prime Minister Berlusconi and a delegation of Italian parliamentarians had come to Bucharest with the same request.[30] 'We are not the guilty ones', Năstase insisted, and as more revelations emerged it seemed he had some grounds for these protestations. Both Romano Prodi, the current President of the Commission and Alvaro Gil-Robles, former President of the European Parliament, had lobbied for the right to allow exemptions for the country's moratorium on international adoptions. Prodi retreated into an embarrassed silence but Gil-Robles openly declared that the moratorium had been a gross over-reaction. He then accused the Bucharest authorities of using adoptions to obtain 'immediate political benefits', not least an invitation to join NATO, without explaining what these were.[31]

Năstase may now have felt that entry for Romania was an irreversible process and the 2001 moratorium could be interpreted selectively. He might also have assumed that the EU was unlikely to treat Romania harshly since some of its best-known officials had been implicated in this affair. This might explain his languid reaction to the criticisms contained in the Nicholson report when it was released on 12 January 2004. 'With all due respect and admiration to Emma Nicholson', he said over a week later, 'nobody can come and tell us how we should manage our child care arrangements'.[32]

Not only Romania but Bulgaria's record in fulfilling entry terms was due to be discussed at the European Parliament. The *rapporteur* for Bulgaria, Geoffrey van Orden, was a British Conservative politician who had taken up the position only in October 2003. His report had been published on 18 December and its tone was very different from the one which Nicholson had produced. Bulgaria was congratulated for provisionally closing 26 of the 31 negotiating chapters. Financial issues were seen as 'at the heart of three of the four remaining chapters'. It was recognised that 'an effective and trustworthy judicial and administrative system' is still a work in progress. There were calls for vigilance to ensure that 'the system for international adoptions' is not abused and 'the welfare of the children to be adopted . . . put first and not the financial revenue accruing to a family, institution, or intermediary'. But there was no call for banning such adoptions and overall van Orden judged that 'Bulgaria's accession negotiations are proceeding without any major problems'.[33]

Bulgaria undoubtedly possessed advantages which enabled it to be seen in such favourable terms. It had known two consecutive governments pledged to reform after a period of corrupt post-communist rule from 1995 to 1997 led to near economic collapse. Ministers appeared to be appointed on merit and not owing to political calculations.[34] Many of the reform challenges were less steep than in Romania. Only 2.6 out of every ten members of the labour market were employed in agriculture compared with four in Romania.[35] The tourist industry was enjoying increasing success and proving to be a showcase for small private businessmen to display their entrepreneurship (a very different situation from Romania where the Black Sea coast continued to be mismanaged). In 2002 Bulgaria had received the coveted EU award of having 'a functioning market economy'. But there were problems with organised crime, the gravity of which went unrecognised in Brussels, and Bulgaria had a lower GDP per head than Romania.

Unlike in 2002, Bulgaria was careful not to call for a decoupling of its membership bid from Romania's once its neighbour's continuing difficulties were underscored. After meeting his Romanian counterpart in February 2004, Solomon Pasi, the Foreign Minister, would declare that problems were 'unfounded'.[36] Despite rumblings in some EU circles, the Commission was keen to preserve a united front between two neighbours which had long been aloof from each other, so as not to disrupt the fifth enlargement process. Milan Velchev, the Interior Minister, had declared in early 2004 that taking Bulgaria into the EU ahead of Romania would create a series of 'logistical problems'. This is why 'we all have an incentive to help Romania'.[37] Foreign Minister Geoană underlined this point: 'Bulgaria and Romania will have to sustain each other reciprocally on the road to EU accession'.[38] But there was little real cooperation and much distrust, extending to societal level. Ioan Rus, Romania's Interior Minister, declared that 'we don't need to look to Bulgarian examples' (regarding eradicating corruption in the police).[39] Adrian Năstase dismissively remarked in his party's inner counsels that 'Bulgaria took down its pants and accepted anything [from the EU]'.[40]

Perhaps only when Arie Öostlander, the Parliament's *rapporteur* for Turkey, called on 22 January for the suspension of negotiations with Romania did Năstase realise that a storm was brewing. But the government's reaction was initially a contemptuous one. There was no recognition that Őostlander might be genuinely appalled at the sluggish pace of reform and the implications for the EU. Bogdan Chirieac, an influential journalist close to the PSD, argued that the Dutch Christian Democrat parliamentarian's gesture was a fit of petulance stemming from the EU's desire to delay Turkish membership.[41] Năstase offered another theory, declaring that because Őostlander was a Christian Democrat, he must have 'a personal problem' stemming from the fact that the PNȚCD was no longer in Parliament.[42] The Transport Minister Miron Mitrea complained at a PSD meeting: 'I don't know how we got into this crisis. Suddenly after an issue over one hundred children, we have a European scandal!'[43]

The government must have hoped that the vast expenditure devoted to boosting the image of the government both at home and abroad might help get it out of trouble. Spending on government publicity in the media reached a record 14.7 million euros in 2004.[44] Năstase insisted on deciding the allocation of advertising revenue personally and independent titles sometimes critical of the government were boycotted. Compliant titles with tiny circulations received large sums for promoting the national railways, the nuclear power industry or state investment in environmental projects. Of course, state television news was even more strictly controlled.

But tight news management failed to stem the crisis. The government could not bury the disclosure from Emma Nicholson on 31 January that she was ready to support Őostlander's motion calling for the suspension of talks with Romania which she had tabled on the 29th. He softened what had been a very tough original motion and both of them tabled a fresh one.[45] It recommended 'the Commission and the Council to suspend entry negotiations with Romania in their present form, so as to make the priority guiding the country forward, establishing the supremacy of the rule of law which is the most important of the Copenhagen criteria'. The amendment asked all three institutions of the EU to cooperate closely to allow Romania to make progress with resuming negotiations for the remaining chapters (perhaps a strong clue that they felt such collaboration had been lacking).[46] This was the signal for a cross-party delegation to rush to Brussels on 3 February to try to limit the damage. It was composed of Viorel Hrebenciuc, a Machiavellian figure inside the PSD (who later in May 2006 would boast that he knew everyone who counted in Moscow). He was from Bacău, the hub of the oil industry, where he had extensive business interests. He was on good terms with businessmen and lawyers in other parties. Călin Popescu-Tăriceanu, who enjoyed a monopoly on the import of Citroen cars to Romania, and Gyorgy Frűnda, a prosperous lawyer, were the other figures in the delegation, being from the PNL and UDMR respectively. But their lobbying appeared unavailing.

Alin Teodorescu, an *eminence grise* who acted as an intermediary between the government and the EU, was aware that soft words and promises of better behaviour might no longer suffice to appease Brussels. For six weeks the man whom Năstase had relied on as a fireman in such difficult times broke off links with him after he had learned of the Italian adoptions scandal.[47] Early in February, Verheugen wrote to Năstase pointing out that Brussels had clear evidence that Romania was not fulfilling the Copenhagen criteria regarding human rights. He warned Năstase that unless the trade in children was halted, financial help would be suspended and Bucharest would be required to reimburse EU funding spent on child protection (totalling 60 million euros).[48]

Both Őostlander and Nicholson became rallying points for the country's beleaguered civil society. On 7 February, 22 public policy and media NGOs sent them (and Verheugen) an open letter, expressing concern over the lack of freedom of expression in Romania 'which they attributed to the political and economic pressure on media outlets and the physical intimidation of journalists'.[49] Both Nicholson and Őostlander could understand a little of the duress they were under because they were trailed by secret policemen while in Romania. They hardly bothered to conceal themselves, which she found amusing (the SIE denying the accusation).[50]

One opposition leader of whom much more would be heard later was very outspoken about the double-standards of well-known European officials. Traian Băsescu, leader of the PD and mayor of Bucharest, accused Năstase of using international adoptions to 'open the doors of offices in Brussels' and he criticised the 'double language' used by certain EU officials in the adoptions issue. On 8 February, he revealed memoranda, from 9 September 2002 and 28 February 2003, which claimed to show that Romano Prodi, the President of the European Commission, had lobbied the government for the adoption of two Romanian children aged two and eight by Italian families.[51] At a press conference Băsescu reproached EU leaders because 'they want us to bend the rules to their own ends'.[52] Emma Nicholson was appalled to find out that Prodi had been one of the chief lobbyists on behalf of childless families.[53] The Romanian government 'must learn to say no' she believed but she appeared willing after that to let the matter rest.

These wounding comments would not have endeared EU grandees to Băsescu who, as President of Romania, often appeared to be isolated from EU circles even when he was attempting to diminish the power of the oligarchy. On 19 February 2004, the foreign affairs committee of the EP voted to 're-orientate' its strategy towards Romania. The critical Nicholson report was accepted with amendments, but one clause omitted from her original report was that Europol start investigations into the alleged ties between the Romanian authorities and child-trafficking networks.[54]

In 2001, when the previous adoption crisis arose, Gűnther Verheugen had told his staff that Emma Nicholson was to be seen as an extension of the Commission and was to be offered all support and assistance.[55] But by 2004 the PSD was no longer seen by the German Commissioner as an alien post-communist force but as a member of the democratic Socialist International. Năstase claimed to his colleagues in 2003 that Verheugen had found Nicholson very wilful. He was also uncomfortable with some of her ideas, namely that Romania and Turkey should join the EU simultaneously in 2009. He relates that both Verheugen and Prodi were amused on learning of the Baroness's idea.[56]

The response of the government to the criticism contained in the Nicholson report, not only about child care but about threats to the independent media and the refusal to implement justice sector reforms, was confused and complacent. Geoană described it as 'a sort of early warning'. For the new Minister of European Integration, Alexandru Farcaş, it was 'a vote of confidence in Romania'. Stănoiu opined that its author was behind the times: 'many problems in the draft resolution have already been solved or are about to be'. Năstase travelled to Brussels on 24 February on 'a counter-offensive' only to be told by Prodi that the Commission shared many of the concerns contained in Nicholson's report.[57]

The main response of the government was an 'action plan' released on 24 February. It has been alleged that the Delegation drew up this rescue plan, which was presented to Năstase on his flight to see Verheugen with the recommendation that he tell the Commissioner this would be the government's bid to defuse criticism of its conduct.[58] It contained 40 measures, the deadline for implementation being June.[59] If this is true, it reveals the Delegation acting as the policy-making civil service which Romania still lacked and Năstase was in no hurry to bring in. Through this rather desperate action, the Delegation was conceding that all its twinning arrangements and action schemes had failed to achieve any decisive improvement in the capacity-making of the public administration. Inevitably, it begs the question as to why Eurocrats waited until 2004 before intervening with specific policies meant to improve Romania's performance when they had had ample scope to draw up a customised strategy for Romania in the previous four years.

Alin Teodorescu was to be the link between the government and the EU during this period of intense activity. The position of Chancellor was created for him. In effect he was to be Minister for the Implementation of the EU *acquis*.[60] But due to Iliescu being angered by an irreverent remark from this sardonic figure, Teodorescu was actually excluded from the cabinet, although he had a staff of six to work with. Soon, there would be no less than five government officials with overlapping responsibility for EU matters. On 8 March a government reshuffle occurred. Stănoiu was replaced as Justice Minister, much to the relief of the Commission. But the influence of this formidable opponent of reform was not curtailed. She became President Iliescu's adviser on security issues. Ioan Talpeş, the intelligence chief who had held this post, actually joined the government as Vice-Premier in charge of European Integration, Justice and Defence.

The EP debated Nicholson's resolution on 10–11 March. The wording was sombre: 'despite progress in a number of areas, Romania currently faces serious difficulties facing the requirements'.[61] But by now Nicholson and Öostlander had made a big concession. They agreed to withdraw their call for negotiations to be suspended and instead called for 'a re-orientation of strategy'. It would never be spelled out just what this required and within a few months, 're-orientation' would begin to look like a chimera. Nicholson spoke firmly: 'we want Romania to join the EU, but not at a price that's too high for Europe's citizens to pay'.[62] She called for the Bucharest elite to be shown 'tough love'. Verheugen even made several significant remarks in his speech to the EP. He said that Bucharest must go after 'the big fish', which from now on was taken as insistence by Brussels that high-profile figures in politics who had enriched themselves through exploiting their public positions needed to be called to account. He also insisted that it was the Năstase government and not the Commission which had pressed for 2004 to be the year when negotiations were closed: 'the Commission had a totally different opinion'.[63] This remark would assume significance at a politically highly charged moment later in the year. The report was passed overwhelmingly, the Socialist group backing it despite its critical tone. Năstase took comfort in the outcome: it 'refuted' the pessimistic prognostications heard recently.[64] The EU's Jonathan Scheele considered that it had brought the government to its senses: 'a cold shower that the government understood very well'.[65] Nicholson flew straight to Bucharest on the termination of the debate 'to eliminate any bid to manipulate' the meaning of the report.[66] She also pointed out that her report could have been more damning, especially about the state neglect of children removed for adoption abroad. But 'I didn't make public these findings because I don't want to criticise the government'. The pro-government journalist Bogdan Chirieac dubbed her 'Baroness Munchausen' and complained that she had subjected the government to blackmail.[67] By now, the government could no longer be in any doubt that unless Emma Nicholson's concerns about child care were taken fully into account, it might be jeopardising Romania's hopes for full EU membership in the near future. On 11 March, on the final day of the debate on her report, a law was hastily passed in Bucharest which closed any further loopholes allowing international adoptions. Ironically, her fixation with children's issues meant that she had far less time for other issues which tarnished Romania's reputation as a democratic state where the interests of citizens were protected. Năstase and his colleagues probably breathed a sigh of relief that most of her energy was channelled in this single direction since it let them off the hook in economic and justice concerns which were far more crucial for their retention of power. They would also have been aware that many EU officials were simply not convinced by Nicholson's solution to the crisis in child care but feared to speak out because of her self-proclaimed expertise on this subject and the effective publicity machine that she could draw upon. This was certainly the perception of a number of American diplomats who doubted the commitment of the Bucharest authorities to maintaining a high level of expenditure on child welfare, especially after EU entry when the number of abandoned children remains high.[68]

As Romania's EU accession efforts were sceptically assessed at the EP, an arguably far more significant event passed almost without notice. This was the resignation as the EU's director of negotiations with Romania of Enrico Grillo Pasquarelli, who had been in the post since 2000. As shown by the Romanian press, he had barely concealed his frustrations with the obstructive approach of the government towards embracing key reforms necessary for Romania if it was to ready itself properly for EU membership and benefit from the process. This punctilious Italian from the city of Turin had been taught by Norberto Bobbio, a renowned political scientist who made an impact on several generations of students by combining a commitment to liberal democracy with a strong aversion to fascism. Pasquarelli was mindful of the legacy of totalitarianism which Romania continued to suffer from and he was watchful of the human rights situation after 2000.[69] But it was over whether, by 2003, Romania fulfilled the criteria to be considered a functioning market economy that he hit the public eye. The 2003 progress report issued in November of that year stated that 'Romania can be considered as a functioning market economy once the good progress made has continued decisively'.[70] Before its release, officials in Prodi's office had looked over the report.[71] This is not unusual. Nor are last-minute changes to the wording. The phraseology had become somewhat ambiguous and Năstase declared that Romania was now recognised by Brussels as having reached that stage.[72] Even though senior officials in the Commission might have been content to allow him to go uncontradicted, Grillo Pasquarelli decided otherwise. In an interview with the Mediafax News Agency, he made it clear that Romania was close to acquiring this status but its confirmation would await measures by the government to 'curb inflation, continue with privatisation and the restructuring of companies, and solve the problem of debts owed to the state by private firms'.[73]

It might not have been easy for the EU official to remain as a chief negotiator after contradicting the Prime Minister of the country he was negotiating with. But he also found himself with a new boss from September 2003, whose pronouncements indicated that he did not share his sceptical outlook about the Năstase government's good faith in its negotiations with Brussels. Fabrizio Barbaso, also a native of Turin, struck a very positive note on his first visit to Romania after being appointed Director-General for Enlargement in September 2003. On 25 November, after meeting Năstase and his colleagues, he said: 'I am very pleased to note that we share the analysis of Romania's state of preparedness for membership and I am impressed by the commitment of the entire government to implement the measures needed to make progress on the ground'. The examples of 'encouraging progress . . . made over the last year' which Barbaso singled out were 'Constitutional reform, a strategy for civil service and judicial reform, child protection and anti-discrimination policies'.[74] These were essentially secondary issues other than administrative and judicial reform which had hardly emerged from the planning chrysalis. It was an acute misreading of the Romanian elite's psyche to assume that encouragement for what were extremely modest efforts usually only undertaken after much pressure from Brussels would produce resolve to make progress with the more difficult accession issues.

Pasquarelli would have probably found it difficult to serve under a director prepared to seize upon mainly public relations trifles as evidence that Romania was honouring its entry conditions. Within four months, he had been promoted to a very different position, in the Transport Directorate of the Commission. Contrary to claims in the Romanian press, there is no evidence that his departure was involuntary or induced by political pressure. But at a late 2003 PSD strategy meeting whose minutes were later leaked to the press, Năstase declared: 'the good news is that they succeeded in getting rid of Pasquarelli and a month from now, there will be another kind of person to answer to . . . I didn't want to ask too much about this'.[75] Pasquarelli's approach to Romania suggests that he hoped to see a home-centred reform process developing which was not reliant on pressure from Brussels for reaching its goals. But by 2003, it was hard to avoid the conclusion that there was little momentum in Bucharest to carry out much needed reforms without constant goading. Instead, a Brussels-centred diplomatic effort focused on closing chapters of the *acquis* gathered momentum. There was often not enough time to consider whether real or enduring reforms were actually occurring as a result. It is not surprising that a pro-active official keen to see Romanian institutions shake off their post-communist character would feel constrained. Pasquarelli was succeeded by Dirk Lange, a German official with little background knowledge of Romania, who would only be in the job for eight months. This was seen as a lucky break for Năstase and his colleagues, who managed to recover quickly from the events of early 2004. The Commission would show increasing readiness to overlook Romania's manifest un-readiness if there was compliance with producing documentation that showed, at least on paper, Romania was grappling effectively with the *acquis*. This would be Alin Teodorescu's mission over subsequent months as he shuttled between Bucharest and Brussels. This efficient manager with a background in civil society endeavours would be a highly convincing emissary of Năstase's. One American official who dealt with Teodorescu on adoption issues recalls him as an artful and highly persuasive technician able to convince Eurocrats that by ticking each of the boxes that made up the *acquis*, they were really contributing to the modernisation of Romania.[76]

Nicholson's report for the European Parliament had already started to appear inconsequential by mid-2004. So did the hard-hitting report on the state of the Romanian judicial system and the commitment of the Justice Ministry to modernising it, ending executive interference and combating corruption, drawn up for the Commission by seven highly experienced legal experts from EU member states in the first quarter of 2004. The report of this advisory team, on the extent of compliance with chapter 24 of the *acquis* in the fields of justice and home affairs, was finalised in April 2004 and shown to the relevant committee of the EP.[77] At that time, it was unprecedented for such an exercise to be carried out during negotiations. That showed the depth of the unease within parts of the Commission, and indeed certain governments closely monitoring Romania's performance, about the dilatory approach to such a key area. The documents submitted by Stănoiu's ministry were badly drafted and consisted of lots of promises of change with little clear indication of how they would be met. The *Judicial System Strategy of Reform 2003–2007* which Stănoiu had overseen was unsparingly dissected. Absent were costings, timetable for reform and who, amidst a swarm of competing and overlapping agencies, would be responsible.[78]

The report drew attention to the complacent picture 'presented by the Romanian administration on paper, and the situation indicated by non-governmental sources'.[79] The government was 'frustrated at what it sees as a lack of recognition of its efforts, and an exaggerated public perception of corruption in Romania'.[80] But the head of the investigating team, a legal figure with a strong reputation for tackling corruption in his own country, was unsparing in his conclusions about the government's unresponsiveness and indeed complicity in corruption: 'corruption in Romania is still clearly at an unacceptable level. It is also obvious that the Romanian government knows quite well where the most sensitive areas of corruption are situated, but seems to tolerate it up to a certain extent'.[81] These devastating claims were backed up by findings which pointed to 'corruption that involves high-ranking members of the state administration, politicians, and high business and/or financial elites . . . Since this *kind of high-level corruption* touches the very heart of government leadership and administration, it is far more dangerous to the democratic structure of the state than the common corruption' which earlier in the report was described as stemming from 'over-regulation, low wages, and a relatively old-fashioned administrative organization'.[82] It is doubtful if, before then, such a searing report had ever been produced about critical shortcomings in a candidate country. But instead of leading to a profound rethink about the timetable for Romanian entry and its ability to assume the responsibilities of membership, the report was mothballed (though its findings would be remembered when a new set of commissioners took office). The fate of this peer review on chapter 24 of the *acquis* showed that no re-orientation towards Romania was occurring. Instead, the EU was surrendering to the Romanian state approach of relying on changes whose existence was confined to documents and regulations which had no impact on existing practices in the areas of justice reform.

A more accurate guide to the thinking of the main EU actors towards Romania was provided by the declaration made by the European Council in December 2003, when it had underscored the 'continuity and irreversibility of the ongoing enlargement process'.[83] Both the Nicholson report and the justice peer review, and Őostlander's motion for suspending negotiating, however well founded they were, proved to be incapable of halting the juggernaut in favour of Romania entering no later than 2008.

Conclusion

Romania went from being the most assiduous NATO candidate in anticipating and complying with the US administration's wishes to being a full member whose government was ready to go back on its commitments if there was political capital to be made at home and the USA persisted in taking what was seen as a moralistic and interfering stance on sensitive domestic political issues. After a period of close cooperation designed to stabilise the Balkans, the EU and NATO increasingly diverged once the Iraq crisis erupted. It is unfortunate that NATO chiefs did not pay more attention to the way Romanian officials went back on undertakings made to the EU since it might have prompted a more alert stance towards Bucharest and not the naive approach exemplified by Defence Secretary Wolfowitz on his visit in May 2004. The discovery that Romania was breaking the embargo on international adoptions agreed with the EU in 2001 led to the threat of entry talks being suspended early in their fourth year. Geoffrey Pridham has written that Romania came close to the possibility of its negotiations being suspended by the EU.[84] But it is doubtful if talks would have been suspended. It would have drawn attention to the fact that officials at the top of the EU had in fact induced Năstase to break the moratorium on international adoptions. Attention was then bound to be focused on the record of the multi-layered system of EU decision-making towards Romania which I tend to argue in this book might not have stood up to such close scrutiny. Besides, the suspension of talks would have looked troubling just as Romania was about to join NATO and with EU chiefs having often emphasised that security reasons were behind the offer of entry talks to a manifestly unprepared Romania.

In fact it is at this time of apparent crisis that the security dimension began to be replaced by an emerging economic trigger for full membership in the short rather than longer term. There were also new political circumstances circumventing the perennial problems with Romania's application. Năstase and the PSD had confirmed a blossoming partnership with the Western European democratic Left by being received into the Socialist International the previous year. The Party of European Socialists in the EP was supportive towards the government during this crisis. Jo Leinen, the German MEP who was the most detached of all the continental left-wing MEPs who took an interest in Romania, argued in February 2004 that negotiations ought to be intensified rather than suspended.[85] Nicholson's broadside was also an opportunity for Năstase to assert his authority in the PSD by compelling President Iliescu to replace his *protégé* as Justice Minister, Rodica Stănoiu, with someone who could sound more in favour of reforms in this problematic sector, however doubtful the commitment was in practice. Soon little more would be heard of a strategy of 're-orientation' towards the candidate for EU membership which presented the gravest challenges to the Union. Indeed, spectacular progress would be made in closing difficult chapters when there appeared to be few grounds for justifying such a rosy attitude in Brussels. Important changes of personnel had occurred in the EU Commission in 2003–04 and figures with scant experience of Romanian conditions were prepared to make extravagant rhetorical gestures towards the Năstase government when the grounds for them appeared meagre. Unable to accomplish institutional reforms, especially where its vested interests were threatened, the PSD mounted a major diplomatic offensive to change hearts and minds in the corridors of power in the Parliament, Council and also at the top of the Commission. The 'continuity and irreversibility of the ongoing enlargement process' had been proclaimed at the December 2003 meeting of the European Council and this is how things would once more start to appear after Baroness Nicholson had been persuaded to resume using superlatives in her public utterances on Romania.[86]

Notes

1 Gallagher, *Theft of a Nation*, p. 58.
2 Mark Almond, *Decline without Fall: Romania Under Ceauşescu*, London: Institute for European Defence and Strategic Studies, 1988, p. 25.
3 See 'Micile secrete ale lui . . . Ioan Talpes', *Bilant* (Bucharest), 5 May 2006.
4 For early signs of promise, see Jeffrey Simon and Hans Binnendijk, 'Romania and NATO: Membership Reassessment at the July 1997 Summit', *Strategic Forum*, No. 101, Washington: INSS, 1997.
5 *The White Book on Romania and NATO, 1997*, Bucharest: Ministry of Foreign Affairs, 1997, chapter 7, p. 6.

6 See Tom Gallagher, 'The West and the Challenge to Ethnic Politics in Romania', *Security Dialogue*, Vol. 30, No. 3, September 1999, pp. 301–2.

7 *Associated Press*, 9 April 2002.

8 *Evenimentul Zilei*, 28 March 2002.

9 'Study on NATO Enlargement', 1 September 1995, para. 70, www.Nato.int.docu/basictxt/enl-9501.htm.

10 *Evenimentul Zilei*, 17 January 2002.

11 *România liberă*, 25 January 2002.

12 Radio Free Europe, *South-East-Europe Newsline*, 16 September 2002.

13 Radio Free Europe, *South-East-Europe Newsline*, 23 September 2002.

14 See Dina Kyriakidou, 'Nato Hopeful Offers Intelligence on Iraq', *Reuters*, 11 November 2002.

15 Interview with Dan Preda, *Radio Romania*, 21 May 2003.

16 Alina Grigore and Cristian Oprea, 'Paul Wolfowitz: Mai sunt multe progresse de făcut', *Evenimentul Zilei* (Bucharest), 20 May 2003.

17 David Ignatius, '"Wolfowitz's War": Not Over Yet', *Washington Post*, 13 May 2003.

18 Nicholas Kralev, 'Romania Moves Ahead', *Washington Times*, 4 November 2002.

19 *România liberă* (Bucharest), 24 March 2001.

20 Mirel Bran, 'Le Roumaine est-elle prête à intégrer l'OTAN', *Le Monde*, 23 May 2002.

21 Kralev, 'Romania Moves Ahead'.

22 Radio Free Europe, *South-East-Europe Newsline*, 2 September 2003.

23 'Iraq Debate Spawns European Identity Crisis', Oxford Business Group, 26 February 2003, www.oxfordbusinessgroup.com.

24 *Jurnalul Național* (Bucharest), 24 June 2006.

25 Răzvan Amariei, 'Romania: A Small Invasion', *Transitions Online*, 12 December 2005, www.tol.cz; Alecs Iancu, 'Local U.S. Bases Sealed with Historic Accord', *Bucharest Daily News*, 7 December 2005.

26 See Bucharest daily press, 16 November 2007.

27 US Embassy press release, 15 November 2007, http://bucharest.usembassy.Gov/US_Policy/Press_releases/Ambassador_Taubman_11; *Hotnews*, 15 November 2007, www.hotnews.ro.

28 *Evenimentul Zilei*, 14 December 2007.

29 Interview with American official stationed in Bucharest in 2002, Washington, 1 April 2008.

30 *Ziarul de Iași*, 23 January 2004.

31 *Ziarul de Iași*, 14 February 2004.

32 *Ziua*, 23 January 2004.

33 *Draft Report on Bulgaria's Progress Towards Accession*, European Parliament, 18 December 2003, PR\515408EN.doc.

34 *Ziarul Financiar* (Bucharest), 23 February 2004.

35 *Ziarul Financiar* (Bucharest), 23 February 2004.

36 *Ziarul de Iași*, 16 February 2004.

37 *Dow Jones newswires*, 13 February 2004.

38 *Ziarul de Iași*, 16 February 2004.
39 *Evenimentul Zilei*, 21 February 2004.
40 Leaked minutes of PSD executive meetings, *Evenimentul Zilei*, 24 November 2004.
41 *Adevărul*, 5 February 2004.
42 *Ziarul de Iași*, 23 January 2004.
43 *Evenimentul Zilei*, 24 November 2004.
44 *Hotnews* (Romania), 26 June 2006, www.hotnews.ro.
45 Conversation with Arie Öostlander, 19 January 2008.
46 *Evenimentul Zilei*, 30 January 2004.
47 Interview with Alin Teodorescu.
48 The letter was leaked to the journalist Bogdan Chirieac. See *Adevărul*, 5 February 2004.
49 Dumitru Balici, 'Romania Caught in the Middle', *Transition Online*, 11 February 2004, www.tol.cz (quote from Balici).
50 *Evenimentul Zilei*, 5 February 2005.
51 *Evenimentul Zilei*, 9 February 2004.
52 Balici, 'Romania Caught in the Middle'.
53 Balici, 'Romania Caught in the Middle'.
54 *Evenimentul Zilei*, 23 February 2004.
55 Interview with senior official based at the EU Delegation in that year, June 2007.
56 *Evenimentul Zilei*, 24 November 2004.
57 Radio Free Europe/Radio Liberty, *Newsline*, 26 February 2004.
58 Geoffrey Pridham, 'The Scope and Limitations of Political Conditionality: Romania's Accession to the European Union', *Comparative European Politics*, No. 5, 2005 (web version, p. 8).
59 Radio Free Europe/Radio Liberty, *Newsline*, 27 February 2004.
60 Interview with Alin Teodorescu.
61 Radio Free Europe/Radio Liberty, *Newsline*, 11 March 2004.
62 Radio Free Europe/Radio Liberty, *Newsline*, 12 March 2004.
63 *Ziarul de Iași*, 11 March 2004.
64 Radio Free Europe/Radio Liberty, *Newsline*, 12 March 2004.
65 Radio Free Europe/Radio Liberty, *Newsline*, 12 March 2004.
66 *Ziarul de Iași*, 12 March 2004.
67 *Adevărul*, 13 March 2004.
68 Interview with American official stationed in Bucharest in 2002: Washington, 1 April 2008.
69 *Directorate C*, DG Enlargement Seminar, Brussels, 8 June 2001.
70 David Cronin, 'Homing In On Reform', *European Voice*, 11 December 2003.
71 Private information.
72 Cronin, 'Homing In On Reform'.
73 *Evenimentul Zilei*, 24 November 2003 (English edition).
74 'EU Chief Negotiator Fabrizio Barbaso Appreciates Government's Commitment to Continue Ongoing Reforms', Delegation of the European Commission in Romania, 25 November 2003.

75 *Evenimentul Zilei*, 24 November 2004.
76 Interview with American official stationed in Bucharest in 2002: Washington, 1 April 2008.
77 *Draft Report of an Advisory Visit under Chapter 24 in the Fields of Justice and Home Affairs in Romania*, p. 146.
78 Interview with official from the European Commission's Justice and Home Affairs department working on Romanian justice issues after 2003, Brussels, 5 June 2007.
79 *Draft Report of an Advisory Visit under Chapter 24 in the Fields of Justice and Home Affairs in Romania*, p. 142.
80 *Draft Report of an Advisory Visit under Chapter 24 in the Fields of Justice and Home Affairs in Romania*, p. 130.
81 *Draft Report of an Advisory Visit under Chapter 24 in the Fields of Justice and Home Affairs in Romania*, p. 142.
82 *Draft Report of an Advisory Visit under Chapter 24 in the Fields of Justice and Home Affairs in Romania*, pp. 130, 129.
83 *Draft Report on Bulgaria's Progress Towards Accession*.
84 Pridham, 'The Scope and Limits of Political Conditionality', pp. 352–3.
85 Victor Iulian Tucam, *Apusul Occidentului nu a venit (incă)*, Cluj-Napoca: Eikon, 2007, p. 202.
86 Draft Report on Bulgaria's Progress Towards Accession.

7

The EU at its most incoherent:
April–December 2004

This chapter documents a series of abdications of responsibility by the EU during the last phase of entry negotiations with Romania. The failure of Brussels to uphold its own rules for entry negotiations during much of 2004 had long-term consequences ensuring that Romania would become a headache for most of its European partners following its accession to the EU in 2007.

The amended resolution tabled in the EP by Arie Őostlander and Nicholson in January 2004 requested the three main arms of the EU, the Commission, the Parliament and the Council, to collaborate closely in order to enable Romania to resume negotiations for the successful completion of the remaining chapters.[1] Such coordination was arguably overdue, especially in relation to an impending entrant which posed as many challenges as Romania. But there were no signs that the EU was going to assume some of the burdens for executing the reforms. This would have involved the Commission allocating more officials to Romania so that it could have greater oversight over funding programmes and strenuously encourage meaningful reform. It would have involved different institutions finally closing ranks. Instead attention focused on Alin Teodorescu, a semi-detached member of the elite with a reformist background who became the newly appointed Chancellor in the government. He was entrusted to work closely with Fabrizio Barboso, Director-General for Enlargement since 2003, in order to accomplish the completion of the *acquis*. A 39-point list of priority measures had been identified at the height of the crisis which formed the basis of an 'Action Plan'. Teodorescu found himself having to meet regularly with EU ambassadors in Brussels. They raised numerous concerns about how Romanian entry might affect their national interests. His businesslike manner, which was devoid of the florid and sometimes bombastic style of speaking which made Romanian politicians immediately distrustful in the eyes of many Western officials, proved a great asset in this mission to convince. He was helped by the fact that a lot of colleagues who, like him, had been office-holders in George Soros's Open Society Foundation, now worked in Brussels for new member states. They often proved to be invaluable allies, speaking up for Romanian efforts in EU meetings and providing him with strategic information that enabled him to overcome problems.[2] Perhaps even more advantageous were his close ties with Emma Nicholson. She respected his earlier work in 2001 to correct serious deficiencies in Romania's approach to child protection and she appeared content to let him get on with the changes, retreating into the background after her high-profile early 2004 intervention.

By the end of April, Verheugen was due to deliver an interim report on the steps Romania was taking in order to revive its membership bid and how the re-orientation strategy of the EU was proceeding. But the report to the EP foreign affairs committee was never delivered. The collapse of his plans to combine EU membership of the Greek-controlled Republic of Cyprus with reconciliation with the Turkish-occupied north of the island proved a source of preoccupation for some weeks. Only a written report was submitted which was never made public. Verheugen stated that with elections for the EP imminent in June 2004, it was not practicable to have a committee hearing.[3] In Bucharest, Năstase publicly declared that the postponement was a vote of confidence in Romania's efforts.[4] Already Dirk Lange, the new chief negotiator, had paid his first trip to Romania, stating that he was impressed by the will of the authorities to move forward.[5] His previous experience as a negotiator had been in the Baltic states, where Romania's venerable traditions of simulating change were generally absent. But concerns remained at the EU Delegation level. Jonathan Scheele was worried about whether judicial independence could be safeguarded in a new bill before Parliament. Speaking in May 2004 at the headquarters of the Superior Council of Magistrates, a body meant to be regulating a justice system supposedly now autonomous from the executive, he detected 'some unclear things about the intentions of the Justice Minister and the government to ensure the independence of the Justice Ministry and of the government to ensure the independence of the justice system' and believed that further discussions were necessary that took account of criticisms of the current proposals.[6]

Another sign of shortcomings in the democratic process was the refusal of Romania's electoral commission to register the Hungarian Civic Union (UCM) as a political party. It was challenging the PSD's ally, the UDMR, and judges and other officials on the commission delivered what was seen as an arbitrary ruling in order to frustrate a challenge that could cause an upset in approaching elections.[7]

But no concerns about the soundness of democratic arrangements in Romania appeared to trouble Verheugen after his meeting with Năstase in Brussels on 12 May. Perhaps he felt the need to single out a success after the Cyprus debacle, when he was easily double-crossed by Greek nationalists into admitting them to the EU without the need to continue working on a peace process with the Turkish north.[8] He said that he was impressed by the government's efforts to speed up accession negotiations and that 2007 was a realistic entry date.[9] All negotiating chapters could be closed by the end of the year (a notably different position from the one he had taken when speaking in the EP just two months earlier).[10] Such complacency after stern warnings in March prompted Gelu Trandafir, one of the closest observers of the EU negotiations in the press corps, to judge that 'the reorientation of entry negotiations was shrouded in mist'.[11]

Verheugen was in Romania from 21 to 23 June. He praised Romania's 'very huge progress', declaring that 'I am absolutely convinced Romania will be successful . . . the remaining problems are more of a technical nature and they have not identified very serious political problems'.[12] The barring of the UCM from participating in elections had just occurred and one month later Paul Florea, the head of the Court of Cassation who, in that position, had protected junior colleagues prepared to resist executive interference in court cases, was removed from his position thanks to moves orchestrated by President Iliescu, according to well-informed press commentators.[13]

Verheugen's one visit outside the capital was to the city of Cluj, where the ultra-nationalist mayor Gheorghe Funar had just gone down to electoral defeat. While there, he reproached Romanians for 'suffering [an] inferiority complex . . . Your country has evolved and is capable of closing negotiations and making all preparations within the timeframe agreed'.[14] The inferiority complex presumably gripped the society and not a self-confident elite that felt it was entitled to the prize even with minimum effort. The commissioner's office had chosen the relatively placid city of Cluj for his showcase visit. Perhaps reality might have broken through if he had gone instead to Bacău, headquarters of the North-East Regional Development Authority. It was the centre of the oil industry and the political stronghold of the powerful PSD politician, Viorel Hrebenciuc, who also headed Parliament's commission on European integration. OLAF had discovered possible irregularities in the use of EU funds involving companies that he was linked to.[15] The newspaper *Evenimentul Zilei* published its report.[16] But the go-ahead for any prosecutions was required from a senior official in the government who, like Hrebenciuc, was one of the PSD's Vice-Presidents: Victor Ponta. He was head of the Prime Minister's Control office that monitored government expenditure, and he failed to see any grounds for prosecution. The lack of coordination in the EU system over this serious issue was painfully evident from an interview given by Scheele in June 2004.[17] The Delegation chief conceded that neither he nor the rest of the Delegation in Bucharest had been following the OLAF investigation into the fate of Phare funds in Bacău. But he revealed that it was OLAF's choice to make Ponta their chief liaison in Romania. They could have sought a less political figure to interact with, one who placed fewer obstacles in the way of acceding to the request for firm action to be taken against those looting EU funds.

Bacău had been one of the centres of loss-making industries controlled by figures close to the PSD. They had been beneficiaries of state aid on political criteria in the form of budgetary credits, non-payment of taxes or guarantees for loans. This was a source of inflationary pressure and low competition in a country with one of the highest inflation and tax rates in the region.[18] Improvements were supposedly in train: new bankruptcy laws to comply with EU standards. A competition council would obtain independence from the government to monitor and act on both anti-trust practices and state aid. But the effectiveness of these measures to curb rent-seeking would depend on vigilance and firm implementation. By quickly lowering its guard after the EP's warning in March, the EU was displaying weakness. The debacle concerning the fate of the OLAF report after clear evidence had been found of serious wrongdoing suggested that no serious re-evaluation of Romania was taking place in Brussels. Indeed, there would be little or no mention of one in official documents.

So there was little sign that the EU realised just how much of a problem case Romania continued to be, nor of the ingenuity its leaders would show in dodging agreed undertakings to carry out proper reforms. The naivety was exemplified by the statement of Bernard Bot, Foreign Minister of the Netherlands, which held the Presidency of the European Council in the second half of 2004. He declared himself to be 'fully confident we will work in a positive spirit, in a positive atmosphere. [Romanians] really are intent on finishing these chapters and on implementation as well as they can'.[19]

From May 2004 onwards, the European Commission was able to give more attention to Romania following the recent completion of the first and largest part of the fifth enlargement. There were stark challenges: Romania was still to receive the status of a functioning market economy. The competition chapter would remain open right up until the end of the year. It and justice were kept in reserve to ensure continuing good behaviour in Bucharest. Vasile Puşcaş said that he faced strong pressure by the EU on hidden state subsidies, especially for the steel industry. Firms benefiting from these subsidies were not ready to accept the new realities without a fight. Puşcaş found himself subjected to unexplained attacks in the influential Bucharest daily *Adevărul*, and it wouldn't have been the first time that groups facing obstacles from government counter-attacked in this way.[20] Indeed, no less a figure than the next president would speak in public about how the state intervened on behalf of favoured clients: when locked in confrontation with a Liberal government, Băsescu revealed in 2007 how favoured clients of the party were able to buy electricity at rates one hundred times less than ordinary consumers. Pharmaceutical companies were also able to keep the price of medication artificially high and make profits that surpassed even those in the energy sector, leaving such medication beyond the reach of ordinary citizens.[21] By now Romania was a full member of the EU and yet the state remained an arena where venal politicians and aggressive business interests made fruitful transactions.

A senior EU official with considerable knowledge of Romania tried to bring such corruption to the attention of Verheugen when they were on a flight to Romania. He brushed aside the matter with the remark that things are really not so different in Bavaria. The crestfallen official felt thereafter that it was pointless to pursue such matters with the Enlargement Commissioner.[22] Ironically, it was a Bavarian politician, Markus Ferber, head of the Christian Social Union group in the EP, who was the strongest critic in public of Verheugen's approach to Romania. He even claimed that Commission officials had been browbeaten to close chapters in order to realise the goal of closing chapters by the end of 2004. Moreover, several officials said that Verheugen allowed his political affiliations to cloud his outlook on Romania.[23] He was a top German Social Democrat (having defected from the rival Free Democrats in the 1980s). Especially after the PSD became a member of the Socialist International in 2003 after years of lobbying, Verheugen began to regard it as a member of his own political family. The PD was already a member but it was thereafter shunned by its former European allies. Antonio Guterres, President of the Socialist International at this time explained this was because the PD was getting too close to the Liberals.[24] But there were no qualms about Năstase's close ties with Silvio Berlusconi or the fact that the PSD delegation turned up at the Socialist International's Sao Paulo conference in a private jet.

The PSD discovered that the trafficking of influences was a practice not confined to Romania or other countries where the public and private spheres were blurred. On 8 December 2003, Miron Mitrea, the Transport Minister, said at a PSD strategy meeting: 'I want to thank Adrian [Năstase] for his visit to Berlusconi because otherwise I would have failed'. This concerned problems that had arisen over the transport chapter in the *acquis*. He continued with the enigmatic remark: 'integration costs money'.[25]

Romania needed to resist strong pressures from the EU over the awarding of a $2.5 billion contract to the US-based Bechtel corporation to build a 450-kilometre highway between Braşov and Borş on the Hungarian frontier near the city of Oradea. EU officials complained that no tender was offered for the contract and the whole selection process lacked transparency. Indeed, in the words of a senior Commission official, 'the whole affair stinks'.[26] It was not in the spirit of free competition and thus threatened prospects of Romania being granted the status of a functioning market economy. But the EU's line had softened by June. Verheugen said that he had received an undertaking from Năstase that a public tender would be held for all such projects in the future.[27] But in August, a one billion euro contract, on the same basis, was signed with the European Aeronautic Defence and Space Company (EADS) in order to provide Romania with enhanced border security and surveillance. (Without the facilities to patrol the largest frontier a member would have with non-EU states, it would be difficult for Romania to join the Schengen zone.) EADS was a consortium of Spanish, French and Dutch companies founded in 2000, with Germany's Daimler Chrysler aerospace being the lynchpin. No less a person than Chancellor Schroeder arrived in person on 12 August to sign the EADS contract and also smaller ones for upgrading Romania's ailing power infrastructure; the smaller deal, worth €650 million, involved modernisation of the power station and electricity transmission firm Transelectrica, the signatories being Siemens, AG, the ABB–AREVA consortium and the German bank, KFW.[28]

These deals were signed in the context of accelerating German investment, more in fact in the first six months of 2004 than in the previous five years.[29] The warning issued by Deutsche Bank in 2003, that Bulgarian and Romanian entry to the EU in 2007 was a very ambitious goal that could only be realised under the most optimistic perspectives, seemed a distant memory.[30] Schroeder was publicly upbeat about Romania's chances of obtaining the status of a functioning market economy and closing negotiations by the end of 2004.[31] A string of Romanian officials from the Interior Ministry and the Police said that the money to finance the EADS contract would be obtained from the EU budget via Phare funds.[32] But EU concerns about the absence of a bidding process produced a *volte-face* on 21 August. Farcaș, the Minister of European Integration, said: 'It seems that the MAI was mistaken'. The contract was not to be financed with EU money. At the end of that month, it was announced that another consortium, the French bank Societe Generale, together with the German banks, FFN and Dresdner, would finance it.[33]

Despite his left-wing orientation, Schroeder had not shrunk from close involvement with top German firms. He had been on the board of Volkswagen when a rising regional politician and, upon retiring as Chancellor in November 2005, he joined the board of directors of the joint venture he had agreed with Russia for a gas pipeline exclusively between the two countries, bypassing other EU states and going under the Baltic Sea. His willingness to establish a 'strategic partnership' with Russia during the twilight of his Chancellorship and describe Vladimir Putin as 'a flawless democrat' raised consternation among those who believed it was vital for the EU to keep its distance from authoritarian leaders.[34] But it is likely that Schroeder's arch-pragmatism went down well inside the PSD. His apparent lack of concern about its lurches towards authoritarianism suggested that life inside the EU might be even more congenial than expected.

Perhaps German and French violation of the Stability Pact and Greek evasion about the country's ability to join the euro zone had taught Iliescu and Năstase that the EU's rules were there to be broken. There were no transparent criteria for entry. The negotiating chapters were flexible targets and it was the core member states which decided whether they had been met or not.

The EU Commission itself appeared disorientated about how to interpret its competition rules, especially when it was core states, and not mere candidates, which appeared to be trashing them. Further discomfiture was provided when the Romanian state awarded another lucrative contract, this time to Vinci constructions, without a tender process. It was to build a sector of a new highway between Bucharest and Braşov.[35] Even before the contract was signed, the Commission declared that EU rules were being flouted. But the government said that no tender was needed since the rules requiring it had not yet become law in Romania.[36] Traian Băsescu, freshly re-elected mayor of Bucharest, and soon to be opposing Năstase in the presidential elections, slammed the ethics behind 'these kinds of contracts'. He characterised them as 'gold mines for those who carry them out and they oblige the Romanian state to pay twice what they would have, if there had been a tender'.[37] On 18 October Băsescu caused a particular stir by saying that Jean-Pierre Raffarin, the French Premier, had 'received his allowance' from the Romanian government during his visit to the country the day before.[38] He accused Năstase of showing servility to particular Western governments in a bid to improve the chances of EU entry. This brought a heated rejoinder from Eugen Bejinariu, a senior government official, that 'if Băsescu comes and calls various presidents and prime ministers frauds and certain European companies bribe takers, then we might not be allowed to travel freely anymore' (in European states).[39]

Pro-Western newspapers now for the first time began to accuse the EU of having double-standards. Dan Turturică, the deputy-editor of *Evenimentul Zilei*, complained about the 'hypocrisy' of top European officials who publicly demanded a struggle against corruption but 'who moderated their language when a case arose in which major figures in continental politics might be implicated'.[40] The same newspaper complained that Delegation officials only found out about the nature of the earlier EADS deal from the local press. It was assumed that Brussels did not see the point about keeping its staff in Bucharest fully informed about such a sensitive matter.[41] Onno Simons, the deputy head of the Delegation, complained in November 2004 that two months had elapsed without the Bucharest authorities providing the Commission with information about the nature of the contract signed with EADS. The government position, according to him, was that the contract was secret, confidential and concerned national security. Toma Zaharia, State Secretary at the Interior Ministry, refuted this and said his ministry had already informed the Commission about the contract.[42] The issue over Vinci was resolved when the Commission admitted that the Romanian law on which the contract was made did not conform with EU legislation, but was still operable.[43] Another messy fudge would later regularise the EADS contract.

Băsescu complained that the people who were already carrying the main burden of entry preparations would be further inconvenienced by the suspect nature of contracts between the state and multinational firms with connections extending deep into the EU system. They would pay not just higher taxes but the fines for all the pre-accession money that the EU discovered had been misappropriated.

Occasionally, without offering evidence, Jonathan Scheele declared that Romanians were indeed players whose voice counted: 'for this process to reach a satisfactory conclusion the effort of all Romanians is necessary'.[44] But there was no sign of an effective partnership, and on plenty of other occasions the EU made it abundantly clear that its main relationship was with the state. At least Scheele was regularly accessible to the media, though his circumlocutory style of expression did not always clarify what the EU position was on sensitive aspects of negotiations. He moved on in 2006 with his popularity largely intact after four years in Romania. He had taken initiatives which few local politicians would have contemplated, such as visiting a leper colony on the Danube Delta. But he was reluctant to detach himself from EU policy towards Romania when it appeared to be mired in confusion. His stock answer when asked to account for controversial actions, such as Verheugen's attempt to close negotiations early, was: 'Mr Verheugen is my chief, therefore he can see the broad picture, and from that vantage-point he is the one who knows what is the best possible course'.[45]

A contrast can be made between his discretion in the face of grave shortcomings in the EU–Romania relationship and the outspokenness of Michael Guest, the United States ambassador to Romania from 2001 to 2004. He had more latitude to criticise corruption and authoritarianism under Năstase and he did so on numerous occasions. A rare counterpart in EU diplomatic circles was Quinton Quayle, Britain's ambassador from 2002 to 2006. The tenor of his statements indicates that he had no wish for Romania to join the EU substantially unreformed, especially in terms of the health of its democracy and the effectiveness of its institutions. A not untypical statement of his, delivered in March 2004, drew attention to the fact that 'too many officials, at all levels, either block reform or do too little to advance it . . . Let's be tough with those who promote their own financial interests ahead of the national interest'.[46] During the last year or more of his ambassadorship, Adrian Năstase completely snubbed Quayle. Britain had been Romania's most active backer for EU entry at the start of the decade, mainly due to regional security issues, but it had no big economic investments in Romania, which perhaps made it possible for Quayle to speak out in this way.[47]

For many in Bucharest diplomatic circles, as well as in Brussels, the opposition remained an unknown and even despised quantity unlikely to do better in electoral terms than the PSD given its previous poor performance in government. Nevertheless, there was a hunger for political change among sections of the electorate in 2004 which contrasted with the widespread sense of despair in 2000 over the complete failure of the reformist coalition to press ahead with long-blocked reforms. Despite the absence of a strong opposition alternative, the PSD had lost ground in the June 2004 local elections. The PNL and PD had formed a Justice and Truth Alliance (DA) in 2003 and this secured victory in a string of major cities. The PSD then endured a month of infighting between supporters of President Iliescu and those of his Prime Minister. In early July, Năstase even threatened to withdraw from the presidential race unless Iliescu stopped undermining his position in the party. A truce was finally arranged between the Iliescu camp, composed of party veterans and members of the intelligence world, and Năstase's more business-orientated, technocratic and generally younger supporters.[48] Năstase was aware that his party's reputation for corruption and arrogance had repelled many voters. He accepted advice to introduce a number of internal party reforms:

1. A Council of Moral Integrity was set up to weed out controversial figures who tarnished the party's image.
2. Primary elections, to enable the half-a-million-strong party membership to select candidates for November's parliamentary elections, were hurriedly arranged.

These innovations were designed to respond to the widespread perception that in order to obtain an eligible position on candidates' lists, individuals need to make huge donations to party coffers which they could then redeem through profitable transactions with the state later on. But the PSD primaries led to fresh infighting as disaffected PSD figures claimed that electoral fraud was being prepared to enable Năstase's younger followers to strengthen their hold over the party.

Năstase was aware that the fatalistic approach among the Romanian public towards corruption in high places was being replaced by a much harsher attitude towards it. He himself had been in the spotlight on account of economic transactions which increased his family wealth substantially.[49] He tried to improve his image as an international player by visiting Presidents Bush and Putin in rapid succession. US advisers were recruited to devise a strategy plan to ensure the continuation of the PSD in power (these included the primaries). But their plan envisaged Năstase staying on as Prime Minister. The American consultants concluded that he wasn't suitable material for President.[50] Polls consistently showed that he stood a grave chance of losing if he went forward for President and he did consistently less well than the PSD was forecast to do in the parliamentary elections. His strongest opposition challenger argued the same. Băsescu declared in September that Năstase 'was born to be beaten. He cannot be elected. He needs to be appointed'.[51]

But Năstase decided to run for the Cotroceni Palace and was unanimously selected by his party on 27 August. He was helped by strengthening economic indicators. The economy was set to grow by 6.5% that year and inflation looked likely to finally accomplish the target of rising by no more than 10%. He also got a boost from Brussels in its annual progress report on entry preparations, Romania finally obtaining the coveted status of a functioning market economy.[52]

Năstase's party controlled the main levers of state and the EU had grown used to dealing with it, despite its infuriating ways. Hardly expecting any upsets, EU officials languidly watched the contest between the rhetorically leftist ruling party supported mainly by peasants, and businessmen relying on state benevolence for much of their wealth. Opposing it was the DA, the electoral pact between the PNL and PD. It enjoyed strong backing from the urban middle-class, much of which had known only years of depressed incomes since 1990. Theodor Stolojan, the PNL leader, had faced internal opposition to the pact, particularly from the oil mogul Dinu Patriciu, who actually subsidised the campaign of both it and the PSD. When Stolojan retired from the presidential race on 2 October, citing ill-health, he was replaced as the DA candidate by 52-year-old Traian Băsescu. A former oil tanker captain, his rallies drew large crowds and he was liked for his lack of aloofness and seeming fearlessness in the face of a PSD that appeared confident of victory. Năstase refused to risk an electoral debate with him unless minor candidates were present. He hoped that the PSD's dominance of the electronic media and the local state, and helpful backing from Iliescu, who was still popular among traditional social sectors, could enable him to prevail.

With the parliamentary opposition dominated by the ultra-nationalist PRM (which had come second in the 2000 elections), the media, particularly several independent-minded daily newspapers, was the main source of informed criticism of government activities. This ought not to have been of undue concern to Năstase. The electronic media was the principal source of information for the population, with 80% of the population regularly watching news on television.[53] State television and radio were run by PSD loyalists and caused few headaches for a Prime Minister who was very sensitive about his portrayal in the media. Private channels were technically autonomous but most of them had incurred huge debts to the state which made them dependent on its goodwill. Research published in the spring of 2004 indicated that pro-government politicians controlled or owned outright about half the local television channels, either directly or through intermediaries.[54] Few television journalists reported being subjected to harassment, but newspaper journalists deemed to be unduly probing or critical of national or local authorities faced numerous difficulties. At a time when privatisation of state assets was escalating and EU funds were pouring into the country, there were numerous stories to pursue about politicians enriching themselves via state money. Journalists working for local newspapers could be subjected to fierce pressures if they uncovered illegalities committed by local officials, such as participating in business activities that were subject to conflict of interest legislation. The pressures ranged from threatening phone calls to having their financial affairs or those of their newspaper minutely scrutinised by tax officials, to suffering assaults of sufficient seriousness to require hospitalisation. These could take place in public places, including court buildings. Elected officials, and even in one instance a judge, could be the culprits, the mayor of one town in the northeast threatening that he 'would kill all journalists' who wrote critical reports about him.[55] In Vrancea County, the only newspaper holding out against the hardline PSD rule of the President of the county council, Marian Oprişan, found it was a constant struggle to get copies on the streets. Several EU ambassadors expressed their concern by visiting journalists who had been hospitalised as result of beatings. On several occasions in 2004, when *Evenimentul Zilei* contained particularly damaging allegations about the government, the newspaper simply never reached provincial cities or else was quickly bought up by PSD loyalists.

Editorial staff and journalists working for the two best-known independent press outlets, *Evenimentul Zilei* and *România liberă*, complained towards the end of 2004 that they were being pressurised by foreign owners to tone down editorial criticisms and avoid politically sensitive stories due to government pressure.[56] The fate of *Evenimentul Zilei* became a *cause-celebre*, its well-known director, Cornel Nistorescu being replaced in September 2004 and most of the staff being locked out in December. Năstase tried to overcome a consistently poor public image by hiring image specialists as the election drew near. The best-known result was a series of interviews conducted with Alin Teodorescu, and published several weeks before election day, called *Adrian Năstase from Karl Marx to Coca Cola.*[57] It suggested that the Prime Minister had followed the emblematic path taken by all Romanians from involuntary association with the communist system to belatedly enjoying capitalist and consumer freedoms.

But what proved to be a damaging blow was the release of complete transcripts of the meetings of the permanent delegation of the PSD which took place during most of 2003–04. Their veracity was admitted by several leading participants, including Rodica Stănoiu. On 20 October 2003 she discussed with party colleagues what could be done with legal files that might implicate Traian Băsescu in criminal wrong-doing. She mentioned that there were two or three crucial files but the snag was that 'our people' were also caught up in them. She declared: 'they are very complicated files and I left them in stand-by to see how we will work on them'.[58] This phrase indicated that in her eyes the separation of powers was still very much a distant dream. Năstase scolded the Minister of Privatisation, Ovidiu Mușețescu, at another strategy meeting for not drawing up files that looked into privatisations carried out under the previous government: 'I'm telling you this now, before the Permanent Delegation . . . you still do not get it . . . you should prepare your papers because the electoral campaign is beginning'.[59] The Prime Minister's help was even enlisted by a PSD notable, Florin Georgescu, who wished the Audit office to stop making checks on PSD members, including Miron Mitrea, the Minister of Transport, whose business affairs had long placed him in the limelight.[60] The Audit office was a regulatory agency whose independence the EU believed to be vital if corruption were to be brought under control in Romania.

Pro-reform sections of the media were increasingly outspoken about a lacklustre EU response in the face of the PSD adopting an increasingly proprietorial attitude towards the state. Rodica Culcer, later head of state television news in 2005–06, wrote in February 2004:

> Romanian ministers know very well that they can play a cat-and-mouse-game with Brussels and laugh in the faces of commissioners . . . If the European institutions refuse to be more alert . . . they will lose their reputation: it won't be the Balkan periphery that is conquered by Europe, but instead the European corridors by the Balkan periphery. Aren't we at the gates of the Orient where all is open to negotiation, including European standards?[61]

Polls generally favoured EU membership by a wide margin, but some revealed acute disappointment with practical effects. One released on 30 August 2004 revealed that 59% of the public and 73% of businesspeople believed that EU funding programmes in Romania were beset by fraud. There was no perceptible sense of accelerating social improvements. This appeared to be borne out by the Human Development ratings produced annually by the UN Development Programme. They show that Romania had only gone up from 74th to 69th place between 1995 and 2005 having been overtaken by Croatia, Macedonia and even Albania in that period.[62]

Romania had got the status of a functioning market economy which Daniel Dăianu, a former Finance Minister, described as a 'tolerant gesture' by the Commission.[63] But Năstase failed to help his cause by descending on Brussels two days before the publication of the report. What was seen as an attempt to 'sweeten the tone of the document' was not received well in some quarters of the Commission. Indeed, a procession of ministers had been virtually camped out in the Commission since the end of the August holidays in order to make the case for swiftly ending negotiations.[64] However, strong criticism was levelled at the inadequate nature of the fight against corruption. The National Anti-Corruption Prosecutor's office, set up in 2002 (at the EU's behest), was seen as failing in its 'core mandate of investigating high-level corruption', pursuing instead 'a large number of petty corruption cases'. Overall the EU's conclusions were unflattering:

> Corruption remains a serious and widespread problem in Romania which affects almost all aspects of society. There has been no reduction in perceived levels of corruption and the number of successful prosecutions remains low, particularly for high-level corruption. The fight against corruption is hampered by integrity problems even within institutions that are involved in law enforcement and the fight against corruption.[65]

In no other pre-accession country has corruption been described in such stark terms within a major EU report. The passage quoted appeared to be describing a kleptocracy not a state which had benefited from five years of EU engagement on the side of reform. Its tenor was an indication of the limitations of Verheugen's power. Decisions were arrived at after being filtered through various bureaucratic layers. 'One person can do damage but never be decisive. In the Commission there are too many layers which decide the fate of a country' was how one insider in the Romanian negotiations described the situation in 2004.[66] There were officials in Brussels unwilling to be steam-rollered by Verheugen. They had powerful weapons, not least the devastating report produced in the spring of 2004 by an advisory team on justice reform led by a highly motivated legal figure with a strong reputation for tackling corruption in his own country. This peer review found little willingness on the part of Mrs Stănoiu's department to carry out reforms required to close chapter 24 and had serious misgivings about commitment to reform under her successor, Cristian Diaconescu.[67] Not only had this report been presented to the EP's foreign affairs committee but it would likely have reached the ambassadors of those EU states which believed that Romania must become a full member by implementing and not merely simulating reforms.

Nevertheless, in the presence of Năstase, Verheugen declared at a press conference held in Bucharest on 5 November that he expected entry negotiations to be completed on the 24th of that month. Two days earlier, his long-term ally, Chancellor Schroeder had said that he believed negotiations should finish that month.[68] It did not appear to matter that Romania was still negotiating three chapters of the *acquis* – justice and home affairs, competition and environment – each of which had been causing particular problems. Uproar soon ensued when it was realised that the pending closure date was just four days before crucial national elections. The timetable Verheugen appeared to be working under seemed ludicrous. Officials from the justice and home affairs directorate were not due to present their final documentation until

17 November.[69] This would leave only a few days for all 25 member states to reach a point of view on a document approximately 300 pages in length and with numerous annexes. He faced ringing criticisms from centre-right MEPs who accused him of incompetence and interference in electoral politics.[70] Jose Vitorino, the Justice Commissioner, like Verheugen a socialist, who had been reluctant to challenge him previously, was very guarded in his public pronouncements. So was the usually dependable Delegation head, Jonathan Scheele. According to one British Liberal Democrat MEP, Chris Davies, Verheugen tried to salvage the situation by claiming that 24 November 2004 had been designated as the date for the closure of negotiations for around one year and that he simply had no idea that it would coincide with the election campaign.[71] This rather stretched credulity. If anything, the EU was in the habit of leaving such decisions to the last minute, as shown in 2005–06 when the date for confirming when Romania would actually join was postponed on successive occasions.

Gelu Trandafir, a Romanian journalist who had closely followed EU negotiations, added to Verheugen's discomfiture by pointing out that in March 2004 he had stood up in the EP and said that it was the government which wanted a 2004 closure date: 'The Commission was of another opinion'. Like Baroness Nicholson, the EP *rapporteur*, Verheugen believed at least then that it would be in the interest of Romania if negotiations were finalised some time in 2005 in order to give it the chance to prepare economically for the shock of entry.[72] This Commissioner was supposed to be acting as the guardian of the interests of member states in trying to integrate such a problem candidate. Diplomats in Bucharest were pointing out that several EU states had particular worries that Romania 'might become a gateway for illegal immigrants, smuggling and organized crime unless it tightens borders and overhauls its judiciary'.[73]

Verheugen had already proven accident prone in the spring of 2004. He had sought to combine the accession of the southern (Greek) part of the island of Cyprus to the EU with acceptance of a UN peace plan which would have helped bridge divisions with the part in the north controlled by Turkey since 1974. He relied on the Greek Cypriot authorities with whom Brussels had been negotiating entry terms to support the plan. But instead they opposed it in a heated referendum and even restricted Verheugen's access to the state media when he tried to rally a yes vote. The Commissioner declared plaintively that the Greek Cypriot side had 'cheated' on him.[74] The outcome was that the Turkish north accepted the plan but in the Greek south it was decisively rejected. Lord Patten, the EU's Commissioner for External Relations, would later state that admitting the (Greek Cypriot) republic without settling its dispute with the Turkish Cypriot north had been a 'mistake'.[75] In April 2004, Verheugen said that those who accepted the UN plan would be rewarded whereas those who rejected it would not.[76] He promised to alleviate the isolation of the Turkish Cypriots but the EU found itself with no powers to sanction the Greek Cypriots who joined the EU a week later. The Turkish Cypriots remained subject to a trade embargo and financial help promised by the EU was not forthcoming since the Greek Cypriots could veto it.[77] Moreover, the Republic of Cyprus is now also in a position to veto the membership of Turkey, which contributes to a rising tide of nationalism in Turkey. In Verheugen's hands enlargement scarcely looked like the EU's most effective foreign policy instrument. After such a *debacle*, most politicians would not expect promotion, but this is exactly what Verheugen got thanks to having such an influential patron, Chancellor Schroeder. From December 2004, he filled the even more important post of Industry Commissioner. The significance of these events was not lost on the Romanian authorities. Cyprus was one of the economic havens where those who had profited from the chaotic nature of the political transition had salted away their riches.

But the biggest lesson absorbed by the PSD after returning to office was that it could obtain legitimacy in Western European political and economic circles by taking the appropriate measures. There was hardly a better-placed observer than Alina Mungiu-Pippidi, head of Romania's leading policy think-tank, the Romanian Academic Society. This redoubtable social scientist had very close ties to the European Commission through the consultancy services provided by SAR. She was a committed advocate of early entry (someone who had upbraided me on occasion for alleged euro-scepticism). But she had noticed a mellowing of Western attitudes towards a still venal Romanian political elite. In particular, she saw how intense lobbying by the Năstase government and an open-door policy towards major firms reduced the level of criticism in Brussels about the state's approach to business and politics. In October 2004 she wrote:

> A great many Westerners, businessmen, large western firms and their political allies (because they also have them in the West) have begun to like the treatment which they receive in Romania. The manner in which these companies and their allies from diverse governments behave makes it look as if Romania is treated as a colony, not the way Westerners would behave in the Czech Republic or Slovakia.

Writing a month before the national elections, she went on to say that: 'this is the first time in the West when the electoral struggle involving the party of Năstase and Iliescu is no longer seen as a struggle between authoritarians and democrats, but as a normal struggle'.[78]

The 28 November 2004 parliamentary and first round of presidential elections featured widespread irregularities in some areas. The problem arose from the existence of 'supplementary voting lists' that enabled voters to cast ballots if they were in transit on election day or were not on the permanent lists. The government had abandoned the use of electoral identification cards, used in 2000, and instead voters were allowed to vote after showing their identity cards. A detachable stamp was then attached to the identity card, and once it had been removed voters could go to another electoral district and cast another vote on the supplementary list there. These lists were not cross-checked with others and there were no computers in Romanian polling stations to try to reduce the likelihood of abuse. More than 10% of those who turned out on 28 November voted on the supplementary lists. The press reported voters being bussed from one polling station to another, particularly around Bucharest. In Ilfov County, the practice appeared to be widespread and there the turnout was 77.66% compared with 57% in the country as a whole. Electoral monitors also noticed the presence of local officials (such as the mayor and the vice-mayor), usually belonging to the PSD, in the vicinity of polling stations, in violation of the electoral law and implying unreasonable pressure on voters. There were also cases in which election observers were threatened after noting irregularities, such as more than one voter being allowed into the voting booth.[79]

No parliamentary bloc won an outright majority. The PSD had a combined 161 seats in Parliament, while the DA had 160, but there were numerous smaller parties whose allegiance was uncertain. A pro-reform government would take office which soon proved to be at the mercy of fickle members unenthusiastic about cleaning up the political system. Some analysts reckon that if fraud had not occurred, reformers would have been in a much stronger position in the last two years before Romania joined the EU. Mircea Kivu, Director of the polling institute, MAS, published findings in January 2005 showing that where a very large proportion of the vote was cast on supplementary lists, or where an unusually large proportion of the votes were invalid, the PSD won by a margin of some 20 percentage points. Conversely, where such factors occurred with far less frequency, victory went to the opposition DA by a margin of some three percentage points.[80]

Pro Democraţia, the NGO with the biggest role as an election observer, announced after the 28 November vote that it was refusing to carry on observing in the second presidential round because of the abuses uncovered. The US embassy appealed for it to reconsider and was more outspoken about electoral irregularities than the embassy of any EU state. Jonathan Scheele plaintively called for steps to be taken to ensure that 'the competent institutions' in overseeing the electoral process be allowed to function fully.[81] The assumption that such institutions were competent or balanced was indeed a bold one to make, given the long history of contested elections and poor oversight of them in Romania since 1989.

The European Commission declared on 1 December, through its spokesperson Krisztina Nagy, that no serious problems regarding the conduct of elections had come to its notice and they appeared to have been carried out in an orderly way.[82] Alina Mungiu-Pippidi, then at the centre of moves to prevent serious electoral fraud, has described the lack of encouragement she and other NGO figures received from Dirk Lange, who served as director of negotiations, during the period when the EU showed most indulgence towards the Năstase government:

> The Commission tends to understate all election problems . . . in the 2004 Romanian elections, evidence surfaced of important irregularities, influencing between 1% and 2% of the total vote. While observers from the OSCE Office for Democratic Institutions and Human Rights [a miniscule mission that had been intended only for ceremonial purposes] were becoming increasingly concerned, DG Enlargement replied to issues raised by Romanian NGOs that as long as both political sides infringed regulations, as they had been informed had happened, there was no reason for concern'.[83]

It was pressure mainly from the USA that compelled the government to take steps to diminish possibilities for fraud, and Pro Democraţia decided to carry on its role as an observer. In the 11 December presidential run-off, the government limited the locations where voters outside of their home districts could vote, thereby reducing the likelihood of multiple voting. However, the official US report on 'Human Rights Practices in Romania' for 2004 reported:

> The lack of sufficient alternate locations and the closure of these locations while many voters were still in line resulted in the disenfranchisement of hundreds and possibly thousands of voters, particularly in the major cities. Members of the center-right opposition accused the PSD of intentionally restricting the vote in this manner as transient voters in urban areas have historically supported the center-right. There were credible reports in some precincts that all officials or partisan election monitors instructed citizens on how to vote and [of] instances of posters being placed too close to [voting booths].[84]

Final official results released on 13 December gave Traian Băsescu 51.23% of the vote to Adrian Năstase's 48.77%. Turnout was 55.21%. The margin of victory was very close. Romania has one of the highest usage of mobile phones anywhere in the world and what may have tipped the balance towards the dark-horse challenger in the final hours of voting was the decision of urban voters to text or phone numerous friends urging them to go and cast their votes.

An OSCE team of election observers published an evaluation report of its mission in February 2005 in which it stated that the 28 November election had fallen short of correct standards and it pointedly mentioned that it had never received a convincing explanation from any government source as to why the government had abandoned the use of electoral identification cards.[85] On 28

January 2005, Prime Minister Tăriceanu ordered a parliamentary investigation into the conditions in which the vote had occurred but nothing further was heard of it after part of the centre-right coalition made common cause with the PSD and smaller anti-reform parties after 2005.[86]

There was an unexpected hardening of mood in the corridors of the EU towards Romania as these dramatic political events unfolded. A new set of commissioners was assuming office in Brussels. Olli Rehn, Verheugen's successor as Enlargement Commissioner, would have studied the very thick file on Romania. He would almost certainly have seen the devastatingly frank report produced in the spring of 2004 for the Commission by legal experts about the unwillingness of the Justice Ministry to approach chapter 24 on justice and home affairs in a serious manner. If he had delved even deeper, he would have seen the reports prepared at desk level by dedicated and informed officials who were determined not to conceal the scale of the problems from the commissioner. These 'very straightforward briefings' helped to balance the passive stance coming not just from Verheugen but also Fabrizio Barbaso, a rather ineffectual Director-General for Enlargement. Certainly Rehn, a Finn, would have been aware that Romania was likely to be an issue which dominated much of his period in office. If he simply inherited his predecessor's approach of trusting the Romanians to implement difficult reforms once the country was a full member and enjoyed all the rights exercised by a sovereign state, he was running a serious risk that matters might blow up in his face. If Năstase had won and his legitimacy had been challenged, perhaps on the streets, as happened with Iliescu in 1990, it would have been deeply embarrassing for the EU. In six months' time two devastating defeats for the proposed European Constitution in France and the Netherlands would bring into question the enlargement process across the EU and if the Bucharest authorities continued to mimic reform it could have ended their membership hopes at least for 2007.

On 17 December 2004 the European Council agreed to sign the accession treaty with Romania in April 2005, apparently paving the way for membership by 2007. But there was a snag. Finland had grown alarmed at the state of the Romanian justice system and was not prepared to ratify Romania on the terms just agreed.[87] Its government invested a lot of importance in the success of Rehn's mission. The Helsinki authorities also had a far more realistic assessment of the nature of the post-communist establishment in ill-reformed countries like Romania because they had spent nearly 50 years trying to keep the Soviet Union at bay.

Olli Rehn conceded that accession without meaningful reform had occurred. He openly admitted that at the end of 2004 when he insisted that key chapters, supposedly satisfactorily resolved under his predecessor, be re-opened. His words are worth quoting in full: 'We should learn that the schedule must not supersede the content. Timetables must not force us to conclude negotiations before we are ready to do so'. According to his Finnish interviewer, he 'complained that EU member states offered Romania and Bulgaria dates for entry into the EU while membership talks were still going on, and before the countries were even close to being ready to meet the requirements of membership'.[88]

He insisted that a number of additional reforms be carried out in the course of 2005, particularly in the areas of competition policy and justice, two of the most sensitive and complex policies of the whole EU *acquis*. If, by the spring of 2006, there wasn't significant progress, he warned that 'a safeguard clause' would be invoked, delaying Romania's entry until 2008.[89] Romania was in fact asked to comply with a list of specific and detailed demands, clearly enlisted in the Treaty of Accession,[90] amid the risk of its accession being postponed by a qualified majority vote in the European Council. Bulgaria also faced a post-ponement clause but it was only of a general nature and more difficult to acti-vate because it required the unanimous agreement of all the member states. This was a sign of the much greater esteem that that country still enjoyed in Brussels. Geoană had publicly expressed his exasperation with the Bulgarians for having accepted this condition in June 2004 as entry talks were being finalised, knowing that it would be hard for Romania to resist similar or even tougher safeguards.[91] The tougher conditions imposed on Romania reflected a greater preoccupation of Brussels officials with Romania's status of prepara-tion for EU membership as the balance swung from passive Commission offi-cials to more activist ones prepared to do hard thinking about the disruption an unreformed Romania could cause for the Union.

Conclusion

The EU's re-orientation towards Romania in March 2004 was essentially an image-preserving device adopted after the watering down of conditions for entry led to serious problems which it was impossible to conceal. Little more was heard of it beyond the spring, Commissioner Verheugen failing to report to the European Parliament on what had been accomplished. Its value was rhetorical, meriting comparison with the 1999 Medium-Term Strategy and the 2002 roadmap although these were far less ephemeral initiatives. By the summer of 2004, when the inability of the EU to get the justice system to act concerning the theft of Phare funds made headlines, it was clear that none of the major EU institutions or individuals playing a watchdog role was willing to do anything about it. The more one is able to judge the erratic role Emma Nicholson played in promoting reform, especially since she stepped down as *rapporteur*, the more it seems that it was personal pique that drove her to threaten Adrian Năstase with the suspension of talks once she discovered how the government was flouting her flagship policy on children's protection. Once she stepped down, her attitude was far more accommodating to his successors even when their efforts to sabotage reforms demanded by the Commission were far more audacious than his had ever been.

The link-up between the PSD and the most accommodating parts of the Commission was resumed after the troubled winter of 2003–04. By the summer of 2004, it had become clear that powerful European business interests were an important new set of actors in Romania's accession process. The Commission appeared powerless to act when two major contracts were issued without a tender, thereby exposing its insistence on adherence to fair competition rules to ridicule. But it did not stop Romania receiving the accolade of a functioning market economy, although two years later than Bulgaria. Nor did it affect the increasingly overt support on the European Council for Romania from Germany. The reverse was in fact the case. The long-running alliance between Verheugen, due to become Industry Commissioner for the next five years, and Chancellor Schroeder, with close interest in and ties to the European energy industry, now redounded to the Năstase government's favour. Both of them talked about the need to conclude negotiations before Romania's elections due on 28 November 2004.

The PSD had grown in the estimation of key European power-brokers since 2000 when its return to government, at the start of the integration talks, had been received with gloom. Major governments and key parts of the EU system appeared ready to pay the ethical price for the apparent stability which the PSD had brought to Romania. A change of government was not expected by diplomats and European policy-makers. Nor was it welcomed. Alina Mungiu-Pippidi has written: 'elections and changes of government during the negotiation years were seen as necessary evils, as Commission country teams, especially where negotiations progressed well, had come to have a vested interest in the continuity of the political and bureaucratic elites with whom they had been working closely'.[92]

Ironically, one of the few strong democratic safeguards was the persistent infighting at the top of the PSD which prevented it from becoming a cohesive authoritarian force. Iliescu's visceral dislike of younger figures eclipsing him encouraged the electoral uncertainty which allowed a substitution in office to occur at the end of 2004. By now, a new set of commissioners were settling in who soon felt the need to adopt a less accommodating approach to Romania than there had been in the Verheugen years. The safeguard clause imposed on Romania was unprecedented in its apparent severity. It was a belated recognition that accession without meaningful reform was in danger of occurring, something which would reveal that top commissioners and leading heads of government had failed to uphold wider EU interest in the manner of their engagement with Romania. The engagement was with small strata of

Romanians who mainly came from the old structures which had successfully regrouped in 1989–90 and then tried with a lot of success to adapt to new times. Verheugen rarely mentioned ordinary Romanians in his public pronouncements nor did he avail himself of opportunities to see how it was they who were bearing the overwhelming burden of a poorly planned accession process. Nor was a meaningful partnership established between the EU and pro-European-minded elements in society with skills and commitment that could have improved the quality of the accession process. This reform-minded constituency remained out in the cold and would continue to be there except for a short interlude in 2005–06. The manner in which the EU engaged with Romania during the final year of negotiations revealed the deeply unsatisfactory nature of a Europeanisation process, much of whose content was drained away in order to enable an unreformed Romania to cross the finishing line in the race to 'rejoin Europe'. Bad examples shown by influential European actors suggested that the pre-conditions for membership were surprisingly light. This would encourage a trans-party set of rulers to turn their back on the promises entered into with Brussels after 2007 in the expectation that the response would be as feeble as it had been in 2004.

Notes

1 *Evenimentul Zilei*, 30 January 2004.
2 Interview with Alin Teodorescu, Bucharest, 18 December 2004.
3 Interview with Verheugen, *Jurnalul Naţional* (Bucharest), 24 June 2004.
4 *Evenimentul Zilei*, 6 May 2004.
5 *Evenimentul Zilei*, 6 May 2004.
6 *Evenimentul Zilei*, 18 May 2004.
7 Radio Free Europe/Radio Liberty, *Newsline*, 28 April 2004.
8 See 'Charlemagne: The Looming Disaster', *The Economist*, 22 July 2006.
9 Radio Free Europe/Radio Liberty, *Newsline*, 13 May 2004.
10 *Ziarul de Iaşi*, 11 March 2004.
11 *Evenimentul Zilei*, 6 May 2004.
12 Lucian Branea, Romania_EU_list@yahoo.com, 24 June 2004.
13 *Evenimentul Zilei*, 14 July 2004.
14 *Jurnalul Naţional* (Bucharest), 24 June 2004.
15 *Evenimentul Zilei*, 30 May 2004.
16 *Evenimentul Zilei*, 3 June 2004.
17 See *Evenimentul Zilei*, 3 June 2004.
18 Radu Marinaş, 'State Aid Remains a Hurdle in Romania's EU Drive', *Reuters*, 23 June 2006.
19 Branea, Romania_EU_list@yahoo.com.
20 Interview with Vasile Puşcaş, Bucharest 20 December 2006.
21 *Hotnews*, 10 May 2007.

22 Private information.
23 Interviews in 2006–07 with Commission members based in Brussels and Bucharest.
24 *Adevărul*, 8 November 2004.
25 *Evenimentul Zilei*, 30 January 2004.
26 Radio Free Europe/Radio Liberty, *Newsline*, 6 February 2004.
27 *Evenimentul Zilei*, 22 June 2004.
28 *Evenimentul Zilei*, 22 August 2004.
29 *Adevărul*, 13 August 2004.
30 *Evenimentul Zilei*, 23 January 2003.
31 'Schroeder Sees Romania Closing EU Talks this Year', *Reuters*, 12 August 2004.
32 Răzvan Amariei, 'Creşte preţul integrării euro-atlantice', *Capital*, 9 September 2004.
33 *Ziarul Financiar*, 31 August 2004.
34 See Edward Lucas, *The New Cold War: Putin's Russia and the Threat to the West*, London: Palgrave Macmillan, 2004.
35 *Evenimentul Zilei*, 20 October 2004.
36 'Romanian Opposition Leader Slams French Highway Deal', *Reuters*, 18 October 2004.
37 'Romanian Opposition Leader Slams French Highway Deal'.
38 Radio Free Europe/Radio Liberty, *Newsline*, 20 October 2004.
39 *Evenimentul Zilei*, 26 October 2004.
40 *Evenimentul Zilei*, 6 November 2004.
41 *Evenimentul Zilei*, 6 November 2004.
42 *Evenimentul Zilei*, 3 November 2004.
43 *Evenimentul Zilei*, 23 October 2004.
44 *Revista 22*, 1–7 November 2005.
45 Gelu Trandafir, 'Optimismul lui Verheugen divizează Bruxelles-ul', *Evenimentul Zilei*, 13 November 2004.
46 *Evenimentul Zilei*, 10 March 2004.
47 Private information.
48 *Jurnalul Naţional*, 8 July 2007.
49 The public declarations of wealth made by Năstase and his wife regularly made press headlines. See *Evenimentul Zilei*, 17 May 2005.
50 Interview with Alin Teodorescu, Bucharest, 18 December 2004.
51 *Nine O'Clock*, 29 September 2003.
52 Vlad Macovei, 'Diplomatic Gift for Romania', *Evenimentul Zilei* (English edn), 6 October 2004.
53 '2004 Country Report on Human Rights Practices in Romania', Bureau of Democracy, Human Rights and Labor, Washington DC, 28 February 2005, p. 4.
54 Radio Free Europe, *RFE-RL Newsline*, 23 March 2004.
55 '2004 Country Report on Human Rights Practices in Romania', pp. 4–5.
56 See the Committee to Protect Journalists report, 'Attacks on the Press 2004', www.cpj.org/attacks04/europe04/romania.html; and 'Row Flares over Romanian Press Freedom', *BBC Romanian Service*, 2 October 2004.

57 Adrian Năstase, *Adrian Nastase de la Karl Marx la Coca-Cola: dialog deschis cu Alin Teodorescu*, Bucharest: Editura Nemira, 2004.
58 *Evenimentul Zilei*, 22 November 2004.
59 *Evenimentul Zilei*, 25 November 2006.
60 *Evenimentul Zilei*, 25 November 2004.
61 *Revista 22*, 27 January–2 February 2004.
62 See Tom Gallagher, *The Balkans in the New Millennium*, London: Routledge, 2005, chapter 8.
63 Macovei, 'Diplomatic Gift for Romania'; *Jurnalul Naţional*, 22 December 2004.
64 Interview with official from the European Commission's Justice and Home Affairs Department, Brussels, 5 June 2007.
65 *2004 Regular Report*, p. 21.
66 Interview with official from the European Commission's Justice and Home Affairs Department, Brussels, 5 June 2007.
67 'Draft Report of an Advisory Visit under Chapter 24 in the Fields of Justice and Home Affairs in Romania, p. 84.
68 Radio Free Europe/Radio Liberty, *Newsline*, 4 November 2004.
69 *Evenimentul Zilei*, 13 November 2004.
70 *Cotidianul*, 11 November 2004; *BBC Romanian Service*, 11 November 2004.
71 *Evenimentul Zilei*, 18 November 2004.
72 *Evenimentul Zilei*, 18 November 2004; for Nicholson, *Evenimentul Zilei*, 8 October 2004.
73 Marcin Grajewski, 'EU Unlikely to Conclude Romanian Entry Talks in November', *Reuters*, 23 November 2004.
74 *The Guardian*, 29 April 2004.
75 John Peet, 'The Ins and Outs', *The Economist* (Special report on the European Union), 17 March 2007, p. 15.
76 'Charlemagne: The Looming Disaster', *The Economist*, 22 July 2006.
77 Peet, 'The Ins and Outs', p. 15.
78 Sabina Fati, 'Diversiunea "Occident"', *Evenimentul Zilei*, 27 October 2004.
79 Information contained in this paragraph derived from the following sources: 'Romania: Declaration on Grave Irregularities in the November 28 Presidential and Parliamentary Elections', statement signed by Pro Demcraţia and eight other NGOs monitoring democratic conditions in Romania and sent to embassies and media outlets on 2 December 2004; interview with Cristian Pîrvulescu, President of Pro Democraţia, published on www.euractiv.com on 8 December 2000; Cristian Ghinea, 'Cum rămâne cu frauda', *Dilema Veche*, No. 63, 1–7 April 2005.
80 Radio Free Europe/Radio Liberty, *Newsline*, 31 January 2005.
81 From memory following the electoral controversy in late 2000.
82 *Ziua*, 3 December 2004.
83 Mungiu-Pippidi, 'EU Enlargement and Democracy Progress', pp. 23–4, quoting letter from Dirk Lange sent to her on behalf of DG Enlargement.
84 '2004 Country Report on Human Rights Practices in Romania', p. 7.
85 *Cotidianul* and *Romania Liberă*, 19 February 2005.
86 Radio Free Europe/Radio Liberty, *Newsline*, 31 January 2005.

87 'Romania Denounces Finnish Demands on EU Membership as a Calvinist conspiracy', www.helsinginsanomat.fi/english, 14 December 2004.
88 *Helsingin Sanomat* (international edition, Helsinki), 16 December 2004.
89 Press release of the EU Delegation in Romania, 14 December 2004.
90 These commitments refer to state aid, competition policy, steel restructuring,
control of the EU external border, implementation of the Schengen action plan,
the reform of the justice system, anti-corruption measures, police reform and anti-
crime strategy. Annex IX, *Treaty of Accession of Bulgaria and Romania, Protocol
concerning the Conditions and Arrangements for Admission of the Republic of
Bulgaria and Romania to the European Union*, OJL 157/29, 21 June 2005.
91 *Evenimentul Zilei*, 11 December 2004.
92 Alina Mungiu-Pippidi, 'EU Accession is No "End of History"', *Journal of
Democracy*, Vol. 18, No.4, 2007, p. 15.

8

The EU regains and loses the initiative: 2005–07

On 12 December 2004 the victory of maverick reformer Traian Băsescu over the unpopular Adrian Năstase in the presidential elections was confirmed. Five days later on 17 December 2004 the EU's Council of Ministers agreed to sign the accession treaty with Romania in April, apparently paving the way for membership by 2007. But there was a snag. Finland had grown alarmed at the state of the Romanian justice system and was not prepared to ratify Romania on the terms just agreed.[1] Verheugen's successor as Commissioner for Enlargement, Olli Rehn, was a Finn. His government invested a lot of importance in the success of his mission. The Helsinki authorities had a far more realistic assessment of the nature of the post-communist establishment in ill-reformed countries like Romania because they had spent nearly 50 years trying to keep the Soviet Union at bay.

Through the decisions he took, Olli Rehn, freshly installed as Enlargement Commissioner, openly conceded that accession without meaningful reform had occurred. He insisted that key chapters, supposedly satisfactorily resolved under his predecessor, be re-opened.[2] When he assumed office in late November, the Commission had finalised a common position on justice and home affairs which had been sent to the Council for approval. But it had not yet done so for competition policy. This gave Rehn his opportunity to look again at these two problematic chapters with the support of his government. The Commission came up with a list of additional measures not just for competition policy but also for justice and home affairs. The outgoing Prime Minister Năstase accepted because he feared that negotiations would not be closed. Under the revised terms, if, by the spring of 2006, there wasn't significant progress, 'a postponement clause' would be invoked, delaying Romania's entry until 2008.[3] It would take a majority of member states to invoke this blocking clause in the case of Romania whereas unanimity was required among all 25 EU states before the same could happen with Bulgaria, a sign of the much greater esteem that country still enjoyed in Brussels. In the case of Romania, there were two postponement clauses. One applied by qualified majority voting to specific commitments in the field of justice and home affairs and competition. The other was identical to that applying to Bulgaria.

Commission President Barroso was stern when he met Tăriceanu in Brussels on 24 January 2005. If the country did not make sufficient progress in fighting corruption or meeting EU standards on competition and environmental protection, he warned that he would propose delaying Romania's accession until 2008.[4] He also insisted that Romania should verify whether the lucrative contracts awarded without a tender by the Năstase government in 2004 conformed with EU legislation.[5] Barroso barely hid his lack of enthusiasm for Romania's bid, rarely visiting the country in 2005–06 despite its preparations for entry being one of the key challenges of his Presidency.

The new Minister of Justice, Monica Macovei, was a former human rights lawyer who had frequently collided with the PSD during its years in power. The President was instrumental in securing her appointment. Small parties such as the Romanian Humanist Party (soon to be renamed the Conservative Party) and the UDMR, with their close ties to the oligarchy, were less keen and their open hostility would spread to the National Liberal Party of the Prime Minister once it was clear how far she intended to go in ending the primacy of politics over the justice system. This chapter will aim to show that the EU failed to revive a reformist momentum in Romania after the PSD's unexpected loss of office. The initiative could only have come from it because domestic reformist forces remained weak and failed to command majority support in the non-PSD government. The Commission prioritised reform of the justice system in ways it had conspicuously failed to do previously. Overt support was offered to Monica Macovei during her period as Justice Minister. But there were no contingency plans available when her reforms started to be blocked from within her own government. The different EU entities, Commission, Parliament and Council, operated independently and there was no effort within the multi-layered EU system to offer a united and concentrated response once it became clear how great the obstacles to carrying out necessary reforms remained in Romania. By contrast, parties that previously had been in different camps showed the coherence and resolve lacking in Brussels. They closed ranks to block changes that weakened their hold over the power structures in Romania. The EU continued to be out of its depth in Romania and reacting to events it often failed to anticipate. A resilient group of local political forces, adamantly opposed to seeing the EU's proclaimed vision of a country governed efficiently and fairly ever taking shape, were poised to dictate the pace of change on a very restricted agenda by 1 January 2007, the date when Romania became the 27th member of the EU.

Exactly two years earlier, upon taking office, a comprehensive reform strategy was elaborated by Monica Macovei aimed at enhancing the independence, efficiency, and accountability of the justice system.[6] A National

Anti-Corruption strategy elaborated in early 2005 contained a bold list of measures to achieve this objective. The most important step was the creation of a specialised National Anti-Corruption Department (DNA) within the General Prosecutor's office to replace the PNA. It had been set up in 2002 but had mainly concerned itself with pursuing lower-level corruption cases.[7] Its head, Ioan Amarie, left undisturbed 'the big fish' in politics alleged to be at the centre of high-level corruption. His brother was a parliamentary candidate for the ruling PSD in 2004 and Amarie would depart in July 2005, having failed to carry out his duties in an efficient manner.[8] The US government commented on the significance of this change as follows:

> [New] legislation . . . placed the DNA under the operational authority of the Prosecutor General's office, although it remained operationally independent. This change was made to ensure that the office would have clear constitutional authority to prosecute cases against members of Parliament. The legislation also amended the DNA's jurisdictional limits to cases involving bribes of more than 10 thousand euros or damages over 200 thousand euros, or to certain designated officials whose rank is too high to be prosecuted by the GPO [the General Prosecutor's office]. Ministry of Justice officials noted that this amendment would improve the DNA's performance by focusing its efforts on the most serious cases of corruption, while leaving minor cases under the purview of the General Prosecutor's Office.[9]

As early as 28 February 2005 Rehn expressed his satisfaction with the results starting to be delivered in the justice field. They were widely seen as critical in enabling the European Parliament to approve entry on 13 April 2005 and on the 25th, at a ceremony in Luxembourg, the accession treaty was formally signed by EU leaders and officials from Romania and Bulgaria. Speaking to a plenary session of the EP, Rehn declared on the 12th that 'Romania has started to seriously tackle accession requirements, in particular in the field of justice reform and the fight against corruption'.[10] This was a clear admission of a perceived lack of seriousness on the part of the Bucharest government in previous years. It was difficult to envisage how enough progress could be made in the remaining 21 months after years of simulated change.

But the position appeared to deteriorate in the months to come. In February 2005, Rehn had declared that postponement was 'only a last resort action' and he had told economics students in Bucharest that 'on our part, all the signs are positive for Romania's entry to the EU'.[11] But in June, warning letters were sent to both states outlining the areas in which they were failing to meet accession criteria.[12] In May Neelie Kroos, the Competition Commissioner, had already warned in 'no uncertain terms' while in Bucharest that failure to enforce anti-trust rules, particularly over subsidies for the steel industry, would mean that there was 'no other option than to propose postponement' of entry.[13]

Referendum defeats on the new European Constitution inflicted by two founder members, France and the Netherlands, in May–June 2005, were producing soul-searching not only about further expansion but about maintaining the timetable for Bulgaria and Romania. But nerves steadied. Rising politicians such as Angela Merkel and Nicholas Sarkozy said that the enlargement process ought to continue.[14] The Austrian Chancellor, Wolfgang Schussel did say that postponement for Romania was preferable.[15] But this was very much for internal consumption and when Austria assumed the EU Presidency in January 2006, his attitude towards Romania had grown more positive, keeping in line with the fast-increasing level of Austrian investment in the country. No major state came out in favour of applying the breaks. Prime Minister Tăriceanu returned from the EU Council summit on 17 June to say that Romania's accession had not been placed in question. The Foreign Minister, Mihai Răzvan Ungureanu, even declared that Romania was 'part of the club' (they were both there as observers).[16] Hopes were pinned on Britain, which was assuming the EU Presidency. No other large state was so strongly in favour of enlargement. But many national Parliaments had yet to ratify Romania's accession and Britain could not influence this.

Already, the failure to agree an EU budget for the 2007–13 period had adversely affected the two remaining candidate states. Under the Luxemburg Presidency's compromise arrangement (which was rejected at the stormy summit of June 2005), the allocation of structural funds to Romania and Bulgaria was cut by a quarter. But postponement until 2008 meant that no provision would be made for them in whatever budget was agreed (and one would eventually be finalised at the start of 2006).

The October 2005 annual report on Romania's progress towards accession contained several big surprises. As late as August Commissioner Kroos had been making downbeat statements about lack of progress in eradicating hidden state subsidies and there were real fears that the safeguard clause, concerning violations of the internal market, might be applied in the area of competition.[17] The government's ability to concentrate on reforms had also been affected by an extended period of severe floods and in August a government reshuffle had resulted in the removal of the Finance Minister. But Rehn told the European Parliament that 'Romania has caught up impressively in the fields of justice reform [and] competition policy'.[18] In briefings to journalists his officials stated that they no longer believed Romania was that much behind Bulgaria.[19] But urgent work still needed to be accomplished in the following fields according to the EU: the securing of borders; the struggle against fraud and corruption; improving veterinary and sanitary conditions; making a payments agency for agricultural funds fully functional; strengthening control mechanisms or regional development funds; protecting the rights of intellectual property, and restricting industrial pollution.[20] Immediately after the adoption of the report, the Commission sent warning letters to both countries, drawing attention to the main shortcomings identified and inviting them to take the necessary remedial action.[21]

Prosecutors were increasingly free from the constant political interference which had hampered their work before 2005.[22] Officials from the Justice and Home Affairs Directorate in Brussels soon noticed a change in atmosphere when visiting the Ministry of Justice in 2005–06.[23] There was an air of purposeful activity and the atmosphere was less formal and hierarchical than it had been in PSD times. It wasn't just the minister and her closest advisers who were engaging in discussions about the nature and pace of reforms with visiting EU officials, but other ministry officials were free to take part. Daniel Morar, a young prosecutor from Cluj, galvanised the DNA when he took charge of it in October 2005. In December 2004 Cristian Diaconescu, the outgoing Justice Minister, had said that 40 dossiers on major corruption were being investigated, but Morar had only discovered a handful.[24] Investigations which had been stalled under the DNA's somnolent predecessor got started and soon 22 cases of major corruption were being investigated. In the winter of 2005–06, OLAF, the EU's anti-fraud agency, sent 17 cases of alleged fraudulent use of EU funds to the DNA that involved individuals who had been in government.[25] By early 2006 indictments were starting to be lodged against powerful political figures. There was also now far less chance of top prosecutors being appointed to their posts on a discretionary basis, since criminal cases were allocated to them through a computerised system. The previously high influence of the secret service over the Justice Ministry was also ended in January 2006 when the minister abolished an intelligence unit whose main purpose may well have been to frustrate pro-reform forces in the justice system.[26] The budgetary allocation for justice was doubled in the 2005–06 financial year which allowed for an increase in very low salaries (seen as an incentive for corruption). The World Bank in 2005 loaned Romania $130 million to modernise the justice system, the largest amount it has ever provided anywhere for judicial reform.

There was a dire need for modern court facilities, more ancillary staff and higher salary rates to attract better-qualified judges. But anti-reform elements remained entrenched within the Romanian justice system. In 2005 individuals who had taken legal courses by correspondence were still sometimes found in influential positions. Members of the two main repressive arms of the pre-1989 state, the *Securitate* and the *Miliția*, enjoyed preferential treatment if they wished to become judges since the system took into consideration the years they had spent in military schools.[27] Legal professionals who supported Macovei's reform efforts drew attention to the scale of the challenge being faced when they launched the Society for Justice in August 2005. They identified 'conservative professional oligarchies that lack social responsibility, but are attached to deeply-rooted privileges . . . The general public perception is that the justice system in Romania is marred by clan politics and subverted by nepotism, conflicts of interests, and lack of performance'.[28]

A 2004 survey carried out by the Justice Ministry and NGOs actually confirmed a severe malaise.[29] The accompanying questionnaire received responses from 3,400 judges and magistrates who described a demoralised profession still subordinated to the executive, and with many vulnerable to corruption. Sixteen per cent knew colleagues who decided cases on the basis of whim or, more likely, after pressure from special interests. One of the reasons why foreign investment had remained sluggish despite improving economic growth rates was distrust about the ability of the courts to make swift and reliable decisions in commercial cases. A sign of how far the justice system needed to go before being free of overt political interference was provided by a case in 2004–05 involving Romania's second richest man, Ion Țiriac. His son, also called Ion, was arrested at Bucharest airport in June 2004 and charged with a serious drugs-related offence.[30] President Iliescu asked prosecutors to proceed with care with the case and those who had arrested Ion Jr were later removed from it.[31] In an embarrassing admission, Ion Țiriac declared on 22 February 2005 that if he had asked Iliescu to intervene in favour of his son, the problem would have been resolved in 48 hours maximum: 'we are after all in Romania'.[32] The Prosecutor-General, Ion Botoș, accused Macovei of political interference after she put the original prosecutors back on to the case and ordered that an investigation into an attempted cover-up be made.[33] In the end, the son of the magnate escaped prosecution but it had been a worrying early sign for the elite about how determined Macovei was to dispense with informal arrangements in managing high-profile criminal cases.

One severe obstacle Macovei encountered was the way that the principle of the separation of powers had been applied in Romania shortly before she assumed her office. Until the revised 2003 Constitution strengthened the principle of the separation of powers, the executive effectively controlled the justice system. But before this change came into effect, the Năstase government managed to install trusted allies in key branches of the justice system. Many of them were officials who had entered the legal service in the pre-1989 communist era when selection and promotion were often on ideological grounds. Other appointees had little judicial experience and were favoured because of their closeness to President Iliescu, who had been keen to ensure that many state structures from the communist era were subject only to cosmetic change. Others were compromised figures who could easily be manipulated by the executive.[34]

The Supreme Council of Magistrates, the chief managerial body of the Romanian justice system, oversees the selection, promotion and disciplining of judges and magistrates and their allocation to particular cases. In December

2004, pro-PSD candidates opposed to energetically tacking corruption triumphed, thanks to the pressure senior judges placed on junior colleagues and to the numerical weight of old-guard figures.[35] Here was a clear sign that the PSD, though in opposition since the end of November, was continuing to exercise great influence over the levers of state. Dan Lupaşcu, the head of the CSM (a rotating annual position), did not conceal his opposition to many of Macovei's changes. There were stormy meetings of the CSM at which they confronted one another in 2005. The Minister was intent on introducing changes which would lead to the retirement of judges and magistrates on grounds of age or owing to professional shortcomings. New measures were also drawn up for appointing judges to the High Court of Cassation and Justice (formerly the Supreme Court, to which all courts are answerable), ones with which the CSM was clearly unhappy as it sought to make selections under the previous system.[36] The CSM conservatives got unexpected assistance from an adviser from Germany who had been seconded to the Justice Ministry under a Phare twinning project to improve the quality of justice in Romania. Dieter Schlafen, a retired judge, urged the CSM to refuse discussions with Macovei on her proposals to reform the judiciary. He believed they violated the Constitution and even breached chapter 24 on justice negotiated with the EU.[37] The Constitutional Court endorsed his position in July and the Minister had to reformulate her proposals. This was embarrassing for the EU Delegation in Bucharest, which issued a terse statement on 12 May 2005, stating that Schlafen was not an EU official and that his opinions were his own and could not be considered to belong to the European Commission or its Delegation in Romania. Yet twinning was a key instrument to ensure that blockages in the path of reform were removed and here was an EU adviser, in a very sensitive position, who had in effect gone native, siding with legal conservatives with whom he had built up a close working relationship, even influencing the drafts of new regulations in place before Macovei's arrival. Even worse, the only person who could withdraw Schlafen, the German ambassador Wilfried Gruber, refused to do so for reasons that have never been satisfactorily explained (much to the discomfiture of the Delegation). But after the October 2005 progress report the Justice Minister was able to rely on increasingly overt backing for her proposed changes. Franco Frattini, the Vice-President of the European Commission, became a strong champion. On 1 December 2005, Christopher Dashwood, the official from Rehn's directorate most concerned with justice and home affairs, spoke in Brussels about the concern in the Commission about the CSM's obduracy. With Macovei by his side, he declared that it was doing harm to Romania being able to fulfil its entry timetable and he called for a more cooperative approach from the CSM.[38]

It was very rare indeed for the Commission to become so publicly involved in a power struggle between such high-placed rivals in a candidate member.

Perhaps it was a recognition not just of the value of her proposed reforms for preserving the EU's already battered reputation in Romania, but an acknowledgement that Macovei was herself increasingly isolated in Bucharest. She belonged to no political party and as long as the forces of civil society were reluctant to become actively involved in competitive politics, she lacked strong allies in politics, excepting President Băsescu whose strength would be eroded in 2006–07.

In the preliminary conclusions prepared for the draft 2005 monitoring report on Romania, recognition was shown of how weak was the momentum behind reform: 'The situation in the justice area remains *fragile* since the many positive developments which have taken place in the past nine months are to be attributed mainly to the *personal commitment of Minister Macovei*. There remains resistance within the [justice] system because . . . some parts . . . continue to serve "other interests"'.[39]

A large trans-party group of parliamentarians (including members of the ruling coalition) viewed Macovei with mounting hostility because of the radical way they felt she was interpreting her mandate on judicial reform. Twice, in 2005 and 2006, crucial justice sector reforms would be overturned in Parliament because government deputies refused to turn up in support. After the second occasion, Frattini felt it necessary to warn Parliament as a whole: 'You are absolutely crazy to play with the future and the accession of your country'.[40]

The origins of the crisis go back to clumsy attempts by Tăriceanu in 2005 to ensure that the President and Macovei showed an understanding attitude to the troubles of Patriciu following his indictment on major corruption charges.[41] In January 2007 Băsescu made public the content of a memo from Tăriceanu which his supporters claimed amounted to a request that the President intervene with the prosecutors investigating Dinu Patriciu's operations in the energy sector.[42] The alliance between both men and their parties had rapidly foundered after the Prime Minister refused to hold early elections once the Constitutional Court had blocked an important part of Macovei's reform package. He cited unhappiness in Brussels at the prospect of months of electioneering delaying preparations for entry.[43] Such strong feelings do not appear to have existed in Brussels but the Commission allowed itself to be manipulated by Tăriceanu by remaining silent and not openly contradicting him. Many in the EU were impressed by Tăriceanu's serious demeanour and businesslike approach to government. Commission documents tended to refer to him in a more positive light than Băsescu, whose informal style clearly grated on some Commission members as well as local advisers in the Delegation who were analysing developments in Romanian politics for them.[44] Thus, the minutes of the meeting which took place in Brussels on 18 July 2005 between Vice-President Frattini and Tăriceanu began by emphasising in bold letters: 'Very friendly meeting with a lot of outspoken support of the VP towards PM Tăriceanu'.[45]

Tariçeanu continued to tend business interests. His car-dealership made a profit of 2.9 million euros in 2006, about 30 times greater than the one registered in 2004 (*Hotnews*, 11 September 2007). Enforcing the competition rules for this industry as a whole was a regular headache for the Commission. He openly defended his business ally, Dinu Patriçiu, after he was detained for questioning in May 2005 concerning alleged irregularities in the post-privatisation activities of an oil-refining company, Petromidia, which he had bought from the state on very good terms.[46] He was already under investigation for tax evasion and money-laundering, to which was added a charge of manipulating the stock exchange.[47] In November 2005, Tăriceanu openly stated that the detention of Patriçiu had been carried out in an 'abusive manner', criticising the state agency responsible. This was no idle matter since shortly beforehand Patriçiu had launched a multi-million dollar law suit in Washington against the Romanian state for actions which damaged the financial standing of the Rompetrol group which he headed.[48] The backing of the Prime Minister was bound to weigh heavily in the minds of any jury eventually hearing a case brought against the state he was in charge of. Tăriceanu's intervention on behalf of the country's best-known entrepreneur, extraordinary in terms of European governance, was not the only one that he made in 2005. In the same year, he summoned Macovei to government headquarters in order for her to suddenly be confronted with Patriçiu, then already under investigation by the justice authorities, a meeting which she refused to take part in. On two other occasions, he telephoned the Prosecutor-General, Ilie Botoş, to request information on the Rompetrol case.[49] By taking steps which in the eyes of many analysts questioned his impartiality in a crucial law case that had enormous bearing on the economic future of the country, he may have 'subordinated the government and the magistrate's independence to the friendship with the head of Rompetrol'. These are the words of the well-known Bucharest commentator Ioana Lupea, who went on to write that: 'The latter's influence on the head of the Executive is so huge that [it] risks deforming the public policy of the central administration and hinder[ing] democracy'.[50]

Moderate Liberals opposed to the influence of Dinu Patriçiu over the PNL were driven out of the party by Tăriceanu in the autumn of 2006. They included his two predecessors as party leader, Theodor Stolojan and Valeriu Stoica. The dissidents formed a Party of Liberal Democracy in December 2006 which they claimed was the true inheritor of the Liberal mantle. After getting 8% of the vote in the European elections of November 2007, only 5% behind what Tăriceanu's party had obtained, the PLD merged in the following month with the PD, the new party calling itself the Democratic Party–Liberals.

The PSD remained the largest party during the life of the 2004–08 Parliament. It controlled the flow of parliamentary business by virtue of having the Presidency of the Senate and Chamber of Deputies. When it lodged a censure motion in June 2005 against a package of judicial reforms, Jonathan Scheele, the head of the EU Delegation, expressed open criticism, saying it would be regrettable if Parliament voted them down. He went further and said that Romania's accession chances might be affected, the motion being narrowly defeated.[51] Such outspoken language from him was unusual. So perhaps was the decision of Frattini to ignore several letters sent to him by Adrian Năstase in the summer of 2005. In them he wrote about 'the brutal pressure of the executive' to modify laws which he believed meant 'the elimination of fundamental guarantees of independence for the justice system'. He even compared President Băsescu with the Italian dictator Mussolini.[52]

It was Olli Rehn, not Frattini, who offered a substantial (as opposed to pro-forma) reply to Năstase in July 2005, saying that the laws he had taken exception to had only been tabled after an intensive process of consultation with judges and prosecutors during which significant modifications had occurred.[53] In what perhaps was meant to be seen as an indirect reply to Năstase, Frattini declared in October 2005 that having been pessimistic about what could be done to accelerate the judicial reform process at the end of 2004, he and his Commission colleagues were fully satisfied by what had been achieved in the past nine months.[54]

At the end of December 2005, Năstase phoned the Commission, requesting to speak with Frattini. He was unhappy at the way that the government side were characterising the PSD's record on reform when it had been in power. Perhaps the ex-Prime Minister assumed that because of the weight of influence the PSD still enjoyed in the power structure, Frattini was bound to speak to him and perhaps ensure that the Commission in its future reports on reform gave the efforts of his government due consideration, but he failed in this attempt to speak to the Commission Vice-President.[55]

But the PSD was able to rely on an understanding attitude from another important player in the EU system, the largest political grouping in the EP, the Socialists. In October 2005, a clear warning was delivered from them to the government that if it adopted an unduly partisan attitude towards the PSD, then there was a risk of the Socialists withholding their support for Romanian entry.[56] These views were expressed by Pierre Moscovici, the EP's *rapporteur* for Romania since the end of 2004. He and his colleagues were unhappy at renewed government efforts to replace Năstase as head of the Chamber of Deputies. His Brussels allies stood by him and his party as they both entered a period of crisis in 2005–06. Poul-Nyrup Rasmussen, the former Danish Prime Minister who headed the Socialist grouping, consistently brushed aside the record of authoritarianism and corruption which had dogged the PSD while in office. After his defeat, Rasmussen declared in December 2004: 'Our friend and colleague Adrian Năstase has done so much for Romania, in particular in guiding the country towards EU membership'.[57] On a visit to Romania in July 2005, he was encouraged to see signs that 'the PSD . . . has embraced social democracy and is transforming into a modern politic party'.[58] He attacked the new authorities for 'trying to control the justice system' and for a witch-hunt against local officials (even though President Băsescu had decided not to exercise his prerogative and had left county council chiefs appointed in 2004 in place).[59] To the mounting chagrin of the European Commission, the Socialists in the EP refused to publicly back justice sector reforms and urge the PSD to withdraw its opposition to them. This led to the anomaly whereby Moscovici in regular reports that he submitted to Parliament declared that Romania was doing enough to merit entry but refused to try to diminish parliamentary opposition to justice sector reforms from his fraternal party, the PSD. It was the first indication that the European party groupings, instead of being a restraining influence on new members from countries where politics remained polarised, would instead actively take sides in their quarrels even if by doing so reforms were jeopardised.

The EU was due to decide in May 2006 whether 2007 would be the entry date for Romania. Over the winter of 2005–06, the Commission required tangible evidence that the momentum behind reforms was high. Calls from European officials were heard that a few 'big fish' must be made an example of, such as prominent tax-evaders, big bribe-takers and figures who had looted the state. Upon becoming head of the DNA, Daniel Morar had said that it might be possible to finalise between five and seven dossiers involving high- or medium-level corruption by February 2006.[60] But under Romanian legislation the balance of proof is on the state to show that someone offered or gave a bribe, or acquired money by irregular means. In fact it has been harmonised to fit in with the norm in EU states. The danger existed that under EU pressure for quick results, elementary mistakes would be made by investigators, leading to the collapse of cases against figures widely regarded as the chief beneficiaries of corruption. Monica Macovei was indeed aware of how real this danger was.[61] The Austrian ambassador, Christian Zeleissen spelled it out in early 2006: 'If there is to be a correct reform of the justice system, you must . . . build up a dossier, construct cases, make investigations, and, on this basis, proceedings can be launched. But you cannot fix a deadline in a few months'.[62]

Nevertheless, a series of criminal investigations was launched against well-known politicians early in 2006. Dan Ioan Popescu, Minister of Industry in Năstase's 2000–04 government, was soon facing trial for failing to explain the origins of assets worth 1.25 million euros. George Copos, a member of the Conservative Party (PC) and a deputy-premier in the coalition, found himself under investigation for a suspect transaction between one of his companies and the national lottery. The biggest headlines were reserved for Adrian Năstase and his wife, who were formally charged with corruption offences on 7 February. The DNA had been investigating a claim in his declaration of assets to Parliament that both of them had inherited cash of US$350,000 and considerable property thanks to the financial wizardry of an aunt who had successfully invested in the Bucharest property market before her death, aged 97, in 2005. The revelations led to his resignation as a president of the PSD in January but he hung on as speaker of the Chamber of Deputies until 15 March, when a revolt in his own party forced him out. Quinton Quayle, the outgoing British ambassador, was quoted as saying: 'How is it possible for politicians to be un-corrupt while their relatives become very rich without explanation'? [63]

In the autumn of 2005 Quayle had expressed his shock that nobody had been condemned for one case of serious corruption in Romania.[64] But Parliament did not share his concern. On 13 February 2006, a cross-party committee showed solidarity with Năstase by rejecting a request from the DNA that some of his properties be searched. He eventually acceded to the request voluntarily. This event revealed that the 2003 constitutional change requested by Brussels to ensure that parliamentarians no longer be able to thwart corruption investigations into their own colleagues was inadequate. A full plenary vote was still required before a search warrant could be allowed. The 2006 peer review on justice issues dawn up for the Commission commented that 'the regulations of the Chamber of Deputies concerning immunity seem to be tailor-made to strangle every corruption investigation at birth'.[65] This was just one example of the EU's tendency to promote a law without ensuring that its content and the way it was applied actually fulfilled the purpose that had been intended.

On 9 February 2006 the absence of many pro-government deputies ensured that a bill giving the DNA permanent legal status was voted down. This was the first sign of how widely the trans-party coalition against reform extended. Macovei visited Brussels one week later to inform Frattini about this problem. Frattini was in Romania a month later and he broke away from a ski-ing holiday to visit Bucharest on 13 March and appeal for a more public-spirited attitude towards EU obligations from Parliament.[66] On this occasion he declared that 'a great part of the success' in Romania improving its credibility in the eyes of the EU was owing to her.[67] But a member of the Commission who had served in many different positions remarked later that 'when we strongly took the side of an individual in the policy-making process, we paid the bill afterwards. The outcome usually depended not on the qualities of the individual but on the constellation of political forces'.[68]

It is not clear whether by now, inside the Commission, second thoughts were occurring about the opposition Brussels had shown towards early elections in 2006. The government had a wafer-thin majority and that existed only by including the PC and UDMR, which had previously been aligned with the Năstase government. Băsescu's popularity suggested that if elections had been called in 2005, the Truth and Justice Alliance of his PD and Prime Minister Tăriceanu's PNL was highly likely to obtain an outright majority. The Commission offered conflicting views on the issue. At one stage Jonathan Scheele had emphasised the consumption of time and energy spent in campaigning which the government could not afford to lose.[69] In July 2005, without being contradicted, Prime Minister Tăriceanu cited the EU's unhappiness with early elections as his reason for going back on an agreement with the President to dissolve Parliament after the Constitutional Court had rejected important justice reforms.[70]

From then on, it became steadily more apparent that Tăriceanu's position on reform increasingly resembled that of the parties in the opposition camp. There was intense manoeuvring to delay unpalatable reforms designed to clean up the profession of politics. He paid lip-service to Macovei's reforms in public but in cabinet the two were often at loggerheads. She spoke out about state contracts being awarded to particular firms without a tender.[71] She opposed ordinances suspending the application of the insolvency law to a range of companies for six months. It was believed that this would enable their owners to sell the assets to their friends. (The government appeared to be emulating its predecessor which in 2004 had been criticised for drawing up a plan to wipe out the debts of 72 state companies.[72]) Not long after receiving the award of 'European woman of the year' from the EP for promoting democratic values, Macovei revealed that at a cabinet meeting in January 2007, she has said to her colleagues: 'This is a corrupt government'. The Prime Minister's only response was to say: 'Good, let's now move on to the next business'.[73] Two months later, he sacked her.

Proposed greater regulation over state finances whose availability to business clients of the ruling party had launched many a fortune had already sharpened hesitation in some business circles about early EU entry. Dinu Patriciu, the oil magnate, increasingly seen as the controller of the Liberals, had placed on record in 2004 his preference for Romania joining at the latest possible date in the EU timetable.[74] This view was shared by Dan Voiculescu, leader of the Conservatives, and Ion Țiriac, a close ally of the PSD.[75] The EU does not appear to have stood back and asked how committed were the ruling Liberals to its reform package given increasing signs of backsliding. Until the spring of 2007, the Commission appeared to prefer the explanation that the differences which paralysed the government sprang mainly from a personality clash between the Prime Minister and President and their respective cabinet supporters.

EU satisfaction with the direction Romania was heading in, despite the increasing isolation of Macovei, its main agent of reform, was reflected in very upbeat statements by Olli Rehn in the early spring of 2006. At the end of

March, he predicted that in May the Commission would make its final decision on the date of entry – 2007 or 2008.[76] On 3 April, he presented a broadly favourable report on Romania and Bulgaria to the foreign affairs committee of the EP. He went as far as to say that 'Romania has practically completed justice reform and has accomplished the first preliminary results in the struggle against corruption . . . It is the first time in the post-communist history of the country when a signal has been given to Romanian society that nobody is more precious than the law'.[77] It was surely a striking admission by an official of his rank that such progress had only been reached within weeks of the country's entry date being finalised.

Rehn was still sounding positive at the end of April 2006 upon being asked by Elmer Brok, head of the foreign affairs committee of the EP, if the period until the end of the year was long enough to ensure that the *acquis* was applied. Referring to justice reform, the struggle against corruption and organised crime, Rehn told the EP that 'both countries have shown evidence of firmness in adopting the necessary reforms'.[78] Emma Nicholson backed him up: 'Successive governments in Romania and Bulgaria have made superhuman efforts to conform with the recommendations of the EU. These efforts aren't easy to see from the outside; it's a question of structural and economic reforms which are not of interest to the mass media'.[79]

But contrary to expectations, on 16 May 2006 the Commission failed to issue a specific date on when both Romania and Bulgaria would join. Unexpected problems had arisen concerning the operation of the justice system in Bulgaria which appeared too serious to ignore. Commission spokesmen denied there had been divergences between them, but the media reported that Frattini had been in favour of offering Romania and Bulgaria a definite entry date but Rehn was now stalling, which meant a decision would be delayed until the autumn.[80] In March, Michael Leigh, from the European Enlargement Department, had said: 'Each country must be judged by its proper merits and not through comparison'.[81] But this was not a true reflection of the situation. As before, difficulties which one candidate encountered impacted on the other. In the past Bulgarians had been annoyed to find that they might be penalised for Romanian shortcomings with entry being postponed until 2008. But the Tăriceanu government reacted with equanimity to the news of yet another delay. Coalition disputes increasingly dominated its life, which meant that entry preparations were not as big a priority as the official rhetoric suggested or Baroness Nicholson hoped. The Finnish Commissioner was aware that Frattini's wishes could probably only have been met if Romania had been decoupled from Bulgaria. Outrage might have greeted any decision to admit Bulgaria given the deplorable state of the justice system. Commission President Barroso declared on 9 May: 'We have to be very credible. I will never say all the conditions are met if all the conditions are not met'.[82]

Barroso hoped that reforms to address outstanding problems, the main one being the crisis of the justice system in Bulgaria, could be implemented 'in three, four [or] five months'.[83] But this was an incredibly rosy view, given that the depth of the problems in the justice system had somehow remained hidden from the view of the EU for the past seven years. In that period, ruthless mafia gangs had carried out hundreds of contract killings, not one of these murders having been successfully resolved.[84] A report carried out for the EU by Klaus Jansen, a German justice official, and released in April painted a shocking picture. He concluded that Bulgarian efforts to tackle organised crime were a total mess and he stated openly that the EU had made a serious mistake in 2004 when it guaranteed that Bulgaria could join by 2008 even if it failed to meet the reform targets.[85] Josep Borrell, the President of the European Parliament, had already criticised the fact that a poorly performing candidate could only be kept out for one year. He remarked in March 2006 that 'it is like saying to a student that he cannot pass his exams now but in one year's time, it will be an automatic pass. Do you think the student will study all the year? Of course not, he will immediately go on holiday'.[86] This appeared to be the Bulgarian attitude from President Georgi Parvanov down. He declared in April 2006 that the European Commission lacked complete information.[87] Roumen Petkov, the Interior Minister, deemed Jansen an 'incompetent' who exaggerated the significance of the problem.[88] But according to Jansen, the Bulgarians 'believed they would get into the EU anyway and I encountered a "kiss my ass" attitude'.[89] He claimed that Bulgarian officials refused to release information to him even on routine matters, insisting that state secrets were involved. His report coincided with another produced for the European Commission by Suzette Schuster, a German judge, which discovered 'open nepotism' in the appointment of judges and characterised judicial reforms as 'chaotic'.[90]

Brussels had not expected that its seven-year engagement with Bulgaria would end in this way. The justice and home affairs chapter had been successfully closed in 2004. The degree of confidence invested in Bulgaria was so high that in 2004 the EU accepted that only the agreement of all 25 states was required before its entry could be postponed. Such solidarity was unlikely, however grim the law-and-order picture, so Bulgarian officials could afford to be confident about entry. This *debacle* raised obvious questions about how well informed EU officials in the Directorates for enlargement really were about conditions in both countries. There appeared a need for last-minute damage limitation efforts and on 16 May it was announced that a decision on the entry date for both states was being postponed until October. Further work on the *acquis* would need to be done. But it was only two weeks later that the Commission put together a list of exact measures Romania and Bulgaria had to carry out before October in order for approval to be certain. They were of course described as 'urgent'.[91] Olli Rehn then used language frequently employed by his predecessor Verheugen whenever there had been blockages on the road to reform: Romania and Bulgaria 'need to make the final effort and go the last mile . . . it is our duty as the guardians of the treaties to ensure that once they join, they really meet our conditions'.[92] But how could such obvious improvisation ensure a qualitative advance in the system of law enforcement, particularly the struggle against organised crime and corruption in high places? To shield longstanding EU states from the negative effects of the entry of both states a range of palliatives were proposed in the spring of 2006. Particularly from Germany there were calls to deny them full membership rights in areas where their standards clearly hadn't improved substantially.[93] Bulgaria would be the main target. It could be excluded from EU legal cooperation and its court judgments would not be recognised by the Union. 'These are the toughest safeguard measures yet, this is something new', one EU official declared in the autumn of 2006. But time would quickly show just how little substance lay behind such a bold claim.[94]

Martin Schulz, head of the German Social Democratic group in the EP, said that 'the stability of a country should in future be a prerequisite for its admission, and no longer an aim'.[95] But supporters of Romania, also mainly on the European Left, believed that the EU must display a leap of faith. Angel Martinez, the Spanish socialist MEP, declared: 'problems remain that can be best resolved inside the EU'.[96] Pierre Moscovici, the EU *rapporteur* since 2005, argued that 'the country has evolved impressively since the dictatorship of Ceauşescu' and that the Commission had been 'too prudent'.[97] But there were doubters scattered across the European political spectrum. Fritz Bolkestein, the outgoing Dutch Competition Commissioner, had declared in December 2004 that Romanian accession was 'based on nothing. But the Romanian diplomacy is so persistent that our ministers buckle under'. In the same interview, he declared that the Council of the European Union was the 'worst performing institution in Europe'.[98] Daniel Cohn-Bendit of the Greens declared sombrely that 'what we are doing now for Romania and Bulgaria will cause us to pay a much higher price in the future'.[99] Most outspoken of all was Roman Herzog, President of Germany from 1994 to 1999, who declared in May 2006 that the accession of the two states was 'a scandal and immense farce', given how far they lagged behind existing members.[100]

During 2006, there was mounting evidence of the failure of the political elite to put aside its internecine quarrels. The lack of coordination inside the government between ministers from the now rival PNL and PD parties meant there was a serious neglect of the administrative reforms and economic restructuring needed to ensure that Romania entered the EU minimally prepared for the enormous challenges that lay ahead. Governmental infighting continued to be matched by opposition obstruction of reforms strongly promoted by Brussels.

Back in Bucharest at the start of August 2006, Frattini expressed his concern about backsliding in the area of justice reform. The CSM, the chief managerial body in the justice system, drew up plans for revoking the prosecutor-general which Brussels considered weakened the office-holder's role as an agent of reform.[101] Since July 2005, there had been a new incumbent, Laura Codruța Kovesi, who was a committed backer of Macovei's reforms, unlike her predecessor, a holdover from the Năstase era. Frattini also discovered opposition inside the coalition to a law allowing the assets of parliamentarians and other elite figures to be closely scrutinised by a body called the National Integrity Agency (ANI). A hundred thousand public officials and elected politicians would have to disclose the extent and origins of their wealth and allow the ANI to access the accuracy of their submissions.

Firm resistance to this law came from the UDMR and the PC, which struck out clauses they were unhappy with in Parliament on 6 September 2006. They and others sought to amend ANI in order to render it 'useless and ineffective', according to the author of the 2006 justice peer review.[102] Two days later, Commissioners Rehn and Frattini wrote directly to both their leaders, asking them not to dilute the law. One particularly pointed passage read: 'we have considerable cause for concern regarding the commitment of all political actors in Romania to combating high-level corruption in a committed, sustained, and irreversible way'.[103] According to the legal expert, it was part of a deliberate strategy of defying commitments made to the EU by simply rejecting the proposals (from Macovei), or by amending the draft-legislation 'in such a way as to render it basically useless in the fight against corruption'.[104]

Bela Marko, the leader of the Hungarian party, the UDMR replied to Frattini, indicating that he would only support the measure if the Commission swung behind a law strengthening the level of autonomy enjoyed by Hungarians. Tăriceanu refused to treat the UDMR's defiance of a key aspect of the Commission strategy as an issue meriting its dismissal from the government. He would expel the PD from the coalition seven months later because it merely objected to the continued postponement of European elections. These were bound to show how unpopular his party was (which was confirmed when they were eventually held in November 2007). The removal of the PC and the UDMR would have swiftly ended the life of the coalition and most likely have led to early elections. This was an outcome Tăriceanu was determined to avoid at all costs. Hanging on to office, mimicking reform, neutralising Băsescu and eventually mounting a determined effort to roll back Macovei's justice reforms became his overriding objectives.

Here was accumulating evidence that the dominant elements in the coalition had scant commitment to reform and that they were determined to link up with the PSD and even the ultra-nationalist PRM to foil unwelcome change. Government deputies (from all the parties except Băsescu's

Democrats) would continue to block the ANI until Romania had joined the EU. Macovei believed that an agency able to monitor the wealth of the elite was indispensable if the justice reforms were to be 'irreversible'.[105] But it was hard to see how that irreversibility could be guaranteed when most of the parties had revealed themselves to be hostile to those reforms that challenged their ability to accumulate wealth from politics. Opposition was also still entrenched in parts of the justice system (though in 2005–06 nearly one-third of judges had retired, many spurred on by new legislation which required them to declare their assets and income on the internet). Macovei was clearly pinning her hopes on a new generation of judges and prosecutors emerging that lacked compromising ties with businessmen and politicians whose fortunes derived from diverting state resources to their own hands. But the CSM was already showing signs of allying with 'rent-seeking elites unwilling to undermine the sources of their domestic power by introducing accountability and transparency in policy-making'.[106]

The European Commission, in its 26 September 2006 monitoring report on Romania, admitted that 'ensuring the sustainability and irreversibility of the recent progress in serious non-partisan investigations into high-level corruption' would be a major challenge. Nevertheless, it referred to 'solid progress' achieved by both countries and considered that they 'will be in a position to take on the rights and obligations of EU membership on 1 January 2007'.[107]

This was a strikingly optimistic assumption given that the 2006 peer review had stated that efforts to reform the judiciary and bring high-level corruption under control 'are isolated and that the progress made is far from irreversible'. It went on to say that 'Romania has failed to deliver on several strategic EU commitments made under the Anti-Corruption Strategy . . . and it is no coincidence this failure concerns the most sensitive aspects of the anti-corruption package (financing of political parties, incompatibilities, conflicts of interest, integrity)'.[108]

It is not clear how much of this sobering view was conveyed by Olli Rehn to deputies in the German Bundestag on 18 October 2006.[109] Along with Denmark, Germany was by now the only EU member still to ratify the treaty. But it ratified the treaty, presumably having been given a sanitised view of Romania's likely impact on the rest of the EU once it became a full member.

Safeguard measures were imposed for Romania and Bulgaria in the area of food safety. The relevant clause allowed the Commission to block exports to the EU of products falling below the veterinary, health and safety standards of the rest of the Union. Mechanisms were also set up for cooperation and verification of progress in judicial reform, the fight against corruption and organised crime. The European Council would consider bi-annual reports on progress made in the justice sector after entry and if problems persisted both countries could be denied full membership rights in the justice and home affairs *acquis*. The Commission demanded continuous efforts in seeing high-level corruption cases through to their conclusion, the introduction of measures to curb corruption at local level, and efforts to ensure the account-ability of the CSM by addressing the question of conflict of interest of some of its members.[110] The ANI was also highlighted as a priority. But the speed and depth of post-entry reform very much depended on the interest which the Commission continued to take in Romania. There was a temptation to walk away from the problem, having absorbed the appropriate lesson of only to take on new members where the commitment to reform was clearcut. Besides, as a full member state Romania would no longer be a supplicant and would enjoy full sovereign rights *vis a vis* the Commission. Therefore, it would be even harder to ensure that its behaviour met the standards contained in the EU treaties. Only a single-minded approach by the Commission could hope to get an unruly Bucharest elite to honour its obligations and such an approach had usually been conspicuous by its absence when Brussels had far more power over Romania. Elmer Brok, the Chairman of the EP's foreign affairs commit-tee, argued in the spring of 2006 that if they fell below EU standards in their behaviour, the voting rights of both new members on EU decisions could be reduced and they could be temporarily excluded from EU ancillary organisa-tions.[111] A sound insurance policy might have been to link compliance in the field of justice reform and anti-corruption efforts with the release of EU struc-tural funds. Such a safeguard might have protected existing member states from the negative effects of membership of countries where corruption was so pervasive. But Rehn's department either failed to advise such tough measures or else backing for them was lacking from within the EU.

Conclusion

Olli Rehn declared on 18 January 2005, in his first major speech devoted to Romanian accession, that 'The new Prime Minister has made EU integration its [the government's] central priority'. But it was difficult to maintain such a rosy attitude once it became clear that Monica Macovei was one of the few champions of reform in the government. Her proposals for trying to ensure that the justice system was commensurate with EU standards enjoyed the backing of President Băsescu but with Prime Minister Tăriceanu increasingly offering only nominal backing for them.

The EU failed to pay close enough attention to the worsening political situa-tion and to come to an assessment of whether there was in fact enough genuine will in the government to carry out reforms. Romania was still on course for entry in 2007 once it had become apparent that an important political rea-lignment had occurred which threatened to crush prospects for meaningful institutional reform. In the course of 2006, differences between opposition and coalition parties (excepting the PD) had dissolved behind a common aim of ousting Macovei, and indeed Băsescu himself if that could be accomplished. Interestingly, the European Council failed to back Băsescu in the way Macovei had been supported by the Commission. Only Great Britain invited him for bilateral talks at the start of his Presidency (a gesture emulated by the USA in July 2006). Barroso, the President of the Commission, never used the weight of his office to urge a greater commitment by the Tăriceanu government to the reforms it had undertaken to accomplish. He usually spoke in bland terms when the situation in Romania grew too difficult even for him to ignore.

If those at the top of the Commission had regarded Romania as a test-case for enlargement rather than an inconvenient problem to be got out of the way as expeditiously as possible, then the EU might have subjected Romanian enlargement to a searching review. This would have involved asking whether the Superior Council of Magistrates could have been trusted to manage the justice system. Commission statements in 2005–06 revealed intense dissatis-faction about its commitment to reform. But there was no appetite for going back to the drawing-board and recommending a management structure less prone to manipulation by the political oligarchy. This might have involved a referendum and a full-scale constitutional crisis. The EU had not relished early elections in 2005 even though there was a strong chance that a majority in favour of comprehensive reforms would have resulted.[112]

It was probably a strategic error on the part of Monica Macovei to assume that many of her reforms were irreversible. This proved not to be the case. If she had urged the Commission to embark on a radical re-think, it might have obliged leading Eurocrats to treat Romania as a far more pressing concern. But she had too much faith in the EU's transformative power whereas most of the Bucharest elite was confident that its impact could be evaded by a combina-tion of subterfuge and brazen defiance. She would have been aware of the deep aversion to using the mechanism which allowed Romania's admission to be postponed until 2008. A simple majority of members was required to institute such a delay. Unanimity would have been required to revoke the treaty signed in 2005 and that would have been highly unlikely.

Taking such steps would only have drawn attention to the often hurried and low-grade approach of the EU to Romania. The EU was even less willing than most major states to hold an unavoidably painful inquest into where an ambi-tious but poorly thought-out policy had gone wrong. Parliament did not have strong inquisitorial powers and the different parliamentary groupings were starting to emerge as lobbies for different factions in Romania as they sought to boost their membership aware that Romania would have 35 seats.

The EU had no plan B for Romania if its attempt to integrate the country based on the formula adopted for previous entrants failed to work. But it was already clear to some Western European politicians and at least one senior ex-Commissioner that the existing roadmap was inadequate in the face of the challenges posed by a country with problems as deep-seated as Romania's. The multi-layered EU system appeared paralysed by Romania. The EU proved to be out of its depth, reacting to events it often failed to anticipate. By contrast, it was a trans-party political elite deriving from pre-1989 structures which possessed a coherent vision of what it wanted – opportunities for entrenching its networks of wealth and power by being at the heart of the world's most successful regional trading bloc, one that even dreamt of becoming a European political and economic union. The mishandling of Romania suggested that immense obstacles lay in the way of this grandiose dream being realised.

Notes

1 'Romania Denounces Finnish Demands on EU Membership as a Calvinist Conspiracy'.
2 *Helsingin Sanomat* (international edition), 16 December 2004.
3 Press release of the EU Delegation in Romania, 14 December 2004. The media usually refers to the 'safeguard clause', which actually refers to something else in the treaty of accession.
4 Radio Free Europe/Radio Liberty, *Newsline*, 26 January 2005.
5 Radio Free Europe/Radio Liberty, *Newsline*, 26 January 2005.
6 Lara Scarpitta, 'The Myth of Compliance: EU–Romania Relations 2004–2007', paper presented at the EUSA tenth Biannual International Conference, Montreal, Canada, 17–19 May 2007, p. 2.
7 See *2004 Regular Report*, p. 21.
8 US Department of State, *Country Report on Human Rights Practices Romania March 2005- March 2006.*
9 *Country Report on Human Rights Practices Romania.*
10 'Parliament Gives its Approval to the Accession of Bulgaria and Romania', 13 April 2005, www.euroactiv.ro.
11 Radio Free Europe/Radio Liberty, *Newsline*, 2 March 2005; *Adevărul*, 1 March 2005.
12 *Cotidianul* (Bucharest), 2 June 2005. The press was a useful conduit for such letters, which were also used in the period prior to the 2004 enlargement where candidates needed to be pressurised in order to try and fulfil various commitments.
13 *Bucharest Daily News*, 13 May 2005.
14 *Reuters*, 28 June 2005.
15 *Ziarul de Iaşi* (Iaşi), 10 June 2005. Only 17% of Austrians supported Romanian accession according to a Eurobarometer poll carried out in all member states later in the year, *Evenimentul Zilei*, 25 January 2006.
16 *Bucharest Daily News*, 20 June 2005.
17 Lieselotte Millitz-Stoica, 'Romania – mai pregătiti de aderare decât Bulgaria', *România Liberă*, 24 September 2005.

18 Speech to European Parliament, Strasbourg, 25 October 2005, Europa.eu/ rapid/press/ReleasesAction,do?reference=SPEECH/05/641&format= HTMLaged=0&language. . .en-23k (accessed 5 December 2008).
19 *BBC Romanian Service*, 25 October 2005.
20 Valentina Pop, 'Raportul UE: aderare in 2007 stă la mâna corupției', *Cotidianul*, 25 October 2005.
21 *CEPS Neighbourhood Watch*, No. 9, Brussels, October 2005, p. 6.
22 Speech to European Parliament.
23 Interview with senior official from the Justice and Home Affairs directorate, Brussels, 25 April 2005.
24 Armand Gosu, 'Cheia aderării: reforma in Justiție', *Revista 22*, 4–10 October 2005.
25 *Country Report on Human Rights Practices Romania*.
26 Cristian Patrasconiu, 'Monica a mers cel mai departe', *Cotidianul*, 30 April 2006.
27 Cornel Nistorescu, 'The Undercover Officers in the Justice System', *Evenimentul Zilei*, 31 January 2005.
28 Press release coinciding with the formation of the Society for Justice, Bucharest, 28 August 2005.
29 Răzvan Saviliuc, *Ziua*, 21 May 2004.
30 *Associated Press*, 22 February 2005.
31 *Evenimentul Zilei*, 24 February 2005.
32 *Hotnews* (Bucharest), 23 February 2005.
33 Radio Free Europe/Radio Liberty, *Newsline*, 25 February 2005.
34 *Ziua*, 21 May 2004.
35 Information gleaned from press sources and contacts in the Romanian justice sector.
36 Gosu, 'Cheia aderării'.
37 *Bucharest Daily News*, 13 May 2005.
38 Notes taken when I was present at this event.
39 Dated 4 October 2005 and copy in possession of the author.
40 *Cotidianul* (Bucharest), 13 March 2006.
41 *Evenimentul Zilei*, 25 January 2006 reported a declaration by Macovei that she was pressurised by the Prime Minister into meeting his controversial business ally.
42 'Evoluția politică a dus la actuala criză', *Hotnews*, 18 May 2007, www.hotnews. ro.
43 See www.hotnews.ro, 19 July 2005 and the Romanian press in subsequent days.
44 See for instance the memo dated 27 January 2006 sent to the Commission by Simina Tănăsecu, long-term adviser in the Delegation, in which she dwelt on President Băsescu's reaction to the report on alleged CIA prisons in Europe drawn up by Dick Marty of the Council of Europe.
45 European Commission, *DG Justice Law and Security*, dated 19 July 2005.
46 *Bucharest Daily News*, 21 July 2005.
47 *Evenimentul Zilei*, 19 February 2004.

48 *Hotnews*, 'Prime Minister Tăriceanu Defends Patriciu in Full International Litigation with the Romanian State', 28 January 2006, www.hotnews.ro.
49 Ioana Lupea, 'Patriciu's Traps', *Evenimentul Zilei*, 26 January 2006.
50 Lupea, 'Patriciu's traps'.
51 *Cotidianul*, 23 June 2005.
52 *Adevărul*, 8 October 2005.
53 *Evenimentul Zilei*, 10 October 2005.
54 *Adevărul*, 8 October 2005.
55 Private information.
56 *Ziarul de Iași*, 1 October 2005.
57 Party of European Socialists' statement, 12 December 2004, www.pes.org.
58 Party of European Socialists' statement, 5 July 2005, www.pes.org.
59 Florin Negruțiu, *Gândul*, 5 July 2005.
60 *Cotidianul*, 22 October 2005.
61 Interview with Monica Macovei, Brussels, December 2005.
62 *Revista 22*, 14–20 February 2006.
63 Răzvan Amarei, 'The Persistence of Scandal', *Transitions Online*, 23 January 2006, www.tol.cz.
64 Interview with Quinton Quayle, *Bucharest Daily News*, 31 October 2005.
65 *Third Peer Review Romania*, p. 6.
66 *Cotidianul*, 13 March 2006.
67 *Evenimentul Zilei*, 13 March 2006.
68 Private information.
69 Iulia Nueleanu, 'Bruxelles-ul nu vede cu ochi buni anticipate în România până în 2007', *Curentul*, 22 February 2005.
70 See www.hotnews.ro, 19 July 2005 and the Romanian press in subsequent days.
71 *România Liberă*, 16 October 2006.
72 Bogdan Preda, *Bloomberg News Agency*, 14 May 2004.
73 *Hotnews*, 25 February 2009.
74 Sabina Fati, 'Frica de UE', *Observatorul Cultural*, 23-29 March 2006.
75 Dan Tapalaga, 'Ce-i unește pe Voiculescu, Vântu, Patriciu și Țiriac', www.hotnews.ro, 6 October 2006.
76 Denisa Maruntoiu, 'Rehn: The Report in May will be Clear', *Bucharest Daily News*, 29 March 2006.
77 Valentina Pop, *Cotidianul*, 5 April 2006.
78 European Parliament, 27 April 2006, www.euroactiv.ro.
79 European Parliament, 27 April 2006, www.euroactiv.ro.
80 'Commissioners in Last-Minute Debate on Bulgaria and Romania Accession', EUobserver.com, 16 May 2005.
81 www.hotnews.ro, 24 March 2006.
82 Jonathan Stearns, 'Romania, Bulgaria May Face Further Entry Test, Barroso Says', *Bloomberg*, 9 May 2006.
83 Stearns, 'Romania, Bulgaria May Face Further Entry Test'.
84 Ilija Trojanow, 'Bulgaria: The Mafia's Dance to Europe', *Open Democracy*, 16 August 2006, www.opendemocracy.net.

85 George Parker, 'Organized Crime Clouds Bulgaria's EU Accession', *Financial Times*, 20 April 2006.
86 *Cotidianul*, 16 March 2006.
87 *B92 News* (Belgrade), 17 April 2006.
88 *Sofia Echo*, 26 June 2006.
89 Parker, 'Organized Crime Clouds Bulgaria's EU Accession'.
90 Parker, 'Organized Crime Clouds Bulgaria's EU Accession'.
91 *Bucharest Daily News*, 31 May 2006.
92 *Bucharest Daily News*, 1 June 2006.
93 *Ziua* (Bucharest), 7 April 2006.
94 George Parker, 'Bulgaria, Romania to face "Tough" EU Entry', *Financial Times*, 5 September 2006.
95 Hans-Jurgen Schlamp, 'The EU's Unpopular Expansion', *Der Spiegel* (international edition), 10 April 2006.
96 *Cotidianul*, 16 May 2006.
97 *Hotnews* (Bucharest), 16 May 2006; *Bucharest Daily News*, 18 May 2006.
98 *Reuters*, Amsterdam, 4 December 2004.
99 *Hotnews*, 17 May 2006.
100 *Gândul*, 22 May 2006.
101 Valentina Pop, 'Frattini i-a pică pe Marko', *România Liberă*, 2 August 2006.
102 *Third Peer Review Romania*, p. 5.
103 *Revista 22*, No. 862, 15-21 September 2006.
104 *Third Peer Review Romania*, p. 5.
105 *Adevărul*, 9 September 2006.
106 Gergana Noutcheva and Dimitar Bechev, 'The Successful Laggards: Bulgaria and Romania's Accession to the EU', *East European Politics and Societies*, Vol. 22, No. 1, p. 115.
107 Directorate-General for External Policies of the Union, Directorate B, 'Update Note on Romania's Preparations for EU Accession', 27 September 2006 (PE 366.235).
108 *Third Peer Review Romania*, p. 11.
109 'Olli Rehn: Romania and Bulgaria Made Enough Progress', *Nine O'Clock*, 1 October 2006.
110 Commission of the European Communities, 'Commission Decision Establishing a Mechanism for Cooperation and Verification of Progress in Romania to Address Specific Benchmarks in the Areas of Judicial Reform and the Fight against Corruption', *C 2006 (6569) Final*, Brussels, 1 December 2006.
111 Schlamp, 'The EU's Unpopular Expansion'.
112 Mungiu-Pippidi, 'EU Accession is No "End of History"', p. 15.

9

Corruption and anti-corruption

Corruption has been a long-term and deep-seated problem in Romania. Its depth and prevalence have acted as a check on the country's economic development, impaired the state even in the performance of its normal duties, and created huge barriers of mistrust between society and the political elite which, on more than one occasion, has stimulated the rise of powerful extremist movements.[1] It is appropriate to locate an extensive appraisal of the phenomenon and attempts to bring it under control to near the end of the book. Corruption has disfigured the entire period of the transition from totalitarian rule to a form of managed democracy which does not challenge the elites that have been the main beneficiaries of the controlled change. The EU was acutely concerned to discover the extent of corruption in Romania and the determination of figures high up in the political system to allow it to remain unimpeded. But as this chapter will show, the measures it insisted were adopted in the anti-corruption struggle were not commensurate with the scale of the problem. In trying to eradicate it, the EU would be far less single-minded and resourceful than those powerful groups determined to ensure corruption would be a way of life even with Romania inside the EU.

In the month when Romania signed the EU accession treaty, Cristian Pîrvulescu, a well-known Romanian political scientist, stated in an interview with *Der Spiegel* that, 'Corruption is a general phenomenon in this country . . . the network of corruption extends to virtually every level within the government bureaucracy, including businesspeople, district attorneys and police officers. They're all part of the system. And it is a powerful system'.[2]

This could have been said with equal validity of the inter-war period when Romania enjoyed the unenviable reputation of being the most corrupt state in Eastern Europe. After 1945, the country appeared to move in a totally fresh direction with the imposition of communist rule. Rigid egalitarian norms were imposed in order to eliminate income differentials between citizens. In 1968, supposedly a time of relaxation in one of the most orthodox of communist states, a law was enacted for controlling the origin of any individual's assets regardless of whether he or she was a public official or a private citizen. Where any disproportion existed between the value of anyone's possessions and their income, the state was entitled to confiscate all suspect assets.[3]

But during the 48-year-long imposition of communist rule, old political practices were revived and given a new intensity beneath a façade of ideological militancy. This was especially true once Nicolae Ceauşescu and increasingly his wife Elena established their personal ascendancy within the system upon the former being appointed General-Secretary of the Romanian Communist Party in 1965. Orthodox communists who believed in the Marxist–Leninist formula for organising society and reflected its puritanical norms in their everyday behaviour were already being pushed aside. They were increasingly substituted by ambitious careerists who used the nationalism legitimised by the Ceauşescus as a tool to acquire privileges and influence. The Ceauşescus themselves were a role model for ambitious *apparatchiks*. Outwardly puritanical and austere, they coveted the trappings of office. The rulers of Western states to which they were invited in the 1970s, when it appeared that Romania was worth cultivating due to it being a maverick state in the Soviet communist bloc, were able to view the ethical standards of the ruling couple and their entourage close up. On the eve of the Ceauşescu's state visit to Great Britain in 1978, France's head of state, Valery Giscard d'Estaing, contacted Queen Elizabeth II to warn her on the basis of his own experience after receiving the Ceauşescus that all unsecured objects of minimal value were at risk of being stolen from Buckingham Palace where the rulers of Romania were being lodged.[4]

One of the reasons for the violent removal in 1989 of this dynastic communist couple was that they denied access to material wealth to the second echelon of Communist Party and state officials. In Poland, Hungary and even the Soviet Union, officials were able to discreetly enjoy the trappings of wealth. Many party and state positions served as vehicles for enrichment. But Ceauşescu kept rotating officials, making it difficult for informal circles of privilege and influence to be consolidated. Only foreign trade officials who enjoyed relative autonomy because they possessed financial knowledge and skills that were not easily replicated, were able to have regular access to video-recorders, other consumer durables, and good food and clothing. These were beyond the limits of most people (including party activists) in the grim atmosphere of the 1980s as Ceauşescu imposed food rationing and power cuts in order to pay off foreign debts and demonstrate to the world Romania's self-reliance.

No real turnover of power occurred in 1989. Second-ranking officials settled their accounts with the Ceauşescus, hastily executed on 25 December, who for too long had prevented their acquisitive instincts being realised. This was a revolution within the communist system which led to a modified version being imposed in which old structures remained dominant beyond a democratising façade. New rulers proclaimed the end of communism and the dissolution of the party. But its assets and means of coercion and control were inherited by the FSN, which promised to establish an 'original democracy'.[5] These words had been proclaimed by Ion Iliescu, who won the loyalty of an army of party and state cadres by establishing the conditions in which they could enjoy not only continued influence but also new-found wealth. After the FSN wrested control of state institutions and won a popular mandate in hastily called elections, a process of transferring state wealth into private hands got underway. Factory managers close to the FSN were able to asset strip their enterprises and become nascent capitalists. An army of former intelligence officers used their contacts within the state system and access to foreign currency to do even better. Interest-free loans were issued by state banks to favoured clients of the new post-communist order. A frenetic attempt to become the owners of wealth which had previously been held in trust for the people by the party got underway. It extended right down to the villages, where the communist rural bureaucracy distributed land to themselves and their clients. This was facilitated by a 1991 law setting an upper limit of land to be restituted to former owners, of only ten hectares. The restitution committees were dominated by ex-communist mayors who controlled the property archives and had the legal power to decide over restitution matters.[6] A predatory elite was thus able to perpetuate itself and flagrant abuses at all levels of economic life meant that Romania soon found itself in number one place for corruption in the former Soviet satellites of Eastern Europe. But in the 1980s this elite had lost valuable time in the race for combining status and power with wealth, so it had to catch up, however crude the means used to accomplish this. By the mid-1990s, Romanian post-communists enjoyed a level of control over the state that went far beyond that enjoyed by any other transitional elites in the region. Iliescu's electoral defeat in 1996 did not alter the balance of power. A coalition of his opponents, in office until 2000, was unable to pass any law which decisively weakened the control over the state machine or economic life of the old structures which had regrouped in 1989 and successfully mutated thereafter. No serious attempt was made to revive the Communist Party as happened in other countries like the Czech Republic. This would have been a pointless gesture since the interests which those committed to some kind of communist recovery wished to uphold had never been displaced in Romania, despite Iliescu and his backers insisting that the country had experienced a genuine revolutionary moment in 1989.

Transparency International, perhaps the most authoritative international agency monitoring corruption, has defined it as 'the misuse of entrusted power for private gains'.[7] The type of political processes which became entrenched after 1989 meant that corruption was bound to extend a long shadow in many areas of national life. Politics was not based on establishing any set of impersonal values or implementing party programmes but instead evolved around group interests. The rationale for participating in politics was more often than not to obtain a range of personal benefits. Parties that began life with higher aspirations found it difficult to avoid succumbing to the rules and conventions established by the FSN if they wanted to enjoy political success. Increasingly, politics appeared to be a ceaseless drive to obtain access to the state and divert its goods and services for the benefit of private interests.

In 2000 an Italian legal expert defined the devastating impact corruption had on societies prone to it: 'Corruption is a serious criminal offence which threatens the rule of law, democracy and human rights, undermines good governance, fairness and social justice, distorts competition, hinders economic development and endangers the stability of democratic institutions and the moral foundations of society'.[8]

Once negotiations for membership began with Romania in 2000, the EU had frequent cause to speak out about the problem of corruption. The statement made by Gunther Verheugen, the Commissioner for Enlargement, on 28 April 2003 was by no means unusual. He called on Romania to firmly tackle corruption at all levels, and outlined the fight against corruption as being one of Romania's top priorities in its effort to meet its EU admission goals.[9] But the EU was handicapped in its approach to Romania in a number of ways. Besides lacking knowledge of the historical and institutional context, it never showed much concern about developing its own methodology for benchmarking corruption. This was a surprising omission given the vast sums due to be channelled to candidate states in the form of pre-accession funds. It might be assumed that trying to document what constituted corruption in this highly specific context, and what would be the most appropriate measures to be employed in countering it, would have been seen as a priority in Brussels. EU funds would have been safeguarded and the chances of eastern enlargement, a key plank in the EU's emerging foreign policy, being blessed with success, would be greatly increased. But there was resistance to establishing such clear benchmarks from within senior member states. Long after it was drawn up, a majority of member states proved reluctant to ratify the 1995 Convention on the Protection of the European Communities Financial Interests, an initiative meant to uphold transparency in the regulation of EU finances.[10] Non-compliance with a measure designed to reduce corruption at central level hardly offered a good example to candidates like Romania.

So was the refusal of Italy to join GRECO. After the EU enlargement process began, GRECO was the only institution monitoring the vast majority of European states according to broad principles of anti-corruption policy. The EU had been content for a long period to allow the Council of Europe to try to improve the quality of European democracy by taking initiatives like this.

But it was striking that despite its greater institutional resources, it showed no inclination to take the lead in mapping corruption and proposing strategies for countering it. Instead, its approach was very much *ad hoc* and not driven by any particular sense of urgency. The first EU initiative on corruption in Romania was the launch of the Phare Inter-Institutional Project on Anti-Corruption in 1999. But it did not actually commence until August 2001, with the start of a project in which the state was twinned with the Spanish 'Fiscalia Anticorrupcion'.[11]

From 2000 onwards, EU officials seeking to implement pre-accession aid programmes soon became familiar with the types of corruption endemic in Romania. In 2008, Cristi Dănileț, a judge who served as an adviser to the Minister of Justice from 2005 to 2007, attempted to chronicle the main types that were prevalent. He identified the following:

- giving or taking bribes;
- trafficking of influence in which someone induces a public official to show favour towards his client;
- receiving a gift in return for showing favour to a supplicant;
- manipulating rules in order to give an advantage to a party such as when competitive tendering is involved;
- fraud, usually involving the falsification of data;
- blackmail, usually involving securing an advantage through pressure or force;
- favouritism in which a public official assists friends or associates to progress in the bureaucracy or the justice system by unfair means;
- favouritism involving nepotism whereby personal relatives benefit from access to public goods or appointments in a manner which contravenes the law;
- embezzlement;
- the use of confidential information to obtain advantage in a public transaction;
- reciprocal commission or kickbacks in which someone commits an illegal act on behalf of another who returns the favour by different means, also illegal. Dănileț cites as an example someone who is promoted in an institution and is rewarded by obtaining material rewards for the one who interceded on his behalf.[12]

This Romanian judge also draws attention to actions which do not constitute corruption but which have greatly deterred the fight against it, such as incompetence, errors in the exercise of justice and negligence. Lawyers defending top public figures facing corruption charges have, on numerous occasions, been able to delay proceedings or get the charges quashed on account of procedural errors. So elaborate are the procedures and with such frequency are laws changed that it is not difficult for a skilful lawyer to find loopholes. In its January 2008 report on the justice system, the European Commission noted with dismay that during the past six months cases involving former ministers or those still in post had been sent back to the prosecutors on account of procedural errors.[13] The same report also noted that the government's plan of action against corruption contradicted current legislation, an indication that it had been carelessly drawn up. In one notorious case during 2007, an army officer facing corruption charges was acquitted because of the absence of a seat in the courtroom.[14]

Politicians from across the political spectrum have proclaimed that corruption is not a problem, or else it is exaggerated. After 2000, the ruling PSD appeared unperturbed by the fact that Romania's ranking in the annual corruption index drawn up by Transparency International fell from 69th in 2001 to 89th in 2004. This was by far the lowest position occupied by any of the post-1997 wave of EU candidates, lower than Turkey and not far behind Russia in 95th place.[15] In September 2003, Adrian Năstase, then Prime Minister, declared that he did not recall too many corruption scandals in Romania and he complained of the Romanian tendency towards 'self-stigmatisation'. He also noted ambiguously that 'others from abroad' obtain satisfaction from any revelation of corruption in Romania, his conclusion being that 'I don't believe that we should victimise ourselves all the time'.[16] A similar message came from his successor as Prime Minister, Călin Popescu Tăriceanu, who in 2006 said to a German journalist: 'With my hand on my heart, I tell you that corruption is no longer a major problem'.[17] Both men were ready to spring to the defence of colleagues accused of corruption. After his Minister of Agriculture had been forced to resign in September 2007 for apparently being filmed in public receiving a bribe, Tăriceanu uttered no word of reproach but instead accused the media of condemning him before he had been found guilty. In 1999, Năstase and numerous other parliamentarians from Iliescu's party marched to the courtroom with one of their colleagues, Gabriel Bivolaru, who was facing trial on corruption charges for which he was later imprisoned.[18] Later, in 2006, a majority of parliamentarians showed solidarity with Năstase himself when they refused to give prosecutors permission to search his home while he was being investigated for corruption.

The cynicism of large sections of the political class was perhaps best exemplified by a public remark made in 2003 by the then Industry Minister, Dan Ioan Popescu, that he had been told in the 1990s by a US businessman that 'corruption is an indication of democracy'. He went on to complain that 'too much noise is being made about corruption in Romania. A certain degree of corruption is found in every country'.[19] It turned out that he had reason for finding the subject distasteful since in 2007 he was sent to trial for failing to explain the origins of assets worth 1.25 million euros.[20]

In 2007, the Justice Minister, Tudor Chiuariu insisted that the Romanian authorities were more expert and knowledgeable than the EU and indeed the World Bank in tackling corruption.[21] In pre-accession times, when it was advisable not to allow frustrations with EU interference to spill into the open, an emollient tone was adopted, indicating that both Brussels and Bucharest were really on the same wavelength despite appearances to the contrary. Thus, in 2003 Vasile Puşcaş, Romania's chief EU negotiator and one of the PSD's more transparent officials, dismissed concerns about corruption emanating from Commissioner Verheugen and US ambassador Michael Guest, by saying that they were really 'a show of support for Romania's current anti-corruption efforts'.[22]

Sometimes, anti-corruption rhetoric was merely a device to scare off or punish rivals. After driving his former ally Petre Roman from the office of prime minister in 1991, Iliescu ordered an investigation into his financial record during his 21 months in office. When he appeared to be locked in a power struggle with his post-2000 Prime Minister, Năstase, he manipulated perceptions of corruption in order to try and retain the advantage. Before their quarrel, all had seemed well. Speaking at the Council of Europe in April 2002, Iliescu argued that democracy had been 'consolidated' in Romania and it was on the way to being a normal country regarding its political and social environment.[23] But by November of the same year his mood had darkened and he urged the government to go beyond declarations and attack at its source what he saw as 'a flood of corruption'.[24] However, he excused ex-Premier Văcăroiu, a close ally, of any wrong-doing despite persistent media speculation that he continued to profit from a failing bank which he had presided over.[25] But he was back on the offensive in February 2003, when he insisted that PSD parliamentarians should resign from profitable positions in state-owned or private companies to avoid conflicts of interest. The same day, the PSD's *eminence grise*, Viorel Hrebenciuc resigned from the board of an insurance company which had won a lucrative tender to insure the fleet of cars used by parliamentarians.[26] The anti-corruption rhetoric then went into abeyance for a year when it appeared that Năstase respected Iliescu's wish to return to lead the party upon retiring as President. But he criticised in similar vein when new tensions erupted after electoral setbacks in mid-2004, complaining about Năstase's reliance on 'Yes men with small brains, fickle characters . . . and the souls of merchants'.[27]

But neither of these men showed any interest in curtailing conflicts of interest when they involved members of their party. Public figures who remained on a private or public board even when a decision was being taken in which they had a personal interest, were not penalised by the law. Introducing such penalties was not something covered by the *acquis* but it would have been an indication of serious intent to crack down on elite figures using public money for private gain if Romania had introduced such legislation on its own volition. Instead, as many citizens were well aware, political power was highly personalised in Romania and it was a rash act to fling around accusations of corruption. Informal mechanisms all too often determined whether action was taken against corruption and often this had a ritualised character. During his final year in office, Năstase centralised an array of investigative functions in the General Control Department, which was answerable only to him. EU advisers expressed alarm that the Department had been transformed 'into a kind of "private" investigation body' at the personal disposal of the Prime Minister, who can order it to 'carry out control . . . on the activities of central and local public institutions and authorities'.[28] Such prerogatives were not lightly ceded by his successor, Tăriceanu, and would start to be utilised when he had an even bigger falling-out with the man who had succeeded Iliescu as President.

Traian Băsescu had been outspoken about corruption during his tenure as mayor of Bucharest. But it is clear that many among the rest of the political elite assumed that once he became President he would not change the rules of a political system which, according to the Open Society Foundation in 2002, generates corruption rather than combating it.[29] The signs looked promising when, at the end of 2004, he admitted the Conservative Party and the Hungarian UDMR, the two political forces which most closely aped the PSD in their conduct, into the newly formed coalition. Prime Minister Tăriceanu felt sufficient confidence in him to request sympathy for the plight of Dinu Patriciu (see p. 233). But Băsescu discomfited each of them by showing disturbing signs that he was committed to creating a justice system that fully matched the EU design of being independent of privileged political forces. The rage of most of the political class was reinforced because he had previously been seen as a political insider who could be relied upon to protect the interests of the political caste which had grown wealthy after 1989, and it led to an attempt to drive him from office in 2007 which involved former allies as well as longer-term opponents.

At least one major Western European state, Italy, a founding EU member, possessed a disorderly and venal political elite which tried to colonise the justice system in order to ensure that politicians misappropriating public funds would never face prosecution. But corrupt politicians, some of them at least, eventually met their match in prosecutors determined to see that the law was applied without fear or favour. Their investigations of corruption in the Christian Democratic Party and smaller allied parties eventually led to the collapse of the party system in the early 1990s. Even when under Silvio Berlusconi fresh attempts were made to ensure that politicians enjoyed immunity before the law, the principle of the separation of powers proved sufficiently robust to withstand efforts to curb the independence of the justice system. But in

Romania, there was no attempt to separate the justice system from executive control until the second decade of post-communist rule. By this time a
political system designed to buttress the power of the networks mainly with
their roots in the pre-1989 era was well established. The different judicial tiers
supposed to guarantee the autonomy of the justice system were dominated by
PSD appointees or close allies (see chapter 8, pp. 184–5). Sentencing practices
were more favourable towards the political establishment than they had been
before the 2003 constitutional revision supposedly guaranteeing the separation of powers. An independent-minded judge, Cristi Dănileț, published evidence in January 2008 which showed a clear preference for issuing suspended
sentences to police officers, fellow judges and lawyers found guilty of corruption charges.[30] In cases of high-level corruption, the European Commission
noted, in its first post-entry report on progress in meeting undertakings in
the field of justice reform, that there were a high number of suspended sentences.[31] Lax judicial sentencing therefore undercut what Brussels regarded as
rigour in the prosecution of high-level corruption.[32] In a seminar organised
in Bucharest in 2007 by the American Bar Association's Central European
and Eurasian Law Initiative (CEELI), participants, who included Romanian
judges as well as foreign experts, concluded that court sanctions and deter-
rence against high-level corruption remained light. Many judges, it appeared,
viewed corruption offences to be less dangerous to society than other offences
such as aggravated theft or violence. It was also claimed that defendants who
ranked highly in the new class system which had emerged in the previous two
decades often benefited from their social status.[33]

One month after this seminar, in December 2007, compelling evidence was
provided of the unwillingness of judges to enforce acceptable standards of
conduct in their own ranks. It concerned a promotion exam which members
of the Supreme Council of Magistrates, the managerial body supervising the
justice system, were taking. The DNA uncovered evidence that Gabriela Ghiță,
a former Deputy-General Prosecutor of Romania, had allegedly made it possible for one of the candidates to obtain the exam topics in advance. But when
the DNA sought from the CSM approval for the arrest of the bribe-giver, the
CSM section for prosecutors rejected the request. The second-highest judicial
body, the High Court of Justice and Cassation, in its turn rejected the DNA's
request to arrest those involved in the alleged fraud (although it prohibited
them from leaving the country for one month).[34] Just like the PSD in the
Bivolaru affair, senior justice figures who had been elected to the CSM by
their peers had no qualms about proclaiming to the world that there were
circumstances when rules meant to ensure good conduct could be overridden,
however compelling the evidence that serious wrongs had been committed.

Bodies like the Council of Europe's GRECO and of course the European
Commission had hoped that intensive training and fully transparent rules

guiding selection and promotion would end such practices. No less than €200 million had been provided by the EU since 2004 for training, the development of efficient managerial practices and electronic equipment meant to speed up the delivery of justice. In fact, the justice system had received more EU funding than any other state sector and the Commission's January 2008 report said that the amount of financial support might be approaching saturation level.[35] But the focus of Western European bodies had been on technical improvements. There had been far less emphasis on evaluating whether the managerial system drawn up by Iliescu and Năstase's PSD supposedly guaranteed the independence of the justice system. Here was a glaring example of the failure of the EU, which was offering Romania full access to the world's most successful regional economic and political entity, to ensure that systems were being put in place to enable the new member to reflect the values of the Union in the conduct of its justice system.

It is clear from looking back at the history of the formal engagement between the EU and Romania that any willingness to tackle corruption had usually only been displayed after pressure from Brussels. For a decade, political elite members happy with the written and unwritten conventions of politics which made their profession one of the most lucrative in the country decided to sit out the rather half-hearted siege mounted by Brussels to improve standards and wait for the offer of full membership, in the expectation that afterwards they would be able to return to their old standards without the rest of the EU being able to do very much about it.

The period from 1999 to 2004 was one consisting of only palid measures to try and rein in corruption. In 2000, a section for anti-corruption and organised crime was established at the Prosecutor-General's office. It was supposed to be the lead organisation according to the anti-corruption law passed in 2000. However, the EU's 2001 regular report baldly stated that 'it has never been functional due to a lack of staff and equipment. Out of 38 posts for prosecutors only 7 are filled'.[36] An evaluation report published by GRECO in March 2002, based on an expert mission in the previous autumn, worryingly concluded that 'the institutions most involved in fighting corruption, including the police and the judiciary, are also affected by the phenomenon'.[37] Under EU pressure, Năstase agreed in March 2002 to set up a well-resourced body dedicated solely to combating serious forms of corruption. This was the PNA. It became operational in September 2002 and had 320 staff, which included 150 police officers and 75 prosecutors. Prosecutors enjoyed six-year tenures but the head was appointed by the President of Romania on the recommendation of the Minister of Justice. He was also subordinated to the Prosecutor-General, and the Minister of Justice had the power to order a reorganisation of his office.[38] The EU pressed the authorities to mount an open and transparent selection procedure in which the respective merit of a range of candidates could be determined in public.[39] Instead, the Minister of Justice recommended a small number of candidates from which the selection was to be made. The EU was also unhappy at the way that the Chief Prosecutor, Ilie Botoş, was appointed in 2003. Both he and Ioan Amarie, the head of the PNA from 2002 to 2005, skyrocketed from relatively unimportant positions within the justice system. Doubts about the PNA's independence had become pronounced by 2004. High-level corruption did not appear to be a major priority. Instead, the PNA became absorbed in pursuing relatively minor instances of corruption.[40] A report published by Freedom House in March 2005, which audited the anti-corruption strategy of the Năstase government, was unflattering about the performance of the PNA. 'It was neither efficient nor autonomous' and, from the moment of its inception, had been used as a political instrument rather than as an arm in the anti-corruption battle. It failed to launch enquiries into senior political figures linked with corruption, or to dubious business affairs such as privatisation of the RAFO oil refinery, or only did so after the PSD left office. Amarie, who quit in July 2005, had a brother who sat in Parliament for the PSD; Freedom House believed this was unacceptable since 'the anti-corruption prosecutor had to be a person without any kind of political connections'.[41]

In the face of additional EU pressure, the government had hurriedly drawn up anti-corruption legislation in 2003. It obliged public officials to fill out income and asset declarations. But those who failed to comply faced few sanctions. The form also omitted property owned abroad, art collections and jewellery. In any case involving the Prime Minister, whose wealth was a growing talking-point, the legislation failed to designate any public agency with the authority to carry out an investigation. Contrary to the advice of the EU, NGOs were not given time to comment on the 50 pages of legislation drawn up by the government. Transparency International identified loopholes which it believed would allow a proliferation of corruption, but the government maintained an attitude of suspicion towards civil society groups monitoring corruption.[42]

Since 1999 the EU has possessed a European Office for the Struggle Against Fraud. It works independently from the Commission but can draw on substantial logistical support from it. Dutch MEP Paul van Buitenen was instrumental in having OLAF set up in 1999.[43] He was then financial controller in the Commission and his investigations into fraud triggered numerous resignations from the Commission, at that time presided over by Jacques Santer. OLAF's first head, Franz-Hermann Bruner, collided with the EU Ombudsman and also with Raymond Kendall, the former Interpol chief who headed the supervisory committee of OLAF during Bruner's first term.[44] He accused him of acting in a high-handed manner by requesting a judge, in 2004, to order the arrest of a German journalist, Hans-Martin Tillack who was investigating fraud in the European Statistics Office (Eurostat). Bruner was re-appointed to a second five-year term in 2005 despite the reservations of many MEPs, including van Buitenen, who declared: 'I don't think he will be a suitable candidate given his track record over the last five years'.[45] In 2005, Bruner was effusive about the record of the Romanian justice system in combating fraud. He even went as far as to say: 'I can tell you that in all our anti-fraud coordination meetings, we used Romania as an example to say, "This is a country that shows it really does its job. Let's be aware of this"'.[46] Yet by then, no major conviction for fraud or corruption had been achieved in Romania. OLAF had around 400 staff, of whom 160 were investigators, but only from 2005 was there an OLAF official permanently based in Romania. This appears a striking discrepancy given the huge amount of pre-accession funding being channelled to the country and its high ranking as one prone to institutionalised corruption.

OLAF establishes a formal partnership with the prosecuting service or else one of the law enforcement agencies to coordinate a response when law-breaking is suspected in the use of EU funds. For reasons never satisfactorily explained, OLAF's partner in Romania was the head of the Prime Minister's Department of Control, a post held by an elected politician and subjected to regular political pressures. A team sent by the Commission to monitor Romanian efforts to bring the justice system up to EU standards remarked in 2004 that: 'There is not one EU-country or EU-candidate country where the OLAF counterpoint is situated so far from its natural position as in Romania'.[47] However, in 2005 Bruner did not feel the need to be particularly vigilant towards Romania. When asked if he had seen any files being examined by Romanian prosecutors, he replied: 'To be honest, we try not to get involved in national activities. These problems must be dealt with nationally. I offer information to institutions because we are, in a way, an organization which makes transfers of information easier. We file reports to point out [that] something illegal is happening. But decisions are made on a national level'.[48] This 'hands off' approach meant it was vital OLAF had as a Romanian partner a body prepared to take the task of eradicating corruption seriously. As has been seen, there was plenty of evidence, above all during the tenure in office of the PSD, that this was not the case.

Even if OLAF had taken the elementary precaution of finding a reliable local partner in the justice field to act on the evidence of corruption it had amassed, it is hard to envisage that convictions could easily have been secured given the preference of so many judges to provide light sentences in corruption cases or else throw them out on a technicality. Rarely did elite figures entangled with the law have harsh words to say about those presiding at their trials. But politicians have persistently accused prosecutors of being biased or punitive in their investigation against corruption. In 2002, before the onset of the so-called separation of power, the Justice Minister had found numerous excuses to remove prosecutors investigating anti-corruption cases. Afterwards, this was not so easy due to the establishment of the DNA in 2005, specialising in high-level corruption. It had important defenders in the President and the Prosecutor-General, who from that year was Laura Codruța Kovesi. The political enemies of the DNA had to increasingly rely on allies in the judiciary to try and restrict its activities. During the eight months Tudor Chiuariu was minister in 2007, the CSM, the body managing the justice system, usually responded positively to ministerial requests to audit the work of the DNA or else to take away from the President the power to suspend ministers facing criminal investigations.

On 27 November 2007, the Constitutional Court decided unanimously that the order to dissolve the special presidential commission that analysed criminal prosecution requests was unconstitutional. The highest court in the land increasingly found itself the arbiter as lower courts suspended corruption trials and referred the cases upwards for its ruling on various unconstitutionality claims submitted by the defence. This move, while procedurally correct, indicated a reluctance by lower courts to take the lead and deal with what were often minor technical issues. It meant that high-level corruption cases were frozen often for well over a year until the higher court delivered its judgment.[49]

On 31 January 2008 the Constitutional Court caused a sensation when it ruled that the work of the National Council for the Study of the Archives of the *Securitate* (CNSAS) had been unconstitutional since its formation in 1999.[50] The CNSAS had been empowered by the state to investigate whether public figures had collaborated with the secret police under the communist regime. The Constitutional Court had thrown out seven previous attempts to declare the CNSAS's work unconstitutional. But it went back on its previous decisions in the case of the media mogul and prominent politician Dan Voiculescu, whom the CNSAS had found to be an informer for the secret police in the 1980s with the code name of 'Felix'. Voiculescu's lawyer was Sergiu Andon, the head of Parliament's justice committee and a prosecutor and longstanding Communist Party member who appeared destined for high political rank until the 1989 revolution.[51] The Court was persuaded by Andon that in the case of his client, the CNSAS had no right to pass judgment and that the constitutional basis for its activities in fact did not exist. Civic bodies committed to strengthening a fragile democracy argued that disestablishing the CNSAS would give clean identity to figures who had carried out controversial activities before 1989 and who had gone on to be prominent in business and politics (Voiculescu just being one among many, albeit the most brazen in his conduct). It was also alleged that old-guard figures in the justice system had an imperative cause for silencing the CNSAS. A law had been passed in 2005 affirming that nobody could continue as a magistrate who had collaborated with the secret police before 1989. It was widely believed that the CNSAS had amassed several dozen dossiers containing incriminatory evidence not just on members of the CSM and High Court of Cassation but also of the Constitutional Court, whose membership had largely been determined by Iliescu after 2000.[52] On 7 February 2008, Germina Nagâţ, the head of the investigations department of the CNSAS, confirmed that 25 out of 118 judges whose files had been checked by the body had worked for the pre-1989 secret police in one capacity or another.[53]

By now a pattern had emerged of the prosecutors involved in anti-corruption investigations relying on the backing of the head of state and the EU for the continuation of their activities while the judiciary and the CSM which managed the justice system displayed increasing common ground with political forces who regarded the high-level anti-corruption investigations as intimidatory and politically inspired. The EU, and external bodies like the American Bar Association spearheading justice reform in Romania, called for prosecutors and judges to work more closely together, but these wings of the justice system increasingly appeared to have different priorities. Judges showed a disinclination to implement changes that increased their professionalism, and informal selection practices started to be revived as soon as the reforming Justice Minister Monica Macovei was ousted in 2007, the year when the EU's oversight role began to diminish.[54] Anti-corruption prosecutors were much younger than most of the officials on the CSM and showed a commitment to pursuing cases of wrong-doing against politically influential people even if it proved an arduous and even risky undertaking.

Opinion polls consistently showed that the justice system lacked credibility. The EU representation in Romania published poll findings on 30 January 2008, from Eurobarometer, showing that confidence in the workings of the justice system had dropped to 26% in 2007 compared with a figure of 35% in the previous year. Confidence in Parliament had fallen even more steeply in the same period, down from 35% to 17%.[55] Over the long term, Parliament had discouraged citizens from playing an active role in combating corruption. Draconian penalties were in place for citizens who submitted information on illegal acts that turned out to be false. In 2001, anyone who provided inaccurate information about the illicit origins of a public official's wealth faced imprisonment ranging from six months to three years. Legislation passed in the teeth of fierce opposition from Parliament in 2007, meant to discourage illicit enrichment by public officials, prevented confidential complaints by the public. These had to be dated and signed which, according to an international specialist in this area, 'may run counter to the purpose of international standards for protection of witnesses . . . such as article 33 of the UN Convention against Corruption'.[56] This law did not envisage whistle-blowing protection for claimants, and effective witness protection during trials had never been a priority, causing changes in testimonies enabling figures facing serious charges of corruption to walk free.[57]

Parliamentarians have taken legislative steps to dissuade members of the public and the media from taking active stands against corruption. The PSD Senator Eugen Nicolicea, continuously in Parliament since 1990, has been particularly industrious in this regard. In 2007, he obtained the support of Parliament for the modification of the Penal Code to allow imprisonment of up to seven years for anyone who published images and transcripts of conversations without the permission of those involved. This initiative was taken shortly after the downfall of the Minister of Agriculture when he was clandestinely filmed allegedly taking a bribe. In January 2008, the same parliamentarian persuaded Liberals, Conservatives and ultra-nationalists to back a further revision of the Penal Code which provided a prison term of between one and five years for anyone threatening the security of the state or its foreign relations by disseminating false information. Monica Macovei had abolished such an offence several years earlier but, according to Nicolicea, this was in order for her to misinform international bodies about the true state of conditions inside Romania. His new addition to the Penal Code included a clause specifically referring to the President and providing either life imprisonment or a minimum jail term of 15 years for high treason.[58] It was clear that by targeting Băsescu and the media, Senator Nicolicea and his numerous parliamentary supporters were issuing a warning to the wider public not to take a stand against corruption, especially if those under scrutiny enjoyed high rank in politics or related occupations.

The Ombudsman (*Avocatul Poporului*), established in 1997 to defend citizens' rights and freedoms in their interactions with public authorities, has failed to invest his office with any authority. Ioan Moraru, a constitutional law professor at Bucharest University, has been a near-invisible figure.[59] But in 2008, he showed concern for the prominent people whom the CNSAS had found had collaborated with the political police, supporting the Constitutional Court in its decision to annul the findings against them.[60]

The trans-party coalition representing the dominant networks of political and economic power was transmitting an unmistakable message that only misfortune would result if the society allowed its frustration with corruption to sharpen into a determination to do something about it. At the same time, parliamentarians lost no opportunity to substantially revise the Penal Code so that corruption was defined in a far more restrictive way than before. In November 2007, they ruled that offences 'with extremely serious consequences' would now involve damage over €9 million, instead of €60,000 as previously specified by the law.[61] This meant that if a high official failed to be protected by the numerous in-built devices meant to avoid a guilty sentence ever being imposed, his sentence would be greatly reduced even if he had been involved in the theft of millions of euros. Earlier, in its June 2007 report on progress in reforming the justice system and combating corruption, the European Commission had expressed misgivings about the serious possibility that Parliament would limit investigations into serious corruption cases to a maximum period of six months. It also drew attention to restrictions on phone-tapping by investigators. It was convinced that such moves 'would seriously limit the potential of the investigators in collecting evidence, particularly when tackling well-established criminal groups or powerful governmental representatives deeply involved with corruption'.[62]

In its follow-up report of February 2008, the European Commission noted that little effort had been made in establishing a functioning and effective agency to monitor and disclose the assets of elected representatives as well as judges and senior administrators. Parliament had felt confident enough to oppose the creation of a National Integrity Agency in September 2006, on the eve of the EU making its final decision on the timing of Romania's accession. The law passed in April 2007 after Justice Minister Macovei had been driven from office was far from what the European Commission had desired since it cast doubt on the independence of the ANI. The Senate, and not the President, as intended by the 2006 bill, would be the appointing body and the ANI authorities would be appointed for a term matching that of the Senate. The author of the most authoritative study on Romanian efforts to tackle illegal enrichment in political life concluded that this greatly increased the likelihood of ANI personnel being appointed not on the grounds of competence but through political negotiations, which was bound to hamper any long-term policy of identifying illicitly obtained assets.[63] In February 2008, the EU clearly indicated that Romania had still to honour its undertaking of establishing 'an integrity agency with responsibilities for verifying assets, incompatibilities and potential conflicts of interest, and for issuing mandatory decisions on the basis of which dissuasive sanctions can be taken'.[64]

Even if the assets of a parliamentarian or judge were far in excess of his or her normal income and no plausible explanation could be advanced for this, the Constitution prevented dignitaries from being deprived of them. Article 4 states that 'legally acquired assets shall not be confiscated. Legality of acquirement shall be presumed'.[65] Therefore the burden of proof lies with investigating authorities to prove that a criminal offence has been committed in the acquisition of unexplained wealth. No other Constitution ring-fences private property as comprehensively as the Romanian one, it has been argued by constitutional lawyers. This is ironic since Romania also enjoys the dubious distinction of probably being the former communist state where the authorities have placed the greatest obstacles on former property owners (and their descendants) whose houses, land and other goods were confiscated after 1945, from securing their return or else just compensation. Leading figures in the political elite occupy such homes, which they obtained at a nominal rent after 1989 and, in many cases, were able to later buy outright for sums well below the market value of the property. The European Court of Human Rights at Strasbourg has been clogged for many years with cases lodged by expropriated owners against the Romanian state. So far, very few of those which have gone to judgment have been won by the Bucharest authorities. Seen in this light, Parliament's obstinate determination to defend private property appears like victors' justice, that of communist office-holders and especially their successors who behaved for much of the 1990s as if state property really belonged to nobody and therefore was ripe for the taking.

A comparative review of sentencing practices on crimes of corruption produced in 2007 shows that countries possessing very different legal traditions have resorted to new legal tools and strategies in order to control most types of acquisitive crime.[66] Encouragement was provided by the European Commission and a 2005 'Framework Decision on Confiscation of Crime-Related Proceeds, Instrumentalities and Properties'. Article 2 of the framework lays down that 'Each Member state shall take the necessary measures to enable it to confiscate, either wholly or in part, instrumentalities and proceeds from criminal offences punishable by deprivation of liberty for more than one year, or property the value of which corresponds to such proceeds'.[67] In Italy, the reversal of the burden of proof applies in cases involving the mafia. In France, the burden of proof is shifted from the prosecution to the defendant in corruption cases, with the latter having to justify the licit origin of the profit where a direct or indirect benefit was obtained. The same principle of reversed burden of proof applies to cases where an individual has a lifestyle that cannot be explained by declared revenues, especially if he or she regularly consorts with known offenders. When applying such procedures, the French courts are obliged to observe certain international guidelines, such as ensuring that specialised judges sit in such cases and defendants can have access to relevant information enabling them to refute the charges.[68] Such legal tools have been upheld by the respective Constitutional Courts of these countries.[69]

Because of a poorly written Constitution which offers numerous loopholes for klepocratic forces adamantly opposed to seeing the profession of politics cleaned up and regulated, Romania appears to be far from reaching the stage France and some other countries have reached in tackling corruption. In the absence of a re-launch of the constitutional process to ensure that a document is drawn up which represents the aspirations not just of the winners in the 1989 political change-over, some practical initiatives have been suggested. As well as greater protection for whistle-blowers, these include a prohibition of suspended sentences for crimes of corruption, by far the ones most favoured by judges. But one objection was that 'risk funds' might be created to rescue members of the oligarchy whenever they were found guilty of corruption and by those means the law would continue to be circumvented.[70]

The pressure on the political elite and allied professions to improve their ethical standards eased considerably upon the removal of Macovei as Justice Minister and the appointment in April 2007 of Tudor Chiuariu, a 29-year-old recent law graduate who had been the personal lawyer of one of the leading political barons in the north-east of the country. It is not an exaggeration to say that a legal counter-revolution almost occurred during his eight months in post during which attempts were made to emasculate the various strategies and instruments which, at the EU's request, the authorities had introduced to try and bring corruption under control. The EU's first opportunity to analyse at length what had occurred was the publication of its *Interim Report on Progress in Romania with Judiciary Reform and the Fight against Corruption*. But the report was studiously measured, referring to 'some concerns on how progress has been evolving' and 'certain weaknesses . . . that could prevent an effective application of EU-laws, policies and programmes'. Bulgaria was also being monitored and the report found cause for concern, citing continuing problems in tackling high-level corruption and also organised crime. There were the same weaknesses in translating intentions into concrete results. There was concern that the action plan for combating corruption at elite but also local government level lacked precise targets and meaningful performance indicators. But by contrast with Romania, praise was extended over continued progress in judicial reform and on fighting corruption on Bulgaria's borders.

Comparisons between the two countries, placed in the same accession grouping because of their perceived similar problems, can be seen as instructive. In Bulgaria, much progress had been made in tackling corruption within the public administration. This was probably easier to accomplish than in Romania because the pre-1989 regime had been less totalitarian and there had been far more of an emphasis on promoting people according to merit than on ideological or informal grounds. In 2007, the respected Bulgarian NGO, the Centre for the Study of Democracy (CDS), produced a detailed report on corruption, efforts to contain it and public attitudes towards it which concluded on a hopeful note. It reckoned that corruption in Bulgaria stood at a level comparable to EU members like Italy and the Czech Republic and was lower than in Romania and also Greece.[71] The general population and local businesses were paying a lower number of bribes than in previous years and reduced corruption was occurring in the context of a lower level of economic development than in any other EU country.

But the 2007 CDS report drew attention to a fact often overlooked in the literature and general discussion about EU enlargement. Not only had the EU failed to acquire its own methodology for benchmarking corruption, but its approach to financing programmes in Bulgaria might be increasing the chances of corruption becoming entrenched.[72] The EU had been slow to accredit managing authorities which would be responsible for the decentralised management of EU resources. Eventually the go-ahead was given by Brussels but the delay shortened the span of time between the announcement of the tendering procedures and the deadline for implementation of projects. This delay makes it harder for the public administration to process the tender application and it gives the bidders far less time to prepare unless they have been tipped off in advance.[73] The CDS warned of the very real danger of corrupt political interests siphoning off EU funding through shell companies or else setting up bodies whose sole purpose was to absorb EU funds. It pointed to tourism, one of the most profitable and well-run industries (by contrast with Romania), where EU funding could be used to replace commercially viable projects with ones that did harm to the industry. Transparent companies offering good-quality services might then end up being driven out by companies whose political connections gave them privileged access to EU funds.[74] The result could be that EU funding had entrenched kleptocratic interests rather than promoting economic development.

Corruption risks were not eased by 'the lack of transparency in the relations between the Bulgarian public administration and the European Commission, including its Delegation/Representation in Bulgaria'.[75] Funds were allocated on 'the basis of non-transparent negotiations' in which both entities were motivated by the desire to defend their own budgets in the future. Delays often resulted in disputes over the selection of specific projects and also bidders. The lack of effective oversight and ability to hold the two administrations to account, in the view of the CDS, 'generates an exceptionally favourable environment for corruption'. The Bulgarian NGO believed that over time, 'a specific institutional culture of intended miscommunication and irresponsibility has developed between the two administrations which, unless adequate measures are undertaken, is a cause for serious concern over the efficient use of EU funds in the period 2007–2013'.[76]

A clear sign of the incoherence in the EU system for managing funds was shown in 2006 following an audit by the Commission into the procedures and structures relating to the implementation of EU assistance programmes in Bulgaria. The auditors found a potential conflict of interest in the appointment of the head of the Financial Unit of the Central Finance and Contracts Unit at the Ministry of Finance. A former employee of a Greek consultancy firm had been appointed head of this unit three weeks after leaving the firm. This happened at the time of evaluation of a tender in which the consultancy was among the bidders. Two months after the appointment of its former employee to the body making the allocation, his former employer was awarded the contract. Contrary to the findings of the Commission's auditors, the EU Delegation denied any conflict of interest in this case, leading the CDS to comment that the body which 'the public expects to be the guardian of the integrity of the spending of EU funds, failed to act'.[77]

Such a worrying incident convinced Bulgarians monitoring the EU's post-entry performance of the need to establish an independent and reliable system to monitor the management of EU funds which would involve collaboration of audit institutions in the EU and Bulgaria and also the non-governmental sector.[78]

The scale of the unease with the EU's performance was shown in 2005 when the head of Transparency International in Bulgaria accused the officer in charge of civil society matters at the EU Delegation of corruption and cli-entelism concerning the management of the Phare civil society programme. Documents disclosed by the media showed how expert evaluations had been manipulated in order for contracts to be awarded to 'the right candidate'. In the eyes of the CDS, there were very real fears that grants to civil society organisations had not been allocated through competitive bidding but as a result of a trade-off between EU Delegation officials and ones in the Finance Ministry, both defending their own nominees.[79] Soon after, a poll of 250 civil society organisations found that one-third of the respondents admitted that the selection procedures under the Phare civil society programme 'lacked any transparency'.[80]

Bulgarian evaluators of the EU's performance believed that the opportunities for corruption could be much reduced if there was a more precise and policy-based allocation of resources. Such an approach was unlikely as long as there was an overriding concern with the absorption of EU funds in order to safeguard individual careers and protect future budgets. There is no sign of a culture shift in Brussels despite the huge sums being allocated to the 2007 EU entrants. This would involve concentrating funding in spheres where businesses are reluctant to invest and where the benefits and returns usually only reveal themselves over the long term. Education, technological development and innovation are areas where funding, if intelligently located, could help to transform a still underdeveloped country's long term prospects. But like the Stability Pact for the Balkans set up in 1999 to promote growth and development and whose performance the EU disparaged, the EU's own funding strategy appears to be very unimaginative and short term in its approach. This leaves the danger that funding will be intercepted or it will be absorbed in mediocre projects that make no impact on the ability of Balkan members to compete effectively with older EU members.

In Romania, there have been none of the serious irregularities alleged of EU officials in Bulgaria. But in 2006, a report by the Court of Auditors roundly criticised the Delegation's management of pre-accession Phare funds.[81] The existence of a vigorous and independent-minded Bulgarian NGO sector provided much-needed oversight of the EU's performance. This was usually absent in Romania, where the NGO sector conspicuously failed to acquire a powerful momentum that enabled it to be both free of EU financial support and capable of offering cogent criticism of the EU's performance when circumstances merited that.

During 2005, a General Anti-Corruption directorate (DGA) was set up within the Ministry of Administration and the Interior. Its aim was to try to reduce the level of corruption in the ministry. EU officials were involved in the DGA initiative. Steve Foster, a British police officer seconded to the EU, headed the Phare anti-corruption project. He helped select as the DGA's head Marian Sîntion, a prosecutor who turned out to be tough and resolute in seeking to identify and root out corruption in one of the most unreformed of the ministries. The MIA has 150,000 staff and was widely viewed as being impossible for a minister to control. Generals and colonels in place over many years appeared to be a law unto themselves.

Considerable EU investment through the Phare programme had already been devoted to improving the police's ability to tackle human trafficking and the smuggling and distribution of drugs. Ending Romania's role as a source and distribution network for these areas of criminality was viewed as vital if Romania was to avoid importing insecurity and lawlessness into the EU. By 2004, the police was beginning to attract personnel who were dedicated, at least in part, to the concept of public service. Even greater attention had been devoted to the Customs authority. The World Bank in 2000 designated it as the most corrupt institution in the country, 66% of companies surveyed believing that nearly all customs officers were corrupt.[82] Corruption in this branch of state activity also involved high-level officials.[83] Brussels was aware that fees collected at the border went to high-ranking officials in the Interior Ministry.[84] A senior Commission adviser detected a marked worsening of corruption in the customs service between 2002 and 2003, with the frequency of bribes being solicited rising from 40% to 79% of crossings.[85] Rigorous controls were introduced afterwards under which staff were checked to determine the money in their possession before and after a shift and this led to a relatively high dismissal rate in terms of the Romanian public service.[86]

The one institution which had not been subject to an overhaul in a bid to reduce corruption had been the main domestic intelligence agency, the SRI. The DNA relied upon it for assistance with communication interception. It had been linked with corruption in the past.[87] It was a serious oversight that the SRI failed to have any preventive campaigns in the corruption field directed at it, but not a surprising one given the influence the intelligence world continued to wield in Romania.

After 2000, the police struggled to evolve into becoming a demilitarised and decentralised force. The previous military structure had isolated it from local communities and transparent systems of selection and promotion were palpably lacking. While successes in demilitarisation were undeniable, an expert assessment carried out by the EU in 2004 found that 'a veneer of efficiency and success was presented whereas in reality under the surface, serious organizational deficiencies existed'.[88]

Giving a sense of urgency to the creation of the DGA had been the collapse of charges against General Toma Zaharia, a former State Secretary in the MIA, and a number of colleagues.[89] In 2005, they had been accused of 'criminal deficiencies' over 'defective contracts' signed to improve Romania's frontier security. Steve Foster, coordinator of Phare's anti-corruption project, thought it would be a good idea if the work of the DGA was supported and evaluated from outside, preferably from within the NGO community. A National Integrity Centre (CNI) would evaluate the effectiveness of the anti-corruption strategy and the work of the DGA.[90] Seven NGOs were involved, from which the Association for Implementing Democracy (AID) was chosen by the others to coordinate the oversight role.

The CNI had previously been given 20,000 euros to promote its work in the anti-corruption field. Funding came from the Dutch and other EU governments through their embassies. The September 2006 report of the EU on Romania's progress towards accession had offered praise for 'raising awareness' about corruption. Sîntion had launched a hotline to report corruption in the MIA. It received 16,000 calls. One coordinator stated: 'We did with 20,000 euros what people don't do with one million. If numerous television stations had not publicised free of charge our bid to involve the public in the anti-corruption campaign, the cost would have been 700,000 euros'.[91] It was carried free by 107 television and radio stations.

The energetic Mr Sîntion investigated the behaviour of generals and even state secretaries in the MIA. Dossiers were built up on leading figures. The sale of MIA houses to officials at a price far below their real value was just one of the abuses uncovered. Sîntion eschewed compromise in trying to clean up the ministry. All those who were responsible for illegalities would have to leave. It seems he hoped that these venal generals would be replaced by captains and majors who were less tarnished. But the MIA had an internal culture which did not prize openness or strict professionalism. Everyone was supposed to adapt to a situation where powerful hierarchies made decisions which benefited informal influence groups.

The files on powerful figures on the MIA were completed in January 2007. Soon a counter-attack was mounted and a commission was appointed to audit its work.[92] It consisted of figures from different parts of the ministry, including several on whom Sîntion had built up thick dossiers. Sîntion resigned on 6 March 2007, saying that the work of the DGA was being sabotaged. He filed a report on the reasons for his resignation which the minister, Vasile Blaga, had classified. Some who had seen it believed that this report was an unprecedented challenge to the closed arrangements which had prevailed in the MIA for many years.[93]

The National Integrity Centre had not been consulted by the ministry when it moved against the DGA. When the scale of the crisis became clear, Transparency International began to scale down its role. Soon, AID was the only NGO still involved. A letter was drawn up setting out how the work of the DGA was being hampered and it was sent to Franco Frattini, Vice-President of the Commission, and other prominent bodies. No reply was forthcoming, but Frattini came to Romania soon after and, when asked at a press conference about the DGA, simply said: 'I trust my friend Mr Blaga. There is no problem'. He also stated that the evaluating body had not been set up at the instigation of the European Commission which flew in the face of all the evidence.[94]

AID sent a report to the Commission in mid-March 2007, but two prominent NGOs, Transparency International and the SAR, declined to be associated with it. As evaluator, the CNI was able to call a public meeting, on 12 March 2007, to draw attention to developments. Shortly beforehand, Sîntion was warned by phone by a senior ministry official that if things got really out of hand he might find himself hauled before a military prosecutor. But there were two others in the room and Sîntion adjusted the phone so that they could hear this conversation.[95]

The 12 March meeting was a dramatic occasion. Blaga, the minister, was flanked by a phalanx of senior officials. Foreign embassies were there and proceedings were broadcast live on television. Sîntion described the pressure he found himself under once it became clear that he meant business and, when asked if high-ranking people whom he accused of corruption were in the room and if he had been threatened by them, he answered both times in the affirmative. For a brief period after giving a lengthy TV interview during which a top MIA official, Virgil Ardelean, had phoned in to dispute his claims, the most active member of the CNI was followed by plain-clothes operatives who did not disguise what they were doing, walking a few paces behind him.[96]

In April 2007, Irinel Păun, the prosecutor who became the new head of the DGA, ordered that the computers which AID had been given to carry on its work be unilaterally seized. This alarmed Ambassador Jaap Werner of the Netherlands whose government had given the strongest backing to the anti-corruption initiative. He asked for clarification about the 'intimidatory methods' which the DGA was now using. He also expressed concern about the fate of anti-corruption work in the ministry, after 'Mr Păun had made clear his intention to change, without warning or consultation, the scope of the project'.[97] The British embassy joined its Dutch colleagues in expressing their concern.[98]

Praise was given for the CNI in the EU's final annual regular report on Romania's performance of 2006 and also in the interim reports on justice reform in June 2007 and February 2008. But this affair did not cast the EU's approach to anti-corruption work in a very inspiring light. The decision to use a consortium of NGOs to oversee anti-corruption work in one of the ministries most resistant to change was a high-risk endeavour. It soon led to splits between the NGOs and at one stage a top EU official even denied the involvement of the EU, which was a preposterous claim. It was only the tenacity of several ambassadors, particularly Werner of the Netherlands, which kept the project alive (although it had become a pale shadow of itself by the spring of 2007). By early 2008, the new Director of the DGA was in open conflict with the Dutch and British governments and was seeking an investigation into how their funding for promoting the civil society partnership with the ministry had been spent.[99]

Conclusion

The EU has been on a painful learning curve since moves began in the late 1990s to include Romania as one of its integral members. Corruption was recognised as a problem in the annual reports issued by the Commission on Romania's progress towards accession. Leading commissioners delivered warnings on the scale of the problem. But it was assumed that new institutions and bodies to enforce their provisions would address the problem of corruption.

Commission officials came from academic backgrounds in development, economics, law and European studies where it was customary to accept the good faith of those with whom negotiations were taking place. The trust, shading into naivety, which a ruthless elite in Bucharest took full advantage of, was painfully displayed as late as 2002 by GRECO. After the EU enlargement process began, GRECO was the only institution monitoring the vast majority of European states according to broad principles of anti-corruption policy. GRECO's first evaluation report on Romania, adopted in March 2002, several times noted 'the existence of the Romanian authorities' clear willingness to attack firmly corruption'.[100] It identified 'the fact that the police is an institution actively involved in fighting corruption'.[101] It believed that 'the most serious forms of corruption in Romania are associated with organized crime' when in fact the kinds of mafia outfits which had emerged in Bulgaria and Serbia were noticeable by their absence due to strength and visibility of the intelligence services.[102] The GRECO report assumed that the ruling PSD stood apart from the phenomenon. It recommended the authorities 'obtain more precise information about the scale of corruption in the country, by conducting the relevant research in order to understand how this phenomenon affects . . . key state institutions, such as the police and the justice system'.[103] It betrayed a lack of awareness about the rules of politics in Romania and the fact that the successor party to the pre-1989 communists had devised an out-wardly pluralist system designed to allow tight-knit political networks major oversight and control over economic resources, particularly ones destined to be privatised. Its naive assumption that the system of government was basi-cally sound and corresponded to Western European norms, merely needing a range of modifications, was shown in its claim that the 'Romanian constitu-tion: [it] and legislation provide adequate guarantees, generally speaking, for the independence of the courts and the immovability of judges'. Already there was considerable evidence to the contrary in the public domain. It also went on to acknowledge the Romanian Parliament's willingness to 'move Romania . . . towards a democracy based on the rule of law and transparency'.[104] Its evidence was 'a vast range of legislative and statutory texts, most of them dating from 1995 to 2000' directed against corruption, as well as Romania's 'actual or promised signature or ratification of various treaties on corruption and organized crime and participation in various international programmes and evaluation processes, including some organized by the Council of Europe and the European Community'.[105] The report based its positive tone on legisla-tion and the existence of a plethora of bodies charged with preventing the theft of public assets. It failed to understand what would become painfully obvious to later external monitors (and which was already evident to the more perspi-cacious ones) that these initiatives comprised a vast displacement exercise to enable Romania to look as if it was tackling corruption when in fact little or nothing was being done, at least about the types involving figures belonging to the political elite and is clients.

OLAF, the EU's fraud-busting agency, showed how far out of its depth it was in Romania by choosing as its local partner agency, the Prime Minister's Department of Control, a post held by an elected politician from the ruling party and subject to regular political pressures. In 2005, its chief, Franz-Hermann Bruner, even issued the astonishing statement that 'in all our anti-fraud coordination meetings, we used Romania as an example to say: "This is a country that really does its job. Let us be aware of this"'.[106] Across the EU, there was a touching belief that transparent structures underpinned by appropriate laws to consolidate judicial independence could decisively address Romania's corruption problems. Independence was duly declared in 2003 with legal officials wedded to post-communist methods of control in key positions in most tiers of the judiciary. There was scant realisation in Brussels that there was an army of judges, prosecutors and indeed ancillary staff who had no desire to aspire to judicial standards known in much of the rest of the EU. They were happy to play their role in a politically captive justice system since it brought them enormous material fulfilment. All the training courses in the world would not alter this world view and indeed the Commission's February 2008 report noted that the amount of financial support to increase the professionalisation of the justice sector might be approaching saturation level. This was at a time when informal selection practices were starting to be revived and judges were closing ranks to shield colleagues against whom corruption charges had been levelled by prosecutors.

The EU also failed to draw appropriate lessons from the point-blank refusal of Parliament to authorise an integrity agency able to verify the assets of elite figures and recommend legal sanctions in the face of clear irregularities. This happened in the final pre-accession period and the EU seemed unwilling to conclude that the elite would be far more obstructive once the country was fully inside the EU. This indeed proved to be the case when, in 2008, a law was passed meant to intimidate citizens who passed on information about corruption that a court could not substantiate with heavy prison terms, while the amount of stolen funds which the law designated as equivalent to serious corruption rose from €60,000 to a staggering €9 million.

Until the creation of the DNA in 2005, the sheer plethora of organisations entrusted with anti-corruption duties was a cause of astonishment and deep frustration for EU officials reviewing progress in this area during 2004. Corruption investigations were conducted by the General Inspectorate of the Romanian Police (Ministry of the Interior), the General Directory for Intelligence and Internal Protection (Ministry of the Interior), the Financial Guard and the National Customs Authority, now centralised under the National Control Authority (Prime Minister's office), the specialised Judicial Police (Ministry of Justice) and the National Control Office, as far as administrative investigation is concerned. It was noted that in many instances fragmentation of competences occurred within these bodies.[107]

Digging deeper, the Western European legal experts asked to audit progress in justice reform in 2004 found that several secret services were engaged in law enforcement tasks without any attempt to coordinate their activities. It was also unclear what rules applied to the evidence gathered by these organisations and in what manner the evidence was, or was not, presented to court. They noted that a relatively minor investigation into corruption could involve no less than four different bodies.[108]

Such a chaotic approach to combating corruption in a country where it was endemic offered numerous opportunities for kleptocratic forces and their legal advisers to frustrate all efforts at cleaning up and regulating the profession of politics.

Despite the gravity of the challenge it faced in its new Balkan members, the EU failed to acquire its own methodology for benchmarking corruption which would have made it easier to commit recalcitrant governments to specific undertakings. Its approach to financing its own programmes, as revealed in Bulgaria, also offered the chances of corruption becoming entrenched. In 2005, weeks before the admission treaty was signed with Romania, the

Commissioner for Enlargement, Olli Rehn, struck an unrealistic, if not out-right irresponsible, note when he said: 'Let us be clear. It is not our job to combat corruption but that of the administration, the government and indeed each Romanian'.[109] This was a posture denoting complete abdication. The EU was providing funds which offered undreamt of opportunities for corruption unless it had rigorous methods in place to frustrate skilled political predators adept at capturing state funds. The EU's responsibility for stemming corrup-tion was also a grave one since it had insisted on the privatisation of large parts of the Romanian state. It had tried to promote regulatory agencies capable of seeing that this process was conducted in a transparent manner. But its reports on progress towards accession candidly admitted that the pace of change in the administrative structure had been painfully slow. How 'each Romanian' could step into the breach and challenge kleptocratic forces when the EU said that it was not its task was never made clear.

These were grave failures on the part of the EU, which was in a position of strength since it was offering Romania full access to the world's most success-ful regional economic and political entity. By failing to ensure that systems were being put in place to enable the new member to reflect the values of the Union in the conduct of its justice system, it was increasing the likelihood that the country would remain under the heel of forces hostile to the European project and capable of disrupting its implementation far beyond the borders of Romania.

Notes

1 See Joseph Rothschild, *East-Central-Europe Between the Two World Wars*, Seattle: University of Washington Press, 1974.
2 'How Fit Are Romania and Bulgaria for the EU?, *Der Spiegel*, 18 April 2005.
3 Guillermo Jorge, *The Romanian Legal Framework on Illicit Enrichment*, Bucharest: ABA/CEELI, 2007, p. 22.
4 Edward Behr, *Kiss the Hand you Cannot Bite: The Rise and Fall of the Ceauşescus*, London: Hamish Hamilton, 1990, p. 43.
5 Vladimir Tismăneanu, 'Semnificaţiile revoluţiei române (III)', *Jurnalul Naţional*, 4 February 2005.
6 Gray, *Evaluation of DFID Country Programmes*, p. 106.
7 www.transparency.org.
8 Edmondo Bruti Libeati, quoted in Meagan Condrey, *A Comparative Review of Sentencing Practices and Norms for Crimes of Corruption: France, Germany, Hungary, Ireland, United Kingdom, and United States*, Bucharest: ABA/CEELI, 2007, p. 1.
9 Eugen Tomiuc, 'Romania: EU Warns Bucharest Over Corruption', Radio Free Europe, 30 April 2003.
10 *Monitoring the EU Accession Process.*

11 *Monitoring the EU Accession Process*, p. 467.
12 'Forme de corupţie', http://cristidanilet.wordpress.com, 5 January 2008.
13 *Interim Report on Progress in Romania with Judiciary Reform and the Fight against Corruption*, Brussels: European Commission, 4 February 2008, Memo/08/72.
14 *România Liberă*, 2 November 2007.
15 *Cotidianul*, 17 March 2005.
16 *Evenimentul Zilei*, 4 September 2003.
17 *România Liberă*, 29 April 2006.
18 Gallagher, *Theft of a Nation*, pp. 220–1.
19 Radio Free Europe, *RFE-RL Newsline*, 4 April 2004.
20 *Hotnews* (Bucharest), 1 October 2007.
21 *Hotnews*, 21 November 2007, www.hotnews.ro.
22 Eugen Tomiuc, 'Romania: EU Warns Bucharest Over Corruption', Radio Free Europe, 30 April 2003.
23 Radio Free Europe/Radio Liberty, *Newsline*, 24 April 2002.
24 Radio Free Europe/Radio Liberty, *Newsline*, 2 December 2002.
25 *Evenimentul Zilei*, 4 December 2002.
26 Radio Free Europe/Radio Liberty, *Newsline*, 4 April 2003.
27 *Evenimentul Zilei*, 15 July 2004.
28 'Fight against Corruption, Fraud and Money-Laundering', in *Draft Report of an Advisory Visit under Chapter 24 in the fields of Justice and Home affairs in Romania, 29 March–2 April 2004*, Brussels: European Commission, April 2004, p. 139.
29 *Monitoring the EU Accession Process*, p. 455.
30 'Corupţia judiciară (8): pedepse pentru corupţie', http://cristidanilet.wordpress.com, 26 January 2008.
31 European Commission, *Report on Romania's Progress on Accompanying Measures following Accession*, Brussels, 27 June 2007, COM (2007) 378 final, p. 15.
32 *Report on Romania's Progress on Accompanying Measures*.
33 *Seminar on 'High Level Corruption and Judicial Sanctions', Summary of Discussions*, Bucharest: ABA/CEELI, 19 November 2007, p. 2.
34 *Seminar on 'High Level Corruption and Judicial Sanctions*, p. 5.
35 *Interim Report on Progress in Romania with Judiciary Reform and the Fight against Corruption*.
36 *2001 Regular Report*, p. 21.
37 *2002 Regular Report*, p. 27.
38 *Advisory Visit under Chapter 24 in the Fields of Justice and Home Affairs in Romania*, p. 134.
39 *Advisory Visit under Chapter 24 in the Fields of Justice and Home Affairs in Romania*, p. 134.
40 See *US Department of Labor 2005 Human Rights Report*, www.state.gov/g/drl/rls/hrrpt.2005.
41 The summary of Freedom House's criticisms of the PNA can be found in 'Online Press Review', 18 March 2005, www.revistapresei.ro.

42 Tomiuc, 'Romania: EU Warns Bucharest Over Corruption'.
43 David Cronin, 'Bruner Determined to Stay but Must Face Competition for Top OLAF Job', *European Voice*, 3 February 2005.
44 Cronin, 'Bruner Determined to Stay . . .'.
45 Cronin, 'Bruner Determined to Stay . . .'.
46 'OLAF Head: There are Politicians Involved in EU Funds Fraud Cases', *Bucharest Daily News*, 25 November 2005.
47 'Fight against Corruption, Fraud and Money-Laundering', p. 139.
48 'OLAF Head: There are Politicians Involved in EU Funds Fraud Cases'.
49 *Report on Romania's Progress on Accompanying Measures following Accession*, p. 16.
50 *BBC Romanian Service*, 31 January 2008.
51 Dan Duca, '"Elita" dosarelor de cadre din Parlamentul României', *Cotidianul*, 15 October 2007.
52 Alina Mungiu-Pippidi, 'Cum a fost assasinat statul de drept', Romanian Academic Society press release, 2 February 2008.
53 *Hotnews* (Bucharest), 7 February 2008.
54 Ioana Morovan, *Hotnews* (Bucharest), 4 February 2008.
55 *Nine O'Clock*, 1 February 2008.
56 Jorge, *The Romanian Legal Framework on Illicit Enrichment*, p. 4.
57 *Seminar on 'High Level Corruption and Judicial Sanctions'*, p. 2.
58 Luminita Pârvu, *Hotnews*, 28 January 2008.
59 *Monitoring the EU Accession Process*, p. 481; for Moraru, see *Cotidianul*, 24 November 2007.
60 *Hotnews* (Bucharest), 31 January 2008.
61 ABA/CEELI, *Romania, Significant Legal Developments*, Bucharest: ABA/CEELI, November 2007, p. 3.
62 *Report on Romania's Progress on Accompanying Measures following Accession*, p. 16.
63 Jorge, *The Romanian Legal Framework on Illicit Enrichment*, p. 28.
64 *Interim Report on Progress in Romania with Judiciary Reform and the Fight against Corruption*, p. 3.
65 Quoted in Jorge, *The Romanian Legal Framework on Illicit Enrichment*, p. 23.
66 Condrey, *A Comparative Review of Sentencing Practices and Norms for Crimes of Corruption*.
67 *Seminar on 'High Level Corruption and Judicial Sanctions'*, p. 3.
68 *Seminar on 'High Level Corruption and Judicial Sanctions'*, p. 3.
69 Jorge, *The Romanian Legal Framework on Illicit Enrichment*, p. 21.
70 *Seminar on 'High Level Corruption and Judicial Sanctions'*, p. 3.
71 *Anti-Corruption in Bulgaria: Key Results and Risks*, Sofia: Centre for the Study of Democracy, 2007, p. 6, www.csd.bg.
72 *Anti-Corruption in Bulgaria*, p. 58.
73 *Anti-Corruption in Bulgaria*, p. 59.
74 *Anti-Corruption in Bulgaria*, p. 61.
75 *Anti-Corruption in Bulgaria*, p. 59.

76 *Anti-Corruption in Bulgaria*, pp. 59–60.
77 *Anti-Corruption in Bulgaria*, p. 63.
78 *Anti-Corruption in Bulgaria*, p. 61.
79 *Anti-Corruption in Bulgaria*, p. 62.
80 *Anti-Corruption in Bulgaria*, p. 63.
81 Mihai Istrate, 'EU Critical of Phare Fund Application in Romania and Bulgaria', *Bucharest Daily News*, 21 June 2006.
82 *Diagnostic Surveys of Corruption in Romania*, Washington: World Bank, 2001.
83 *Monitoring the EU Accession Process*, p. 456.
84 Private information from inside the Commission.
85 'Fight against Corruption, Fraud and Money-Laundering', p. 130.
86 'Schengen Action Plan, Blue Borders, Danube, Danube Delta and SIS', in *Draft Report of an Advisory Visit under Chapter 24 in the Fields of Justice and Home Affairs in Romania, 29 March-2 April 2004*, Brussels: European Commission, April 2004 p. 26.
87 See Gallagher, *Theft of a Nation*, p. 235.
88 'Functioning of the Police and Fight against Various Forms of Organized Crime', in *Draft Report of an Advisory Visit under Chapter 24 in the Fields of Justice and Home Affairs in Romania, 29 March–2 April, 2004*, Brussels: European Commission, April 2004, pp. 116–17.
89 *Gândul*, 27 December 2006.
90 *Curierul Național*, 9 February 2006.
91 Interview with civic activist involved, Bucharest, 13 and 20 June 2007.
92 *România Liberă*, 14 March 2007.
93 Interview with civic activists involved, Bucharest, 13 and 20 June 2007.
94 Interview with civic activists involved, Bucharest, 13 and 20 June 2007. For a report of the press conference, see *Gardianul*, 15 March 2007.
95 Private information.
96 Interview with civic activists involved, Bucharest, 13 and 20 June 2007.
97 *Cotidianul*, 26 April 2007.
98 *Cotidianul*, 23 July 2007.
99 *Curentul* (Bucharest), 8 February 2008.
100 *Evaluation Report on Romania*, Strasbourg: GRECO, 4–8 March 2002, p. 18.
101 *Evaluation Report on Romania*, p. 21.
102 *Evaluation Report on Romania*, p. 24.
103 *Evaluation Report on Romania*, p. 18.
104 *Evaluation Report on Romania*, p. 17.
105 *Evaluation Report on Romania*, p. 17.
106 *Bucharest Daily News*, 25 November 2005.
107 'Fight against Corruption, Fraud and Money-Laundering', p. 138.
108 'Fight against corruption, fraud and money-laundering', p. 141.
109 *Jurnalul Național*, 2 March 2005.

10

The expiry of reform after 2007

Jonathan Scheele, the head of the European Delegation from 2002 to 2007, was the international official who ought to have had the deepest awareness of how problematic Romania's bid to join the EU would turn out to be. But in the spring of 2004, just after the EU had briefly panicked abut Romania's state of unpreparedness, he had declared that accession would mark 'the beginning of much work to help the country to fully integrate into the European Union'.[1] Such complacency was followed by the prediction of Prime Minister Tăriceanu made shortly before accession on 1 January 2007 that this event merited comparison with the unification of the country in 1918 when it emerged greatly expanded in size after choosing the winning side in the First World War.[2]

Instead, what followed was an extended period of infighting within the political elite which has been characterised as 'a war of the palaces' between Prime Minister Tăriceanu in Victoria Palace, the seat of government, who was allied with the bulk of parliamentary forces, and President Băsescu, whose only strong asset was the high popularity that he enjoyed among the electorate.

On 17 January 2007, Băsescu published a memo he said he had received in 2005 from Tăriceanu, asking him to intervene with the prosecutors who had still to lay formal charges against Patriciu.[3] Tăriceanu contended that the handwritten note merely raised the issue of abuse of their powers by officials and did not amount to a plea for intervention. On the following day, the PSD announced that his party would seek to remove Băsescu from office and on 12 February the proposal to suspend him was laid before Parliament. The next day, the Senate overwhelmingly backed a vote of no confidence in Justice Minister Macovei, many government supporters also endorsing it. She had complained of a lack of support from the Prime Minister for reforms hailed in Brussels and widely seen as the breakthrough which allowed Romania to join the EU on schedule. A flagship policy of hers, which the EU viewed as vital if corruption were to be reduced, was a law allowing the assets of parliamentarians and other elite figures to be scrutinised. On 1

February 2007 the Liberals ensured its defeat in Parliament. Norica Nicolai (who was twice considered for the justice minister position when it later fell vacant) attended a routine meeting in Brussels rather than attend the session of the parliamentary committee where her vote would have avoided the bill being defeated.

On 29 January EU Commission President Jose Manuel Barroso described the crisis as 'normal turbulence'.[4] One senior figure in his Vice-President's staff some months later described Romania to me as a colourful Latin country with Slavic undertones that was merely trying to discover itself politically.[5] Here was further evidence of how deficient the attention-span of EU grandees was towards Romania and how strong the temptation was to regard power-struggles over whether the political class could be made accountable to the rule of law, in superficial terms.

Băsescu seemed committed to establishing a law-based state where politicians needed to improve their conduct and be accountable to the electorate and more transparent in their behaviour. But, beyond calling for uninominal elections, a single chamber Parliament and a crackdown on corruption, Băsescu's plans for rebuilding the state and establishing the partnership hitherto lacking with society were not clearly formulated. He has failed to build a strong presidential office that could act as a brains trust and enable him to seize the initiative decisively from the squabbling politicians. Until the summer of 2006, he appeared too reliant on secret service chiefs whom he had inherited from his predecessor. Nevertheless, he remained the most popular politician due to his eloquence, informality and readiness to challenge vested interests long seen to be profiting at the expense of ordinary citizens. Without being able to rely on strong allies on the parliamentary scene, this popularity would be the only strong card he enjoyed in the confrontation with his opponents in 2006–07. Certainly, his party, the Democrats (PD), ruling in uneasy coalition since 2004 with Tăriceanu's Liberals, often appeared an unimpressive advertisement for reform since it contained no lack of figures content with the money-making opportunities a political career offered.

Open warfare had existed between the two former electoral allies, the PNL and PD, since January 2007 when the PD decided to form separate lists for European elections to take advantage of its current popularity. On 10 March Tăriceanu retaliated by postponing the European elections from May until the autumn. On 26 March he demanded the resignation of the two chief supporters of the President in his cabinet, the Interior Minister, Vasile Blaga, and Justice Minister Monica Macovei after they had refused to approve his decision. Personal relations between the head of state and Tăriceanu had collapsed some time ago. On 21 January the Prime Minister, said Băsescu, 'conducts himself . . . like the head of state of a former Soviet republic' and is intent on setting up a regime of personal authority. In a television confrontation on 20

February, Tăriceanu branded the President a liar for accusing him of tolerating 'a mafia' in the energy sector.[6]

Getting rid of Macovei was a key objective after she had resisted efforts from the heart of government to intercede with prosecutors on behalf of Dinu Patriciu and had proved determined to introduce justice reforms that made the political class accountable to the law. Tăriceanu would have been aware of the high esteem with which Macovei was held by the Commission in Brussels. This made it all the more imperative to assert Romania's prerogative as a sovereign member of the EU to plot its own course in the area of justice reform even if it risked the imposition of the safeguard clause. What a Commission official wrote in October 2005 remained even more true 18 months later as Macovei faced her last days in office: 'The situation in the justice area remains *fragile* since the many positive developments which have taken place in the past nine months are to be attributed mainly to the *personal commitment of Minister Macovei*'.[7]

The two favourites to succeed her were hardly the types of politicians whom the EU had viewed as torch-bearers for a European-style justice system. Norica Nicolai, who had quietly mobilised opposition to some of Macovei's key reforms in Parliament, had previously been funded by Rompetrol, as indeed had several other anti-reformers in the PNL camp.[8] Tudor Chiuariu was a 29-year-old PNL backroom official best known for having worked for the law firm of the most visible of the economic barons from the city of Iaşi in the north-east, Radu Fenachiu. [9] Iaşi was an oasis of civility in one of the poorest areas of the country. In 2003, it emerged that 33 people had accumulated enormous wealth (between 736 and 797 million US dollars) in a region where 30% of the population were poor and 25% extremely poor.[10] Many of these millionaires acquired privatised state assets for nominal sums without proper validation or competitive bidding. This grand theft was easier to accomplish in poor regions where exploitative relations had long been the norm.

Perhaps because he was an unknown quantity whose violent antipathy to disrupting the incestuous ties between the oligarchy and the justice system was yet to be made clear, it was Chiuariu and not Nicolai who was appointed.

On 19 April 2007 322 parliamentarians voted to suspend Băsescu from office and he was replaced as President by Nicolae Văcăroiu, the President of the Senate pending a referendum on 19 May in which the electorate could decide whether or not to endorse Parliament's action. He was suspended the day after the Constitutional Court published the basis of its 5 April ruling that none of the charges of his parliamentary opponents about Băsescu's alleged misconduct had any foundation. The Court also endorsed the view that the President should have an active role in political life, not the merely ceremonial one apparently desired by his opponents.[11]

Băsescu was able to project himself in the campaign as the underdog. He named a list of powerful figures, mainly in business, who he claimed controlled the trans-party alliance that had formed against him. He campaigned even in Spain among the nearly one million Romanians who had emigrated there, drawing large crowds which he often did at home. On 19 May, 74% of voters, on a 44% turnout, overturned his suspension from office. For the first time in electoral politics since the establishment of multi-partyism in 1990, the turnout of young, urban and middle-class voters surpassed that of the countryside where most Romanians still live. These groups swung massively behind Băsescu while his opponents found it hard to mobilise their mainly rural supporters. Over half of the supporters of the two parties in government, the Liberals and the Hungarian party, backed Băsescu and he picked up considerable support from nationalists and populists.

This referendum revealed a sharp gulf between the popular mood and hitherto dominant parties intent on clinging to arrangements which preserved the abundant privileges they could obtain from politics and keep out new rivals. But it turned out to be a skirmish rather than a decisive victory. Băsescu decided not to form a new party that would transcend the anaemic PD and seemed unsure of what to do next. But his opponents were more resolute. On paper, it was hard to see how they could hold out for long against a popular President. By mid-2007, the PNL had 22 seats and the UDMR 10 in the 137-seat Senate, with 51 and 22 seats respectively in the 332-seat Chamber of Deputies. But these tiny percentages masked the fact that the parties supposedly on the other side of the ideological spectrum, the PSD and the ultra-nationalist PRM, backed the Tăriceanu government because of its readiness to defend the interests of the cohesive trans-party oligarchy. Elected on a party list system, most of the parliamentarians were numb to the principle of accountability, had no links whatsoever with their constituencies and sometimes delegated their relatives to vote for them when they could not be bothered going to a plenary session (as in the case of Norica Nicolai in 2007).[12]

The ruling Liberals and their allies decided to go on the political offensive. Their target was the package of justice reforms whose future appeared uncertain in the absence of their chief architect, Monica Macovei. The offensive would be directed at the EU and the USA, who were told to mind their own business in tones which not even Iliescu's PSD had dared use towards the country's chief international allies. Tudor Chiuariu, the Justice Minister, accused the European Commission, which had been monitoring Romanian efforts to combat corruption since he was a teenager, of blocking anti-corruption efforts in Romania. He insisted on 20 November 2007 that it 'was obstructing efforts to combat corruption through its backing of fragmented structures in the Prosecuting service'.[13] He was unhappy that Brussels refused to give its backing to the absorption of the specialised anti-corruption department DNA within the General Prosecutor's office into a larger structure. The National Anti-Corruption Department had been set up in 2005, when the Commission's influence was probably at its maximum, to try and make it less easy for politicians to divert large sums of public money for their own benefit and bring to justice the most flagrant law-breakers influential in politics. DG Justice and Home Affairs was well aware that its head, Daniel Morar, was one of the few senior figures in the prosecuting system 'committed to obtain quick . . . [and] visible results' in the struggle against top-level corruption. Diluting the DNA in an amorphous anti-corruption body similar to its ineffectual predecessor, the PNA, would have led to the demise of a body that 'concentrated exclusively on high level and political corruption'.[14]

Chiuariu enjoyed support across Parliament among parties which feared that legal scrutiny of the business activities of leading members could endanger their survival. His nine months as Justice Minister were dominated by a war of nerves between him and the prosecutors investigating the business affairs of past and present members of the Tăriceanu government. In May, he tried to remove Doru Tuluş, the prosecutor handling top-level cases, accusing him of lethargy and poor organisation. But this move was foiled thanks to the strong public backing Tuluş received from the EU and a string of Western ambassadors. On 16 May five EU ambassadors took the unprecedented step of attending a meeting of the managerial body of the Romanian judiciary at which it was feared that a prosecutor investigating top figures in the coalition would be removed. Instead, a decision was postponed but Cristian Diaconescu, the PSD's Minister of Justice in 2004, had already denounced the interference of Western governments in Romania's internal affairs and Tăriceanu declared that the approach of foreign diplomats had not been helpful.[15]

Internal state agencies monitoring the use of public funds had been ordered not to cooperate with the DNA. The Minister ordered an audit of the work of Tuluş which in September accused him of a range of mistakes that independent analysts felt were minor ones.[16] The DNA in turn accused the inspectors appointed by Chiuariu of disclosing confidential information in their report which prejudiced the outcome of ongoing corruption investigations.[17] In an extraordinary move, Chiuariu tried in advance to water down the 27 June report on justice reform produced by the European Commission, insisting that it had been misinformed about 'the impressive professionalism of anti-corruption prosecutors'. EU sources claimed that this was the first time ever a government official had tried to undermine an EU report which was praising his own officials.[18]

The Minister has also claimed that the DNA was set up through subterfuge in 2005. On 23 September, he accused the well-known NGO Freedom House of conspiring with Macovei to produce a damning audit on the DNA's ineffective predecessor in order that partisan prosecutors could be appointed who would target politicians that were the President's enemies.[19] Chiuariu said that the proof was in the failure to have a tender for this auditing work. But since the EU had insisted that the audit be carried out within three months in order that it could have a clear picture of the state of justice sector reform, it had been agreed that a request for offers from interested parties would suffice and Freedom House was the only one to submit a proposal.[20]

Midway through his stormy period as Minister, Chiuariu was insisting that 'the DNA has become an instrument in a political struggle'.[21] This position enjoyed the backing of the government and indeed most members of Parliament. Not a few of its members who had profited financially during the interminable political transition in Romania were gripped by a sense of panic that their good fortune would run out if codes of conduct governing people in public life were at last introduced. Upon taking office, Chiuariu had said that 'it would be disastrous after having had a Joan of Arc, if the Romanian justice system had to endure a Robin Hood'.[22] But he proved to be a Robin Hood for those eager for a champion uninhibited about insisting that government and opposition politicians were targets of legal vengeance by politically motivated prosecutors. He raised the stakes in September 2007 by accusing top DNA officials of receiving orders directly from Băsescu. The President responded by saying that if this were true it would be impossible to keep it concealed and he pointed to the fact that the DNA had recommended criminal charges against leading figures in his own party, the PD, including a city mayor who is his God-child.[23]

Chiuariu won a crucial victory over the President when, on 7 October, Parliament voted that the DNA could no longer request criminal investigations to be launched and that only the prosecutor-general could do so. Parliament also suspended the presidential commission, composed of prosecutors, which had the power to recommend the removal from office of ministers under criminal investigation.[24] This relieved the pressure on a string of ministers against whom the DNA had presented evidence of possible criminal wrong-doing.[25] They included Chiuariu himself, who in August 2007 was accused by the DNA of intervening on behalf of a private interest to ensure that a hectare of land belonging to the postal service in central Bucharest was sold at disadvantageous terms to the state.[26] The Constitutional Court decided on 27 November that the order to dissolve the special Presidential commission that analysed criminal prosecution requests was unconstitutional. But on 10 March 2008, it ruled that he could not exercise this power against former or serving ministers if they were members of Parliament.[27] Here was another indication that politicians still enjoyed immunity from prosecution and Parliament was a sanctuary in which they could shelter irrespective of their behaviour. The EU's insistence in 2003 that the revised Constitution strike out such a clause because of the difficulties it caused for bringing top-level corruption under control now seemed a distant memory, as the Constitution was revised on the floor of Parliament to buttress the privileges of its members and the interests they served, and strip the President of many of the rights he had previously been able to exercise.

Once Chiuariu's conduct led to mounting concern among Romania's allies, numerous messages of support for him were posted on the message board of a leading daily which had been typed on a computer traced back to his own ministry. A petition supporting Chiuariu which supposedly originated in October 2007 with students from Petre Andrei University in Iași, which he had graduated from some years previously, had also been drawn up on one of the ministry's computers.[28] At the end of that month, the President publicly described Chiuariu as 'a brazen young mafia-type'.[29] Chiuariu quit in December rather than give Băsescu the satisfaction of sacking him, which he was then able to do since the Constitutional Court had temporarily restored this right to him on 27 November. He promised to return, judged himself proud of all that he had attempted to do as Minister, and soon after was appointed the Prime Minister's chief adviser on legal affairs, obviously a sign of the esteem in which Tăriceanu held him for the zeal with which he had defended the power networks and their parliamentary allies.[30]

Complaints about EU ignorance from Chiuariu were reinforced by an extraordinary attack directed at Nicholas Taubman, the US ambassador in Romania, which was made by Bogdan Olteanu, a God-child of the Prime Minister, who had secured the position of President of the Chamber of Deputies for him in 2006. On 15 November 2007, shortly after the ambassador had publicly expressed alarm about the latest parliamentary moves to thwart the fight against high-level corruption, Olteanu declared that he had obtained his position in a way that would have been regarded as corrupt in Romania.[31] Instead of this being an opportunity for EU ambassadors to show solidarity with a colleague, a businessman who had never hidden the fact that he was appointed because of his closeness to the Bush administration, they all remained silent with the exception of the British ambassador who rallied to his defence. A week later Gunther Kirchbaum, the head of the European affairs committee of the German Parliament, declared that if a similar outburst had come from Olteanu's counterpart in Germany, he would have been forced to resign as a speaker of Parliament.[32]

In March 2008, a similar lack of inhibition was shown by Lidia Bărbulescu, the newly appointed head of the Superior Council of Magistrates.[33] She berated the US State Department after the annual report of its Bureau of Democracy, Human Rights and Labor had suggested that the justice system in Romania was not independent.[34] She asked for proof, apparently oblivious of the fact that a few days earlier, in a report released by Transparency International, 24%

of judges considered the system was not independent from political pressure, a sharp increase on the previous year's figure.[35] Perhaps the most damning proof had been provided by some of her leading colleagues in December 2007, when prosecutors produced evidence that they had been involved in bribe-taking in order to enable examinations for judicial promotion to be passed through cheating. A vote in the prosecutors wing of the CSM decreed that those under investigation should be shielded from arrest.[36] Thus, the body tasked with preserving the impartiality of the judiciary appeared to have as much disregard for its own transparency and accountability as the political elite had for maintaining decent standards of behaviour within its own ranks. The CSM under Bărbulescu has reacted with nonchalance to Parliament's repeated bids to limit top-level anti-corruption investigations to six months and under certain circumstances to inform the subjects of the investigation that their phone lines were about to be tapped or their houses searched.[37]

Bărbulescu owed her eminence to Rodica Stănoiu, the 2000–04 Justice Minister who brought her to Bucharest from Oltenia, where the old politi-cal structures were arguably more entrenched than anywhere else in the country.[38] One of her first decisions was to remove the personal files of all judges from the Justice Ministry to the CSM, where control, especially over judges unwilling to allow court verdicts to favour political interests, could be more easily exercised. Many such files were contained in the intelligence service of the justice system which Macovei had dissolved in 2006, but which it was assumed in the media that Bărbulescu was interested in re-activating.[39]

In February 2008, just as old-guard figures were extending their grip over the justice system and synchronising their moves with parliamentary forces, the European Commission sent a report to the Parliament and the Council of the EU on the justice system. It was one of a bi-annual series due to be produced during the two years after entry, a period when the justice system continued to be monitored by Brussels. The efforts of the DNA to combat high-level corruption were praised and concern was expressed about the unwillingness of judges to take it seriously. Overall, the report was unable to discover much progress in justice reform.[40] Soon after, Prime Minister Tăriceanu made a point of visiting the CSM head, Bărbulescu, and he expressed his hopes that the monitoring process which the Romanian justice system was subject to would soon be wound up.[41]

Whether it was wound up or not, there was mounting evidence from both Brussels and the EU's formal mission in Bucharest that no strong voices in the EU were determined to ensure that Romania adhered to the promises it had made to fight corruption and ensure the creation of a justice system free of political interference.

The scope of the EU's mission in Romania was greatly reduced from the autumn of 2006 onwards, after Scheele's hasty departure. By late 2007, its role was primarily a public relations one designed to raise awareness about the EU in Romania. This was certainly needed, as would be shown in the elections for the European Parliament in 2007 when no debate occurred about what position Romania ought to adopt in any of the major debates concerning the EU's future. Donato Chiarini, a diplomat approaching retirement who had considerable experience of the western Balkans, was Delegation chief from November 2006 to early 2008. He was hardly visible, perhaps because the Romanian state was supposed to coordinate publicity for the EU Representation (the new name since 2007 for the Delegation). In this, as in so many areas, it proved deficient and the tempo of activities of the mission appeared very feeble. Because of Romania's ongoing problems a strong case could be made for having preserved a Delegation with a strong oversight role. This would have been at variance with the EU custom in post-accession countries. So would direct funding for civic projects meant to strengthen the quality of democracy. But some EU embassies were pressing for Brussels to continue funding initiatives which were designed to preserve a fragile pluralism in the civic and human rights field. The fact that such an approach was necessary proved another illustration that the consolidation of democracy had not been a by-product of the EU's engagement with Romania. Catherine Day, Secretary-General of the Commission, on past experience was unlikely to view support for a range of projects to preserve tenuous checks and balances in Romania with much enthusiasm. As head of the Phare programme in the late 1990s, she had phased out projects designed to nurture grassroots democracy and community engagement in favour of unwieldy and expensive programmes strictly tied in with accession-based objectives.

Ironically, nearly a decade later, in April 2007, she was lobbied by the ambassadors of five EU states (including Britain, France and the Netherlands) who asked her for a clear and firm application of the monitoring process that applied to Romanian and Bulgarian efforts to combat corruption and reform the justice system. They secured a meeting with her, where concerns about the EU's handling of a problematic new member were not masked: 'We have to have a transparent system [of monitoring] not one that hides problems' said one ambassador.[42]

But from 2008, it was unclear what the quality of information Brussels would be receiving from Romania would be like. The EU's Directorate for Communications (DG Comm) appointed as head of the Representation Nicolae Idu, who had been a channel of communication between the EU and those anti-reform forces mainly in charge of negotiations after 2000. DG Comm had little idea of the critical struggle being waged in Romania about what the pace of Europeanisation ought to be. Therefore, the advice of Leonardo Orban, the former chief negotiator who was now a Commissioner and who previously had been ready to minimise the serious failings of Romania in getting ready to face the challenges of membership, counted for a great deal. Idu shared much of his outlook and there is no doubt that his appointment was a victory for the old guard in Bucharest which wants a restricted circle of people to enjoy benefits from EU membership without public life in Romania becoming influenced by EU models of behaviour. Under the 2000–03 Minister for European Integration, Hildegard Puwak, Idu quietly assisted the PSD in ensuring that the civic world never grew into a formidable body which the EU could mobilise to promote its ideas for changing Romania. As the perennial head of the European Institute of Romania, he confined it to translating the *acquis* and holding unexciting seminars on technical aspects of accession.[43]

On 12 February 2008, a revealing incident occurred when Jonathan Scheele was receiving an award from the Group for Social Dialogue at the Bucharest offices where they faced the threat of eviction. As he tried to articulate concerns he had about Romania's performance since joining the EU, he was cut short by Idu, who clearly had little patience with them.[44] There is the risk that, in his reports to Brussels, he will provide a sanitised account of the political struggle in Romania, however nasty it grows. The Commission already has strained relations with the Romanian diplomatic mission to the European Council, which is the largest Romanian diplomatic mission abroad. Often, its role appears to be to minimise attempts by Brussels to promote change in Romania and it has been known to refuse cooperation with the Commission even on routine issues. By contrast, EU institutions in Brussels have recruited many young Romanians committed to the best EU values, people often blocked from performing public service at home, despite their aptitude for it, owing to the backwardness of much of the public administration. So ironically, the EU itself has become a venue for a struggle between progressive Romanians committed to seeing European ideals blossom in their country and those sent abroad by the Foreign Ministry often to simulate change and block inconvenient changes.[45]

The old power networks not only wished to disinform the EU about the extent to which Romania was failing to carry out the undertakings it had given in negotiations with Brussels but were also determined to muzzle the independent media.

Jonathan Scheele had got the matter the wrong way round in 2004 when he suggested that Romania would only have a completely independent press when economic growth generates sufficient advertising revenue from a sufficiently broad market place. But instead those who had emerged on top in a far from transparent privatisation process were determined to muzzle the independent media and curb its investigative powers. This was done by taking over previously independent titles and offering tempting inducements to those editors who had resisted the PSD's more brutal crackdown on the media. Once they started to enjoy immense private wealth, some editors who had proved serious thorns in Năstase's side switched sides and became fierce opponents of attempts to create an independent justice system. They turned on NGOs which previously had been their allies and accused Băsescu of being determined to establish a personal dictatorship despite his adherence to procedures and his support for efforts to decouple the justice system from the oligarchy.

In a bid to rein in the independent media, Romania's economic barons faced no opposition from the EU, which had never concerned itself with the need to ensure a plurality of ownership continued to exist in a fragile democracy where the media had often played a key role in ensuring that unaccountable politicians were held to some sort of public account. With the independent media facing its worst crisis in many years during 2007 (with many journalists finding it impossible to practise their profession unless they wrote to order for politically active economic moguls), the EU issued no pronouncements on the matter. Indeed, its evaluation of the extent to which Romania was honouring its commitments to combat corruption proved remarkably tepid in 2007, as shown when it released its first monitoring report in July 2007. Officials were influenced by the fact that, once inside the EU, Romania could no longer be subject to active pressure to conform to club rules. Thus 'the safeguard clause' devised to ensure compliance was a dead letter. The *Financial Times*, commenting on the Tăriceanu government's unwillingness to proceed with justice reform, wrote:

> The EU is discovering that the penalties for new members that fail to meet the club's rules are toothless. The only remedy available is for the EU to refuse to recognise the court judgments of Bulgaria and Romania – in effect declaring that their legal systems cannot be trusted.
>
> 'The problem is that the innocent would get hurt', says a senior Commission lawyer. Divorces obtained in Sofia might no longer be recognised elsewhere in Europe; foreign companies operating in the two countries could run into serious legal problems. 'We are seeing if there is anything we can do that protects innocent parties but it is not easy', says a lawyer.[46]

Referring to both Romania and Bulgaria, the *Financial Times*, in June 2007, was unsparing about the EU performance:

> This cowardly approach undermines the reformers in both countries by robbing them of some powerful weapons they could use in their domestic battles. It deprives the people of Romania and Bulgaria of the full benefits of membership. It undermines the impact of future membership on other potential members which might also hope to slide around their obligations. It compromises public support for further expansion at a time when it is already dangerously weak. Finally, it exposes the whole union to ridicule: how can the EU fight for the rule of law elsewhere in the world when it cannot impose it on its own members.[47]

Some national governments were also very apprehensive about what the impact of a large delinquent state inside the EU might be. Jaap Werner, the

Dutch ambassador, publicly expressed fears about the direction in which Romania was going, which no Commission official went on record with. Asked about whether concerns existed in the Netherlands about the rule of law in Romania, the evolution of reforms in the justice sector and the anti-corruption struggle, the ambassador replied that 'Yes, there are worries in each of these regards . . . the process of reforms in the justice system no longer possessed the rhythm that it previously had had'.[48] Such a forthright statement could be contrasted with that issued by Mark Gray, a spokesman for the Commission after Tudor Chiuariu had accused the EU of blocking progress in the fight against corruption. He declared that the Justice Minister's 'views were well-known' and that the Commission had repeatedly defended 'the need for stability and continuity in the existing anti-graft structures'.[49] On a visit to the EU Representation in November 2007, I was informed that this statement was considered to be a tough one in Commission circles.[50]

In the same month Ambassador Werner declared that in January 2008 'we want a detailed and good-quality report from the Commission' on justice issues and, as if to underline the point, he went on to say: 'we take the mechanisms for cooperation and verification very seriously . . . I want to stress that not only are we critical observers, but we are implicated as well . . . I see the European Union as a community of laws, a community of values, a common internal market, and a political union. And that means . . . we are inter-connected and dependent on each other. Thus, the way the justice system evolves here is relevant for us . . . That's why we are expressing these worries'.[51]

The EU did, however, threaten to penalise Romania over economic failings. On 7 October 2007, it emerged that Romania was in danger of losing up to one-quarter of the €8 billion of aid allocated for agriculture. The Agriculture Commissioner, Marianne Fischer Boel, had found serious deficiencies in the work of the APIA, which had been supposed to begin providing financial support in agriculture from 1 January 2007 but which was paralysed by internal difficulties.[52]

The Agriculture Minister, Traian Decebal Remeş, was days away from resigning on 11 October after state television had broadcast a leaked tape, allegedly showing him taking a 15,000 euro bribe and the promise of €4,555 in goods, including home-made sausages and plum brandy. The person allegedly passing on the bribe was a former agriculture minister himself facing charges, who the press alleged was acting on behalf of a businessman seeking an advantage in a public auction for a state contract.[53] A second embarrassing tape was not broadcast due to government pressure, with Parliament quickly passing a law reserving heavy jail sentences for journalists who published covertly filmed material on politicians (one that would later be rescinded).[54]

Remeş's successor, Dacian Cioloş, was one of the few ministers who enjoyed technical expertise in the policy area he was in charge of. This agronomist was given the autonomy to carry out a lightning series of changes in a sector plagued with chronic difficulties, and on 19 December 2007 the EU announced that it would not after all be imposing the safety clause on agriculture. Once again the EU had become dependent on a particular individual to drive forward change when it was clear that there were systemic faults preventing the Agriculture Ministry performing effectively – something which was beyond the ability of one individual to change, especially an isolated figure like Cioloş, one liable to be dismissed if he challenged any vested interests in the agricultural sector.[55] But Brussels was less forgiving of the Tăriceanu government for giving state assistance to one of its main car plants in Romania before it was sold to Ford Motor. By doing so, Romania had violated EU competition policy and it was ordered, in early 2008, to recover €27 million from the US firm.[56]

This was despite the stark peer review report sent to senior European officials in November 2007 by Willem de Pauw, the Belgian Deputy Prosecutor at the Court of Appeal in Ghent, who had issued four such reports at the request of the EU from 2001 onwards. He described how 'many of the measures that were presented before Accession, to be instrumental in the fight against corruption, have been deliberately blunted by Parliament or the government immediately after Accession'.[57] He pointed out that 'all major trials concerning high-level corruption, started just before Accession and only after many years of hesitation, have now been aborted and are, most probably, definitely abandoned for all practical purposes'.[58] He concluded that 'if the Romanian anti-corruption effort keeps evaporating at the present pace, in an estimated six months' time, Romania will be back where it was in 2003'.[59]

In June 2008, the ambassadors of Great Britain and the Netherlands issued grave warnings that the amount of protection parliamentarians wished to give serious criminals, whether from their own ranks or else the wider fraternity of drug-bosses and human traffickers, undermined the interests of their own states, damaged bilateral cooperation with Romania and undermined the security of the rest of the EU.[60] Ambassadors Robin Barnett and Jaap Werner had turned up in person at a meeting of the parliamentary commission' on the judiciary to voice these concerns. But it was hard to disguise the fact that they were concerned at the passivity of the European Commission, which had issued an anodyne report on justice reform in January 2008 with all the indications already in place that the next one, due to be published in late July of that year, would not significantly diverge from it, and would not impose the safeguard clause introduced precisely to penalise such defiance of undertakings previously made to the EU by the Tăriceanu government concerning the fight against corruption. The Justice and Security Commission had become rudderless after the sudden departure of Commissioner Frattini to be Foreign Minister in the Italian government. It is likely that the concern of middle-ranking officials lay behind the leaking of the entire 2007 de Pauw report in *The Economist* of 3 July 2008. 'The EU Conceals Romania's Backsliding on Corruption' was the sub-heading of the article. It revealed the dismay felt among officials who had tried to impose proper norms of conduct on the Bucharest authorities but whose efforts were sabotaged by the indifference of senior figures in the Commission and core EU states, France being mentioned in the article. This revelation followed hard on the heels of the Irish voters' rejection of the Lisbon treaty on 12 June which promised to give the top echelons of the Commission the trappings of statehood in important policy areas. Senior figures in the Franco-German core states openly discussed pushing Ireland to the outer limits of the EU for holding up the drive towards supra-national unity and Ireland's ejection from the EU was even discussed in some quarters.[61] Such severe punishment was being seriously considered for Ireland by Eurocrats who disliked the result of a referendum, which its Constitution compelled it to hold, as simultaneously the very same people were overlooking the way that most of the Romanian political elite was reinforcing corrupt networks that threatened to pollute the whole EU. It suggested that the era of post-democracy has arrived not just in Bucharest but in Brussels also.

Such myopia only spurred on most of the political elite and the managers of the justice system in Romania to close ranks and ensure that only cosmetic reforms would be permitted. The evidence therefore accumulated that the failure to promote a system of justice that was independent of the legislature and protected the interests of the weak as well as the strong was perhaps the EU's single biggest blunder in its engagement with a set of rulers who scorned its values but were eager to enjoy the privileges of membership.

Beyond spasmodic initiatives, the EU had never shown much need to strengthen civic forces in Romania so that they might act as a counterweight to a venal political elite. NGOs were not always transparent in their conduct but the strongest pro-European sentiment was to be found in the civic sector. However, once the EU's influence started to wane and its funding programmes were scaled back, even NGOs with a democracy-building agenda found it difficult to resist the overtures of oligarchical forces.

The Timişoara Association had a distinguished record of coordinating civic action in this western Romanian city where the flag of revolt had first been raised against Ceauşescu in 1989 and where, afterwards, there was strong resistance to the old political structures re-imposing their control. But in 2007 it was ensnared by Bogdan Olteanu, who proposed to use his position as lower house speaker to promote a law on lustration which would have imposed penalties on communist-era officials and those who had actively assisted the dictatorship. But Olteanu quickly abandoned the idea after obtaining some capital for positioning the PNL as a party still in tune with the aspirations of those who had resisted communism and tried to reduce its influence after 1989.[62] The emptiness of such a claim was shown when he was instrumental in placing Daniel Dăianu, an economist and former employee of the pre-1989 intelligence services, near the top of the list of PNL candidates for the 2007 European Parliament elections. He and other leading Liberals also closed ranks around the PNL's most eminent intellectual figure, Constantin Bălăceanu Stolnici, after it emerged that he had been an informer for the *Securitate* for decades with the code name of 'Laurenţiu'.[63] There was genuine shock when it emerged that this respected octogenarian had passed on detailed information about the home of Vlad Georgescu, a celebrated broadcaster in the Romanian section of Radio Free Europe before his death in 1988 (it being widely assumed that he had been irradiated by Ceauşescu's secret police).[64] Stolnici remained in the PNL, whose government sponsored an Institution for the Investigation of Crimes against Communism in Romania (IICR). Its leading figures, Marius Oprea and Stejărel Olaru, had no qualms about continuing to rely on Liberal patronage and they were widely suspected of leaking information designed to compromise popular opponents of the Tăriceanu government such as the politician Mona Muscă and the journalist Carol Sebastian.[65] The IICR received a budget of 6 million euros from the Prime Minister's office to finance its activities and Olaru ran on the PNL ticket in the 2007 European elections.

Heading the PNL list was Renate Weber, formerly the longstanding President of the Soroş Foundation in Romania. Having previously been a senior adviser to President Băsescu, she broke with him over the lengths he was prepared to take reform of the justice sector. Professional and personal rivalry with Monica Macovei contributed to the rupture, the NGO world in Romania frequently being disfigured by such quarrels.[66] Having previously been aligned with forces committed to releasing the grip of oligarchical parties on the justice sector, she became an ally of Tudor Chiuariu. During the 2007 campaign, she refused to criticise the unprecedented offensive that he mounted against anti-corruption prosecutors, Weber having been earlier hired by Tăriceanu to advise him on legal issues.

Criticism of the Tăriceanu government's controversial record could prove costly. After leading members of the Group for Social Dialogue sponsored a letter broadly defending Băsescu and Macovei's position on justice reform, Parliament passed a motion in 2007 to evict the oldest pro-democratic civic body from its Bucharest headquarters.[67] Gabriel Liiceanu, the most prominent civic supporter of the President, found himself arraigned in the pro-government press for alleged intellectual fraud, and soon after his publishing house, Humanitas was subject to a painstaking financial audit by the tax authorities.[68] Such methods of control had been associated with the PSD, but the PNL did not hesitate to apply them with even more rigour than before. The worsening situation persuaded other civic bodies with a record of defying state-sponsored authoritarianism to keep a low profile. A good case in point is the Civic Alliance under Cristian Mititelu (he had been at the centre of controversy in 2003 when, as Director of the BBC Romanian Service, he allowed the sacking of its most popular broadcaster, Traian Ungureanu, which led to the resignation in solidarity of leading colleagues in the Romanian service).

Under Ana Blandiana the Civic Alliance had been a leading proponent of greater pluralism in the 1990s. After she switched her energies to creating a memorial for the victims of communism at Sighet in north-west Romania, her NGO, along with others, pressurised Traian Băsescu to issue a formal condemnation of communism and the crimes committed in its name in Romania, only to retreat from public view. After some hesitation, Băsescu threw his weight behind setting up an official commission of investigation of the repression between 1948 and 1989. A commission of experts headed by the well-known historian of communism, Professor Vladimir Tismăneanu, concluded that communism was an illegal regime imposed by external armed force in the mid-1940s, one which stayed in power through blanket oppression that left many hundreds of thousands of victims. It also concluded that the structures and mentality of Romanian communism persisted long after 1989, thereby distorting the transition to political and economic pluralism.[69] When the President read out its findings to a special sitting of Parliament on 18 December 2006, there were disorderly scenes. Ultra-nationalist members and their supporters (unimpeded by parliamentary officials) disrupted his speech and threatened the supporters of the commission who were in the visitors' gallery, including ex-political prisoners.[70]

Russia offers plenty of helpful examples of how an autocratic state can bend civil society to its will. In February 2008, the PNL, along with its allies on the Left and the ultra-nationalist camp, passed a law threatening NGOs with dissolution if they did not change their names whenever a risk existed that they might be confused with the name of a state body. Twenty-five NGOs signed a letter of protest accusing the government of using tactics already tried out in Russia to punish civic associations which refused to toe the line.[71] The EU for its part has kept an awkward silence. The worrying trajectory of events blows away its often-expressed hopes that democracy will be consolidated after 2007.

Perhaps the issue which perplexed the EU the most in relation to Romania was how to integrate the large Roma (gypsy) population who had lived on the margins of society for centuries. In 2006 the World Bank/UNDP placed the population at between 1,800,000 and 2,500,000.[72] They faced discrimination from state and society but had their own social customs which were often at variance with those of mainstream society. Once visa restrictions were lifted on Romanians in 2001, member states were soon complaining about the conduct of some Roma which greatly complicated the task of Romania's negotiators.[73] By 2002, French state officials were claiming that about 1,000 Roma children were on the streets of Paris, where they were forced into begging, prostitution and other crimes.[74] Peter Schieder, President of the Council of Europe's Parliamentary Assembly, told the Romanian Parliament in November 2002 that Romania's image was being harmed thanks to large numbers of gypsies emigrating to Western Europe and that he hoped Romania would make important investments in projects aimed at keeping them at home.[75] The OSCE staged a large conference in Bucharest in 2001 designed to promote strategies which would respond effectively to pressing problems faced by the Roma in South-East Europe. These ranged from the vulnerability of Roma women and children and the lack of adequate housing and education, to the need for greater protection under the law, protection for refugees displaced by conflict and the need to strengthen Roma participation in public life.[76] In 2001 the Năstase government launched a strategy to improve the situation of the Roma population.[77] But only a year later, Adrian Năstase admitted that the strategy for improving the social conditions of the Roma people 'has been enacted, but then forgotten in a drawer'.[78] The dispiriting comments made by successive EU annual reports on Romania suggested that little had really changed for the better. The European Roma Rights Centre complained about the absence of a coherent programme for action along with an effective budget. This well-known Roma advocacy body argued that, 'the strategy is in reality a plan committing the government in many areas, to little more than more planning over the next four years'.[79] A key weakness it identified was the lack of coordination between the national and local authorities in understanding their joint responsibilities and implementing objectives to improve conditions for the Roma. A 2004 local-level monitoring report by the European Union noted the low level of implementation, stating, 'the objectives of the strategy have not been successfully translated to the local level, and there is a general lack of awareness of how the strategy should be implemented in practice'.[80]

One of the greatest hurdles faced by policy-makers when confronting the socio-economic difficulties faced by Roma is the diversity of the group itself. Far from being a uniform group, they are highly heterogeneous.[81] A common expression applied to Roma diversity is a mosaic, one that is built upon multiple subgroups, which are based on language, history, religion and occupation.[82] One group which is undoubtedly among the worst off is Roma women. From the early 1990s, they have become increasingly vulnerable to a wide range of abuses, from domestic violence to prostitution and human trafficking, with the impetus for the trade often coming from within the Roma community.[83] In addition, they are subject to a lot of customary laws and pressures from within their own communities.[84] The Roma Women Association of Romania has stated that 'when a woman breaks the rules and does not respect the rules of the family, her extended family does not respect her anymore and her parents are also less respected by the community'.[85] These roles and responsibilities are reflected by the estimated average age of Roma women at marriage, which is 18.5 years compared with an average age of 22.2 for the entire population. Roma women also have an estimated average of 4.35 children in comparison to 1.79 for the entire population.[86]

Not all Roma were on the margins of society; indeed the PSD had made a political alliance with Roma leaders in 2000 and Roma figures participated in the informal economy, enjoying control over areas of the black market such as food distribution in some cities and even the property business in parts of Bucharest. Sometimes, members of the community could be vexatious for the rest of society. Thus, in 2007 the Prefect of Timiş, Ovidiu Drăgănescu, made headlines when he said that the police must take firm action against Roma who intimidate the owners of flats in the middle of the city into selling them. This followed the complaint of a physics professor from the main university that the police had refused to do anything to restrain a Roma family threatening him after he had refused to sell his apartment to them.[87] Other examples of anti-social behaviour indicated that there were Roma who found it difficult to obey the customary rules of society. But not a few had managed to integrate whereas huge numbers lived in abject poverty, being illiterate, jobless and sometimes being subject to exploitation by unscrupulous figures in the hierarchical clan system which prevailed in the Roma world. So this was a community, or set of communities, facing a deep crisis, as the trades which had enabled them to eke out a precarious existence had vanished due to mass production.

The former Foreign Minister Adrian Severin has insisted that this crisis was a European one and that it was at this level solutions would have to be found.[88] It was ill-chosen words by a successor, Adrian Cioroianu, which brought fresh prominence to the Roma issue across Europe. On 2 November 2007, while on an official visit to Egypt, he stated on television with reference to Roma who had committed crimes abroad that the government should buy land in the Egyptian desert 'to place there those who embarrass us'.[89] There were uncomfortable echoes to remarks made in August 1998 by Corneliu Vadim Tudor, leader of the Greater Romania Party, when he unfurled a ten-point programme to run the country which included 'isolating the Roma criminals in special colonies' in order to 'stop the transformation of Romania into a Gypsy camp'.[90] In May 2007, in a private conversation which was picked up on tape, Traian Băsescu used the term 'stinking gypsy' to refer to a journalist who had been harassing him. Vasile Dâncu, a well-known PSD parliamentarian, referred on 18 June to 'the difference between Social Democracy and

Gypsy-like attitudes' and on 2 July Prime Minister Tăriceanu reportedly associated the Roma with criminality.[91]

Foreign Minister Cioroianu's outburst had followed the high-profile killing
in Rome of the wife of an Italian admiral for which Romulus Mailat, an
illegal immigrant of Roma origin, was arrested. Amidst the resulting uproar,
Giuliano Amato, the Interior Minister of the centre-left government, accused
Romanian immigrants in Italy of carrying out large numbers of thefts, sexual
attacks and killings.[92] A wave of arrests followed and plans were announced
to deport large numbers of Romanians, but these were dropped (after the
furore started to abate) because they violated EU laws. Franco Frattini, the
Vice-President of the Commission, promised to meet soon with gypsy leaders
in order to assure them of the EC's backing for 'the elimination of the discrimination towards them that currently exists in Europe'.[93] But when he took one
month off to campaign in Italy's spring 2008 general election, he connected
Romanians with the growing crime rate and promised zero tolerance in the
efforts to contain the problem.[94]

The EU's principal anxieties about Romania continued to be focused on
economic matters. On the surface, Romania appeared to be a resounding
success story. There was rapid credit, expansion and spiralling asset appre-
ciation. Since 2001 GDP had grown between 4% and 7% per year. But from
2007, there were warnings from the IMF and Mugur Isărescu, the head of
the National Bank, about the dangers of economic over-heating.[95] A jump
in inflation and a yawning current account deficit were particular causes of
concern.[96] In November 2007, the well-known ratings agency, Standard and
Poor, downgraded Romania's prospects from stable to negative.[97] In March
2008, the Economist Intelligence Unit warned that Romania was one of the
most vulnerable countries in Eastern Europe as the international financial
world faced serious problems. It pointed out that foreign investment was likely
to slow down as the privatisation process ended and therefore the government
would lose a key lever for controlling the current account deficit.[98] Foreign
investment had failed to significantly expand the labour market. By 2007, the
49 companies doing business worth 1 billion euros[99] or over in Romania used
only 3.8% of the labour force.[100] Productivity was lagging behind. Steep falls
in output in the textile sector which had driven industrial production since
the closure of most heavy industrial plants were noticeable after 2004. Maria
Grapini, head of the Federation of Light Industry Owners, said that joining the
EU spellt doom for textile firms. Romanian employees received an average of
one euro per hour while the average European wage was 18 euros. The growing
labour shortage meant that wages would have to rise, resulting in firms
transferring to low-wage economies elsewhere in the Balkans and in Asia.[101]

The food sector also registered heavy falls due to labour shortages and bad
weather.[102] Leonard Orban, later to be Romania's first EU Commissioner,

warned in 2005 that very many meat- and dairy-processing companies would not be able to adapt to EU requirements in terms of food safety. 'Around 80% of these companies will have to cease trading', he warned.[103] In the same year, Scheele pointed out that 43% of firms were totally unprepared for EU entry. Only 12% had estimated what the entry costs would be for them.[104] Ovidiu Nicolescu, the President of the National Council for small and medium-sized enterprises, had similarly warned in May 2005 that 20% to 25% of SMEs could close after 2007 because of their lack of competitiveness. He believed that those most at risk were in the food-processing and service industries, noting that between 15 and 30% of SMEs had closed when the Mediterranean entrants joined the EU in the 1980s. He believed that the only way to stem the rate of closures was by a training, consultation and information campaign.[105]

The weakness of a competitive business ethic also greatly disadvantaged Romania as it faced formidable competition from other EU states. The economist Ilie Şerbănescu stated in 2006 that many Romanian companies 'don't stand a chance. They are not competitive and will not be able to resist the shock of accession. Many of them still live under the impression that one can do business by making phone calls to their political clientele or [by] cheating on the state'.[106] In March 2008, Adel Murad, the Iraqi ambassador, argued that Romanian companies were lazy and still operating in the communist style and therefore missing out on huge investment opportunities in his country.[107] Romanian products all too often were over-priced and of poor quality.[108]

The lack of initiative displayed by many businessmen in relation to the EU and emerging markets is ascribed to deep-seated psychological conditioning, according to the social psychologist, Claudiu Ganciu. Writing in 2006, Ganciu believed mentality played an important role in determining Romanian expectations towards the EU: 'the tendency to wait for others is a permanent characteristic. Romanians don't make history. They endure it. They see in the EU an authority not a partner. . . . What the Romanian does not understand is that in order for living standards to get better it is necessary to act on your own initiative indifferent as to whether Romania is inside the EU or not'. Romanians waited for the Russians to liberate them from the Turks and the Americans from the communists. 'This perception has marked us through our history – we lack our own goals, our attitude towards reality is to demand nothing and to wait for everything to be done by others . . . In this situation [of EU accession] the Romanian acts like the child who waits for his father to bring him something to eat'.[109]

The persistence of a dependency outlook meant that, having gone through traumatic changes to prepare for EU membership, Romania risked suffering damage by remaining unprepared to face the challenges of entry. In late 2006, the public administration only had 1,000 people trained to access structural funds, 10% of the minimum required, according to a survey carried out by the

Romanian Institute for Training for funding procurement.[110] Thus it faced a critical shortage of experts in the very ministries that it was anticipated the bulk of funding would flow into in order to strengthen administrative efficiency, modernise agriculture and increase economic competitiveness.[111] Six months later the European Delegation reported that the situation had hardly changed. Incredibly, the Ministries of Commerce, Agriculture, Transport, Administration and the Interior, and European Integration, up until the end of 2006, had no training programmes to prepare staff to acquire competence with applying for and managing EU funds.

Mircea Geoană, the leader of the PSD, had declared categorically on 30 April 2006 that Romania would be incapable of accessing more than 15–18% of the structural and cohesion funds money (30 billion euros) to be allocated to it from 2006–13. The country was not yet ready to co-finance European funds or absorb them.[112] The government did not deny this and Emil Boc, the leader of the second largest coalition party, soon after said that Romania risked becoming a net contributor to the EU budget unless projects were devised by the mainline ministries for a broad range of modernisation tasks, ones which Brussels found acceptable. Sebastian Vlădescu, the Finance Minister, in his turn asked the Prime Minister to galvanise members of his government to ensure that they obtain 800 million euros of Phare funds for the 2004 and 2005 period which otherwise would revert to Brussels.[113] He feared that part of the 2005 Phare allocation for infrastructure would be lost unless feasible projects had been submitted by September 2006. Anca Boagiu, the Minister of European Integration, had already revealed the loss of 266 million euros for the development of human resources (re-integration of the unemployed and improving skills) because of delays in submitting projects.[114] But perhaps the most striking failure in the issuing of EU funds has been in transport and environment (which come under Ispa). By June 2006, only 11% of allocated funds for the previous six years had been used. One reason was the failure of the Bucharest authorities to follow transparent procedures for public tenders, leading to the disqualification of projects for funding from Brussels.[115]

In the event, little funding came in 2007 except for projects considered vital for EU security, such as the protection of Romania's borders, for which Romania received over €500 million. The procedures which needed to be mastered to access structural and cohesion funds were simply beyond the capabilities of a poorly performing bureaucracy. Every member state needed to submit operational programmes indicating how the funds would be spent in each sector. These programmes had to be approved by the Commission before any payments could be made. Moreover, any member state needed to prove that it had the auditing structures necessary to be able to give a proper account of how EU funds had been spent.[116] But these were tasks for which a government mired in infighting with the President and whose members tended their own private interests had neglected to adequately prepare. As a result, Romania became a net contributor of aid to the EU in 2007 when it paid some €1.35 billion to the EU budget, equal to about 1.3% of its GDP.[117] The situation was likely to be little different in 2008, which caused Isărescu, the National Bank Governor, to warn that if radical improvement did not occur in the state's approach, 'Romania would remain in the position of being a poor and underdeveloped country which was also a net contributor to the European budget'.[118]

Lacking was a strong central managing authority for funding with the right degree of high-level political backing. Regional authorities, through which much of the funding was supposed to flow, had serious flaws and even exceeded the defects of the central bureaucracy.[119] Some degree of decentralisation is necessary given the size of Romania and the often weak capacity of the central state. But due to abundant evidence that local and regional authorities sometimes duplicate and even exceed the defects of the central bureaucracy, a strong central managing authority with the right degree of high-level political backing would be essential, according to the head of the IMF in Romania during 2008.[120] From January 2007, around 3.5 billion euros were due to be spent on regional development projects. But problems arose when the political complexion of the beneficiaries differed from the councillors whose final approval was needed. The south-east region is the best-known one where projects are blocked on political criteria. Besides this, funding was given for bizarre and ephemeral projects such as the protection of a small area in Transylvania inhabited by a sub-species of the common viper. A Cluj-based NGO obtained €388,000 to safeguard its habitat, the state providing an additional €100,000 which the press dubbed 'the golden viper'.[121]

Herbert Bosch, an Austrian MEP who had acquired a reputation as a stern watchdog of EU finances, had already insisted in the autumn of 2005 that Romania was not ready to access structural funds and that therefore it should be excluded from the EU budget in 2007.[122] But Danuta Hubner, the Commissioner for Regional Policy, believed that Brussels possessed 'strict auditing measures' able to protect from corrupt interception the €20 billion Romania was due to receive in regional funds.[123] However, it remains to be seen how effective well-known audit and consultancy companies now employed by the EU to audit some of its programmes will prove to be. They often hire as local managers figures who enjoyed close links with the economy and financial system when it was state controlled. Some of them have pursued aggressive marketing strategies to increase the profits of the Romanian division which even involves advising private clients on how best to access structural funds. It is important that these external auditors retain high standards because the autonomy enjoyed by state auditors has been whittled away.[124] In 2008, Sebastian Bodu, head of the National Agency for

Fiscal Administration from 2005 until his removal in 2007, as a result of the infighting which wrecked the ruling centre-right alliance, warned of political interference. He complained that staff involved in overseeing the customs service had been shifted to other parts of the country which was bound to erode efforts to maintain probity in what had been one of the most corrupt branches of state activity.[125]

There was mounting evidence at the heart of government of the revival of the outlook that the main business of politics was to satisfy the appetites of the interest groups who had grown wealthy through maintaining close links with all sides in Parliament and the power structure as a whole. Three days before Bodu's criticism, Carl Bildt, the Swedish Foreign Minister and someone with considerable experience of the Balkans after the 1995 Dayton peace agreement, openly admitted that in Brussels the sentiment that Romania and Bulgaria had been granted full membership too early was expressed with growing frequency. He complained that both countries had not stuck by the promises that had secured entry for them in 2007 and that the instruments meant to continue the reform process were not functioning. One inevitable consequence in his view was that future candidates would face much stricter monitoring and that this would slow the pace of EU expansion.[126] So here was an admission from the member of the European Council with arguably the most experience of the Balkans that the EU's belief that these countries could be trusted to proceed with the broad reform agenda had been misplaced.

But Romania was the seventh largest EU member and the EU would have to get used to dealing with the political and business networks which increasingly dominated the political process. A great deal changed during the first 18 months of full membership of the EU. In May 2007, the power of this oligarchy appeared to be tottering when voters decisively rejected a bid to drive the President from office. But it has come back with a vengeance assisted by the crushing of much of the independent media and relying on the willingness of judges to acquit, give derisory sentences or postpone the cases of politicians who come before them on corruption charges.

The PSD performed well in the June 2008 local elections thanks to mistakes by Băsescu and the failure of his party to offer a powerful contrasting alternative to its rivals in terms of a programme for change and even its ethical standards. The PSD's recovery also derived from the strength of provincial barons, especially in the south and east of the country. They had built up formidable local machines whose influence extended beyond local government to encompass the media, local business and sometimes also the courts. The most autocratic and ruthless ones were re-elected and their power is likely to be consolidated since they will be responsible for far greater local budgets thanks to decentralisation measures insisted upon by the EU.

With Adrian Năstase back in the leadership and the PSD confident about forming the next government after parliamentary elections due in late 2008 (and also the Presidency in 2009, perhaps running a unity candidate), reform hopes appeared to be in ruins. The mood of most Romanians who had expected that the implication of the EU in their affairs would result in a transformation of political standards was a desolate one by 2008. It was particularly well summed up by 'Catalin Z', writing in the readers' forum of *The Economist*:

> The governing National Liberal Party broke the anti-corruption alliance it formed with the Democratic Party and, instead, allied itself with the representatives of the old corrupt PSD . . . The alliance, never validated at the polls, is led by the cronies of . . . Romanian moguls, former members of the Securitate and high rank officials of the former Communist Party, people who participated in the robbery of former state banks, robbery of former state assets through the so-called privatisation process, robbery of state budgets and, recently, robbery of EU funds which will surely continue in the years to come, should they keep their hold on power after the next elections. The alliance always opposed any judicial reform, sacked those who promoted it, and drafts a new penal legislation that transforms Romania into a true Camorra-like state, where high-rank corruption will become immune from a legal system which, many say, does not even exist in Romania. All eyes are now focused on the reaction of the EU officials in their next report on the state of the Romanian judicial reforms, and whether it will finally sanction a corrupt state and a corrupt system of clientele that always changes its colors but never changes itself. It is, after all, the people, 'the new Europeans' that suffer the most from corruption under the indulgent and sometimes blind eye of EC surveillance'.[127]

Notes

1 *Evenimentul Zilei*, 18 May 2004.
2 *România Liberă*, 11 January 2007.
3 *Cotidianul*, 18 January 2008.
4 *Cotidianul*, 30 January 2007.
5 Private information.
6 *Revista 22*, 2–8 March 2007.
7 Dated 4 October 2005 and copy in possession of the author.
8 D.T., *Hotnews*, 17 December 2007.
9 *Hotnews*, 3 April 2007.
10 *Evenimentul Zilei*, 14 November 2003.
11 *Hotnews*, 17 April 2007.
12 Valentina Pop, 'Romanian Parliament will Stick Out Like a Sore Thumb in the EU', 8 January 2007, www.euobserver.com.
13 *Hotnews*, 21 November 2007, www.hotnews.ro.
14 Commission document dated 4 October 2005.

15 *Hotnews*, 17 March 2007.
16 *România Liberă*, 9 October 2007.
17 Dan Tăpălaga, *Revista 22*, 21–27 September 2007.
18 Dan Tăpălaga, *Revista 22*, 21–27 September 2007.
19 *România Liberă*, 24 September 2007.
20 *Hotnews*, 25 September 2007.
21 *Hotnews*, 20 September 2007.
22 *BBC Romanian Service*, 13 April 2007.
23 *Ziarul Financiar* (Bucharest), 22 January 2008.
24 *Hotnews*, 5 October 2007.
25 *Evenimentul Zilei*, 9 October 2007.
26 Dan Tăpălaga, *Hotnews*, 21 September 2007.
27 Dan Tăpălaga, *Hotnews*, 11 March 2008.
28 *Cotidianul*, 29 November 2007.
29 *Hotnews*, 1 November 2007.
30 *Hotnews*, 15 January 2008.
31 *Evenimentul Zilei*, 16 November 2007.
32 *România Liberă*, 22 November 2007.
33 *Rompres News Agency*, Bucharest, 13 March 2008.
34 See 'Romania: Country Report on Human Rights Practices in Romania – 2007', Washington: US Department of State, 2008 www. state.gov/g/drl/hrrpt/2007/100580.htm.
35 *Hotnews*, 11 March 2008.
36 ABA/CEELI, *Romania, Significant Legal Developments*, Bucharest: ABA/CEELI, December 2007, p. 5.
37 Thomas Escritt, 'Prosecutors Caught in Tangle of Intrigue', *Financial Times*, 7 March 2008.
38 Andreea Pora, 'Clona lui Stănoiu la CSM', *România Liberă*, 1 January 2008.
39 *Cotidianul*, 19 January 2008.
40 Commission of the European Communities, *Interim Report on Progress in Romania under the Cooperation and Verification Mechanism*, Brussels, 4 February 2002, COM (2008), 62 final.
41 *Hotnews*, 28 February 2008.
42 Oana Lungescu, *BBC Romanian Service*, 18 April 2007.
43 For the ultra-cautious approach of Nicolae Idu during the years of accession negotiations, a perusal of the contents of the *Romanian Journal of European Affairs*, which he supervised, provides ample evidence.
44 For the debate on 12 February, see *Revista 22*, 19–25 February 2008.
45 Private information obtained from European officials in Brussels and Romanian journalists and civic activists.
46 George Parker, Kerin Hope and Christopher Condon, 'Europe's Errant Entrants', *Financial Times*, 13 June 2007.
47 'Maintain Standards', Editorial in the *Financial Times*, 29 June 2007.
48 *România Liberă*, 28 November 2007.
49 *Hotnews*, 21 November 2007.

50 A copy of Mark Gray's statement was given to me on this visit to the EU Representation.
51 *România Liberă*, 28 November 2007.
52 D. Mihai, *Hotnews*, 6 October 2007.
53 Associated Press, 'Romanian Agriculture Minister Forced to Resign amid Corruption Charges', *International Herald Tribune*, 11 October 2007.
54 See the Bucharest press for 12 and 13 October 2007.
55 *Evenimentul Zilei*, 19 December 2007.
56 *Reuters*, 27 February 2008.
57 W. de Pauw, *Expert Report on the Fight against Corruption/Cooperation and Verification Mechanism*, Bucharest, 12–15 November 2007, p. 22. (Published on the website of *The Economist*, 3 July 2008, www.economist.com.)
58 de Pauw, *Expert Report on the Fight against Corruption/ Cooperation*, p. 23.
59 de Pauw, *Expert Report on the Fight against Corruption/ Cooperation*, p. 23.
60 Luminita Parvu, 'Stenograma sedintei in care ambasadorii din UE I-au criticat pe parliamentari pentru frinarea luptei anti-coruptie', *Hotnews*, 3 July 2008.
61 See Wolfgang Műnchau, 'Europe's Hardball Plan B for the Lisbon treaty', *Financial Times*, 16 June 2008.
62 *România Liberă*, 13 December 2007.
63 *Cotidianul*, 24 April 2007.
64 *Cotidianul*, 28 November 2007.
65 Alexandru Lăzescu, 'Forţa residuală a vechilor structuri', *Hotnews*, 4 February 2008.
66 Alina Mungiu-Pippidi, 'Lupta logicii cu talentul', *România Liberă*, 3 May 2007.
67 *Hotnews*, 20 December 2007.
68 Andreea Pora, 'Guvernul-spălătorie', *Hotnews*, 8 October 2007; Cristian Ghinea, 'Demascarea ticăloşilor din ONG-uri', *România Liberă*, 1 March 2007.
69 Vladimir Tismăneanu (coordinator), *Raportul Final al Comisiei Prezidenţiale pentru analiza dictaturii comuniste în Romania*, Bucharest: Humanita, 2007.
70 See the Bucharest daily press for 19 December 2006.
71 *Hotnews*, 27 February 2008.
72 UNICEF, *Breaking the Cycle of Exclusion; Roma Children in Southeast Europe*, Paris: UNICEF, February 2007, p. 14.
73 Interview with Vasile Puşcaş, 17 November 2006.
74 *Reuters*, 21 October 2002.
75 *Evenimentul Zilei*, 13 November 2002.
76 OSCE *Conference, Equality of Opportunities for Roma and Sinti: Translating Words Into Facts, Bucharest, 10–13 September 2001*, Bucharest: OSCE, 2001.
77 'Proiectul UE Phare RO 9803.01 – Îmbunătăţirea Situaţiei Rromilor din România', *Buletin informativ Nr 5*, Bucharest: Guvernul României, August 2001.
78 Minelres, 'Romania: Ethnic Diversity', Brief No. 23, 20 September 2002.
79 The European Roma Rights Centre, *States of Impunity: Human Rights Abuse of Roma in Romania*, p. 121, located at http://errc.org/publications.
80 Open Society Institute and EU Monitoring and Advocacy Program, *Monitoring Local Implementation of the Government Strategy for the Improvement of the*

Conditions of the Roma, Budapest, 2004, p. 10, available at http://www.eumap. org/topics/minority/reports/roma.

81 Jean-Pierre Liegeois and Nicolae Gheorghe, *Roma/Gypsies: A European Minority*, London: Minority Rights Group International, 1995, p. 29.

82 Dena Ringold, Mitchell A. Orenstein and Erika Wilkins, *Roma in an Expanding Circle: Breaking the Poverty Cycle*, Washington, DC: World Bank, 2005, p. xiii.

83 UNICEF, *Breaking the Cycle of Exclusion*, p. 6.

84 Isabel Fonseca, *Bury me Standing: The Gypsies and their Journey*, London: Vintage Books, 1996, pp. 80, 130.

85 Roma Women's Association of Romania, '*The situation of Roma/Gypsy Women in Europe*, Bucharest: Roma Women's Association 2003, available at http://www. romawomen.ro.

86 Zoltan Barany, 'Romani Marginality', in Henry F. Carey, *Romania since 1989: Politics, Economy and Society*, Maryland: Lexington Books, p. 257.

87 *Evenimentul Zilei*, 23 May 2007.

88 *Ziua*, 10 November 2007.

89 See Romanian press on subsequent days.

90 'When Van der Stoel Touches the "Untouchables" of the Balkans', AIM, Athens, 19 May 2000.

91 'Romania: Country Report on Human Rights Practices in Romania – 2007'.

92 *Gândul*, 27 June 2007.

93 *Hotnews*, 16 November 2007.

94 *Hotnews*, 18 March 2008.

95 Juan J. Fernandez Alonso, 'Post-Accession EU Funds for Romania: Issues and Challenges', 16 April 2007, www.imf.ro (the author was the IMF's regional representative in Romania)/(accessed 15 September 2007).

96 Thomas Escritt and Stefan Wagstyl, 'Romanian Boom Rings Economic Alarm Bells', *Financial Times*, 22 November 2007.

97 *Hotnews*, 5 November 2007.

98 *Hotnews*, 18 March 2008.

99 *Capital* (Bucharest), 4 November 2004.

100 Ilie Şerbănescu, 'Impactul investiţiilor străine (3)', *Revista 22*, 11–17 March 2008.

101 *Hotnews*, 12 July 2007.

102 'Ce sectoare ne duc în UE şi ce ne trage în jos', 26 January 2006, www.eurActiv.ro.

103 www.EuroActiv.ro, 26 May 2005.

104 *Evenimentul Zilei*, 26 February 2005.

105 *Bucharest Daily News*, 23 March 2005.

106 Mihai Istrate, 'Romania: Business Ambivalent About EU Accession', *Balkan Insight*, 13 July 2007.

107 *Hotnews*, 18 March 2008.

108 Dan Strāuţ, 'Buşteanul şi şifonierul', *Adevărul*, 2 August 2008.

109 *Evenimentul Zilei*, 16 July 2006.

110 Oana Cracium, 'Specialisti sa fie, ca fonduri UE avem', *Cotidianul* (Bucharest), 10 September 2006.

111 *Cotidianul*, 9 September 2006.
112 *Bucharest Daily News*, 1 May 2006.
113 *Adevărul*, 10 May 2006.
114 *Adevărul*, 10 May 2006.
115 Mark Percival, 'EU Funds and the Competence of Romania's Public Administration', *Bucharest Daily News*, 6 June 2006.
116 *Monitoring Report on the State of Preparedness for EU Membership of Bulgaria and Romania*, Brussels: European Commission, 26 September 2006, com (2006) 549 final, p. 8.
117 *Emerging Romania*, London: Oxford Business Group, 2007, p. 51.
118 *România Liberă*, 14 March 2008.
119 Fernandez Alonso, 'Post-Accession EU Funds for Romania'.
120 Fernandez Alonso, 'Post-Accession EU Funds for Romania'.
121 *Ziua*, 15 June 2007.
122 *Averea*, 21 October 2005.
123 *Hotnews*, 25 September 2007, www.hotnews.ro.
124 See Tom Gallagher, 'Autohtonizarea firmelor occidentale?', *România Liberă*, 17 December 2007.
125 *Curierul Național* (Bucharest), 19 March 2008.
126 *România Liberă*, 16 March 2008.
127 The letter appeared in the electronic edition after the article 'Corruption in Romania', *The Economist*, 3 July 2008.

Conclusion

In conclusion, it is clear that Romania joined with the accession criteria relaxed or even set aside in key areas. Victory was declared on a flimsy basis with reforms in vital policy sectors waiting to be accomplished and an elite with no appetite for this work reaping the main benefits of membership. Confounded by the challenge it encountered, the EU revealed itself to be an institution which had great difficulty projecting democratic values and indeed ethical forms of capitalism into inhospitable terrain. Perhaps the task would have been easier if it had entered into partnership with the USA, which since 2001 has sent a number of impressive ambassadors committed to Romania achieving the reforms to which the EU also said it was committed. These envoys were usually more outspoken than Brussels when Romanian officials tried to dodge their undertakings. But a disdain for the USA, most noticeable within the Franco-German axis of the EU, prevented any such alliance ever being consummated.

Brussels has always proclaimed that it was entering into a partnership with the populations of candidate states like Romania after entry negotiations started. But, except spasmodically, it failed to connect with the most committed pro-European forces in the general population. Too often visiting auditors and some of its own top officials were prepared to accept the loud assurances of local politicians that they should be trusted when their performance did nothing to merit such confidence. The main entities of the EU allowed themselves to be misled and disarmed by a calculating local elite well versed in simulating change. Values seen as central to the EU project, such as political accountability, clean government and active citizenship, failed to acquire much meaning in the Romanian context. Political power continued to be wielded by a narrow set of parties and economic interest groups, enjoying a symbiotic relationship with one another who were determined not to be accountable before the law or to face too many external constraints.

In its defence, the EU responds that it was really up to the leaders, and indeed citizens, of Romania how well they used the opportunities to modernise the country offered by Brussels when talks were opened in 2000.[1] The EU merely gave them a chance to succeed and it was up to Romania if it wanted to grab that chance. But this is a rather disingenuous argument. The timetable, the decision to emphasise some policy areas and ignore others like education, the privatisation of most strategic sectors of the economy, the lifting of price controls, the form of regionalisation through which funds were channelled, were all worked out in advance by the EU.

The shape of the *acquis communautaire* determined the nature of the EU's engagement with Romania. This roadmap was worked out to assist countries with a far more robust political and socio-economic profile than Romania's. Indeed, the accession strategy was finalised in the mid-1990s for East-Central Europe when it was widely assumed that Romania would not be in contention for EU membership for a very long time to come. It was a huge error of judgment not to adopt a modified approach suitable for engaging with a country with a grim totalitarian legacy, a battered economy and a moribund bureaucracy unable to carry out even routine problem-solving tasks. The failure to take account of these stark challenges meant that the EU was unlikely to succeed in establishing an effective partnership with the population. Instead, it would slowly but surely find itself dancing to the tune of the post-communist elite. That has surely been confirmed by the fact that today those ruthless former communists who became extraordinarily rich through blocking reform are among the main beneficiaries of EU structural funds. EU taxpayers will be giving dozens of millions of euros in structural funds to the new landed class drawn from communist-era rural managers as well as shrewd foreign investors. By contrast, the EU has been unable to ensure that most families deprived of land and property after 1945 have enjoyed any kind of fair restitution.

In a 2005 interview Olli Rehn, the Enlargement Commissioner, said: 'it is not our job to combat corruption but that of the administration, the Government and indeed each Romanian'.[2] But, having insisted that millions of Romanians make huge personal sacrifices, it was indeed the job of Messrs Rehn, Verheugen, Scheele and not forgetting Baroness Nicholson to ensure that they were the ones who finally enjoyed the benefits. This is not the way it worked out. Billions of euros have been provided in pre- and now post-accession support which provide undreamt of opportunities for corruption. This mega-welfare relief for the oligarchy means that its members are more determined to cling to power by whatever means it takes. It is EU unpreparedness which has contributed to Romania at times appearing to be something close to an elective dictatorship in its first year of full membership.

In the seven years when it closely engaged with Romania and when its leverage was at its maximum, the EU failed to make a significant impact on the corruption, clientelism and very low standards in public life that characterised Romanian politics. Its ability to shield Romanian citizens from a delinquent political elite, which is the public manifestation of a cohesive oligarchy, is now far less than it was. It failed to set transparent standards which Romania had to meet in order to be eligible to join the Union. The opaque *acquis communautaire* was nothing of the sort, as shown by the fact that Romania joined with this roadmap for entry complete but the country still unreformed in crucial respects. This mediocre outcome did not merit the sacrifices demanded of the Romanian people in the pre-entry years. A huge human exodus resulted which continues unabated, especially among professional people, now that Romania is inside the EU. No arm of the multi-layered EU distinguished itself in relation to Romania although individual figures in the Commission and the Delegation in Bucharest behaved with credit as they saw the train-wreck that was approaching. Entities like the EU squander their credit when they behave in such an unimpressive way towards the challenge of modernising a country with challenges as steep as those encountered in Romania. Jonathan Scheele was being rather disingenuous when he argued, shortly before leaving Bucharest in 2006, that the EU was in fact a secondary player in the enlargement era and the initiative lay with Romanian leaders to develop a political project that would result in successful modernisation (see the Appendix). It remains the case that Brussels assiduously pushed particular reforms in the judicial and administrative spheres, as well as projects designed to improve infrastructure at all levels of the country. These barely scratched the surface of the problems being addressed because of the leisurely way the Eurocrats carried out their own programmes, their failure to grasp the degree of opposition to genuine change at the top, and their refusal to acquaint themselves with the Romanian context. The EU also established a privileged partnership with political forces with a questionable commitment to democracy and an inability not to plunder public funds even in the full gaze of Eurocrats. It became dependent on predatory political actors delivering reforms and became committed to their electoral success (even when elementary democratic rules were being violated), as shown in 2004. So the EU was a crucial actor and Mr Scheele found himself playing a role in Romanian history whose significance he still refuses to acknowledge.

The EU had the political weight and the resources to steer Romania in a new direction so that a long period marked by political misrule and a failure to take advantage of the country's natural resources and human capital could be replaced by a more achievement-orientated era. Instead, its mishandling of the Romanian application means that a large, under-developed state now finds itself inside the Union. There are few examples in history of a political entity whose ambitions are as vaulting as the EU's managing to fulfil them after making a blunder as great as this one. Indeed, its dilatory approach to a clutch of problems in South-East Europe – in Bosnia and Kosovo in particular, where it has replaced the UN as the key peace-building actor – suggests that there are serious design flaws in its strategy for projecting its influence into a still deeply troubled part of Europe. Nations, civilisations and even hybrid entities like the European Union usually die from suicide not murder. If those who believe the EU is still capable of shaping Europe's destiny in a new century are consistent, they need to explore what went wrong in Romania and try to put right many of the errors made. It is pointless to hide behind arcane theories concerning the complex and often contradictory workings of the EU's opaque system of multi-level governance. Otherwise, the EU will be a transitory force even in its own neighbourhood, in different parts of which deeply illiberal forces are already capable of challenging its increasingly brittle authority.

Notes

1 See the speech of Jonathan Scheele made in Iaşi on 26 May 2006 on the occasion of his being made a *doctor honoris causis*. The speech is reproduced in the Appendix and can be found at http://ww.infoeuopa.ro/under 'Presa'.
2 *Jurnalul Naţional*, 2 February 2005.

Appendix

Speech given by Jonathan Scheele Cuza University Iaşi, 26 May 2006

Mr. Rector
Deans
Your Holiness
Mr and Mrs Professors

Dear students,

Of course, the honour you do me today is hard to be described in words. To receive this honorary title from the oldest[1] and one of the most prestigious Romanian universities, from the heart of the cultural capital of Moldavia, is an absolute privilege.

Being the chief of the Delegation from the European Commission in the last five years was also an absolute privilege that life has offered to me. Therefore, I receive this title in the name of the entire Delegation team. Without them, I wouldn't be able to achieve anything.

In this period we mark the ending of a major historical phase in the history of Romania, started back in 1821 or even earlier and consisting of the gradual detachment from the Orient, represented back then by the Ottoman Empire, and the country's movement towards Europe. This phase was marked by convulsions, recoveries and devastating historical dramas.

The political or geopolitical integration, not simple at all, being the subject for international power struggles in the past, has been achieved through the country's adhering to NATO and it will be strengthened by adhering to the European Union, a moment that will mark the end of my mission in your country. However, this type of integration, extremely useful, will only be an integration of substance, meaning that it will not necessarily make Romania a Western-like society. The true challenge is the integration through a deep transformation, by modernising the country and its institutions, followed by a gradual re-orientation of mentalities. The true challenge remains the filling of substance with essence. The debate on this topic from the Romanian culture is well known for you.

Romania's integration in the European Union means that important steps have been made towards the *'filling of the substance with essence'*. The European Union has exported its regulations – *the substance* – in Romania, and then it pressed on for these to be applied, *which means to fill the substance with essence*. Theoretically, the integration can take place only when these two dimensions *overlap or are about to overlap*. But is Romania's modernisation problem solved this way? Not by a long shot.

One of the greatest and most frequent mistakes made by Romanians, including the intellectual ones, is that they sometimes think that the country's integration into the European Union also means a profound and integral transformation of the country, of the economy and the society. It really isn't like that.

The famous European *acquis* is not made to build modern states in fact most of it assumes that modern and functional states already exist. The *acquis* is just what these states, members of the European Union, decided to be considered as common rules. *It is limited because of its nature*. It might mean good regulations, applied in a certain domain of activity, but it might be missing in others. Especially in the domains tied to the political organisation of the state, the *acquis* is absolutely inexistent. The *acquis* transfer has positive effects on the reform and transformations going on in a candidate country, but it does not mean complete modernisation it does not mean the reforming of the state, for instance. *The complete modernisation of Romania, the reconciliation between substance and essence, through the combining of local specifics with the European-like universality, can only be the result of a Romanian political project, a political project of the elites and the Romanian society.*

In other words: the integration in the European Union does not mean that Romania will suddenly change for the better, if Romanians will not make it better. The integration in the European Union will not save Romania from reality. Only you, Romanians, and not someone else, from Brussels or God knows where, can be the miracle.

The European and Euro-Atlantic integration of Romania project also had a negative effect for Romania, mainly because it offered everything as granted – *prêt à porter* – saving the political and the elite class from the effort of judging by themselves and deciding what needs to be done for Romania, both in specific domains, *as well as overall, including fundamental data of the country's evolution*. Through misunderstanding, it was expected that Europe will somehow solve the problems of the Romanian rural area, the problems in the Romanian justice, the Romanian administration etc.

What can be the outlines of a Romanian political project? First of all, the Romanian political class should proclaim a number of ideals, that belong to it and to the nation, rather than import already made ones, copied or assumed through rebounding. Ideals that are meant to make a difference in people's lives. Ideals like:

- corruption is a crime against the nation and the political class, 'helped' by an independent justice system, will give up legal immunity, choosing real equality with the rest of the citizens; in this process, the political class will be forced to change itself;
- that in ten years Romania will possess one of the strongest economies from Central and Eastern Europe, with the friendliest business environment in the area;
- that in ten years, not a single talented child from the countryside will be left without education, because of poverty;
- that in ten years, the indicators for the quality of the health and education system will be at the European average;
- that in ten years, a rich and reformed Romania will be a model for the Republic of Moldavia and a regional power, by being an example (and not by showing discursive progressions);
- that through a modern and efficient administration, Romania will truly become the seventh power in the European Union, contributing to the Union's progress and fulfilling its own identity and mission.

Some of these ideals are certainly realistic, but for others a lot of hard work needs to be done. What's most important is that they have to be formulated in the most serious and credible way possible, *so that they can be debated*; once they reach the public conscience, sooner or later they will become an electoral offer, obligations assumed by politicians, they will become the nation's project.

The fundamental role of this project is for Romania to defeat its biggest complex, the lack of trust in itself.

I think this is the most important message I can send you, today, here: *that you are all free people and responsible of your own destiny and of this country's destiny, that Europe is a favourable context that will help you tremendously, but Europe cannot live and make performance in your place, the Romanians.*

The Romanian intellectual elite, your university, your students, you all can and have to contribute to the creation of the Romanian political project, as well as to its application.

As long as I will represent the European Commission in Bucharest, but also in the future, I will stand beside you and you can count on me if you will need my experience or my ideas. I am a person who learned to love Romania, who wishes Romania all the best and will always remain beside Romania.

Thank you once again for the honour you gave me and I wish you a lot of success!

Note

1 1860.

Index